Lecture Notes of the Institute for Computer Sciences, Social Informatics and Telecommunications Engineering   **167**

More information about this series at http://www.springer.com/series/8197

Yin Zhang · Limei Peng
Chan-Hyun Youn (Eds.)

Cloud Computing

6th International Conference, CloudComp 2015
Daejeon, South Korea, October 28–29, 2015
Revised Selected Papers

 Springer

Editors
Yin Zhang
Zhongnan University of Economics and Law
Wuhan
China

Limei Peng
Ajou University
Suwon
Korea (Republic of)

Chan-Hyun Youn
Department of Electrical Engineering
KAIST
Daejeon
Korea (Republic of)

ISSN 1867-8211   ISSN 1867-822X (electronic)
Lecture Notes of the Institute for Computer Sciences, Social Informatics
and Telecommunications Engineering
ISBN 978-3-319-38903-5   ISBN 978-3-319-38904-2 (eBook)
DOI 10.1007/978-3-319-38904-2

Library of Congress Control Number: 2016938677

Printed on acid-free paper

This Springer imprint is published by Springer Nature
The registered company is Springer International Publishing AG Switzerland

Preface

It is a great pleasure to present the Proceedings of the 6th International Conference on Cloud Computing (CloudComp 2015). This year's conference continued its tradition of bringing together researchers, developers, and industry professionals to discuss recent advances and experiences in clouds, cloud computing, and related ecosystems and business support. The conference also provides a forum for presenting the recent advances and results obtained in the wider area of cloud computing, giving users and researchers alike a chance to gain better insight into the capabilities and limitations of current cloud systems.

CloudComp 2015 received 89 paper submissions, from which the Technical Program Committee (TPC) selected 36 regular papers for presentation and publication in these proceedings after rigorous reviews by expert TPC members. The acceptance rate is 40.44 %. The conference consisted of six symposia that covered a broad range of research aspects. In addition to these paper presentations, CloudComp 2015 also featured two inspiring keynotes on software-defined cloud systems and cloud-assisted big data application. We hope that the conference proceedings will serve as a valuable reference to researchers and developers in the area.

Located in the charming and cultural city of Daejeon at an enchanting time of the year, CloudComp 2015 was an exciting and stimulating event. It advanced our understanding of cloud computing and opened up new directions for research and development.

October 2015

Yin Zhang
Limei Peng
Chan-Hyun Youn

Organization

General Chairs

Chan-Hyun Youn   KAIST (Korea Advanced Institute of Science
and Technology), South Korea
Eui Nam Huh   Kyung Hee University, Korea
Min Chen   Huazhong University of Science and Technology (HUST),
China

Technical Program Committee Chairs

Honggang Wang   University of Massachusetts at Dartmouth, USA
Yin Zhang   Huazhong University of Science and Technology, China
Limei Peng   Ajou University, South Korea
Wei Xiang   University of Southern Queensland, Australia
Hak Young Kim   ETRI, Korea
In-Young Ko   KAIST, Korea

Organizing Committee Chairs

Wan Choi   ETRI, Korea
Youngjoo Chung   GIST, Korea
Bong Hwan Lee   Daejeon University, Korea
Young Ik Eom   Sung Kyun Kwan University, Korea

Workshop Chairs

Zhengguo Sheng   University of Sussex, UK
Kan Zheng   University of Waterloo, Canada

Publication Chairs

Chi Harold Liu   Beijing Institute of Technology, China
Zohreh Sanaei   YTL Communications and Xchanging Malaysia, Malaysia

Publicity Chairs

Chin-Feng Lai   National Ilan University, Taiwan
Kai Lin   Dalian University of Technology, China

Web Chair

Ran Li   Huazhong University of Science and Technology, China

Sponsorship and Exhibits Chair

Daeyoung Kim   KAIST (Korea Advanced Institute of Science
                                and Technology), Korea

Local Chair

In-Young Ko   KAIST (Korea Advanced Institute of Science
                                and Technology), Korea

Conference Manager

Anna Horvathova   European Alliance for Innovation

Steering Committee Chair

Imrich Chlamtac   Create-Net, Italy

Contents

Virtualization and Management on Cloud

Automated Overlay Virtual Networking Manager for OpenFlow-Based
International SDN-Cloud Testbed   3
   Junsik Shin and JongWon Kim

An Educational Virtualization Infrastructure   12
   Mohamed K. Watfa, Vincent A. Udoh, and Said M. Al Abdulsalam

A Study of Resource Management for Fault-Tolerant and Energy Efficient
Cloud Datacenter   22
   Dong-Ki Kang, Fawaz Alhazemi, Seong-Hwan Kim,
   and Chan-Hyun Youn

User Isolation in Multi-user Multi-touch Devices Using OS-Level
Virtualization   30
   Minkyeong Lee, Minho Lee, Inhyeok Kim, and Young Ik Eom

A VM Vector Management Scheme for QoS Constraint Task Scheduling
in Cloud Environment   39
   Kyung-no Joo, Seonghwan Kim, Dongki Kang, Yusik Kim,
   Hyungyu Jang, and Chan-Hyun Youn

An Adaptive VM Reservation Scheme with Prediction and Task Allocation
in Cloud   50
   Jisoo Choi, Yungi Ha, Gyubeom Choi, and Chan-Hyun Youn

A Cost-Effective VM Offloading Scheme in Hybrid Cloud Environment   60
   Myeongseok Hyeon, Heejae Kim, and Chan-Hyun Youn

Dynamic Virtual Machine Consolidation for Energy Efficient Cloud
Data Centers.   70
   Dong-Ki Kang, Fawaz Alhazemi, Seong-Hwan Kim,
   and Chan-Hyun Youn

Resource Management, Models and Performance

A New Framework for Cloud Business Process Management   83
   Mohamed K. Watfa, Nafez A.L. Najjar, Jad Cheikha, and Nayef Buali

On Increasing Resource Utilization of a High-Performance
Computing System   93
   Lung-Pin Chen and Yu-Shan Cheng

A Game Theory Based Automated SLA Negotiation Model for Confined
Federated Clouds   102
   Asma Al Falasi, Mohammed Adel Serhani, and Younes Hamdouch

Experiences on Setting up On-Premise Enterprise Cloud Using OpenStack. . .   114
   R. Ananthalakshmi Ammal, K.B. Aneesh Kumar, Beniwal Alka,
   and B. Renjith

Performance Evaluation of Scientific Workflow on OpenStack and
OpenVZ.   126
   Amol Jaikar, Syed Asif Raza Shah, Sangwook Bae, and Seo-Young Noh

An Science Gateway with Cost Adaptive Resource Management Schemes . . .   136
   Woojoong Kim, Seung-Hwan Kim, and Chan-Hyun Youn

Hybrid Workflow Management in Cloud Broker System   145
   Dongsik Yoon, Seong-Hwan Kim, Dong-Ki Kang,
   and Chan-Hyun Youn

Mobile Cloud and Media Services

Mobile Cloud Computing System Components Composition Formal
Verification Method Based on Space-Time Pi-Calculus   159
   Peng Wang, Ling Yang, and Guo Wen Li

Monitoring Prayer Using Mobile Phone Accelerometer   168
   Reem Al-Ghannam, Eiman Kanjo, and Hmood Al-Dossari

A Prospective Cloud-Connected Vehicle Information System for C-ITS
Application Services in Connected Vehicle Environment   176
   SeongMin Song, Woojoong Kim, Seong-Hwan Kim, GyuBeom Choi,
   Heejae Kim, and Chan-Hyun Youn

Video and USB Transmission Devices for Cloud Desktop Service   184
   Chanho Park and Hagyoung Kim

A Feature-Oriented Mobile Software Development Framework to Resolve
the Device Fragmentation Phenomenon for Application Developers in the
Mobile Software Ecosystem   189
   Younghun Han, Gyeongmin Go, Sungwon Kang, and Heuijin Lee

Improving Data Access for Smart World   200
   Tariq Lasloum and Ahmad S. Almogren

Pervasive Cloud Applications, Services and Testbeds

Implications of Integration and Interoperability for Enterprise Cloud-Based
Applications   213
  Justice Opara-Martins, Reza Sahandi, and Feng Tian

Building and Operating Distributed SDN-Cloud Testbed with
Hyper-Convergent SmartX Boxes   224
  Aris Cahyadi Risdianto, Junsik Shin, and JongWon Kim

On Providing Response Time Guarantees to a Cloud-Hosted Telemedicine
Web Service.   234
  Waqar Haider, Waheed Iqbal, Fawaz S. Bokhari, and Faisal Bukhari

Modeling Parallel Execution Policies of Web Services.   244
  Mai Xuan Trang, Yohei Murakami, and Toru Ishida

A Hybrid Cloud Computing Model for Higher Education Institutions
in Saudi Arabia.   255
  Muhammad Asif Khan

A Methodology to Select the Best Public Cloud Service for Media Focussed
Enterprises   260
  Subhranshu Banerjee, Vikas Mathur, and Sreehari Narasipur

A Cloud Computing System Using Virtual Hyperbolic Coordinates
for Services Distribution   269
  Telesphore Tiendrebeogo

Enabling SDN Experimentation with Wired and Wireless Resources:
The SmartFIRE Facility   280
  *Kostas Choumas, Thanasis Korakis, Hyunwoo Lee, Donghyun Kim,
  Junho Suh, Ted Taekyoung Kwon, Pedro Martinez-Julia,
  Antonio Skarmeta, Taewan You, Loic Baron, Serge Fdida,
  and JongWon Kim*

Cloud-Enabling Techniques and Devices

A Buffer Cache Algorithm for Hybrid Memory Architecture in Mobile
Devices   293
  Chansoo Oh, Dong Hyun Kang, Minho Lee, and Young Ik Eom

Protocol for a Simplified Processor-Memory Interface Using High-Speed
Serial Link   301
  HyukJe Kwon and Yongseok Choi

The Trapping Device Implementation of Wireless Sensor Network   311
  Hendrick Hendrick, Guo-Sheng Liao, Kuo-Ying Lu, Chun-Yen Lin,
  and Gwo-Jia Jong

A Formal Approach for Modeling and Verification of Distributed Systems. . .   317
  Gang Ren, Pan Deng, Chao Yang, Jianwei Zhang, and Qingsong Hua

Design of a Security Gateway for iKaaS Platform   323
  Seira Hidano, Shinsaku Kiyomoto, Yosuke Murakami,
  Panagiotis Vlacheas, and Klaus Moessner

KVM-QEMU Virtualization with ARM64bit Server System   334
  Jin-Suk Ma, Hak-Young Kim, and Wan Choi

A System Interconnection Device for Small-Scale Clusters   344
  Ye Ren, Young Woo Kim, and Hag Young Kim

Author Index   355

Virtualization and Management on Cloud

Automated Overlay Virtual Networking Manager for OpenFlow-Based International SDN-Cloud Testbed

Junsik Shin and JongWon Kim[✉]

School of Information and Communications,
Gwangju Institute of Science and Technology (GIST), Gwangju, Korea
{jsshin,jongwon}@nm.gist.ac.kr

Abstract. With the development of virtualization and cloud technology, cloud data centers have been emerging for ICT infrastructure market. In order to link resource pools (i.e., servers, storages, and switches) over distributed data centers, tunneling-based overlay networking can maintain L2 connectivity with reasonable scalability. However, in properly managing all the switches and tunnels, the complexity of underlying network topology causes uncontrollable difficulties. Thus, in this paper, we discuss how to automatically manage overlay virtual networking by employing an OpenFlow-based OvN-Manager (Overlay vNetworking Manager) tool. The verification results for implemented OvN-Manager tool are also presented over OF@TEIN international SDN-Cloud testbed.

Keywords: OpenFlow-enabled software-defined networking · Future internet testbed · DevOps-based automation · Tunneling-based inter-connection · Overlay virtual networking

1 Introduction

The hyper-scale cloud data centers from Amazon, Google, and Microsoft are already established across the world and have been providing public cloud services [1]. These cloud data centers are equipped with a large number of servers, storages, and switches, distributed over multiple data centers. Due to their scales ($>$10,000 servers per center) and underlying network technology [2, 3], they are exposed to complexity problems in networking aspects. In linking resource pools among cloud data centers, it is important to maintain connectivity with reasonable scalability. However, the complexity of underlying network topology can cause uncontrollable difficulties in properly inter-connecting resource pools together.

Meanwhile, the emerging SDN (software-defined networking) paradigm is increasingly embracing OpenFlow and Open vSwitch (OVS) as a de-facto protocol interface and virtual switch, respectively. Aligned with this trend, by leveraging hyper-convergent SmartX Boxes and OpenFlow-enabled OVS, GIST and OF@TEIN collaborators have been building and operating an international OF@TEIN SDN-Cloud testbed [4]. Diverse operational experience is built to address the real-world challenges including the complex overlay tunneling management.

© ICST Institute for Computer Sciences, Social Informatics and Telecommunications Engineering 2016
Y. Zhang et al. (Eds.): CloudComp 2015, LNICST 167, pp. 3–11, 2016.
DOI: 10.1007/978-3-319-38904-2_1

Thus, in this paper, we discuss how to improve overlay virtual networking management by utilizing an automated OpenFlow-based OvN-Manager (Overlay vNetworking Manager). The proposed OvN-Manager is implemented and verified over OF@TEIN international SDN-Cloud testbed. Then, in Sect. 2, we introduce the OF@TEIN international SDN-Cloud testbed. In Sect. 3, we detail the design and implementation of automated OvN-Manager. We also provide the functionality verification results for the proposed OvN-Manager tool. Finally, we conclude this paper in Sect. 4.

2   OF@TEIN: International Distributed SDN-Cloud Testbed

2.1   SDN-Cloud Playground Interconnecting Multiple OpenFlow Islands

The OF@TEIN project (from July 2012) aims to provide OpenFlow-enabled SDN testbed (i.e., playground) for international researchers [4–6]. As shown in Fig. 1, an initial 6-site testbed has grown to more than 8 sites with hyper-convergent SmartX Boxes. Note that SmartX Box refers to a hyper-convergent resource box, which integrates compute, storage, and networking resources in a single box.

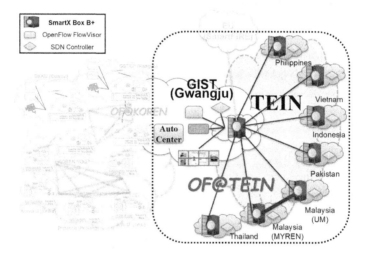

Fig. 1. OF@TEIN testbed infrastructure (June 2015).

To link SmartX Boxes distributed in multiple international sites, virtual overlay networking with NVGRE(Network Virtualization using Generic Routing Encapsulation)/VXLAN(Virtual eXtensible Local Area Network) tunnels establishes OpenFlow-based inter-connection over underlying TEIN (Trans Eurasian Information Network) network. Figure 2 illustrates the operation concept behind OF@TEIN testbed setup and configuration. Each site has three types of nodes. First, nodes under VMs at the end of each site contain hypervisors to provide VMs (virtual machines). OpenFlow Switch nodes are managed by user controllers that are policed by FlowVisor [7]. Also, Capsulator nodes are in charge of NVGRE/VXLAN tunnelling. Note that, in early days of

OF@TEIN, some switches/capsulators are supported by hardware switches and FPGA-accelerated servers, but all hardware switches are now replaced by OVS virtual switches.

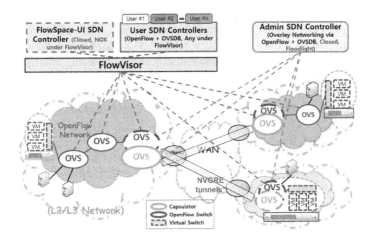

Fig. 2. OF@TEIN sites and operation setup (concept version).

By replacing networking devices from hardware to software, as depicted in Fig. 3, all SmartX Boxes have the same virtual networking topology as long as there are no site-specific modifications. Xen-hypervisor VMs connect to "xenbr0" bridge (for Internet connectivity) and "xenbr1" bridge (for VM to VM connectivity). For data traffic between VMs, bridges "br1", "br2", and "brcap" are placed and subsequently connected beyond "xenbr1". Furthermore, "br1" and "br2" are connected to user's choice of controllers, e.g., ODL (Open Daylight) SDN Controller [8]. With its own SDN controllers and open-shared bridges (e.g., "br1" and "br2"), users can do their own SDN experiments over their overlay networks. However, as shown as a line from Admin's ODL SDN Controller to "brcap" bridge in Fig. 3, "brcap" connects only to Admin's ODL SDN Controller, which manages all the NVGRE/VXLAN tunnels.

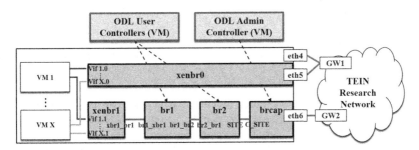

Fig. 3. Common bridge configuration of SmartX Box (Type B+).

2.2   Automated Inter-Connection Provisioning Tools

To provision overlay virtual networking for OF@TEIN playground, we should take care of combined configurations for bridges, tunnels, and flows. It is apparent that managing them is very difficult without an automated tool. Thus, to assist the configuration of tunnel-based inter-connections, in 2014, we deployed a script-based automated inter-connection tool [9]. This inter-connection tool is focused on linking multi-point Open-Flow islands by utilizing OVSDB (Open vSwitch Data Base) configuration protocol [10] to automate the configuration procedures for all OVS-based bridges and tunnels. Note that, in Fig. 2, bridges and tunnels are matched with OpenFlow Switch nodes and Capsulator nodes.

However, although the existing tool in [9] can help the automated provisioning, it is limited in terms of software flexibility since it narrowly focuses on how to automate with scripting. First, with the existing tool, it is hard to dynamically manipulate diverse networking configurations. It simply combines together pre-arranged automated site-specific scripts for all SmartX sites. Only those who know the details of all configurations, commands, and APIs are possible to modify the automated scripts. Next, the existing tool lacks fine-grained configuration capability and aims only to automate the provisioning procedures. Specialized configurations in building bridges, making flows, and creating tunnels are not supported. Thus, the operators should manually configure fine-grained parameters, whenever needed. Finally, there is no automated tool to find and recover inter-connection problems, which are occurred in the OF@TEIN playground. The operators can notice inter-connection problems based on user's claims during their experiments. Even though the existence of inter-connection problems is noticed, the operators have to spend a lot of time to figure out the root cause. Besides, even after the operators find out the root cause, the existing tool could not cover the recovery configurations. Thus, finding and recovering inter-connection problems are sometimes slower than the brute-force automated provisioning procedures that flush all existing configuration and reconfigure them. These inflexibilities of existing tool verify the observations such as "hard to manipulate the tool", "lack of fine-grained configuration capability", and "no support for finding and recovering inter-connection problems", which puts additional burden to the operators of OF@TEIN playground.

3   Overlay VNetworking Manager

3.1   Design

To overcome the limitations of existing tool discussed earlier, we have refactored it for flexible inter-connection management under the name of OvN-Manager. The OvN-Manager tool is designed to satisfy the following requirements.

- All configuration procedures are automated from creating the virtual switches (i.e., bridges) to downloading flow rules.
- Anybody can easily design his/her own overlay virtual networking and change its configuration.

- The inter-connection status and resource are repeatedly monitored at each site and the spotted problem is reported for automatic recovery attempts. Also, the operators are notified about the spotted problems and their recovery progress.
- Easy-to-use configuration is supported for bridges, ports, tunnels, and flows at all sites in a fine-grained manner. Also, according to inter-connections among sites, flows can be dynamically created and modified.

The important design concept of OvN-Manager is networking template for flexible provisioning and management. To realize flexible configuration for the operators, the OvN-Manager tool configures each site according to the specified networking template, which contains the customized details. The OvN-Manager tool has only one common code to automate different provisioning cases based on template files. Figure 4 represents an example networking template that is being used for managing the SmartX Box in Pakistan site. The networking template contains detailed configurations for bridges, DPID (data path identifier), ports, and so on. With this networking template, the SmartX Box in Pakistan site can be automatically configured for overlay virtual networking as represented in Fig. 3. Furthermore, we manage an additional tunneling list file for automated tunnel management. All tunnels required for overlay virtual networking are listed in this file.

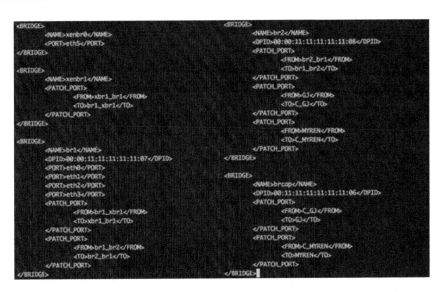

Fig. 4. OvN-Manager networking template for Pakistan site.

3.2 Implementation and Working Procedure

The OvN-Manager tool, implemented in a bash shell script, is working at a centralized management box in GIST. From this management box, the OvN-Manager tool provisions, monitors, and recovers the overlay virtual networking of all remote SmartX Boxes in OF@TEIN playground. The implemented OvN-Manager tool works by following the procedure depicted in Fig. 5. This tool operates in 3 different main phases: Bridge, Tunnel, and Flow Management Phases. Figure 5 represents Bridge-Tunnel-Flow Management Phases with detailed working procedure. After completing all 3 phases, the checked errors are saved into a report file. This report file is automatically sent to the operators by e-mail. Also, the OvN-Manager tool recycles again after 30 s.

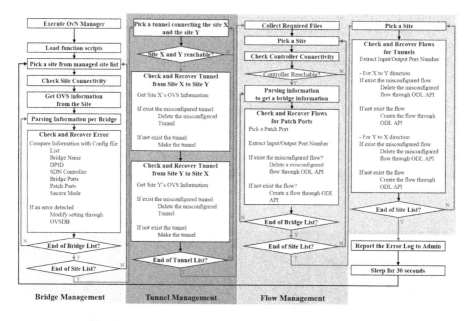

Fig. 5. OvN-Manager: Flow diagram for working procedure.

First, in Bridge Management Phase, the manager collects current OVS configurations from all sites through the OVSDB protocol. All bridges in each site are automatically checked by comparing against listed bridges in the networking template one by one. If any listed bridge is missing, it is automatically created or recovered.

Next, Tunnel Management Phase takes care of managing all tunnels listed in the tunneling list file. In this phase, unlike Bridge Management Phase, each tunnel should be checked at both tunneling endpoints to ensure bi-directional connectivity. The manager first checks the connectivity (e.g., ping) and OVS configuration in one direction. After that, it also checks in the reverse direction. The spotted problems are fixed by configuring the tunnel patch ports through the OVSDB protocol. Note that, since all bridges and tunnels are instantiated with OVS virtual switches and all sites are internationally distributed, the OvN-Manager tool mainly utilizes the OVSDB protocol to configure overlay virtual networking for remote sites.

Lastly, in Flow Management Phase, all flows are dynamically enabled according to the OVS configuration and the OpenFlow flowtable at each site. To manage the flows effectively, we divide Flow Managements Phase into two distinct steps. One step manages flows between internal bridges and another step covers only tunneling-related flows. Initially, the manager checks the connectivity between bridges at each site and the ODL SDN controller, because all flows are managed by the SDN controller. Next, all flows between internal bridges are checked by comparing with the OVS configuration and flow tables originated from the SDN controller. Then, the missing or misconfigured flows are automatically configured through ODL APIs. After finishing the internal flow management for all sites, tunneling-related flow management begins. Again, flows should be checked in both directions by following similar checking and recovering mechanism for internal flow management. Also, all flows are automatically arranged according to the existing rules on port names. For example, if all packets coming from "xbr1_br1" should be forwarded to "br1_xbr1", the flow from "xbr1_br1" to "br1_xbr1" is defined and configured. Note that, in this regard, the applicability of OvN-Manager tool is restricted to OF@TEIN playground yet.

3.3   Evaluation: Features and Limitations

The OvN-Manager tool provides several features for the OF@TEIN operators, coming from its functionalities, to effectively manage testbed infrastructure. The operators can provision overlay virtual networking. The template-based configuration alleviates the burden of operators in modifying networking configurations. The problem recovery and reporting can also improve the management efficiency by reducing trouble-shooting time. Also, due to template-based automation support, the OvN-Manager tool can be generalized. By decomposing into Bridge-Tunnel-Flow Phases, the OvN-Manager tool can leverage specific functionalities of each isolated phase. It can be easily generalized by plugging with other tools. Thus, Bridge, Tunnel and Flow Phases give improved scalability by increasing the number of manageable nodes at a time. The time-consuming procedure of the OvN-Manager tool is collecting information through OVSDB, SSH, and ODL APIs. In each phase, all boxes provide the same type of information to the manager. Thus the manager can simultaneously collect information from distributed SmartX Boxes. Moreover, we can easily add additional functionality due to phase-based procedures.

On the other hand, the OvN-Manager tool is limited, mostly from the implementation. The OvN-Manager tool can address tunnel-based connectivity for overlay virtual networking. However it is suitable only for overlay virtual networking in the OF@TEIN testbed. Similarly, the operator may have to spend time to apply the OvN-Manager tool on one's own environment.

3.4   OvN-Manager: Functionality Verification

To verify the monitoring and recovering problems, we apply a simple experiment to the SmartX Box at Pakistan site. We detach the SDN controller from all bridges. Then, according to the Pakistan networking template, we define additional bridge "testbr" and a patch port connecting "TEST_A" to "TEST_B". Also, another experiment removes a tunnel connecting between SmartX Boxes at Malaysia site (MY2) and Pakistan site (PK1).

Finally, the reports from OvN-Manager are represented as shown in Fig. 6. The OvN-Manager tool can detect and distinguish problem types in a fine-grained level (i.e., Bridge/Port/Tunnel/Flow/Controller problems, repectively), and send a report to the operators. If the default recovery fails, the OvN-Manager tool includes recovery failure notification. Additionally, the OvN-Manager tool repeats its operation every 30 s, which is sufficiently freqent for dynamic operator intervention.

Fig. 6. Problem Reports from OvN-Manager.

4   Conclusion

In this paper, we introduce OvN-Manager, an automated tool for overlay networking management, which can check and recover problems for multi-point international OF@TEIN sites. In future, we plan to improve its recovery features by adding VMs and package recovery and integrate the OvN-Manager tool with GUI-based efficient visibility [11].

Acknowledgments. This work makes use of results produced by the SmartFIRE project, which is supported by the International Research & Development Program of the National Research Foundation of Korea (NRF) funded by the Ministry of Science, ICT and Future Planning (MSIP, Korea) (Grant number: K2013078191) and the Seventh Framework Programme (FP7) funded by the European Commission (Grant number: 611165).

References

1. Right Scale: Right Scale 2014: State of the cloud report. Survey Report (2014)
2. Koomey, J.G.: Growth in data center electricity use 2005 to 2010. Analytical Press, New York (2011)
3. Microsoft: Microsoft had more than 1 million servers in 2013. http://news.microsoft.com/2013/07/08/steve-ballmer-worldwide-partner-conference-2013-keynote/

4. Kim, J., et. al.: OF@TEIN: An OpenFlow-enabled SDN testbed over international SmartX Rack sites. In: Proceedings of the APAN–Networking Research Workshop, Aug 2013

5. Risdianto, A.C., Na, T., Kim, J.: Running lifecycle experiments over SDN-enabled OF@TEIN testbed. In: Proceedings of the IEEE International Conference on Communications and Electronics, July-Aug. 2014

6. Risdianto, A.C., Kim, J.: Prototyping media distribution experiments over OF@TEIN SDN-enabled testbed. In: Proceedings of the APAN Network Research Workshop, Nantou, Taiwan, Aug. 2014

7. Sherwood, R., et al.: Flowvisor: A network virtualization layer. Technical Report Openflow-tr-2009-1, Stanford University, July 2009

8. Medved, J., Varga, R., Tkacik, A., Gray, K.: OpenDaylight: Towards a model-driven SDN controller architecture. In: Proceedings of the IEEE International Symposium on A World of Wireless, Mobile and Multimedia Networks, June 2014

9. Na, T., Kim, J.: Inter-connection automation for OF@TEIN multi-point international OpenFlow islands. In: Proceedings of the International Conference on Future Internet Technologies (CFI 2014), Tokyo, Japan, June 2014

10. Pfaff, B., Davie, B.: The open vSwitch database management protocol. In: IETF RFC 7047, Dec. 2013

11. Risdianto, A.C., Kim, J.: Flow-centric visibility tools for OF@TEIN OpenFlow-based SDN testbed. In: Proceedings of the International Conference on Future Internet Technologies (CFI 2015), Seoul, Korea, June 2015

An Educational Virtualization Infrastructure

Mohamed K. Watfa[(✉)], Vincent A. Udoh, and Said M. Al Abdulsalam

University of Wollongong in Dubai, Knowledge Village, Dubai, UAE
MohamedWatfa@uowdubai.ac.ae, bamiboy89@gmail.com,
saidabdulsalam@gmail.com

Abstract. Virtualization is a key cost-cutting technology developed from the concept of cloud computing which provides efficient IT Solutions in corporate and educational sectors. We present an original structural framework for which the effects & implications of virtualization technology are measured based on a real campus wide deployment. The Virtual Desktop Infrastructure (VDI) provides academic members access to virtual applications and personalized virtual desktops on and off-campus for easy convenient access to academic resources. This paper provides intricate analysis on the perceived and categorical perspectives on the usefulness, effectiveness and values of this technology in an academic environment. Among other significant results, our results indicated that students and academic staff had positive experiences using virtualization technologies and have generally improved accessibility to their course documents and academic materials which enabled them to perform course work more effectively.

Keywords: VDI · I.T · Virtualization technology · Academia · Virtual lab application · Cloud computing

1 Introduction

Information Technology is with no doubt a key part of any educational infrastructure. Since educational institutions often lack the IT resources, virtualization and cloud computing technologies are often utilized in the teaching-learning process [1] where academic professionals can access the needed academic resources using virtual classrooms. Universities have utilized the benefits of virtual technologies in a number of university level subjects [2]. Cloud computing affects the way technological services are invented, and utilized The potential of cloud computing affects the functionality of existing information technology services and enables new functionalities that are thus far infeasible as it has massive effects on the cost of deployment and development of new IT services and tools which were preventing a number of key decision makers. Cloud computing exemplifies two major IT developments: IT efficiency and Business Agility. IT efficiency is exponentially increased by using advanced hardware and software tools and resources. On the other hand, Business agility also advances by using real time rapid deployment and parallel processing offering a competitive advantage to any company. In a related context, virtualization which can be considered as a subsidiary of cloud computing is defined as a set of software tools which divides a server into virtual resources called Virtual Machines (VM's) reducing power and expanding computing

© ICST Institute for Computer Sciences, Social Informatics and Telecommunications Engineering 2016
Y. Zhang et al. (Eds.): CloudComp 2015, LNICST 167, pp. 12–21, 2016.
DOI: 10.1007/978-3-319-38904-2_2

resource allocation and data storage [3]. Virtualization is one of the key areas being widely explored by many academic institutions given its high potential in offering computing resources to a large number of students with minimum cost of deployment and maintenance.

In this research work, we provide intricate analysis on the perceived and categorical perspectives on the usefulness, effectiveness and value of virtualization technology in an academic environment. Our analysis is based on extensive qualitative and quantitative data resulting from the deployment and implementation of virtualization technologies at a university. The platform of virtualization desktop infrastructure was provided by Citrix technology, one of the pioneers of virtualization technology amongst others such as Microsoft and VMWare. This research paper is outlined as follows. Section 2 states the research problem and its corresponding research questions highlighting the significance of this research work. Section 3 summarizes the related research work. Section 4 summarizes our research design and methodology and results. Section 5 concludes this work.

2 Problem Statement

Cloud computing is an emerging topic in the IT industry. Presently, universities have been considering the adoption of virtualization technology which is an application under cloud computing for various reasons. Adopting virtualization in a campus wide location is a very costly venture and when compared to the traditional method of installation and management of applications, it raises some concerns as to whether it delivers rewards that can substantiate its initial high cost of implementation. Our research will attempt to justify this investment in terms of resulting benefits for students, staff and academic members as a whole. To put things in technical perspective, we focus only on the implications of the virtualization platform on academia. The environmental configuration consists of hardware with a host OS, virtualization software and series of virtual machines. A citrix configuration [4] was utilized. Some important technical implications of such a deployment include:

- In the main office, the console is set up on a computer that is close to the server for fast data collection. This is referred to as the Presentation server. The IT department at the university must create user accounts for each remote user. These users can then access the console quickly over HTTPS to improve security.
- The university can benefit from load-balancing to spread the remote accesses.
- The main bottleneck for a console running on Citrix is memory size. If the console (in a computer lab or in an academic faculty office) runs out of memory, its performance decreases sharply which results in some application crashes (as will be noted in some negative student experiences).
- The second constraint is CPU power. During refreshes, the console works best with a full CPU core. This implication would be evident in extensive interviews with academic staff running CPU intensive applications.

- The final concern is disk space for the console cache. There should be enough disk space to provide one cache file for each console operator. This requirement results in some negative side effects on individual student consoles in computer labs.

2.1 Research Questions

Leading from the above problem statement, our research focus was centered on the following research question: "What is an optimal framework for measuring the Effects and implications of Virtualization on an academic institution?" We start by considering the effects of virtualization as an application of cloud computing on academic institutions. The aim of this research is to discover the fundamental approaches used in the deployment, lease and workload, as well as the utility, benefits and justification of this technology in an academic institution. The research extended the literature on studies conducted at a few prominent U.S universities that already employ virtualization technology. However, from the literature and previous works done on virtualization in academia, there have been no known framework for measuring the effects of Virtualization on academia. In this paper, we provide an appropriate framework which can be utilized to assess the effects of Virtualization in an academic institution. This research focuses on capturing and analyzing the student learning curves, work load, usability of virtualized applications and privacy amongst others to eventually validate its positive and/or negative outcomes.

2.2 Significance of This Study

Virtualization technology has been noted to be one of the contemporary and pioneering trends in information technology today. As such, it is relevant to carry out a research study to analyze the optimal deployment of the virtualization infrastructure as well as to view the benefits and effects which this state-of-the-art technology can bring to other institutions in the UAE as well as other parts of the world. This study can help other business ventures, especially educational institutions such as universities looking to adopt virtualization technology in their enterprise, by providing relevant information entailing the outcomes and consequences in adopting this technology to assist decision-making by stakeholders. We provide intricate analysis on the perceived and categorical perspectives on the usefulness, effectiveness and value of this technology in an academic environment using statistical analysis.

3 Related Work in Virtualization

Virtualization technology supplements cloud computing and can is considered as a set of software tools which divides a server into virtual resources called Virtual Machines (VM's) reducing power and expanding computing resource allocation and data storage [3]. Applications running within an Operating System (OS) independently can also be configured using virtualization. Cost effective solutions for academic institutions has been a major driver in current decision making. Chawdry and Lance [5] discussed computer virtualization techniques used at a university in California University highlighting the potential paybacks virtualization can offer to academic institutions. They also explained the IT infrastructure needed to successfully implement such innovative tools. Condensed costs and minimized energy consumptions were the two key benefits highlighted. Microsoft, Citrix, and VMware were discussed as possible solutions and how the size and structure of the different universities would require different settings for the virtualization deployment to maximize benefits. The virtualization concept started in 60 s where it was explained that different operating systems can potentially be installed in the same computer [6]. The concept of the virtualization was widely expanded since then [7] distinguishing between different virtualization types. Academic institutions usually allocate an IT budget to develop new software/hardware solutions as we as maintain existing IT solutions to maximize technological benefits in the teaching and learning process. The high costs of existing desktop computers as well as the complex network configurations and software licenses result in a careful re-thinking of existing IT deployments. A number of researchers have investigate the use of virtualization in universities worldwide. For example, [9] discussed how teachers used virtual network labs to teach an IT course. The authors in [8] discuss the concept of a virtual computer laboratory where students can access tools virtually. The authors in [10] investigated the use of virtualization in a management information security course. [11, 12] discussed the effective uses of virtualization in different contexts to deliver course learning outcomes. In [13], the authors discussed the deployment and implementation of a unique innovative virtualization infrastructure used for educational training allowing remote access to software tools using a web portal. They discussed the use of a hypervisor which isolates each server's virtual machine protecting the different virtual machines from each other. Desktop virtualization provides a solution to this problem by enabling older operating systems the ability to install and run applications that are only compatible in newer operating systems. The remarkable improvements virtualization brings to educational applications are nowadays widely documented and consolidated. Castiglione, et al. [14] explained how visualization can be used to increase the course learning outcomes by providing exercises to the students which they can access using PCs. Garcia et al. [15] described different hosting technologies that can be used to build up a suitable virtualization infrastructure in an academic environment. A university learning lab was thoroughly discussed as an example to showcase the virtualization potentials. The separate components of the lab were summarized.

To summarize, existing research on virtualization have discussed the fundamental benefits derived from the adoption of this technology in the academic environments including the choice of various vendors specializing in virtualization technology and what features (e.g. cost, compatibility with existing IT infrastructure, etc.) influenced their selection of a particular vendor. However, no existing work has provided a framework to test the implications of the use of such technologies on the performance of the students and existing teaching methodologies.

4   Research Methodology and Analysis

Our research will include quantitative analysis and the target population is set to be university students and faculty staff members. We would like to investigate the perceived benefits of virtualization at the university and its implications on the aforementioned stakeholders. We conducted a series of interviews, surveys and correlated research searches to discover firsthand the virtualization technology effects on past and current students as well as on academic staff. The sample frame for the survey was selected from current student and faculty staff directory. This provided adequate means to reach all registered students and staff to deliver effective results.

4.1   Sample Size and Description

The population selected for this research consists of all enrolled and currently registered students as well as faculty members of the university. The plan for selecting sample units includes:

(a) a manual cluster sample survey for students where 300 enrolled students in random cluster classes (final year classes and newer classes) were asked to fill a survey accurately.
(b) a manual survey/interview for faulty members where five randomly selected non-IT faculty staff members and five randomly selected IT faculty staff members were interviewed and surveyed.

4.2   Proposed Survey Measures

Based on prior research, we summarize our theoretical framework in Fig. 1. Our framework includes significant measures and attributes of virtualization on the students as well as on academic staff. These attributes were divided into five main categories including: (i) Accessibility; (ii) Usability; (iii) Privacy; (iv) Performance and (v) Applications. More specifically, the interviews conducted for the faculty members were standardized open-ended interviews for the IT and Non-IT faculty member while the questionnaire for students focused on answering the following questions (and sub-questions): "Does virtualization have effect and to what degree on:"

(1) Student general academic performance.
(2) Ease of access of online material for both student and staff.
(3) Usability and satisfaction when accessing applications and academic materials online.
(4) Convenience in Accessing virtual computer labs and MyDesktop online.
(5) Student and staff credential security and Privacy when accessing virtualized platforms.
(6) Effect on staff for enabled Access to document management system within and outside the campus, caused by campus virtualization (RMS).

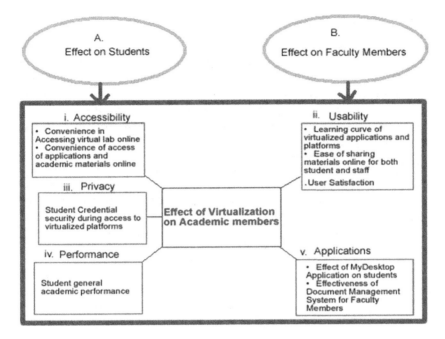

Fig. 1. Framework for measuring the effects of virtualization on academic members

We also divided our questions into the different categories as follows:

1. *Experience/Behavior Questions*: Aimed at eliciting description of experiences, behaviors, actions and activities that would have been observable had we have been present. Examples of questions asked included: If I had been in the program with you, how would we have utilized virtualization in a project? What experiences would I observe you having in an assignment requiring an application not available in your local pc?

2. *Opinion/Values Questions*: These questions are aimed at understanding the cognitive and interpretive processes of the students as well as the academic staff.

3. *Feeling Questions*: These questions are aimed at understanding the emotional responses of the students/staff to their experiences and thoughts.

4. *Knowledge Questions*: These questions try to find out what factual information the students/staff has. Examples included: What are some of the rules and regulations of the virtualization program? What kinds of services are provided?

5. *Sensory Questions*: The purpose of these types of questions is to allow us to enter into the sensory apparatus of the students/staff. An example of questions asked included: Describe to me what I would see if I was using the virtualization tools at your university?

6. *Background/Demographic Questions*: These questions concern the identifying characteristics of the student/staff being interviewed.

4.3   Data Collection and Analysis

The surveys were broken down into two parts, interviews with selected faculty members and hard-copy questionnaire surveys delivered to enrolled students to complete in their classes. For the manual hard copy questionnaires, we used cluster sampling (probabilistic) where we selected random classes for students. Convenience (non-probabilistic sampling) was used for interviews with selected Faculty academic staff. The survey was carried out over a period span of two weeks. Questionnaires were distributed to students in their classes for courses based on two major categories:

A. New students (IT and non-IT majors) who got enrolled after implementation of campus virtualization, and
B. Old students (IT and Non-IT majors), who have been enrolled prior to the implementation of virtualization.

The groups were verified based on their subject code enrolled in the current semester and through this we were able to identify the old from the new students as well as IT from non-IT students. For the faculty members, interview sessions were conducted with three Associate Professors from the Faculty of Computer Science and Engineering and two Associate Professors from the Faculty of Business and Management. After conducting the surveys, 223 accurately completed student questionnaires and 8 uncompleted student questionnaires were received.

4.3.1   Statistics Relating to Students

- Virtualization platforms are effective and new non-IT students access it weekly more than other categories of students as shown in Fig. 2(a).
- Half of the students are satisfied with the user experience of virtualized platforms. 41 % are unsure about it with most stating reasons such as interface issues and slow performance as shown in Fig. 2(b).

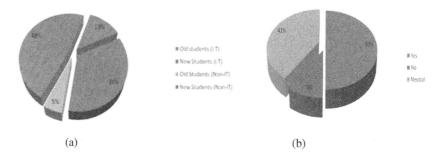

(a)   (b)

Fig. 2. (a) Weekly student usage of virtual platforms; (b) Overall student satisfaction.

- Except for newer students that are unsure about privacy, on average, 79 % of the students feel their credentials are secured when accessing VDI platforms (Fig. 3(a)).
- More than 50 % of students make use of VDI platforms in their course work and assignments as shown in Fig. 3(b).

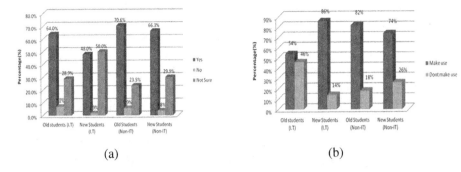

(a)   (b)

Fig. 3. (a) Student perceived credential security using virtual platforms; (b) Effectiveness of VDI on student course work (Usage).

- Generally newer students are more satisfied with the Virtual storage space of 100 MB provided than senior students as shown in Fig. 4(a).
- Students averagely have good accessibility but some face login errors, Virtual labs PC freezing and lag in some applications as shown in Fig. 4(b).

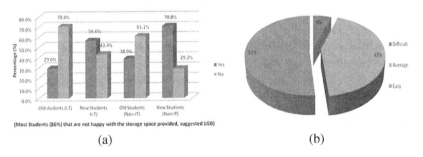

(a)   (b)

Fig. 4. (a) Student Satisfaction with VDI provided storage space (100 MB per student); (b) Student ease of accessibility to virtual computer labs.

- Overall 80 % of students feel virtualization has helped them in better communicating with their lecturers. However, the other 20 % unanimously expressed their dissatisfaction in that the virtualized platforms provided for communication was only suited for a one-way medium – from lecturer to student and not the other way around.

4.3.2   Statistics Relating to Academic Staff

- *Seamless Transition:* All interviewed faculty members alleged that there was no perceived difference in the new virtualized systems implemented as opposed to the older traditional system as there was an absolute and seamless transition.
- *Performance Issues:* Especially for IT faculty staff and students, high Memory Utilization Apps such as RobotC, Arena, Matlab, Lightwave and Unity tend to have declined performance having been virtualized. These virtualized lab applications are generally slow, and seen as highly time-consuming by its users. This leaves the

academic members who utilize these virtual apps frustrated as well as giving the new I.T students a bad impression about the course offered.

- *Access:* Virtualization provides improved/convenient access to academic materials off-campus. However, there is lack of control for some virtual apps especially ones used by the IT faculty. Some apps such as Cyber-cage, which is a 3D scenario based IT security application used, may require some admin modifications to its configurations. Virtualization prevents such modification to be accomplished, leaving IT faculty members frustrated.
- *Interface:* 60 % of faculty members interviewed expressed that even though they utilized some virtualized platforms, the Interface is unsatisfactory and in some cases cumbersome. They stated that virtualized platforms such as RMS, and WebMail can and need to be improved in terms of the interface and usability.
- *User Rights:* 50 % of interviewed IT faculty member stated that RMS, which is a document management system used by faculty members to share documents, has some difficulty in enabling user-rights to documents intended for sharing and furthermore suggested that granting of rights should be made more transparent in the RMS interface.
- *Storage:* Due to Virtualization, there is improved effectiveness especially with the greater email storage space provided by the technology.
- *Security:* The interviewed faculty members pointed out that security and privacy remains uncompromised with virtualized platforms, however a general sense of insecurity remains with the fact that their data is stored remotely away from their close and immediate reach with virtualization.
- *Licensing:* For Academic members, virtualization technology provides access for utilizing applications online. However, there is a limitation in that some applications cannot be accessed off-campus due to license restriction. Therefore, the faculty members express their hopes for future availability of licenses for those applications which they and their students would immensely benefit from if virtualized and made available remotely off-campus. Such applications include Matlab, Arena and Lightwave.

In an extended version of this research, inferential hypothesis test results would be presented regarding the effectiveness of virtualization in academia.

5   Conclusions

We can conclude that virtualization is effective in academia as proven by the developed framework and survey analysis conducted within the campus. Student and faculty member feedback yielded positive results, even though the majority expressed that there is room for future improvement concerning availability of licensed applications, usability of interfaces, and performance of some specialized virtual lab applications with the implemented virtualization technology. Conclusively, we hope to see more and more universities move on to adopt virtualization technology in their campuses as an application of cloud computing to improve convenience and efficiency of academia as well as save costs in the IT infrastructure development and maintenance in the long run.

References

1. Kurilovas, E., Dagiene, V.: Learning objects and virtual learning environments technical evaluation criteria. Electron. J. e-Learn. **7**(2), 127–136 (2009)
2. BouSaba, C., Burton, L., Fatehi, F.: Using virtualization technology to improve education. In: 2nd International Conference on Education and New Learning Technologies, pp. 201–206 (2010)
3. G5Networks–Technology Partner (2013). http://www.g5networks.net/virtualization.html. Accessed 22 March 2013
4. Citrix. Virtualization: Meeting the Higher Education IT Challenge. Citrix Application Delivery Infrastructure, 1–14 (2009)
5. Chawdhry, A., Mance, C.: Virtualization: providing better computing to universities. Inf. Syst. Educators Conf. ISECON, Nashville, USA **27**(1401), 1–6 (2010)
6. Anisetti, M., Bellandi, V., Colombo, A., Cremonini, M., Damiani, E., Frati, F., Hounsou, J.T., Rebeccani, D.: Learning computer networking on open paravirtual laboratories. IEEE Trans. Educ. **50**(4), 302–311 (2007)
7. Scarfone, K., Souppaya, M., Hoffman, P.: Guide to Security for Full Virtualization Technologies. National Institute of Standards and Technology (2011). http://www.nist.gov/manuscript-publicationsearch.cfm?pub_id=907776
8. Murphy, M.C., McClelland, M.K.: My personal computer lab: operating in the "Cloud". Inf. Syst. Educ. J. **7**(93) (2009). http://isedj.org/7/93/
9. Dobrilovic, D., Zeljko, S.: Using virtualization software in operating systems course. In: International Conference on Information Technology: Research and Education, pp. 222–226 (2006)
10. Lunsford, D.: Virtualization technologies in information systems education. J. Inf. Syst. Educ. **20**(3), 339–348 (2010)
11. Fuertes, W., Lopez de Vergara J.E., Meneses, F.: Educational platform using virtualization technologies: teaching-learning applications and research use cases. In: Proceedings of the II ACE Seminar: Knowledge Construction in Online Collaborative Communities, pp. 1–6 (2009)
12. Galan, F., Fernandez, D., Fuertes, W., Gomez, M., Lopez de Vergara, J.E.: Scenario-based virtual network infrastructure management in research and educational testbeds with VNUML: application cases and current challenges. Ann. Telecommun. **64**(5–6), 305–323 (2009)
13. Miseviciene, R., Ambraziene, D., Tuminauskas, R., Pazereckas, N.: Educational infrastructure using virtualization technologies: experience at kaunas university of technology. Inf. Educ. **11**(2), 227–237 (2011)
14. Castiglione, A., Cattaneo, G., Luigi, C., Ezio, C., Carlo Fulvio M.: Virtual Lab: a concrete experience in building multi-purpose virtualized labs for Computer Science Education. Dipartimento di Informatica - Universit`a degli Studi di Salerno, Italy, pp. 1–15 (2010)
15. García, C.R., Quesada-Arencibia, A., Candela, S., Carrasco, E., González, A.: Teaching information systems technologies: a new approach based on virtualization and hosting technologies. Int. J. Online Eng. **8**(4), 32–41 (2012)

A Study of Resource Management for Fault-Tolerant and Energy Efficient Cloud Datacenter

Dong-Ki Kang, Fawaz Alhazemi, Seong-Hwan Kim, and Chan-Hyun Youn$^{(\boxtimes)}$

School of Electrical Engineering, KAIST, Daejeon, Korea
{dkkang, fawaz, s.h_kim, chyoun}@kaist.ac.kr

Abstract. In cloud computing datacenters, the reliability and energy consumption have been studied as main challenges to achieve the reputation of cloud service users and the cost efficiency. To overcome the system fault of the datacenter, VM request load has to be distributed on multiple hosts to minimize the effect to the running cloud applications. Moreover, Dynamic Right Sizing (DRS) which adjusts the number of active hosts and sleep hosts in order to reduce the energy consumption in view of the resource usage cost. To do this, we propose the resource management scheme based on the portfolio diversification which has been studied in economics. The proposed scheme is able to reduce the fault of application significantly by finding the near Pareto optimal solution through Simulated Annealing approach We show the efficiency of our proposed scheme through the simple analytical results.

Keywords: Fault-tolerant · Cloud computing · Energy efficient · Resource management · Load balancing

1 Introduction

Nowadays, cloud computing datacenters are facing the system fault and the power consumption problems. In google datacenter [1], the thousand servers experience the fault at least in the first year per one cluster which consists of 1800 servers in general and the hard disk failure is the main factor of the system fault. Moreover, if the error is occurred in the power distribution unit of the datacenter, then $500 \sim 1000$ server machines are disabled during 6 h at least. In general, 50 percents of the cluster are experience overheat.

To solve this problem, many traditional fault-tolerant schemes have employed the data replication mechanism. That is, they replicate the data of the cloud service application to the backup host, and recover the replicated data from the backup host

---

D.-K. Kang—Please note that the LNICST Editorial assumes that all authors have used the western naming convention, with given names preceding surnames. This determines the structure of the names in the running heads and the author index.

© ICST Institute for Computer Sciences, Social Informatics and Telecommunications Engineering 2016
Y. Zhang et al. (Eds.): CloudComp 2015, LNICST 167, pp. 22–29, 2016.
DOI: 10.1007/978-3-319-38904-2_3

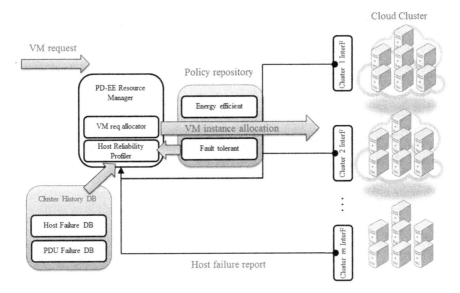

Fig. 1. PD-EE resource manager structure

when the failure is occured in the original host. However, this procedures require the additional host to do replication, this causes the performance overhead by replication process and increases the resource usage cost. In addition, the inconsistency problem may be occurred between the origianl data and replicated data, therefore the synchronization is required consistently. This is inefficient.

In this paper, we propose the dynamic resource balancing algorithm for fault-tolerant resource management without any inefficient replication scheme. Our proposed algorithm is based on the portfolio diversification in economics. In the portfoilo diversification the asset is not invested into the single items but rather is distributed to multiple items, therefore the economic risk is able to be minimized. In this mechanism, the reliablity is increased according the average value and the risk is decreased by reducing the variation value. We find the resource allocation solution with maximized average and minimized variation by searching the near Pareto optimal solution since the allocation solution is kind of the multi objective problems. We apply the Simulated Annealing Procedure as a heuristic algorithm to derive the desirable VM balancing solution. The additional objective for the datacenter resource management is the energy consumption which is a main part of the resource usage cost. The VM instance balancing solution increases the number of active host, the resource usage cost is increased by increasing power consumption. Therefore, it is important to derive the resource management strategy to achieve the reasonable fault-tolerancy with energy efficient resource allocation. To do this, we propose the algorithm satisfying these two objectives. We show that our proposed algorithm outperforms with the random and existing packing schemes through the simulation testbed based on nodeJS servers.

2 System Structure

Figure 1 shows the structure of our proposed Portfolio Diversification based Energy Efficient Resource Manager (PD-EE RM) module. When the VM request is submitted to the interface of the system, PD-EE RM determines the desirable host of the cloud cluster by predefined VM packing scheme and allocate the VM instance through the VM request allocator. In this case, the weight values for the energy efficiency and fault-tolerancy are set in the Policy repository module. In Cluster History DB, the reports of the not-working Power Distribution Unit (PDU) or not-working host in each distributed cluster are written. The reliability of the whole datacenter is derived based on the stored DB in the PE-EE RM module and the parameters for the resource allocation are adjusted according to the derived reliability.

3 Portfolio Diversification Based Resource Management Scheme

In this chapter, we describe the resource management strategy based on the Portfolio diversification. Our proposed scheme is based on following two equations.

$$E[R_x] = \sum_{i=1}^{n} w_i E[R_i] = w_1 \mu_1 + \cdots + w_n \mu_n \tag{1}$$

$$Var(R_x) = E[R_x - E[R_x]]^2 = \sum_{i=1}^{n} w_i^2 \sigma_i^2 + \sum_{i \neq j} w_i w_j Cov[R_i, R_j] =$$

$$\sum_{i=1}^{n} w_i^2 \sigma_i^2 + \sum_{i \neq j} w_i w_j \sigma_i \sigma_j \frac{Cov[R_i, R_j]}{\sigma_i \sigma_j} = \sum_{i=1}^{n} w_i^2 \sigma_i^2 + \sum_{i \neq j} w_i w_j \sigma_i \sigma_j \rho_{ij} \tag{2}$$

where x is the resource allocation solution, and w_i is the allocated weight for the host i. μ_i represents the average reliability of the host i, and n is the number of physical hosts. $E[R_x]$ is the expected success ratio of the resource allocation solution x. σ_i is the standard deviation of the physical hosts and $Cov[R_i, R_j]$ is the covariation between the physical host i and the physical host j. ρ_{ij} is the correlation of the physical host i and physical host j, this value is same to $\frac{Cov[R_i, R_j]}{\sigma_i \sigma_j}$. That is, the average value in Eq. (1) represents the reliability of the cloud resource allocation and as the bigger, the better. The variation value in Eq. (2) represents the risk of cloud resource allocation. For instance, there are two resource allocation solution A and B, and the reliability of A and B is average 80 % in the same. In this case, if the variation of A is 20 and the one of B is 10, then it means that the reliability of B is better than the one of B because the risk of A is bigger than B even the average values are same. When the failure is occurred under A, whether all the VM instances are free from the failure or many VM instances are affected, the moderate effect is not exist. Contrastively, some VM instance are affected when the failure is occured under B, however the effect level is smaller than the case of A. That is, the smaller variation, the better reliability.

Reliability : Expected return

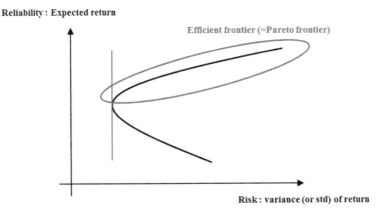

Fig. 2. The curve of average and variation for reliability

Figure 2 shows the performance curve in views of reliability with average and risk as evaluation metrics of the resource allocation solution. The upper part of the curve in graph represents the Pareto frontier of the reliability and the risk. That is, the points within the Pareto frontier represents the optimized resource allocation solutions in view of the fault-tolerant and the points outside the Pareto frontier are not optimized resource allocation solutions.

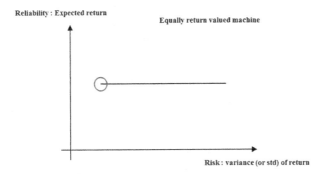

Fig. 3. Reliability and risk curve in the homogeneous host set

Figure 3 shows the performance curve of the homogeneous host set with the same reliability values. In this case, every resource allocation solutions have same fixed avaerage value and only variation values are different. The variation value is minimized when the VM instance workload is distributed perfectly and this solution is the only one optimized solution. Based on Eqs. (1) and (2), we apply the heuristic scheme to find the near optimal resource allocation solution. Our deployed heuristic scheme is based on Simulated Annealing search [3] and this is kind of the local searching techniques. This scheme searches optimal solution by adjusting the searching direction based on the solution searching running time. Our proposed algorithm based on Simulated Annealing is shown in Table 1.

Table 1. Algorithm 1 simulated annealing based VM allocation

Algorithm 1. Simulated Annealing based VM allocation scheme

1. select the random resource allocation solution.
2. Evaluate the reliability and risk by calculating the reliability average and variation of each neighbor solution of the staring solution.
3. Get the weighted sum of reliability and the risk.
4. Get the objective funtion values of each solution and derive the switching probability according to the function values.
5. Select next solution according to the switching probability
6. Update the temperature parameter
7. When the delta E values of all the neighbor slutions are under the pred efined threshold value, the searching of the solution is stop and final resource allocation solution is chosen.

Algorithm 1 considers the VM allocation policy with Simulated Annealing scheme. The objective function based on reliability and variation values is defined by using weighted sum approach as follows,

$$f(x) = \alpha \cdot E(R_x) + \beta \cdot Var(R_x) \tag{3}$$

where α is the weight for average value of the solution x and β is the weight for the variation value representing the risk. The switching probability of the neighbor solutions is calculating according to the objective function value as follows,

$$p(x_{neigh}) = e^{\frac{\Delta E = f(x_{neigh}) - f(x_{origin})}{kT}} \tag{4}$$

$$T_t = z \times T_{t-1}, 0 < z < 1 \tag{5}$$

where k is Bolzman constant. During the solution searching procedure, the temperature value T is decreased and the switching probability to the worse solution is near zero. When the delta E is under the threshold E_{th}, the solution searching is finished and the last chosen solution is the final solution.

4   Analytical Results

In this chapter, we show the efficiency of our proposed algorithm through simple analytical results. Figure 4 shows the the example of the VM instance allocation of the 5 homogeneous host machines with the same success rate and failure rate. The number of allocated VM instances is 5 and the their required flavor types are same. The failure return is represented as the number 0 and the success return is 1, the average reliability of each host is 0.8 and all the values are same. Figure 5 shows the variance and covariance of all the possible host pairs. The variances and the covariances are same since the average reliability of all the homogeneous host is same.

PM1	PM2	PM3	PM4	PM5
failure rate				

	PM1	PM2	PM3	PM4	PM5
failure rate	20%	20%	20%	20%	20%
success rate	80%	80%	80%	80%	80%

Fig. 4. Five host machines with same success rate

	Variance / covariance				
	PM1	PM2	PM3	PM4	PM5
PM1	$\sigma_1^2 = 0.34$	$\sigma_{12} = 0.16$	$\sigma_{13} = 0.16$	$\sigma_{14} = 0.16$	$\sigma_{15} = 0.16$
PM2	$\sigma_{21} = 0.16$	$\sigma_2^2 = 0.34$	$\sigma_{23} = 0.16$	$\sigma_{24} = 0.16$	$\sigma_{25} = 0.16$
PM3	$\sigma_{31} = 0.16$	$\sigma_{32} = 0.16$	$\sigma_3^2 = 0.34$	$\sigma_{34} = 0.16$	$\sigma_{35} = 0.16$
PM4	$\sigma_{41} = 0.16$	$\sigma_{42} = 0.16$	$\sigma_{43} = 0.16$	$\sigma_4^2 = 0.34$	$\sigma_{45} = 0.16$
PM5	$\sigma_{51} = 0.16$	$\sigma_{52} = 0.16$	$\sigma_{53} = 0.16$	$\sigma_{54} = 0.16$	$\sigma_5^2 = 0.34$

Fig. 5. Variance and covairance with each host pair

Figure 6 shows the case of the all-in VM consolidation. In this case, the weight of host 1 is one and the weights of other hosts are zero since all the VM instances are allocated to the host 1. The average reliability of the allocated solution is 0.8 and the variation is 0.1156. Figure 7 shows the case of equally weighted resource allocation which distributes all the VM instances to the hosts. The number of VM instance is five and the number of hosts is also five, each host has one allocated Vm instance. In this

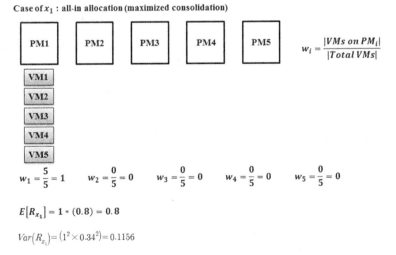

Case of x_1 : all-in allocation (maximized consolidation)

$$w_i = \frac{|VMs\ on\ PM_i|}{|Total\ VMs|}$$

$$w_1 = \frac{5}{5} = 1 \qquad w_2 = \frac{0}{5} = 0 \qquad w_3 = \frac{0}{5} = 0 \qquad w_4 = \frac{0}{5} = 0 \qquad w_5 = \frac{0}{5} = 0$$

$$E[R_{x_1}] = 1 * (0.8) = 0.8$$

$$Var(R_{x_1}) = (1^2 \times 0.34^2) = 0.1156$$

Fig. 6. Average and variance values of all-in allocation

28   D.-K. Kang et al.

case, the weight of host is 0.2 and the average relilability is 0.8, these values are same to the case of Fig. 6. However, the variance of the solution is 0.087 and this value is smaller than one in Fig. 6. This means that there is no error in every running VM instances if the failure is occurred from host 2 to host 5 but all the VM instances experience error if the failure is occurred in the host 1 in the case of Fig. 6. In this case, the risk is high. In the case of Fig. 7, there is absolutely the error VM instance if the failure is occurred from host 1 to host 5, but the number of error occurred VM instance is just one. That is, other 4 VM instances do not have any error. In this case, the risk is small.

In conclusion, we derive that the case of Fig. 6 has the better performance than the case of Fig. 7.

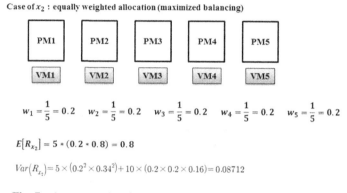

Fig. 7. Average and variance values of equally weighted allocation

5 Conclusion

We propose the fault-tolerant VM instance allocation scheme for the cloud computing environment. Our proposed scheme uses the average and variation of the reliability of the allocation solution based on the portfolio diversification. In order to find the near Pareto optimal solution satisfying both of the reasonable average and varaition, the Simulated Annealing heuristic is imployed in the proposed algorithm. In the analytical results, the performance of each solution with simple homogeneous hosts and VM instance submission. In ongoing works, we demonstrate that our proposed algorithm outperforms traditional algorithms through various simulation results.

Acknowledgments. This work was supported by 'Electrically phase-controlled beamforming lighting device based on 2D nano-photonic phased array for lidar' grant from Civil Military Technology Cooperation, Korea.

References

1. Google. www.google.com
2. Belly, Z.Y.: Socially responsible investing and portfolio diversification. J. Financ. Res. **28**(1), 41–57 (2005)

3. Bandyopadhyay, S., Saha, S., Maulik, U., Deb, K.: A simulated annealing-based multiob-jective optimization algorithm: AMOSA. IEEE Trans. Evol. Comput. **12**(3), 269–283 (2008)
4. Xiao, Z., Song, W., Chen, Q.: Dynamic resource allocation using virtual machines for cloud computing environment. IEEE Trans. Parallel Distrib. Syst. **24**(6), 1107–1117 (2013)
5. A-Eldin, A., Tordsson, J., Elmroth, E., Kihl, M.: Workload classfication for efficient auto-scaling of cloud resources. Umea University, Sweden (2013)

User Isolation in Multi-user Multi-touch Devices Using OS-Level Virtualization

Minkyeong Lee[1], Minho Lee[1], Inhyeok Kim[1], and Young Ik Eom[2(✉)]

[1] College of Information and Communication Engineering, Sungkyunkwan University,
Suwon 440-746, Korea
{krong96,minhozx,kkojiband}@skku.edu
[2] College of Software, Sungkyunkwan University, Suwon 440-746, Korea
yieom@skku.edu

Abstract. Providing multi-user isolation is one of the most important issues in computing environments with multi-touch displays because multi-touch devices such as tabletops allow multiple users to interact simultaneously. However, existing window manager, which is commonly used to control the placement and appearance of windows, never provides isolation among the users. In this paper, we present a method that provides isolation in multi-touch multi-user computing systems using OS-level virtualization and show the effectiveness of the method with serveral experimental results. Our experimental results show that OS-level virtualization sucessfully provides both multi-user interaction and isolation in multi-touch devices.

Keywords: Multi-user environment · Multi-touch device · User interaction · User isolation · OS-level virtualization · Docker

1 Introduction

As multi-user computing systems with multi-touch devices become increasingly available, users can interact more easily in those environments [1]. In those multi-user environments, user isolation is important to prevent negative interferences among the users. However, it is difficult to provide multi-user isolation in such computing systems, because they were designed only for a single user. To support multi-user functionalities, there are two major considerations: (1) user interaction and (2) user isolation.

First, user interaction is necessary to share data of each user. Generally, user spaces are logically partitioned in multi-user systems, and to support user interaction in such systems, window manager should be used [2], which is a software layer between kernel and application, and manages window placement on the screen and provides control of common actions (e.g., click, drag and drop). For user interaction, the window manager exploits Inter-Process Communication (IPC) which has lower overhead than Remote Procedure Call (RPC). However, this makes it more difficult to achieve multi-user isolation. Second, isolation of user space should be guaranteed to exclude negative interferences among the tasks of users. To do this, previous works used full virtualization or para-virtualization on mobile devices, desktops, and servers [3]. However, these technologies are inappropriate for multi-user multi-touch devices, because they use multiple guest kernels for multiple execution environments. In these technologies, window manager is difficult to provide efficient interactions via UNIX domain sockets. In contrast, OS-level virtualization can efficiently support user interactions because all the separate user spaces share only a single kernel. Moreover, it facilitates isolation by partitioning user space with containers.

In this paper, we verify that OS-level virtualization is suitable for user isolation in multi-user multi-touch systems. For evaluation, we performed experiments using Docker, which is a framework based on OS-level virtualization [4]. In case of Docker, it has some advantages: (1) there is no modification of kernel and applications, and (2) it reduces waste of space by managing file system images via AuFS, which provides a layered stack of file systems. Experimental results show that Docker has just 0.5 % performance degradation, compared to native system. Furthermore, the overhead of Docker is less than 1 % in the experiments that measure frame rates of User Interface (UI) applications and costs of client-server communication and UNIX domain socket communication.

The remainder of this paper is organized as follows. Section 2 discusses related work, including window manager and virtualization technologies. Section 3 describes the reason why it is necessary to use OS-level virtualization in multi-user multi-touch systems. Section 4 presents experimental results. Finally, Sect. 5 concludes this paper and describes a future direction.

2 Related Work

In this section, we describe window manager and discuss typical virtualization technologies.

2.1 Window Manager

Window manager is a software package that manages windows on a screen and processes user's inputs on appropriate windows [5]. In addition, it performs not only framing windows but also controlling user's actions [6].

X window system is one of the standard window systems. It is based on client-server model and handles shaping and staking of windows, which are separate spaces on a screen. In this system, applications are connected to the server called a compositor, which handles rendering of changed windows. Even though X is commonly used for UNIX-like systems, it has a problem; X has become increasingly heavy, while it used for decades [7]. In other words, it includes unnecessary functions and is difficult to apply new technologies. In order to replace this system, many researchers have developed a novel lightweight window system, Wayland, by removing unnecessary remote-assisted functions and using open source API [8]. It uses the reference compositor called Weston [9], which has the same role of the server in the X window system.

2.2   Virtualization Technologies

To run multiple OSs on a single hardware device, virtualization technology is commonly used. In virtualized system, since the guest OS in each virtual machine does not have permission to directly access hardware resources, it cannot execute privileged instructions. For this reason, hypervisor handles requests of the guest OS to mediate between guest OS and hardware resources. In accordance with its control mechanism, virtualization technologies can be classified into two cases: (1) platform-level virtualization (full virtualization and para-virtualization) and (2) OS-level virtualization.

Full virtualization. Exploits either Binary Translation (BT) or hardware assistance. BT is a software-based approach. When guest OS tries to access hardware resources with privileged instructions, hypervisor translates the instructions and allow guest OS to access the hardware resources, as shown in Fig. 1(a). In case of hardware assistance, hardware such as Intel VT-x and AMD-v supports the process of translation [10].

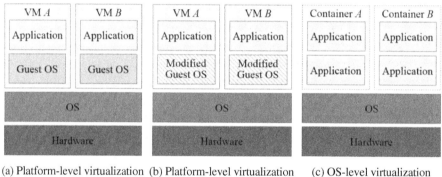

(a) Platform-level virtualization   (b) Platform-level virtualization   (c) OS-level virtualization
    (full virtualization)   (para-virtualization)

Fig. 1. Architectures of virtualization technologies

Para-virtualization. Allows modified guest OS to directly access hardware resources [11]. Modified guest OS translates privileged instruction into *hypercall*, a software *trap* from guest to hypervisor, by inserting control codes in the guest OS, as shown in Fig. 1(b). By doing so, para-virtualization reduces interference of hypervisor. So, it outperforms full virtualization in terms of I/O performance.

OS-level virtualization. Packages several guests into containers. Guest does not have its own kernel unlike full virtualization or para-virtualization. In other words, all the guests share a single kernel of the host, as shown in Fig. 1(c). Since OS-level virtualization does not have interference of hypervisor, its performance is similar to non-virtualized system. Moreover, it consumes fewer resources compared to full virtualization or para-virtualization, because it has a single kernel [12].

2.3   Case Study

Hwang et al. proposed a prototype of platform-level virtualization for Xen on ARM CPU architecture [13]. It provides mobile phone security for high trusted computing capability by using Xen hypervisor. In addition, it supports secure execution by classifying secure guests and non-secure guests in user mode. However, it is unsuitable for user isolation in multi-user multi-touch devices, because para-virtualization has communication overhead, where each guest should communicate with other guests via RPC. Linux VServer was proposed for isolation of servers by using OS-level virtualization technology [14]. In this system, user space is separated into Virtual Private Server (VPS) by the container. VPS is almost identical to a real server and is able to be regarded as a guest on the systems of full virtualization or para-virtualization. Soltesz et al. verified the effectiveness of VServer, compared to Xen [15]. They showed that VServer provides more efficient user isolation, in that VPS has no additional software layer such as guest kernel.

3   Why OS-Level Virtualization is Necessary

As aforementioned in Sect. 2, virtualization technology is commonly used for user isolation. However, both full virtualization and para-virtualization are inappropriate to provide user interactions. In virtualized system, each guest has its own kernel, and thus it is difficult to share data among the guests, although it is not impossible. Even if RPC can be used for interactions such as sharing data, it has higher overhead than IPC, due to a long communication path [16]. On the other hand, OS-level virtualization can provide interactions among the guests by using IPC. This is because it just separates user space into containers and makes guests share a single kernel. Thus, it can share file descriptors and exploit shared memory. In other words, it can support both user interactions and user isolation. For this reason, OS-level virtualization is suitable for multi-user multi-touch systems such as tabletops.

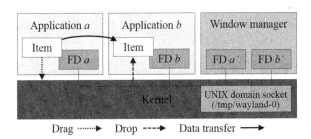

Fig. 2.   Process of drag and drop

Now, let us explain the advantage of OS-level virtualization by describing the process of drag and drop. As shown in Fig. 2, when application *a* gets drag event, the application registers *data source* of the item at window manager. Then application *b* receives the item by using the *data source* from window manager and processes drop event. These two applications can communicate with each other on a single kernel. In this way, window manager exploits UNIX domain socket and file descriptors. Figure 3 depicts that it is possible for applications to communicate on OS-level virtualization framework, because all the applications share a single kernel, even though they belong to different containers that allow them to be isolated logically. In contrast to OS-level virtualization, full virtualization does not allow applications in different guests to communicate in the way of OS-level virtualization, as shown in Fig. 4. The reason is that it has multiple kernels, and *data source* of the item in application c cannot be transmitted from guest c to guest d via UNIX domain socket. In case of para-virtualization, it also has a number of kernels. For this reason, it is difficult to apply both full virtualization and para-virtualization in multi-user multi-touch devices.

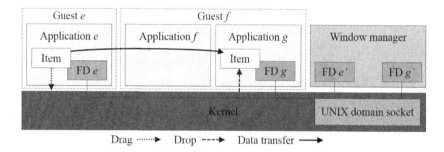

Fig. 3. Process of drag and drop in OS-level virtualization

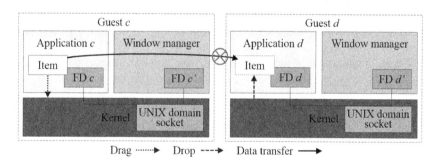

Fig. 4. Process of drag and drop in full virtualization

4   Evaluation

4.1   Experimental Setup

We performed our experiments on a system equipped with Intel Core i5-3570, 4 GB of RAM, and 1 TB Samsung HDD. We set two types of system configuration. The first system configuration is Ubuntu 14.04 LTS with Linux kernel 3.16.0. In this environment, we used two virtualization technologies: (1) Docker and (2) KVM with QEMU and hardware assistance of Intel-VTx. To verify the effectiveness of Docker, we measured the performance with a series of common benchmarks including Sysbench, ApacheBench, and IOzone. The second system configuration is Ubuntu 15.04 with Linux kernel 3.19.0. We installed Wayland 1.7.0 with Weston 1.7.0 on the system and compared Docker with native system, in terms of frame rate and costs that is incurred by client-server communication and UNIX domain socket communication.

4.2 Experimental Results

CPU performance. We first evaluated CPU performance of each virtualization technology by using Sysbench, which is a multi-threaded benchmark tool [17]. We performed calculation of n prime numbers. As shown in Fig. 5, the performance of Docker is similar to that of native system. It indicates that Docker does not have CPU overhead for the calculation. In contrast to Docker, KVM has the performance degradation by up to 11.68 %, compared to the native system. This is because it has interference of hypervisor and should pass additional layers, such as guest kernels, to access hardware resources.

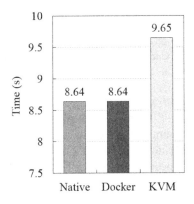
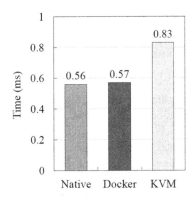

Fig. 5. Comparison of CPU performance   **Fig. 6.** Comparison of network performance

Network performance. To evaluate network performance of each virtualization technology, we created a server on host and then sent 100 requests to the server with 10 concurrency levels by using the ApacheBench [18], which is a tool for benchmarking Apache Hypertext Transfer Protocol (HTTP) server. We measured round-trip time, which takes for a request to travel from an application to the server and back to the application. As shown in Fig. 6, the performance of Docker is approximately equal to that of native system with only 0.89 % performance degradation. On the other hand, KVM has higher round-trip time by up to 47.32 %. The major reason is that it performs additional processes such as a request transmission between guest and host.

Performance of file operations. We performed experiments related to the operation of directory by using fileop, a file operation benchmark in IOzone [19]. The fileop performs file operations such as access, chdir, stat, open, and close. In this experiment, Docker has the worst performance as shown in Fig. 7. On average, its elapsed time is

1.46x higher than that of native system. This is because Docker has the overhead of namespace isolation and *cgroups*. However, since UI application used in multi-user multi-touch system consists mainly of CPU-bound and network-bound tasks, it is a negligible overhead.

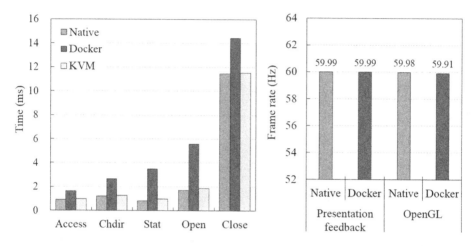

Fig. 7. Comparison of performance of file operations

Fig. 8. Comparison of frame rate of UI application

Frame rate of UI applications. We first measured frame rate of an animation using Presentation feedback, which delivers information of display synchronization to the application [20]. As shown in Fig. 8, both native system and Docker have about 60 Hz frame rate. In case of frame rate of the animation using OpenGL, Docker and native system have 59.90 Hz and 59.98 Hz frame rate, respectively. It indicates that Docker does not incur performance degradation for running UI applications, although user space is partitioned with the containers.

Client-server communication. We measured round-trip time, taken for a dummy message to travel back and forth between window manager and application in a container. For comparison, we used *Weston-simple-shm*, which is one of the UI applications in Weston. As shown in Fig. 9, Docker has higher round-trip time by up to 2.55 %, compared to the native system. It implies that there is little overhead of communication between window manager and an isolated application.

UNIX domain socket communication. To evaluate communication costs between two applications, where one is in a container and the other is not, we set up request size as 10 bytes and then sent 1,000,000 requests by using UNIX domain socket in Wayland (/tmp/wayland-0). As shown in Fig. 10, total execution time of Docker has delays of only 0.01 s. In other words, applications inside and outside containers can communicate with each other by using UNIX domain socket without overhead.

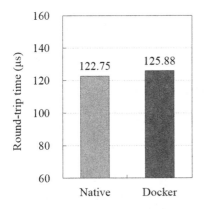

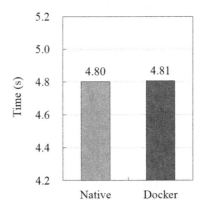

Fig. 9. Comparison of communication costs between window manager and application

Fig. 10. Comparison of communication costs between applications

5   Conclusion

In multi-user multi-touch systems, user interaction and user isolation should be carefully considered for collaboration of users and tasks and prevention of interferences between tasks. However, since full virtualization and para-virtualization have communication overhead between kernel and applications, OS-level virtualization can be more appropriate candidate for multi-user environment. Moreover, it guarantees user isolation by partitioning the user space into containers.

In this paper, we verified the effectiveness of Docker, which is based on OS-level virtualization, in terms of system performance and window manager operations. To compare Docker with native system and KVM, we performed experiments by using some common benchmarks, such as Sysbench, ApacheBench, and IOzone. Experimental results show that Docker has little performance degradation, despite overheads of namespace isolation and *cgroup*. Moreover, the performance of Docker is nearly equal to that of native system in the experiments that measure frame rates of UI applications and costs of client-server communication and UNIX domain socket communication. Therefore, we demonstrated that Docker is greatly appropriate for multi-user multi-touch systems, when we consider system performance, user interaction, and user isolation.

In future work, we will perform additional evaluation including Xen, which make use of para-virtualization, and then compare it with native system, Docker, and KVM. In addition, we will evaluate the performance of Docker by applying it to a practical device for multiple users and multiple applications.

Acknowledgments.   This work was supported by ICT R&D program of MSIP/IITP. [R0126-15-1065, (SW StarLab) Development of UX Platform Software for Supporting Concurrent Multi-users on Large Displays]. Young Ik Eom is the corresponding author of this paper.

References

1. Gartner Identifies the Top 10 Strategic Technology Trends for 2015. http://www.gartner.com/newsroom/id/2867917
2. Hamdan, N., Voelker, S., Borchers, J.: Conceptual framework for surface manager on interactive tabletops. In: CHI 2013 Extended Abstracts on Human Factors in Computing Systems, pp. 1527–1532. ACM, USA (2013)
3. Reshetova, E., Karhunen, J., Nyman, T., Asokan, N.: Security of OS-level virtualization technologies. In: Bernsmed, K., Fischer-Hübner, S. (eds.) NordSec 2014. LNCS, vol. 8788, pp. 77–93. Springer, Heidelberg (2014)
4. What is Docker? https://www.Docker.com/whatisDocker/
5. Scheifler, R., Gettys, J.: The X Window System. ACM Trans. Graph. 5(2), 79–109 (1986)
6. Stern, D., Herbrich, R., Graepel, T.: Matchbox: large scale online bayesian recommendations. In: 18th International Conference on World Wide Web, pp. 111–120. ACM, USA (2009)
7. Wayland: Motivation. http://wayland.freedesktop.org/docs/html/ch01.html#sect-Motivation
8. Wayland. http://wayland.free-desktop.org/
9. Wayland: the Compositing Manager as the Display Server. http://wayland.freedesktop.org/docs/html/ch01.html#sect-Compositing-manager-display-server
10. Walters, J., Chaudhary, V., Cha, M., Guercio, S., Gallo, S.: A comparison of virtualization technologies for Hpc. In: 22nd International Conference on Advanced Information Networking and Applications, pp. 861–868. IEEE, USA (2008)
11. Barham, P., Dragovic, B., Fraser, K., Hand, S., Harris, T., Ho, A., Neugebauer, R., Pratt, I., Warfield, A.: Xen and the art of virtualization. In: 19th ACM Symposium on Operating Systems Principles, pp. 164–177. ACM, USA (2003)
12. Yu, Y.: Os-level Virtualization and Its Applications. ProQuest, USA (2007)
13. Hwang, J., Suh, S., Heo, S., Park, C., Ryu, J., Park, S., Kim, C.: Xen on arm: system virtualization using xen hypervisor for arm-based secure mobile phones. In: 5th Consumer Communications and Network Conference, pp. 257–287. IEEE, USA (2008)
14. Linux Vserver. http://linux-vserver.org/Overview
15. Soltesz, S., Potzl, H., Fiuczynski, M., Bavier, A., Peterson, L.: Container-based operating system virtualization: a scalable, high-performance alternative to hypervisors. In: 2nd ACM SIGOPS/EuroSys European Conference on Computer Systems, pp. 275–287. ACM, USA (2007)
16. Kim, K., Kim, C., Jung, S., Shin, H., Kim, J.: Inter-domain socket communications supporting high performance and full binary compatibility on xen. In: 4th ACM SIGPLAN/SIGOPS International Conference on Virtual Execution Environments, pp. 11–20. ACM, USA (2008)
17. Sysbench. http://imysql.com/wp-content/uploads/2014/10/sysbench-manual.pdf
18. Apache Http Server Benchmarking Tool. http://httpd.apache.org/docs/2.2/en/programs/ab.html
19. Iozone Filesystem Benchmark. http://www.iozone.org/
20. Weston 1.7.0 Presentation Extension. http://lists.freedesktop.org/archives/wayland-devel/2015-February/019977.html

A VM Vector Management Scheme for QoS Constraint Task Scheduling in Cloud Environment

Kyung-no Joo$^{(\boxtimes)}$, Seonghwan Kim, Dongki Kang, Yusik Kim,
Hyungyu Jang, and Chan-Hyun Youn

Department of Electrical Engineering, KAIST, Daejeon, Korea
{eu8198, s.h_kim, dkkang, yusiky326, chyoun}@kaist.ac.kr

Abstract. To reduce operational costs in computing service, there have been many researches on resource utilization improvement. In cloud environment, virtualization technology, coupled with virtual machine migration, can improve utilization of physical machines by server consolidation. Cloud service providers will consolidate virtual machines in order to reduce the number of physical machines running, therefore reducing their operational cost. Capacity of resources used by virtual machines can be set by users who schedule their tasks, minimizing resource waste by underutilization. However, it is difficult for a user to find the optimal virtual machine with respect to the resource capacity in minimal cost. To solve this problem, cloud service broker is required between users and cloud service providers. Task scheduling in cloud service broker solves finding virtual machine with lowest cost while satisfying SLA. Previous methods using mixed integer programming have showed difficulties in complexity and as system got larger and more complex, they could not solve the problems effectively. In this paper, with preliminary experiment, we propose vector modeling on virtual machine types and tasks can be applied and used in VM management. The allocated computing resources for each task components showed low complexity in operation of VM managements and effectiveness in task consolidation.

Keywords: Cloud computing · Scheduling workloads · SLA

1 Introduction

Cloud computing service provides computing resources such as CPU, RAM, storage and network through internet as much as users want to use, as long as they are willing to pay. This model is called "pay-per-use model" and it is one of the major characteristics of cloud computing service. Cloud computing provides scalable, theoretical infinite computing resources to users with low risk of resource waste because they can always stop using the service with no penalty or investment made whenever demand for resources has disappeared [1, 2].

Users who are willing to use cloud service to process their requests must decide which resource to use. There are many cloud service providers providing many different types of virtual machines (VM) with different computing power and price. Not only that, there is no standard to compare performance of different VM types across different cloud

© ICST Institute for Computer Sciences, Social Informatics and Telecommunications Engineering 2016
Y. Zhang et al. (Eds.): CloudComp 2015, LNICST 167, pp. 39–49, 2016.
DOI: 10.1007/978-3-319-38904-2_5

service providers. As a result, users find it difficult to compare performance across different cloud service providers. Moreover, SLAs guaranteed by cloud service providers [3, 4] are limited to resource capacity and availability with given prices. Since performance level for each specific application is not guaranteed, users find it difficult to make optimal decision in choosing which resource to buy. One solution to this problem is to have a brokering service layer to solve resource allocation decision problem instead. The broker needs to translate user requesting SLA consisting of time and cost constraints to SLA which cloud service providers provide to users: resource capacity, price and availability. Then, users can simply request jobs with time and cost constraints and cloud broker service can decide whether or not the job can be processed within constraints.

In cloud computing, with virtualization technology [5], one physical machine (PM) runs more than one virtual machines (VM). Therefore, through virtualization, multi tenants can be served by a single physical machine. This approach is called server consolidation and it allows efficient usage of computing resources by running as many as VMs possible in a single PM as long as performance is not affected [6]. Addition to server consolidation, scheduling multi-requests to a single VM is also introduced [7]. Resource capacity of VM types provided by cloud service providers are relatively coarse-grained and there are not many tasks which can fully utilize given computing power with a single task alone. However with task consolidation, brokering service can improve resource utilization [7, 8]. There are two issues in task consolidation: how many tasks can we consolidate execute with a given VM type's resource capacity? And which tasks should be consolidated together to maximize resource utilization?

We want to solve a decision problem: choose a VM type provided by multi cloud service providers to schedule a QoS constraint application to minimize operational cost for cloud service broker. To maximize brokering service's profit, maximizing resource utilization is necessary. Some previous works [6, 9] used linear programming (LP) optimize the scheduling problem. However, using LP solver as optimizer has complexity issue: if system is complex, such as hybrid cloud environment, optimizing process takes too long to schedule tasks on-line. Also, they do not consider how the services are placed taking into account load balancing constraints in terms of individual resource components. Others [7] scheduled multi requests to a single VM in order to fully utilize a VM resource as long as SLA violations do not occur. However, they do not consider balance between resource components. If any resource component is fully utilized by scheduling specific resource-intensity tasks into same VM, other resources can be waste because no more task can be scheduled due to fully utilized single re-source component. Memory is fully almost fully utilized while CPU is underutilized. In this case, no more tasks can be scheduled because there is no sufficient memory resource left although CPU is underutilized. CPU resource becomes resource waste.

In this paper, we propose a VM vector management scheme which consolidates tasks to improve resource utilization of cloud resources. We define vectors representing VM types and tasks. We used vector sum and vector dot products to define scheduled total tasks, latency factor and balance factor. Using this information, we propose a scheduling scheme with low complexity. We deployed the proposed VM vector management scheme into scheduler in the brokering system

We will discuss the performance of the proposed system with experimental result in Sect. 3.

2 VM Vector Management Scheme in Task Scheduling

2.1 Modeling Task Consolidation in Cloud Computing Environment

To schedule incoming requested tasks online while consolidating them to minimize number of VMs running, we need an efficient way to calculate expected overall utilization of a VM after scheduling. If the VM is expected to have overutilization after scheduling the task, then the task must be scheduled to different VM. Otherwise, every task on the VM has a risk of violating SLA due to context switch delays.

To test how resource utilization changes when tasks are consolidated, we performed preliminary experiments in a cluster of cloud computing environment with OpenStack cloud plat-form installed. Detailed explanation on experimental environment is in Sect. 3.1. For simplicity, we focused on a single VM type with 1 VCPU, 1 GB RAM, and 10.0 GB disk resource capacity. We monitored resource utilization of RAM using System Information Gatherer And Reporter (SIGAR) [10]. MapChem task, which is a CPU-intensive sequencing task used in bioinformatics, is consolidated in a VM during the experiment. Table 1 shows how resource utilization changed as tasks are consolidated in the same VM.

Table 1. Memory utilization changes when tasks consolidate

	Number of tasks consolidated			
	0	1	2	3
Memory utilization	0.183593	0.023664	0.278868	0.328247
Change	–	+0.0530	+0.0422	+0.0494

Memory usage when no task is scheduled comes out to be about 0.18. This is because the VM is running Ubuntu 12.04 Server OS and other daemon processes such as Tomcat server to receive MapChem application requests from the broker. As one additional task requested and executed in parallel in the same VM, memory utilization increased by 0.048218 in average (Table. 2).

Table 2. CPU utilization changes when tasks consolidate

	Number of tasks consolidated		
	1	2	3
Execution time (s)	40.992	92.706	128.243
CPU utilization	0.20496	0.46353	0.641215

CPU utilization was difficult to measure with just SIGAR because it approaches 1.0 when VM is executing any CPU-intensive task. Therefore, we redefined CPU utilization for **QoS constraint applications** which have required deadline to execute and if deadline is not met, the broker loses profit. In other words, CPU Utilization for QoS Constraint Applications are defined as

$$U_{CPU} = \frac{(Used\ CPU\ Cycles\ by\ Given\ Task)}{(Total\ CPU\ Cycles\ Available\ Until\ Deadline)} \tag{1}$$

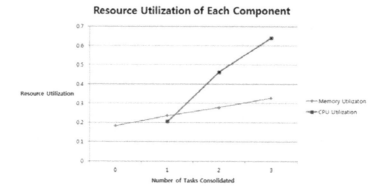

Fig. 1. Resource utilization when tasks consolidate

Both memory and CPU utilization changes come out to be linearly proportional to number of tasks consolidated in the VM currently. Linearity is shown in Fig. 2.

From this preliminary experiment, we found that resource utilization changes have linearity when tasks are consolidated. Each resource component follows different amount of change as shown in the Fig. 1: different resource component has different slope. We model multiple resource components' utilization changing with linearity with vector model. It is described in detail in Sect. 2.2.

2.2   Vector Models

There are many VM types provided by multi cloud service providers. They are categorized with different capacity of resources each VM type uses. Different VM types which different cloud service providers provide as service make it difficult for users to decide optimal choice of VMs online. To ease solving such complex decision problem online, we use vector modeling to represent each VM type and tasks.

We define a VM type vector as a unit vector: (1.0, 1.0...). Each value represents utilization value when the entire resource component is used. Therefore, task vectors differ as the task. A task vector is relative to which VM type it is going to be executed

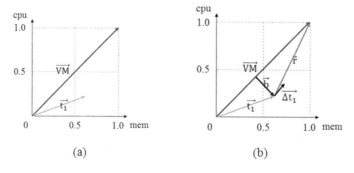

(a)   (b)

Fig. 2. (a) A VM vector, task vector, and balance factor in a vector model (b) latency factor considered in scheduling

with. Magnitudes of each component represent average utilization of the resource component. The values can be calculated based on historical data of each task. Figure 2 describes relationship between a VM vector and a task vector.

We defined the The task vector $\vec{t}$ of task T as following.

$$\vec{t} = (c, m) \tag{2}$$

Where c is the average cpu utilization and m is the average memory utilization while executing T. Axises may be added or deleted elastically such as network I/O axis and storage axis. The values can be acquired by monitoring the VM while executing tasks. Let $\text{cpu}_T(t)$ and $\text{mem}_T(t)$ are obtained by monitoring the VM which runs the task T for time τ. Then, the c and m value can be calculated by

$$c = \frac{1}{\tau} \int_0^\tau \text{cpu}_T(t) \tag{3}$$

$$m = \frac{1}{\tau} \int_0^\tau \text{mem}_T(t) \tag{4}$$

When there are some tasks running on the same VM, the total task vector can be calculated by simply adding the all task vectors.

$$\vec{t}_{\text{total}} = \sum \vec{t}_i \tag{5}$$

$\vec{t}_{\text{total}}$ is the total task vector where each component of the vector is representing resource utilization of each resource components. $\vec{t}_i$ is a single task vector consolidated in the VM. When a task has finished execution, the task vector is removed from total task vector for corresponding VM. The total task vector represents overall resource utilization of all tasks executing on the VM.

We define a balance vector which is the vector perpendicular to a VM vector to a tack vector. We used vector dot product to get the balance vector. And the magnitude of this vector is defined to be balance factor. Balance factor represents level of unbalance of resource utilization between different resource components. Even an application which uses one resource component intensively requires at least some minimum amount of other resource types. If a VM's resource usage is unbalanced and any of resource component utilization goes near 1.0, no task can be scheduled on the VM and other underutilized resource components cannot avoid being wasted until fully utilized resource components get freed. Therefore, we use balance factor as task scheduling criteria to avoid such case of resource waste.

Definition 1 Balance Vector ($\vec{b}$) and Balance Factor ($|\vec{b}|$)

$$\vec{b} = \vec{t}_{total} - \left(\vec{t}_{total} \cdot \overrightarrow{VM}\right)\overrightarrow{VM} \tag{6}$$

We obtain balance vector and balance factor, which are presented in Fig. 2(a). The magnitude of balance vector is described in Eq. 7. (c, m) is set of CPU and memory resource utilization respectively.

$$\left|\vec{b}\right| = \frac{|c - m|}{\sqrt{2}} \tag{7}$$

Also, we should consider a performance degradation when multi tasks run in parallel in a single VM. Such variation has several causes. One of them is interference effect caused by other VMs running on same PM [6]. Also, context switching between multi tasks running on same VM can cause performance degradation. Since our paper does not focus on causes of such degradation, we focus on dealing with performance degradation during scheduling more than one task to a single VM. We defined latency factor and when sum of task vectors and sum of latency factors have any resource component greater than 1.0, we scale the same VM type to avoid SLA violation.

Latency vector of task t is defined to be the standard deviation of utilization multiplied by κ

$$\vec{\Delta t} = \kappa\left(\sigma_t^{cpu}, \sigma_t^{mem}\right) \tag{8}$$

Where σ_t^{cpu} presents the standard deviation of $cpu_T(t)$, σ_t^{mem} denotes the standard deviation of $mem_T(t)$ and κ represents the latency factor. The meaning of the latency vector is the maximum value that the task vector can cover. When we monitor the VM resource while running tasks, we can see that resource utilization varies in time. In order to avoid degradation, we should take the maximum value of resource utilization into account.

κ is determined based on 68-95-99.7 rule since we assumed that the resource utilization follows the normal distribution of $N(\vec{t}, \vec{\sigma})$. If we take $\kappa = 1$, resource utilization underlies $\vec{t} + \vec{\sigma}$ with probability of 84 %. This value may not be correct since the resource utilization do not follow the normal distribution. However, we can notice that almost all values are covered if we set κ near 2. The more κ value we set, the more probability of $\vec{t} + \kappa\vec{\sigma}$ coverage. In our paper, we set basic κ value 2.

We defined total latency vector by adding all latency vectors of each task as in Eq. (9). Figure 4 shows the graphical representation of latency vectors. We can see there are additional black vectors presented in Fig. 4. Blue lines stand for the task vector which is the average value of resource utilization. Also, by adding black latency vector to task vector, it shows the estimated maximum coverage of the task.

$$\vec{\Delta t} = \sum \vec{\Delta t_i} \tag{9}$$

2.3   Task Scheduling Algorithm with VM Vector Management Scheme

The proposed scheduling scheme is presented as heuristics. There are four steps:

Step 1. Determine VM type candidates which can satisfy SLA requirement user request task based on historical data.

Step 2. Generate task vectors for each VM type generated in Step 1.

Step 3. Remove VM type if adding new task vector will have latency factor with any component greater than 1.0 and can violate SLA requirement due to performance degradation.

Step 4a. Find VM type which has minimum balance factor

Step 4b. If no VM type is available, VM type with minimal cost in Step 1 is allocated.

In Step 1, Based on task profiles and VM type profiles from historical data stored in repositories, available VM types which expect to satisfy SLA requirement are retrieved. Already allocated resources in resource pool are considered first. If there are no available allocated resources and auto-scaling process must proceed, cheapest VM type which can satisfy SLA requirement is chosen. In Step 2, task vectors are generated. Resource utilization differs by which VM type the task will execute on; therefore, each task generates many task vectors. Task vectors include both average utilization and standard deviation of the utilization for each resource components. Average utilization is used to calculate balance factor and the standard deviation of the utilization is used to calculate latency factor. In Step 3, VM types which already allocated in the resource pool and have high resource utilization are removed from the candidate list using latency factor. If any resource component utilization becomes greater than 1.0 after the scheduling it is expected to violate SLA requirement. Therefore, we decide not to schedule any more tasks until any of already executing task terminates. In Step 4, since any of remaining VM types in the available VM list can be used to execute the requested task we choose the VM type which has minimum balance factor. In this way, we manage all VMs utilized with balance between all resource components. We avoid resource waste because resource usage is unbalanced. If there is no VM type which satisfies by now, scaling number of VMs is necessary. We allocate new VM for the VM type which has lowest cost and satisfies SLA requirement of the given task. Algorithm 1 shows the entire procedure of vector-based balance scheduling algorithm (Fig. 3).

3   Experiments and Evaluation

The user request consists of workflow topology W and the service level agreement SLA. We used colored Petri-net model in order to represent the workflow topology W. In our experiments, all Physical Machines (PMs), controller node and compute nodes have two quad-core processor with hyper-threading (Intel Xeon Processor E5620), 14 GB of RAM and 1000 GB of disk. Ubuntu 12.04 server is installed in all PMs and OpenStack computing environment is installed on top of the operating system.

Algorithm 1. Vector-based Balance Scheduling Algorithm

Input: user request task $\mathbf{t_{req}}$, deadline $\mathbf{DL_{req}}$

Output: scheduled VM

01: Get available VM types and put into **AvailableVMList**
02: Calculate task vector $\mathbf{t_{req}}$ for all possible VM types
03: ProposedType = VM Type which is available and the cheapest
04: **for** all VMs $\in$ **AvailableVMList do**
05:     Let $\{\vec{t_1}\}$ be the scheduled task vector list inside the VM where $i \geq 0$
06:     **if** $\sum(\vec{t_1} + \overrightarrow{\Delta t_1}) + \vec{t}_{req} + \overrightarrow{\Delta t}_{req}$ has element which is larger than 1.0 **then**
07:         **continue**
08:     $\vec{t}' = \sum \vec{t_1} + \vec{t}_{req}$
09:     Calculate $|\vec{b}|$ using eq. 7
10:     **if** $|\vec{b}|$ is smaller than min_b **then**
11:         $min_b = |\vec{b}|$
12:         scheduledVM = VM
13: **if** scheduledVM is null **then**
14:     scheduledVM = new VM with type = proposedType
15: schedule and run $\mathbf{t_{req}}$ **onto scheduledVM**
16: $\overrightarrow{\textbf{scheduledVM}} = \overrightarrow{\textbf{scheduledVM}} + \overrightarrow{\textbf{t}_{req}}$

Fig. 3. Vector based balance scheduling algorithm

3.1 Performance Metric

We defined two performance metrics: total cost and SLA violation rate. Each VM type has its own VM cost. Therefore, we define total cost as the sum of each VM's cost.

$$TC = \sum_{i \in K} C^i \cdot m_{BTU}^i \tag{10}$$

We also defined SLA violation rate. User requests with time constraints and we choose which VM type to execute the task with based on the constraint. However, if SLA is not satisfied, we count it as SLA violation case. SLA violation rate is the ratio of such case to all user requests. Therefore, SLA violation rate is defined as follows:

$$VR = \frac{\text{number of requests not satisfying deadline}}{\text{number of requests}} \tag{11}$$

3.2 Application Service Scenario

To evaluate our proposed scheme, we experimented with other schemes as well to compare as following:

Single-Request Single VM (SRSV) scheme [8] – Only a single request is scheduled to a single VM. This scheme rarely violates SLA requirement, however it has lowest utilization compared to other schemes.

Multi-Request Single VM (MRSV) scheme [8] – Multi requests are scheduled to a single VM and executed in parallel. This scheme does not consider balance between usages of different resource components (CPU, memory, and disk I/O etc.).

Vector-based Balanced Scheduling (VBS) – Multi requests are scheduled to a single VM and executed in parallel. This scheme uses balance factor as scheduling criteria in order to balance between usages of different resource components. It also considers performance degradation with latency factor as auto-scaling criteria, to reduce SLA violation rate.

All of above schemes are tested with same set of request inputs. We generated random requests which are combination of CPU-intensive task and memory-intensive task. The amount of workload for each task also differs and randomly selected. As we assumed with more resource capacity, performance increases. For example, VM type with 2 CPU cores finishes task execution with only half of time, which VM type with 1 CPU core would use. We experimented multiple times with average inter-arrival time being different starting from 10 s to 20 s. (λ = 10, 12, 14, 16, 18, 20) Input request follows Poisson 'arrivals. To be fair, we used same input sets for all schemes.

We evaluated the proposed scheme for three times with different pricing models. First scenario charges $0.03 per CPU core and $0.03 per Gigabyte RAM. Therefore, the price ratio between CPU and memory units is 1:1. Second scenario charges $0.03 per CPU core and $0.02 per Gigabyte RAM. The price ratio between CPU and memory units is 3:2. Third scenario charges $0.03 per CPU core and $0.04 per Gigabyte RAM. Therefore, the price ratio between CPU and memory units is 3:4. Total cost and violation rate measurement experiment result is shown in Fig. 4.

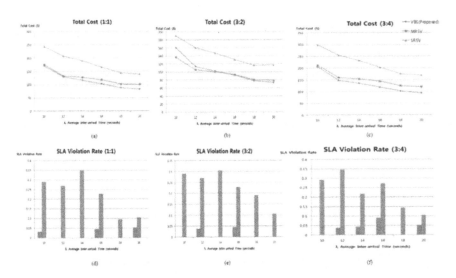

Fig. 4. Total cost and SLA violation rate as inter-arrival time varies when price ration is 1:1, 3:2, and 3:4

Both MRSV and VBS, which use task consolidation, have lower total cost spent for all inter-arrival time scenarios compare to SRSV. SRSV does not fully utilized resource of VM types which is set in coarse-grained manner. Our proposed scheme, VBS has even lower total cost compared to MRSV, because we have better resource utilization as we balance usage between different resource components. Compare to other schemes [8], total cost decreased as shown in the following figure. This is because, scheduling while considering balance between resource components increased utilization rate throughout the experiment. On the other hand, violation rate is decreased. This is because we scale number of VMs considering performance degradation due to executing too many request on a single VM causing latency by context switching. Also, interference effect also decreased because balance between resource usages reduces interference effect between tasks.

4   Conclusion

In this paper, we proposed vector models for VM types and tasks and QoS constraint task scheduling heuristics with low complexity. Task vector is a simple model to represent resource utilization made of each resource components in VM types. Based on resource utilization historical data, task vectors are generated to calculate expected resource usage before scheduling. Also, expected performance degradation is considered to minimize SLA violations due to scheduling too many tasks into a single VM.

With the experiment, we proved our scheme improved in terms of total cost and SLA violation rates compared to other schemes such as MRSV and SRSV. With balance factor as scheduling criteria, our scheme improved resource utilization of VMs because we avoid cases of being unable to schedule new task because one resource component being fully utilized and other resource components being under-utilized. This resulted low operational cost as shown in the experiment. Also, with latency factor as auto-scaling criteria, our proposed scheme minimized SLA violation which occurs during task consolidation. This can lead to increase in profit of cloud service broker because penalty fee related to SLA violation is minimized.

Acknowledgement. This work was partly supported by 'The Cross-Ministry Giga KOREA Project' grant from the Ministry of Science, ICT and Future Planning, Korea and Institute for Information & communications Technology Promotion(IITP) grant funded by the Korea government(MSIP) (No. B0101-15-0104, The Development of Supercomputing System for the Genome Analysis)

References

1. Smith, T.F., Waterman, M.S.: Identification of common molecular subsequences. J. Mol. Biol. **147**, 195–197 (1981)
2. May, P., Ehrlich, H.-C., Steinke, T.: ZIB structure prediction pipeline: composing a complex biological workflow through web services. In: Nagel, W.E., Walter, W.V., Lehner, W. (eds.) Euro-Par 2006. LNCS, vol. 4128, pp. 1148–1158. Springer, Heidelberg (2006)

3. Foster, I., et al.: The Grid: Blueprint for a New Computing Infrastructure. Morgan Kaufmann, San Francisco (1999)
4. Czajkowski, K., et al.: Grid information services for distributed resource sharing. In: 10th IEEE International Symposium on High Performance Distributed Computing, pp. 181–184. IEEE Press, New York (2001)
5. Foster, I., et al.: The Physiology of the Grid: an Open Grid Services Architecture for Distributed Systems Integration. Technical report, Global Grid Forum (2002)
6. National Center for Biotechnology Information. http://www.ncbi.nlm.nih.gov
7. Ren, Y.: A cloud collaboration system with active application control scheme and its experimental performance analysis. In: KAIST (2012)
8. Kang, D.K., et al.: Enhancing a strategy of virtualized resource assignment in adaptive resource cloud framework. In: Proceedings of the 7th International Conference on Ubiquitous Information Management and Communication. ACM (2013)
9. Lucas-Simarro, J., et al.: Scheduling strategies for optimal service deployment across multiple clouds. Future Gener. Comput. Syst. **29**, 1434–1441 (2012)

An Adaptive VM Reservation Scheme with Prediction and Task Allocation in Cloud

Jisoo Choi[(⊠)], Yungi Ha, Gyubeom Choi, and Chan-Hyun Youn

Department of Electrical Engineering,
Korea Advanced Institute of Science and Technology (KAIST),
Daejeon, South Korea
{jisoochoi,yungi.ha,mosfetlkg,chyoun}@kaist.ac.kr

Abstract. In a cloud environment, it is important for cloud broker to provide a cost-effective VM utilization. In this paper, we suggest a predicting scheme that can be applied for RVM provision by calculating demands. And there are some resource difference with respect to user's needs on the process measuring clients' needs. We also propose a method called M-C-VMA to handle the cost caused by the difference between real user demand and RVM provision. Performance evaluation showed that the proposed heuristic with VM Replacement is more efficient than C-VMA in cost performance. When M-C-VMA works on the VM allocation procedure, the result shows the higher RVM utilization than the not-modified method and consequently, it can lead the cost-efficient operation in broker system.

Keywords: Cloud service brokers · Prediction · VM reservation · VM replacement allocation

1 Introduction

Many devices extract a lot of raw big data and they have the potential to make information to change the world. In the process to generate useful data, prediction is getting important. There are several methods to predict the future. And one of the most famous prediction model developed from time series analysis is ARIMA (Auto Regressive Integrated Moving Average) [1, 2].

Cloud computing is one of the hottest technique to handle the generated big data using virtualization technology [3]. But some users were hard to use the cloud services so Cloud Service Brokers (CSB) have been created and for the users and CSB, Reserved VM (RVM) service was made by Cloud Service Provider (CSP) that Amazon EC2 [4] is a representative of. In CSB system, it will be beneficial to merging a prediction scheme into RVM reservation policy. Because CSBs contract Service Level Agreements (SLA) with both CSPs and Cloud Service Clients (CSC). All predictions always have an error and there should be a way to cover this error but it is hard.

For prediction mechanism, Kim et al. [5] suggested the scheme to set the proper number of RVMs to be leased on the CSB's side. They propose an idea called C-VMR (VM reservation scheme) is adaptively choosing RVM number to be leased based on

© ICST Institute for Computer Sciences, Social Informatics and Telecommunications Engineering 2016
Y. Zhang et al. (Eds.): CloudComp 2015, LNICST 167, pp. 50–59, 2016.
DOI: 10.1007/978-3-319-38904-2_6

predicted method called ARIMA and its algorithm gives a basic idea to our step 1 algorithm in the Sect. 2. Also Shumway et al. [6] provides ARIMA modeling method with giving R application examples. In the process to reduce the prediction error, we choose to use the VM replacement concept as our Replacement policy that abstractly suggested by Kang et al. [7] who proposed the A3R (Recycle, Replacement, Reposition) algorithm. It focuses on how to cost-efficiently broker VMs in cloud computing services. The VM replacement scheme just gives a concept that when the CSPs have no RVM to supply to the user corresponding to the user-requested RVM, they can lease the RVMs with larger capacities than the demanded RVMs'.

In this paper, we integrate ARIMA prediction model to RVM reservation policy. We also use the replacement scheme based on Kang et al. [7] to cover the occurring error related to the demands on RVMs. Simply, in broker system, if there is no RVM to lease to users and there are some RVMs that have larger capacities than RVM that user requested, then CSB will let the larger ones be leased to users to get more benefits. Briefly, the rest of the paper will be illustrated as follows. Section 2 introduce the prediction-based RVM reservation policy and applied RVM Replacement method. Section 3 is the experiment with its evaluation. Lastly, Sect. 4 concludes the paper.

2 VM Reservation with Prediction and Job Allocation

2.1 Problem Statement

As an aspect of commerce, if the providers can predict the future demand from the historical data collection, they will become more beneficial. In the cloud computing, the same concept can be applied for CSB and the prediction of VM requests is getting important. Figure 1(a) shows relationship of SLAs in cloud computing environment. SLA contract between clients and brokers needs some information such as deadline and budget of the users. From this data, brokers are easy to provision their resources. If resource demand varies as depicted in Fig. 1(b), there exists over-provisioning by wasting cost and under-provisioning by violating SLA. So the uncertainty of the resource demands is an inevitable problem and by predicting the demand, reserving the proper number of resources is hard to solve.

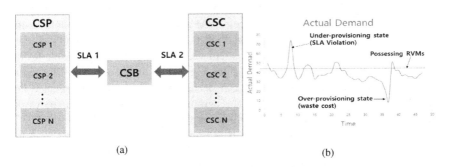

(a)   (b)

Fig. 1. CSB constraints: (a) SLA relationship of cloud broker between consumers and providers, (b) Demand variation causing QoS problem

To resolve the problem, many prediction models [8] can be considered and Kim et al. [5] suggested the C-VMR method in order to reserve VMs from ARIMA model. Kim's approach was based on Eq. (1), where we try to improve operation scheme. We consider a different prediction model, prediction, and others. Thus, we expect good performance in VM reservation. In this case, applying Eq. (1) for VM reservation could cause over-provisioning or under-provisioning problems because distinctive values like $\max D_p(t)$ and $\min D_p(t)$ over each T_p will mislead non-average number to lease RVMs.

$$n_{RVM}^l(t) = \left\lfloor \frac{1}{T_p} \sum_{k=t}^{t+T_p-1} D_p(k) - n_{RVM}^e(t) \right\rfloor \tag{1}$$

Kang et al. [7] proposed a method cost efficient VM brokering. One of the scheme that they suggested was the replacement algorithm and the concept was that larger capacity RVMs can be borrowed by smaller capacity RVM on the VM allocation request of smaller VM. We can improve this method in two ways. First A3R scheme is for the situation that the prediction is not applicable however, if we use this scheme when VM allocation proceeds with a prediction method, the replacement algorithm will act as an error controller to cover the difference between real VM demand and reserved VMs. Second, they proposed the scheme with abstracted explanation and did not prove its availability on cost policy and it needs to be concreted as an algorithm with a specific form.

2.2   A Proposed Model Description

Figure 2 is the proposing model to overcome the problems discussed in Sect. 2.1. Below the dotted line, historical demand acts as an input of the prediction model and the module will generate the future demands that are predicted values. From the information of predicted number of VMs to lease, a heuristic algorithm that we propose supports CSB reserving VMs. The result of VM reservation affects the broker's VM pool. From the number of RVM and OVM that broker has, the cost can be calculated. In Fig. 2, when user request comes to the brokers, it needs to be allocated. The scheme C-VMA (VM Allocation Scheme) [5] is applied for task allocation. First, and the replacement algorithm works. In this process, VM allocation algorithm module let the brokers know how many OVM to lease and when they need to get more OVM, they check the VM pool first to find RVM that is replaceable. If there is a replaceable RVM, by using VM replacement method, OVM leasing cost will not happen. The entire process represents VM allocation and it can be used to check the performance utilization. So this model is whole conceptual diagram how the proposing scheme works and the specific algorithm and formula will be explained.

The prediction scheme in this paper is based on C-VMR [5], the demand from the time t during T_p that is prediction period. Then, $n_{RVM_\alpha}^l(t)$ denotes the number of RVMs to be leased at the time t, $D_\alpha(t)$ is the predicted demand at time t and α is the type of RVMs so it is represented as {S, M, L}. $n_{DRVM_\alpha}^e(t)$ is the number of existing predicted

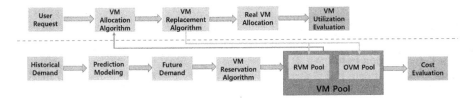

Fig. 2. The proposed model for VM reservation using M-C-VMR (Modified C-VMR) and task allocation based on M-C-VMA (Modified C-VMA)

demanded RVMs in the VM pool at time t. $n_{ADRVM_\alpha}^e(t)$ is the number of existing actual demanded VMs in the VM pool at time t. $n_{RVM_\alpha}^e(t)$ is the number of RVMs in the VM pool at time t. $opt(n_{RRVM_\alpha}^e(t))$ is the optimized number of Replaceable RVMs in VM pool at time t but we are focusing on applying the demand prediction on the original VM Replacement scheme so that we assume this term might be negligible in this experiment.

Equation (2) is the average demand during T_p and it means that deleting the maximum and minimum values of the predicted demands on measuring the average will result the better fitted mean on the T_p. Equation (3) is about how many RVMs to lease from the result in Eq. (2). α is a VM type that can be all VM types, and β is the VM type that is made for designating Replaceable RVMs (RRVMs) which is applied for the Replacement policy. The number of RRVM on β type can be calculated by using Eq. (4). With the RRVM concept, Eq. (5) represents the maximum number of RVMs to be leased to user. The VM reservation equations are as follows.

$$n_{DRVM_\alpha}^e(t) = \frac{1}{T_p - 2}\left\{\left(\sum_{k=t}^{t+T_p-1} D_\alpha(k)\right) - \max_{k\in[t,t+T_p]} D_\alpha(t) - \min_{k\in[t,t+T_p]} D_\alpha(t)\right\} \quad (2)$$

$$n_{RVM_\alpha}^l(t) = \left\lfloor n_{DRVM_\alpha}^e(t) - n_{RVM_\alpha}^e(t) - opt(n_{RRVM_\beta}^e(t)) \right\rfloor \quad (3)$$

$$n_{RRVM_\beta}^e(t) = n_{RVM_\beta}^e(t) - n_{ADRVM_\beta}^e(t) \quad (4)$$

$$\max(n_{RVM_\alpha}^e(t)) = n_{RVM_\alpha}^e(t) + \sum_{\beta > \alpha} n_{RRVM_\beta}^e(t) \quad (5)$$

In step 1 of algorithm 1, we need to set prediction method to get the RVM demand in each type. From the historical data, we can measure the future demand on all RVM types. The output let the broker know what will be the approximated demand and how many RVMs to lease. Step 2 will be the stage to generate RVM actually by the result of the step 1. $n_{RVM_\alpha}^e(t)$ will be the number of RVMs to maintain from the prediction and $NG(t)$ is the number of RVMs to be newly generated (Fig. 3).

Algorithm 2 will be the stage to make up the difference between the actual demand and predicted demand occurred on the previous Algorithm 1 because of the RVM reservation error by the prediction method. This method will be done in the process of

Algorithm 1. Prediction-based VM Reservation

M-C-VMR
Step 1. Generation Policy
Input: Historical data HD(t) for time interval $[t - T_p, t - T_p + 1, ..., t - 1]$ to make demand prediction before decision-making time t
Output: Prediction demand $D_\alpha(t)$ for time interval $[t, t + 1, ..., t + T_p - 1]$
1: **while** true **do**
2:    Feed $HD(t)$ to the prediction model
3:    Generate *ACF* and *PACF* for *HD(t)* to decide the degree of ARIMA model
4:    Produce prediction model by regression
5:    **if** the model passes verifying step
6:       Apply the model to generate $D_\alpha(t)$
7:    **else**
8:       Go back to **4**
9:    **end if**
10: **end while**

Step 2. RVM Generation

Input: Number of maintained RVM $n^e_{RVM_\alpha}(t)$
Output: Number of newly generated RVM *NG(t)*

1:**while** true **do**
2: Prediction model produces forecasted demand D_α *(t)* for time interval $[0, T_p, ..., 3T_p]$
3: Obtain *NG(t)*
4: **if** *NG(t)>0* then
5:    Lease *NG(t)* additional reserved VMs
6: **else**
7:    return
8: **end if**
9:**end while**

Fig. 3. Prediction-based VM reservation scheme

VM allocation. We used C-VMA and modified it with the RVM Replacement method that is abstractly suggested. When CSB allocates the user-requested tasks to VMs that the CSB has, CSB will first look into the OVM pool to find the OVM which satisfies that the value, residual time - the predicted application execution time is larger than δ. If true, the OVM will be used for the task. And there is no OVM to satisfy the condition then search RVM to use. Lastly, when RVM is not available, the replacement section will be executed and RVM which has larger capacity than the past RVM has will be used. Through even these entire searching procedures, if there is no VM to allocate the task on, CSB will lease OVM from one of the CSPs (Fig. 4).

Algorithm 2. Job Allocation

M-C-VMA with Replacement Scheme

Input: $n_{ADRVM_\alpha}^e(t)$, $n_{RRVM_\alpha}^e(t)$, RT_{OVM_α}, PET_{OVM_α}, and $\alpha, \gamma \in \{S, M, L\}$

Output: Renewed $n_{RRVM_\alpha}^e(t)$, and the number of OVMs to lease notated as $n_{OVM_\alpha}^e(t)$

1: **while** true **do**
2: **for** all α from small to large type
3:    **if** there exists $n_{OVM_\alpha}^e(t)$ which satisfy $\delta < RT_{OVM_\alpha} - PET_{OVM_\alpha}$
4:      Apply the MBF algorithm on the $n_{OVM_\alpha}^e(t)$ with the replacement scheme
5:      Allocate the task to one of the $n_{OVM_\alpha}^e(t)$
6:    **else if** there exists $n_{RRVM_\alpha}^e(t)$
7:      Allocate the task to one of the $n_{RRVM_\alpha}^e(t)$
8:    **else**
9:      **if** there presents $n_{RRVM_\gamma}^e(t)$, where $\gamma \geq \alpha$
10:       Allocate the task to one of the $n_{RRVM_\gamma}^e(t)$
11:     **else**
12:       Lease one of the $n_{OVM_\alpha}^e(t)$ from one of the CSPs
13:     **end if**
14:    **end if**
15: **end for**
16: **end while**

Fig. 4. Task allocation using replacement scheme

3 Performance Evaluation

3.1 Prediction-Based VM Reservation with M-C-VMR

In this part, first we generated the demand of CSCs to lease VMs in each type from the CSB for 4 years. The generated demand is measured the user VM requests per day. From the demand, we calculated the average number of VM requests per week and also from the data, we could get the predicted average number of VM requests per week. To do this, we use the R application [9] with ASTSA package with ARIMA model for prediction. Graphs in Fig. 5 describes the procedure to get predicted demand that explained.

We checked the cost policy of GoGrid [10] which is shown in a chart in Table 1. Minimum time to lease of OVM (MT_O) is an hour, and Minimum Time to lease of RVM (MT_R) is a month. We considered that the broker initially has small, medium, and large type of RVMs leased from CSPs. As shown in Fig. 6, we changed the initial VM numbers on each type like 70/70/70 means small/medium/large VM numbers that the broker has. And it is on the horizontal axis. The vertical axis stands for the actual total cost that broker needs to pay. The total cost is measured by Eq. (5) and the ratio (δ) can

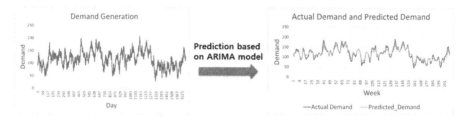

Fig. 5. Demand prediction process using ARIMA model

be $\frac{MT_O \times MT_O}{MT_R} \leq \delta \leq \frac{MT_O \times MT_R}{MT_R}$ and we set OVM using time as MT_O in this evaluation. It reflects the fact that OVM is leased in shorter term than RVM's. If the OVM leasing event happens, then OVM cost will be considered, otherwise not considered.

$$C_{TotalSum} = \sum_{\alpha} \{C_{RVM_\alpha}^{MT_R} \cdot n_{RVM_\alpha}^e(t) + C_{OVM_\alpha}^{MT_O} \cdot n_{OVM_\alpha}^e(t) \cdot \left\lfloor \frac{\delta \times MT_R}{MT_O} \right\rfloor \} \qquad (6)$$

The lines of the result graphs in Fig. 6 mean as follows. The diamond point line is the case that only OVMs are used without any RVM. The circle point line stands for the concept that with RVM introduced, initial leased RVM number will be maintained and on under-provisioning state, the CSBs will lease OVM from CSP to prevent breaking SLA with their CSCs. Especially at the 90/90/90 stage, it shows the minimal cost of the circle point line and it is because leasing about 90 VMs on each type draws the cost-efficient conclusion by leasing proper number of RVMs. The plus point line is for the C-VMR prediction modeling and it shows overall smaller cost than the circle point line since the prediction was introduced. The cross point line is the proposing prediction concept and the cost is smaller than the plus point line about $200 to $1200. The square line is added the replacement concept on the plus point line. It shows cheaper result than the plus point line. Sometimes the cost flow trend goes up, and this is because when the large RVMs are replaced to the medium RVMs and large RVMs are needed, the broker needs to lease OVM from the CSP. However, when a lot of RVM are reserved comparing to the actual demand, replacement algorithm is effective to get the cost reduced. Lastly, the triangle point line is applied by the proposing scheme and replacement. By excluding the points that have a chance to be way far from the average, and using replacement scheme, it leads the most minimal cost Fig. 6.

3.2   VM Utilization with M-C-VMA

Through experiment, we evaluated the performance of M-C-VMA with comparing the C-VMA. Our testbed was implemented as shown in Fig. 7. Each machine specification is Intel(R) Xeon(R) CPU E5620 with two quad-core CPUs providing hyper-threading. They have 8 GB main memory and 1,000 GB hard disk and are clustered to provide the cloud services by using OpenStack [11]. We prepared two VMs of three types (small, medium, large) for the RVM set and a VM of the same type for the OVM.

Table 1. GoGrid cloud cost policy [6]

GoGrid VM Cost Policy	RVM Cost / Month	Equivalent RVM Cost / hour	OVM Cost / hour
Small	$32.85	$0.05	$0.06
Medium	$65.70	$0.09	$0.12
Large	$131.40	$0.18	$0.24

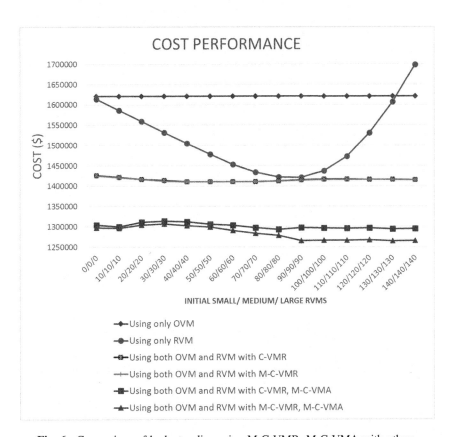

Fig. 6. Comparison of budget policy using M-C-VMR, M-C-VMA with others

We assume the situation that users want to execute the three different types of the Montage scientific applications [12] in cloud (m105-1.5, m106-1.7, m108-1.7) and their requests which require some specific types arrive by following a Poisson process

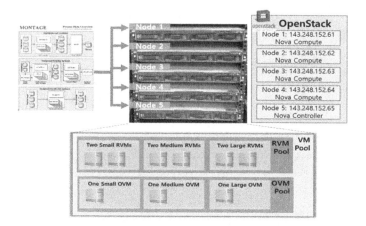

Fig. 7. The experiment environment for M-C-VMA performance evaluation

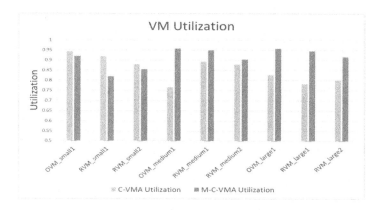

Fig. 8. The comparison of average utilization in VM

with its mean value, 30 s. Also the RVM minimum leasing time is set to 2 h and the time for OVM is 5 min. The factors are scale-downed in terms of the reality.

Figure 8 shows the VM utilization result of M-C-VMA comparing with the C-VMA. The bar graph indicates that the VM utilization on medium and large types is better by using M-C-VMA and C-VMA works well only on small type. This is because the proposing replacement scheme used in the task allocation process affects the VMs to be replaced. This method is about managing the VMs that have larger capacities than the requested type of VM. When a VM for some specific applications is out of stock, the C-VMA need to lease the new VM. However, the M-C-VMA finds the Replace-able VM first, letting the application run on the larger size VM, whose specification is proper enough to run on smaller VM. This is the reason why the small type VM utilization of the proposing scheme is lower than the C-VMA. In other words, it is explained in the same aspect of the replacement scheme that the VMs of the small type do not have many chance to be utilized. By using the proposing algorithm, two things get better. First, M-C-VMA does not need to lease OVM from the beginning and it means that RVM utilization will increase, so that the cost that was supposed to be wasted will be saved. This explanation can be proved by the cost comparison result of Fig. 6. And second, the execution time can be decreased by making the task that was supposed to be executed on smaller type run on larger type.

4 Conclusion

In this paper, we proposed an adaptive prediction-based VM replacement scheme in cloud to solve the difficulties about managing VM pool for CSBs. To maintain RVMs cost-effectively, we suggested the prediction scheme by introducing the prediction model and heuristics named M-C-VMR to get the RVM number to newly lease. And the M-C-VMA applying replacement method in VM allocation phase offsets the extra cost that occurs because of the prediction error. Evaluation about cost showed that M-C-VMR and M-C-VMA can decrease the budget. VM Utilization explained that the proposing scheme gives many benefits related to cost by increasing the VM utilization, and in terms of the execution time by giving a chance to run a task on the larger VM. For the future works to do will be to improve the proposing prediction method such as meta-heuristics and to propose another scheme to cover the difference error due to the prediction.

Acknowledgement. This research was supported by the MSIP under the ITRC (Information Technology Research Center) support program (NIPA-2014(H0301-14-1020)) supervised by the NIPA (National IT Industry Promotion Agency), and 'The Cross-Ministry Giga KOREA Project' grant from the Ministry of Science, ICT and Future Planning, Korea.

References

1. ARIMA. https://onlinecourses.science.psu.edu/stat510/node/66
2. http://people.duke.edu/~rnau/411arim.htm
3. Virtualization defined by VMware. http://people.duke.edu/~rnau/411arim.htm
4. Amazon Cloud. aws.amazon.com/cloud
5. Kim, H., et al.: A VM Reservation-Based Cloud Service Broker and Its Performance Evaluation. CloudComp (2014)
6. Shumway, R.H., Stoffer, D.S.: Time Series Analysis and Its Applications
7. Kang, D., et al.: Cost Efficient Virtual Machine Brokering in Cloud Computing. KIPS (2014)
8. Steven, F.: Predictive modeling. In: Predictive Analytics, Data Mining and Big Data. Myths, Misconceptions and Methods, 1st edn. (2014)
9. R. http://www.r-project.org
10. GoGrid. http://www.gogrid.com
11. OpenStack. https://www.openstack.org/
12. Montage. http://montage.ipac.caltech.edu/docs/grid.html/

A Cost-Effective VM Offloading Scheme in Hybrid Cloud Environment

Myeongseok Hyeon$^{(\boxtimes)}$, Heejae Kim, and Chan-Hyun Youn

School of Electrical Engineering, KAIST, Daejeon, Korea
{tidusqoop, kim881019, chyoun}@kaist.ac.kr

Abstract. Video streaming service is offered by various content provider with cloud content delivery network like a Netflix, Youtube. In this environment, for content deliver, cache servers need to be placed properly in cost-effective manner with guaranteeing streaming performance. In this paper, as contents providers, to minimize the cost of using public cloud and to maximize performance of video streaming service, we suggest cost-effective VM offloading algorithm in hybrid cloud environment (CVOH). The CVOH considers performance degradation in internal cloud and cost for public cloud using penalty cost model and learning curve model, respectively. As the result of evaluation for CVOH, we got about twice better performance than a maximal consolidation case, and 9.1 % better than a maximal offloading case.

Keywords: Video streaming · Hybrid cloud · VM placement

1 Introduction

For offering video streaming service effectively, the architecture of video streaming service has developed into a way to place a cache server to a cloud environment for content delivery. In cases of Netflix and Youtube, content providers, they are using Amazon Web Service and Google Cloud respectively for serving their content [1, 2].

It has been reported that the great number of content consumers' request for streaming service can burst in a short time period, and also refer to needs for network resource in server to handle the peak demand which can appear frequently by Aggarwal et al. [3]. If content provider have to deal with such a dynamic demand by using their own computing resources, it is hard to estimate an amount of demand properly and it is inefficient to construct and to manage servers in respect to cost. Hence, the way using a hybrid cloud environment rises, that a private computing resource is used in dealing with universal demands and in dealing in other specific demands such a peak demand resource of the public cloud can be used.

To use cost-effectively such a hybrid cloud environment, there are two main challenges. First one is to maximize resource utilization in the internal cloud and the other one is to minimize the cost occurring by using other public cloud resource. To satisfy both objectives to guarantee QoS of streaming service being supported by the internal cloud and to minimize cost of management datacenter, content provider have to manage his computing resource properly by placing the cache server properly. The other reason is the cost occurring by using other public cloud resource increases as the

Y. Zhang et al. (Eds.): CloudComp 2015, LNICST 167, pp. 60–69, 2016.
DOI: 10.1007/978-3-319-38904-2_7

quantity of computing resource that content provider uses increases. As a related issue, Bossche et al. [4] proposes cost-optimal scheduling in hybrid IaaS clouds for deadline constrained workloads.

We present a cost-effective virtual machine offloading algorithm in hybrid cloud environment (CVOH), the optimization problem to find a cost-effective solution of virtual machine (VM) placement as a cache server in video streaming service in hybrid cloud computing environment. To guarantee performance of streaming service and to lower cost with VM placement in hybrid cloud environment, the algorithm CVOH considers both performance degradation in the internal cloud and the cost model in public cloud referred by Amit and Xia [5].

2 Problem Description and Scenario

Streaming content provider needs suitable number of cache server placed as a form of VM in datacenter for offering content to end-user's request with a stable performance. Kim et al. [6] analyze resource performance for inter- and intra- datacenter resource management under cloud CDN environment.

Streaming Performance with Consolidation. Experiment presented by Kim et al. focus on measurement of resource performance in respect to a number of VMs with applications using different computing resource.

The cache servers in form of VMs are placed in physical machines (PMs) and measure performance degradation caused by interference from other VMs within same PM executing application of different computing resource.

Table 1 [6] shows the completion time of video streaming service offered through a cache server placed in one PM of internal cloud, and it is in scale of msec. With decreasing network I/O performance, the completion time of video streaming service increases because of delay, buffering for downloading a content from a cache server. In the Table 1, using a same type of computing resource more can make performance degradation more.

Table 1. Measured network I/O performance. In the PM where a cache server for streaming service is placed, VMs using different computing resource is placed with a different number and Measuring the completion time of streaming service. [6]

	Video streaming completion time (msec)			
n	0	1	2	3
Compress-7zip [7] (CPU intensive)	220595	223811	222687	223674
Cachebench [8] (memory intensive)		221652	223008	220740
Bonnie ++ [9] (Disk I/O)		231943	253414	258503
Video streaming (Network I/O)		**230158**	**234090**	**268448**

The right side graph in Fig. 1. [6] shows the measurement of bandwidth with increasing a number of cache servers using same computing resource, network I/O, in a same PM. In this figure, network bandwidth converges with time, and it achieves more slowly as n is larger. That is performance degradation in streaming service appearing as a delay in a settling time. By the result showing, tendency of streaming performance degradation can be figured out when streaming cache servers are placed in consolidation manner in internal cloud.

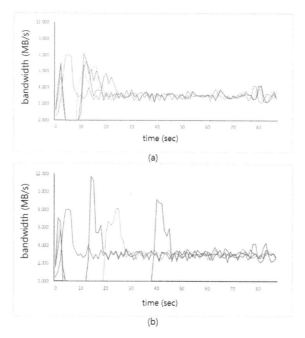

Fig. 1. Bandwidth of video streaming cache server measured with placing other VMs in same PM. Blue, red, green, and purple represent the number of other VMs n = 0, 1, 2, 3 respectively with Compress-7zip (a) (CPU intensive), streaming cache server (b) (network I/O intensive) [6] (Color figure online).

2.1 Video Streaming in Hybrid Cloud Environment

In this paper, we consider hybrid cloud Environment to decrease performance degradation of streaming service when computing resource in content provider's internal cloud is insufficient due to large scale of end-users' requests.

Figure 2 show architecture and flow of video streaming in hybrid cloud computing environment. In this environment, content provider send cache server request to both internal cloud and public cloud he uses after considering end-users' requests and a number of cache server needed. The cache server is placed in each PM in datacenter or public cloud as a VM. In this procedure, the VM placement module make a request set of proper VM placements with considering performance degradation profiling data in internal cloud and cost occurring by using public cloud resource.

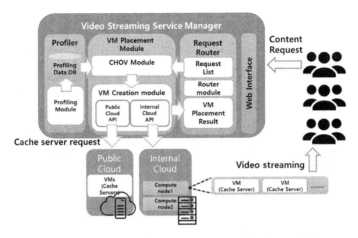

Fig. 2. Video streaming flow in hybrid cloud computing environment

The profiling data used in the VM placement module contains information of videos which content provider offers and about specification of internal cloud, performance degradation with cache server consolidation. The profiling data of videos are bit rate, size, video length and etc. In respect to an internal cloud, it contains specification of nodes in a datacenter, power consumption, performance degradation tendency of VM and etc.

We focus on an algorithm deciding how many VM has to be placed in public cloud and PMs in datacenter in VMP module, namely cost-effective VM offload in hybrid cloud environment. Main objective of the algorithm in this paper is to find an optimal solution when there exits tradeoff between minimizing cost of using public cloud and performance degradation in internal cloud.

3 CHOV Model

In this section, we present the CHOV used in VMP module for finding a solution of optimal VM placement. As an important consideration, we introduce two models, one is penalty cost model about performance degradation in datacenter and the other one is cost model occurring from using resource in public cloud. The CHOV is expressed by sum of those two models, and the solution of VM placement is the point that minimizes the sum of two models.

$VM = \{VM_0, VM_1, \ldots VM_n\}$ is a set of whole cache servers which needed to deal with end-users' requests, each cache server VM_i is placed in PM of internal cloud or public cloud as a VM. Equation (1) is a decision variable and **VM** depicts a definition of matrix of VMs.

$$vm_{ij} = \begin{cases} 1, & when\ VM_i\ is\ placed\ in\ PM_j \\ 0, when\ VM_i\ is\ placed\ in\ PM_k\ and\ k \neq j \end{cases} \tag{1}$$
$$i \in \{0, 1 \ldots n\}, j \in \{0, 1 \ldots m\}$$

In Eq. (1), $PM = \{PM_0(= PC), PM_1, PM_2, \ldots PM_m\}$ is a set of PMs in internal cloud which content provider can manage and public cloud depicted as PC. PM_0 is a public cloud PC.

Cost model for public cloud. The cost model occurring from using resource in public cloud is Eq. (2) which Amit and Xia suggest. l denotes a number of VMs placed in public cloud, K is the cost of the first unit. $\alpha \in (0, 1)$ is the learning factor of public cloud the content provider uses.

$$\text{Cost}(l) = \frac{K \cdot l^{1 + \log_2 \alpha}}{1 + \log_2 \alpha} \tag{2}$$

$$l = \sum_{i=1}^{n} vm_{i0} \tag{3}$$

The cost model Eq. (2) is based on the learning curve model. It assumes that as the number of production units are doubled the marginal cost of production decreases by a learning factor. It has been reported that for a typical Cloud provider like a Amazon EC2, the learning factors has typically value in range (0.75, 0.9).

Penalty Cost for performance degradation. Equation (4) denotes the penalty cost for performance degradation in internal **cloud** which content provider can manage.

$$\text{PenaltyCost}(\mathbf{VM}) = \beta \cdot Pd(\mathbf{VM}) = \beta \cdot \left(\frac{\sum_{VM} Completion\ time}{\sum_{VM} Video\ Length} - 1 \right),$$
$$\beta > 0 \tag{4}$$

Video Length is the time from start to end of videos which content provider offers through each cache server, *Completion time* is the time really took from start to end when it is offered to end-user by streaming. As lower performance of streaming service make a buffering, delay happen, more completion time increases.

Thus, optimal problem considering penalty cost and cost for public cloud in hybrid cloud environment is denoted by Eqs. (5), (6) and (7).

$$\text{minimize}\ \ \text{totalCost}(\mathbf{VM}) = \text{PenaltyCost}(\mathbf{VM}) + \text{Cost}(l)$$
$$= \beta \cdot Pd(\mathbf{VM}) + \frac{K \cdot l^{1 + \log_2 \alpha}}{1 + \log_2 \alpha} \tag{5}$$

$$\text{Subject to}\ \sum_{j=0}^{m} \sum_{i=1}^{n} vm_{ij} = n \tag{6}$$

$$vm_{ij} \in \{0, 1\}, \forall i \in \{1, 2 \ldots n\}, \forall j \in \{0, 1 \ldots m\}\ \text{and}$$
$$vm_{ij} = 1\ if\ VM_i\ is\ placed\ in\ PM_j. \tag{7}$$

To find a solution for this problem stated, implementation is under.

In a set of VMs, $VM = \{VM_0, VM_1, \ldots VM_n\}$, place each VM to the PM of the internal cloud in order of decreasing in expected network bandwidth based on profiling data. There are threshold values, $BW_{PM_j}^{thres}$ in each PM based on profiling data. This threshold values refer to range of network bandwidth where the performance degradation is marginal and measured experimentally. In this procedure, place the VMs maximally consolidated but not exceed the threshold in each PM denoted by Eq. (8).

$$\sum_{i=0}^{n} vm_{ij} \cdot Bw(VM_i) < BW_{PM_j}^{thres} \qquad (8)$$

$Bw(VM_i)$ is expected network bandwidth in VM_i based on profiling data about content offered by content provider.

Algorithm 1. CHOV	
INPUT	1. *VM* : Set of VMs needed to provide streaming service to end-users' request 2. *PM* : Set of PMs in internal cloud and Public cloud. PM_0 is a public cloud.

PHASE1. VM Placement only in PMs without degradation.

> While $(VM \neq \emptyset)$
> $\quad vm = max\,BW\,VM_{\text{max}\_bw}\,in\,VM$
> $\quad$ Foreach $PM_j, j \in \{1, 2 \ldots m\}$
> $\quad\quad$ If $BW_{PM_j}^{thres} > (\sum_{i=0}^{n} Bw_{PM_j}(VM_i) + vm)$
> $\quad\quad\quad PM_j \cup \{vm\}\,and\,VM/\{vm\}$
> $\quad\quad\quad$ Break foreach
> $\quad\quad$ End if
> $\quad$ End foreach
> $\quad$ If vm can be placed in $\forall PM_j, j \in \{1, 2 \ldots m\}$
> $\quad\quad PM_0 \cup \{vm\}\,and\,VM/\{vm\}$
> $\quad$ End if
> End while
> TotalCost = totalCost(**VM**)
> Solution = **VM**   /* current placement */

PHASE2. Find optimal placement to minimize totalCost(VM)

> While $(PM_0 \neq \emptyset)$
> $\quad vm = min\,BW\,VM_{\text{min}\_bw}\,in\,PM_0$
> $\quad PM_{\text{min}\_bw} = min\,BW\,PM_k\,in\,PM, k \neq 0$
> $\quad PM_{\text{min}\_bw} \cup \{vm\}\,and\,PM_0/\{vm\}$
> $\quad$ If TotalCost > totalCost(**VM**)
> $\quad\quad$ TotalCost = totalCost(**VM**) and Solution = **VM**
> $\quad$ End if
> End While

Fig. 3. The proposed CHOV algorithm.

After that, if VMs needed in streaming service remain, it denotes computing resource of internal cloud is insufficient to deal whole end-users' request without performance degradation. Hence there is need to offload VMs to the public cloud. To find the solution minimizing totalCost(**VM**), initially assume that all remaining VMs placed to public cloud. In order of increasing in delta of PenaltyCost, in other words, place the VM with minimal bandwidth in public cloud to the PM with using minimal bandwidth one by one until no VM is placed in public cloud, maximally consolidated.

Estimated Performance Degradation. To estimate **PenaltyCost**, approximation performance degradation estimation is needed. Equations (9) and (10) denotes performance degradation estimation based on profiling data about datacenter specification. It is found experimentally.

$$Pd(\mathbf{VM}) \approx Pd_{estimated}(\mathbf{VM}) \frac{1}{2} \qquad (9)$$

$$= \begin{cases} \gamma \cdot \left\{ \sum_{j=1}^{m} \left(\sum_{i=0}^{n} vm_{ij} \cdot Bw(VM_i) > BW_{PM_j}^{thres} \right) \right\}^2 \\ \qquad \text{where } \sum_{i=0}^{n} vm_{ij} \cdot Bw(VM_i) > BW_{PM_j}^{thres} \\ 0 \text{ where } \sum_{i=0}^{n} vm_{ij} \cdot Bw(VM_i) \leq BW_{PM_j}^{thres} \end{cases} \qquad (10)$$

$Pd_{estimated}(\mathbf{VM})$ reflects the fact that performance degradation becomes more severe as difference between estimated bandwidth and threshold in each PM. γ is a control parameter for scaling (Fig. 3).

4 Evaluation

4.1 Experiment Setting

To evaluate the CHOV, we form the experiment setting as shown in Fig. 4. To construct internal cloud of content provider, Openstack [10] is used. This cloud environment consists of a control node, 2 compute nodes and their specification is denoted as shown in Table 2.

The VMs used as cache servers have a 1 VCPU, 2 GB of memory, 20 GB Disk. For public cloud environment, we choose Amazon EC2 [11], and as cache servers VM instances with a 1 VCPU, 1 GB of memory, EBS only storage.

The videos that a content provider offers are shown in Table 3 with their profiling data.

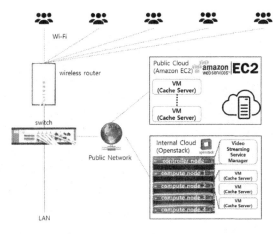

Fig. 4. Experiment setting in CHOV

Table 2. Internal cloud environment setting using Openstack.

	Control node	Compute node 1	Compute node 2
Functions	Cloud controller node, network, volume, API, scheduler, image services, Nova compute	Nova compute	Nova compute
Specification	16 cores (Intel® Xeon® CPU E5-2650 v2, 2.60 GHz),		
	32 GB memory, 242 GB Disk, Ubuntu 14.04.3 LTS	16 GB memory, 258 GB Disk, Ubuntu 14.04.2 LTS	

Table 3. 3 videos used in experiment and their profiling data. Each of them has a different bit rate, size, video length.

	Video 0	Video 1	Video 2
Bit rate	313 Kbyte/s	707 Kbyte/s	3008 Kbyte/s
Video length	231.6 sec	227.0 sec	227.0 sec
Video size	72.5 MB	160.5 MB	683 MB

4.2 Experiment Result

Figure 5 shows severe performance degradation is measured in case of maximal consolidation but comparing CVOH and maximal offloading, the whole performance degradation of VMs have similar aspect. The performance degradation is defined as Eq. (11).

$$\text{performance degradation} = \left(\frac{\sum_{VM} Completion\ time}{\sum_{VM} Video\ Length} - 1 \right) \qquad (11)$$

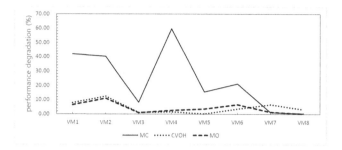

Fig. 5. Performance degradation graph of VMs placed as cache servers. MC, CVOH, MO denote respectively maximal consolidation, cost-effective VM offloading in hybrid cloud environment, maximal offloading cases.

In Fig. 6(a), as the worst case, performance degradation of video streaming results 23.5 % in case of MC, and CVOH is worse than maximal offloading case but there is small difference comparing to MC case as 4.58 %, 4.15 % are shown respectively in CVOH and MO. By the result shown in (b) and (c), CVOH is more cost-effective solution than other cases to content provider.

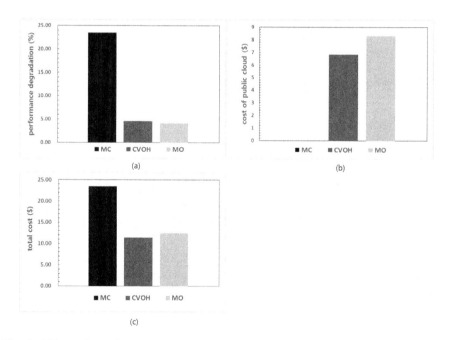

Fig. 6. This graph set shows the results of experiment in each case of MC, CVOH, MO. MC, CVOH, MO denote respectively maximal consolidation, cost-effective VM offloading in hybrid cloud environment, maximal offloading cases. (a) Entire performance degradation graph of each case. (b) Cost of using public cloud instances in each case. (c) Total cost in each case.

5   Conclusion

In this paper, we suggest cost-effective VM offloading algorithm for video streaming services in hybrid cloud environment. The CVOH considers cost model for using public cloud based on the learning curve model, and a penalty cost of performance degradation in internal cloud. From the result of experiments, CVOH shows that it has better performance than maximal consolidation in dealing end-users' request and it is also more cost-effective than maximal offloading. Comparing with a maximal consolidation case, CVOH has about twice better performance in total cost and comparing with a maximal offloading case, it has 0.4 % worse performance, but in total cost it has 9.1 % better.

Acknowledgments. This research was supported by the MSIP under the ITRC (Information Technology Research Center) support program (NIPA-2014(H0301-14-1020)) supervised by the NIPA (National IT Industry Promotion Agency), and 'The Cross-Ministry Giga KOREA Project' grant from the Ministry of Science, ICT and Future Planning, Korea.

References

1. AWS Case Study: Netflix. http://aws.amazon.com/ko/solutions/case-studies/netflix/
2. Google Cloud Boosting YouTube Upload Speeds. http://blogs.wsj.com/digits/2011/02/14/googlecloud-boosting-youtube-upload-speeds/
3. Aggarwal, V., Gopalakrishnan, V., Jana, R., Ramakrishnan, K.K., Vaishampayan, V.A.: Optimizing cloud resources for delivering IPTV services through virtualization. In: COMSNETS (2012)
4. Bossche, R.V.D., Vanmechelen, K., Broeckhove, J.: Cost-optimal scheduling in hybrid IaaS clouds for deadline constrained workloads. In: CLOUD 2010
5. Amit, G., Xia, C.H.: Learning curves and stochastic models for pricing and provisioning cloud computing services. Serv. Sci. **3**, 99–109 (2011)
6. Kim, H., Hyeon, M., Jang, H., Youn, C.: An analysis of resource performance for inter- and intra- datacenter resource management under cloud content delivery network environment. In CIAPT (2015)
7. Phoronix Test Suite. http://www.phoronix-test-suite.com/
8. LLCbench. http://icl.cs.utk.edu/projects/llcbench/cachebench.html/
9. Bonnie++. http://www.coker.com.au/bonnie++/
10. OpenStack. http://www.openstack.org/
11. Amazon EC2. http://aws.amazon.com/ec2

Dynamic Virtual Machine Consolidation for Energy Efficient Cloud Data Centers

Dong-Ki Kang, Fawaz Alhazemi, Seong-Hwan Kim,
and Chan-Hyun Youn$^{(\boxtimes)}$

School of Electrical Engineering, KAIST, Daejeon, Korea
{dkkang, fawaz, s.h_kim, chyoun}@kaist.ac.kr

Abstract. As a cloud computing model have led clusters to the large-scale data centers, reducing of the energy consumption which imposes a crucial part of the whole operating expense for data centers has received a lot of attention of a wide public. At cluster-level viewpoint, the most popular method for energy efficient cloud is Dynamic Right Sizing (DRS), which turns off idle servers those do not have any of running virtual resources. To maximize the energy efficiency through DRS, one of primary adaptive resource management strategies is a Virtual Machine (VM) consolidation which integrates VM instances into as few servers as possible. In this paper, we propose Virtual machine Consolidation based Size Decision (VC-SD) approach migrates VM instances from under-utilized servers which are supposed to be turned off to sustaining ones according to their monitored resource utilizations in real time. In addition, we design a Self Adjusting Workload Prediction (SAWP) method to improve a forecasting accuracy of resource utilization even under irregular demand patterns. Through experimental results based on real cloud servers, we show various metrics such as resource utilization, energy consumption and switching overhead caused by application processing, VM migration and DRS execution to verify a necessity of our proposed methodologies.

Keywords: Cloud computing · Virtual Machine migration · Dynamic Right Sizing · Workload Prediction

1 Introduction

In modern cloud data centers, resource allocation with high energy efficiency has been a key problem as a fraction of cost caused by energy consumption has increased in recent years. According to an estimation from [1], a cost of power and cooling has increased 400 % over 10 years, and 59 % of data centers identify them as key factors limiting server deployments. Consequentially, challenges about energy consumption and cooling have led to growing push to achieve a design of energy efficient data centers. At the data center level, a promising candidate called Dynamic Right Sizing (DRS) to save energy is to dynamically adjust the number of active servers (i.e., servers those power is switched on) in proportion to the measured user demands [2]. In DRS, the energy saving can be achieved through allowing idle servers that do not have any running VM instances to go low-power mode (i.e., sleep, shut down). In order to maximize the energy efficiency via

© ICST Institute for Computer Sciences, Social Informatics and Telecommunications Engineering 2016
Y. Zhang et al. (Eds.): CloudComp 2015, LNICST 167, pp. 70–80, 2016.
DOI: 10.1007/978-3-319-38904-2_8

DRS, one of primary adaptive resource management strategies is a VM consolidation in which, running VM instances can be dynamically integrated into the minimal number of cloud servers in accordance with their resource utilization collected by hypervisor monitoring module [3]. That is, running VM instances on under-utilized servers which are supposed to be turned off could be migrated to power-sustainable servers. However, it is difficult to efficiently manage cloud resources since cloud users often have heterogeneous resource demands underlying multiple service applications that experience highly variable workloads. Therefore, the inconsiderate VM consolidation using live migration might lead to undesirable performance degradation due primarily to switching overheads caused by migration and turning off servers on [4]. Running service applications with reckless VM migration and DRS execution might encounter serious execution time's delay, increased latency or failures. As a result, a careful resource management scheme considering switching overheads is necessary to reduce efficiently the energy consumption of cloud servers while ensuring acceptable Quality of Service (QoS) based on Service Level Agreements to cloud users.

In this paper, we propose Virtual machine Consolidation based Sizing Decision (VC-SD) approach to address above challenges for cloud data centers. The energy consumption model based on VC-SD approach is formulated with a performance cost (reputation loss) caused by the increased delay from downsizing active servers and an energy cost of keeping particular active servers, and a cost incurred from switching off servers on. Subsequently, we develop the design of an automated cloud resource management system called Dynamic Cloud Resource Broker (DCRB) with VC-SD approach. Moreover, we introduce our novel prediction method called Self Adjusting Workload Prediction (SAWP) to increase the prediction accuracy of users' future demands even under the unstatic and irregular workload patterns. The proposed SAWP method adaptively scales the history window size up or down according to extracted workload's autocorrelations and sample entropies which measure periodicity and burstiness of workloads [6]. To investigate performance characteristics of the proposed approaches, we conduct various experiments to evaluate a resource utilization, completion time's delay and energy consumption by live migration and DRS execution on real testbed based on Openstack which is a well known cloud platform using KVM hypervisor [5]. Through meaningful experimental results, we find that our proposed VC-SD approach and SAWP method provide significant energy saving while guaranteeing acceptable performance required by users in practice.

2 System Model Formulation

In this chapter, we introduce a system model based on reputation cost and energy cost by DRS with VM consolidation using live migration. Several notations for the system model are described as follows,

n: a total number of running VM instances

m: a total number of physical servers

$\boldsymbol{x}^t = \left(x_1^t, x_2^t, \ldots, x_n^t\right)^T$: a resource allocation vector at period t, x_i^t is an index of physical server assigned VM instance i at period t.

$pm_j^t = \{i | x_i^{t-1} = j, \forall i = 1, \ldots, n\}$: a set of running VM instances on physical server j at period t.

$d_{j,i}^{t,k}$: a flavor demand of resource k by VM instance i on physical server j at period t.

c_j^k: a capacity of resource k on physical server j.

C_{total}^t: a total cost at period t.

C_{repu}^t: a reputation cost (i.e., affects the future purchase of users) at period t.

C_{energy}^t: an energy cost for maintaining active servers and processing wake-up of off servers by DRS at period t.

C_{intf}: a constant value. An unit cost caused by interference of running VM instances.

C_{mig}: a constant value. An unit cost caused by live migration.

C_p: a constant value. An unit power cost for active servers.

P_{active}: a constant value. An unit power consumption for active servers.

P_{switch}: a constant value. An unit power consumption for turning off server on.

T_{mig}: an execution time for live migration of VM instances.

T_{switch}: an execution time for turning off servers on.

ω_k: a weight value for resource component k (e.g., cpu, memory, and I/O bandwidth, etc.).

$r_{j,i}^{t,k}$: a resource utilization of VM instance i on resource component k of physical server j at period t.

r_{thr}^k: a threshold value of resource utilization representing over-utilization of resource component k.

Based on above defined notations, cost models based on live VM migration and DRS can be formulated as follows,

$$C_{total}^t = C_{repu}^t + C_{energy}^t \tag{1}$$

$$C_{repu}^t = C_{intf} \sum_{j=1}^{m} \sum_{k=1}^{l} \omega_k \left| pm_j^t \right| \cdot \left(\frac{\sum_{i=1}^{n} r_{j,i}^{t,k}}{r_{thr}^k} - 1 \right)^+$$
$$+ 2 C_{mig} T_{mig} \left| \{ x_i^{t-1} | x_i^{t-1} \neq x_i^{t-2}, \forall i = 1, \ldots, n \} \right| \tag{2}$$

$$C_{energy}^t = C_p P_{active} \sum_{j=1}^{m} \left(\left| pm_j^t \right| \right)^-$$
$$+ C_p P_{switch} T_{switch} \left(\sum_{j=1}^{m} \left(\left| pm_j^t \right| \right)^- - \sum_{j=1}^{m} \left(\left| pm_j^{t-1} \right| \right)^- \right)^+ \tag{3}$$

where $(x)^+ = \max(x, 0)$ and $(x)^- = \min(x, 1)$. The first term in the right hand of Eq. (2) represents that as the number of concurrent running VM instances on single physical server is increased, the number of users experiencing undesirable performance degradation is also increased. We multiply by the cost of live migration by 2 as shown in the second term in (2) since two physical servers obviously are required for migration.

The purpose of our algorithm is to derive an optimal consolidation plan x for resource allocation at next period iteratively. At period $t - 1$, the proposed VC-SD approach aims to minimize the cost function (1) by finding a solution x^{t-1} as follows,

$$minimize_{x^{t-1}} \quad C^t_{total} = C^t_{repu} + C^t_{energy} \tag{4}$$

$$subject\ to. \quad \sum_{i=1}^{n} d_{j,i}^{t,k} \leq c_j^k, \quad \forall j = 1, 2, \ldots, m \tag{5}$$

$$state\left(pm_{x_i}^t\right) \neq off, \quad \forall i = 1, 2, \ldots, n \tag{6}$$

where $state(\cdot)$ represents the state of physical server; *on* or *off*. For simplicity, we assume that any additional VM requests are not submitted to our system during VC-SD approach execution. In general cases, this assumption is not trivial, we therefore consider this issue in future works.

To solve the objective cost function (4), we prefer a well known evolutionary metaheuristic called Genetic Algorithm (GA) in order to approximate the optimal plan x^* at each period since Eqs. (1)–(3) have non-linear characteristics. In next chapter, our proposed system with VC-SD approach and DRS method is introduced in detail.

3 Proposed System Structure

In this chapter, we introduce the architecture of an automated Dynamic Cloud Resource Brokering (DCRB) system with our proposed algorithms. In Fig. 1, two main components of DCRB are shown; VC-SD manager and SWAP manager.

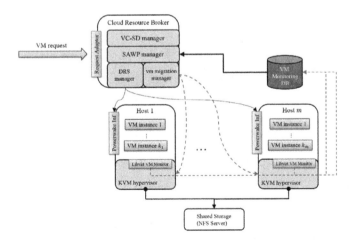

Fig. 1. Cloud Resource Broker with VC-SD manager and SAWP manager for greening the cloud data center

First, the process of VC-SD approach includes following four steps: (1) to monitor and collect resource utilization data of VM instances on each physical server through attached Libvirt based monitoring tools; (2) to go step 3 if the average utilization of whole active servers are significantly low (i.e., below the predefined threshold), otherwise go step 4; (3) to choose active servers which are supposed to be turned off, migrate all the VM instances on them to other servers and trigger DRS execution; (4) to determine the number of off servers to be turned on and send magic packets to them for wake-up if the average utilization of whole active servers are significantly high (i.e., above the predefined threshold), otherwise maintain the current number of active servers.

Figure 2 shows the procedure of the proposed VC-SD approach in DCRB. $\overline{r^k} = \frac{1}{m}\sum_{j=1}^{m}\sum_{i=1}^{n} r_{j,i}^{t,k}$ is an average resource utilization of whole active servers and $r_{thr_{green}^{low}}^{k}$ and $r_{thr_{green}^{high}}^{k}$ are threshold values of resource utilization to make a decision whether to turn active servers off or to turn off servers on. A term $\alpha \cdot \max_{k} \frac{\overline{r^k}}{r_{thr_{green}^{high}}^{k}}$ affects the number of off servers that supposed to be turned on, where α is a predetermined constant value. Second, the process of SAWP method also includes following four steps: (1) to analyze user demand history data based on a Workload Analysis and Classification tool (WAC) [6] and calculate fluctuation and burstiness of demands; (2) to go step 3 if derived values of fluctuation and burstiness are high (i.e., above the predefined threshold), otherwise go step 4; (3) to increase the history window size in proportion to the values of fluctuation and burstiness; (4) to decrease the history window size in proportion to values of fluctuation and burstiness if they are significantly low (i.e., below the predefined threshold), otherwise maintain the current history window size.

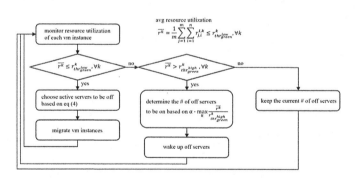

Fig. 2. Procedure of VC-SD approach

Figure 3 shows the procedure of the proposed SAWP method in DCRB. The irregularity function $g(\varepsilon, \delta)$ represents a level of unpredictability of future resource utilization where ε is its fluctuation value (i.e., levels of unstability and aperiodicity) and δ is its burstness value (i.e., levels of sudden surge and decline), both values are calculated based on [6]. According to predetermined threshold values g_{thr}^{high} and g_{thr}^{low} with $g(\varepsilon, \delta)$, the history window size σ is adaptively updated at each prediction process.

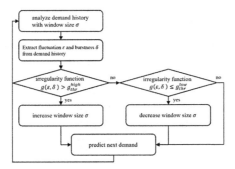

Fig. 3. Procedure of SAWP method

Algorithm 1. Genetic Algorithm (GA) for VC-SD approach

Input : $x^{t-1} = \langle x_1^{t-1}, x_2^{t-1}, \ldots, x_m^{t-1} \rangle^T$, an allocation vector at period $t - 1$

Output : $x^t = \langle x_1^t, x_2^t, \ldots, x_m^t \rangle^T$, an allocation vector at period t

00: initialize $pop^h = \{x^{h,1}, x^{h,2}, \ldots, x^{h,P}\}$, $P = size\ of\ population$, and even number

01: **while** $h \leq h_{max}$

02:    **for each** $x^{h,i} \in pop^h$

03:      $fv^{h,i} = f_{C_{total}^t}(x^{h,i}, x^{t-1})$

04:    **while** $! (\forall x^{h,i} \in pop^h\ are\ selected\ as\ parents)$

05:      $(x^{h,i}, x^{h,j}) \leftarrow$ select parents randomly from pop^h

06:      $offspring^h = \cup$ crossover $(x^{h,i}, x^{h,j})$

07:    **for each** $off\_x^{h,i} \in offspring^h$

08:      $off\_fv^{h,i} = f_{C_{total}^t}(off\_x^{h,i}, x^{t-1})$

09:    sort $pop^{h\sim} = \{x^{h,1}, \ldots, x^{h,P}, off\_x^{h,1}, \ldots, off\_x^{h,\frac{P}{2}}\}$ in ascending

       order of solutions' corresponding $fv^{h,i}$ and $off\_fv^{h,i}$

10:    $pop^{h+1} = \{pop_1^{h\sim}, \ldots, pop_P^{h\sim}\}$

11:    **if** $f_{C_{total}^t}(pop_1^{h+1}, x^{t-1}) \leq fv_{thr}$ **then**

12:      $x^t = pop_1^{h+1}$ and exit

13:    $h + +$

14: $x^t = \text{argmin}_{pop_i^{hmax} \in pop^{hmax}} \left(f_{C_{total}^t}(pop_i^{hmax}, x^{t-1}) \right)$ s.t. (5), (6)

15: **if** $x^t = \emptyset$ **then**

16:    $x^t = x^{t-1}$

A relatively long history window size is not suitable to react to recent changes of workload but is tolerant of varied workload patterns in a short time while a short history window size is favorable to efficiently respond to latest workload patterns but is not good for kaleidoscope of workloads. Consequently, the SAWP method generally outperforms traditional prediction schemes at drastic utilization changes from various cloud applications since it is able to cope with temporary resource utilization (i.e., not reflect overall trends) by adjusting the history window size σ. Now, we introduce a metaheuristic called Genetic Algorithm (GA) for solving approximated optimal solution of Eq. (4) with VC-SD approach. GA is a kind of well known guided random search techniques for combinatorial optimization problems [7]. In GA for VC-SD approach, the value of gene represents an index of physical server as an integer value where the position of gene represents an index of the allocated VM instance. Consequently, each chromosome formed of multiple genes represents a possible solution (not feasible solution) x to the objective cost function (4).

Algorithm 1 describes GA for VC-SD approach in detail. pop^h is a population with size P (even number) at h^{th} generation. h_{max} is a maximum of GA iteration count. At line 03, $f(\cdot)$ is a fitness function of total cost with both of parameters; candidate solution x^t and x^{t-1} based on Eq. (1). At line 04–06, two candidate solutions are iteratively chosen randomly from pop to generate offsprings by crossover until there are no remaining unselected solutions in pop. At line 07–08, the fitness function values of each offspring are calculated similar to line 03. At line 09, all the parent solutions in pop and generated offsprings are sorted in ascending order of their corresponding fitness function values. At line 10, the next population including only P solutions that achieve good performance from the union of original pop and derived offsprings is generated to improve a quality of final solution. At line $11 \sim 12$, to reduce a time complexity of GA procedures, when we encounter a first solution which has a fitness function value below the predetermined fitness threshold value fv_{thr}, it counts as a final solution for next period and the algorithm is finished. At line 14, if we cannot find a solution satisfies fv_{thr} until the iteration count reaches h_{max}, then we select a solution which has minimum fitness function value in the population satisfies conditions Eqs. (5) and (6) as a final solution for next period. If there are not any solutions satisfy conditions Eqs. (5) and (6), then we just preserve the current resource allocation vector as shown at line $15 \sim 16$. For population of GA, mutations often applied in order to include characteristics of offsprings that are not inherited trait by parents. We do not consider mutations in our GA in this paper, but it can be used to improve the quality of GA for VC-SD approach in future work.

4 Experimental Results

In our experiments, we have measured various metrics which affect the parameter decision for our proposed algorithms. To do this, we set five cluster servers for cloud platform, one server for DCRB with Mysql DB system, power measuring device of Yocto-Watt [8] and a laptop machine called VirtualHub for collecting and reporting the information of measured power consumption as shown in Fig. 4. The hardware specification of each server for cloud compute host which has Intel i7-3770 (8-cores, 3.4 GHz), 16 GB RAM memory, and two 1 Gbps NICs (Network Interface Cards). In order to measure efficiently the power consumption of cloud cluster server, we use power measuring device model called YWATTMK1 by Yocto-Watt. This model has a measurement unit 0.2 W for AC power with error ratio 3 % and 0.002 W for DC power with error ratio 1.5 %. The VirtualHub collects the information of power consumption from YWATTMK1 through Yocto-Watt Java API and reports them to power

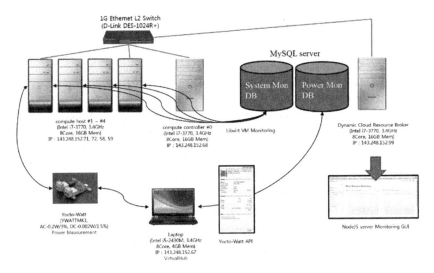

Fig. 4. Experimental environment

monitoring table of Mysql DB system in DCRB periodically. The dynamic resource utilizations by each VM instance are measured via our developed VM monitoring modules based on Libvirt API and are sent to resource monitoring table of Mysql DB system periodically. In addition, SATA 3 TB hard disk called G-drive is deployed as a NFS server in our testbed for live migration [9]. We adopt Openstack kilo version which is a well known open source solution based on KVM Hypervisor as a cloud platform to our testbed. Finally, we use Powerwake package [10] to turn remotely off servers on via Wake on Lan (WOL) technology for DRS execution.

In Table 1, we show the average power consumption and resource utilization of two running applications: Montage m106-1.7 projection and ftp transfer. Montage project is an open source based scientific application and it has been invoked by NASA/IPAC Infrared Science Archive as a toolkit for assembling Flexible Image Transport System (FITS) images into custom mosaics [11]. The m106-1.7 projection in

Table 1. Average power consumption and resource utilization by Montage and ftp transfer

Host state		Power Consumption (Wh)	CPU utilization	Mem utilization	Net bandwidth
Idle		55Wh	1.5 %	3 %	20 Kbps (bytes)
Active	Montage m106-1.7 (projection)	75Wh	15 %	3.7 %	20 Kbps (bytes)
	test.avi downloading (ftp, 1.5GB)	60Wh	2 %	3.7 %	3.7 Mbps (bytes)
aSleep (to Power Off)		70-80Wh (5-7s)	1.8 % (5-7s)	3 % (5-7s)	20 Kbps (bytes)
Power Off (hibernating)		2.5Wh			
aWake (from Power Off)		78Wh (50s-1min)			

Montage is a cpu-intensive application while the ftp transfer is a network-intensive one. Therefore, m106-1.7 causes the power consumption about 75 Wh and the cpu utilization about 15 % whereas the power consumption by ftp transfer for 1.5 GB test.avi file is about 60 Wh and the network bandwidth usage is about 3.7 Mbps. That is, the cpu usage is a main part to affect the power consumption of server. In view of DRS execution, the power consumption by an off server is about 2.5 Wh (note that this value is not zero since the NIC and its some peripheral components are still powered on to keep standby mode to receive the magic packet from Powerwake controller) while aSleep and aWake procedures which cause switching overhead for DRS require the power consumption about 80 Wh to turn active servers off or to turn off servers on, respectively. The aSleep procedure is trivial since it requires a short time (i.e., 5 ∼ 7 s) to complete even though its power consumption is considerable whereas the aWake procedure requires a relatively long execution time (i.e., above 1 min) supposed to be considered carefully. The overhead for aWake procedure would be more serious problem in practice since the execution time by aWake procedure is generally far long (i.e., above 10 min) for multiple servers of rack in the data center. Therefore, it is essential to consider the switching overhead for aWake procedure to reduce efficiently the resource usage cost of the data center.

Figure 5 shows the dynamic resource utilization by several applications on running VM instances measured via Libvirt based VM monitoring modules. The instance-00000010 runs m101-1.0 mProj, instance-0000000f runs m108-1.7 mProj and

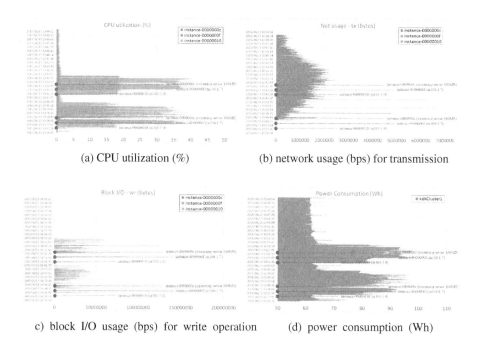

(a) CPU utilization (%)   (b) network usage (bps) for transmission

c) block I/O usage (bps) for write operation   (d) power consumption (Wh)

Fig. 5. Measured resource utilization and power consumption by Libvirt API based VM monitoring module and YWATTMK1 device

instance-0000000c runs a streaming server with a 180 MB movie file. Especially, Fig. 5(d) demonstrates that the Montage projection which is the cpu-intensive application increases the power consumption significantly of server whereas the streaming server which is a network-intensive application produces consistently very little effect on the power consumption by comparison with results of Table 1. Figure 6 shows cpu utilizations of a source server and a destination server for live migration. The instance-00000033 is supposed to be migrated from kdkCluster2 - source server to kdkCluster1 - destination server and the instance-00000034 is a fixed running VM instance on kdkCluster2. The instance-00000033 is migrated to kdkCluster1 during its application - m101-1.6 - execution. The completion time for live migration of instance-00000033 is longer than half an hour, therefore this overhead might cause a significant performance degradation of application and an undesirable waste of energy. All the results from experiments in this paper obviously verify that our proposed VC-SD approach and SAWP method considering switching overheads by live migration and DRS execution are necessary for real cloud environments.

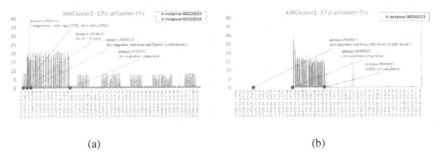

(a)   (b)

Fig. 6. cpu utilizations during VM migration (instance-00000033) from (a) a source server: kdkCluster2 to (b) a destination server:kdkCluster1

5   Conclusion

In this paper, we introduced a Dynamic Cloud Resource Broker (DCRB) with Virtual machine Consolidation based Size Decision (VC-SD) approach for energy efficient resource management by a real time based VM monitoring in cloud data center. Our proposed approach is able to reduce efficiently the energy consumption of servers without a significant performance degradation by live migration and Dynamic Right Sizing (DRS) execution through a considerate model considering switching overheads. Through various experimental results based on Openstack platform justify that our proposed algorithms are supposed to be deployed for prevalent cloud data centers. Moreover, the novel prediction method called Self Adjusting Workload Prediction (SAWP) is proposed in order to improve an accuracy of forecasting future demands even under drastic workload changes. In future works, we demonstrate that our proposed algorithms outperform existing approaches for energy efficient resource management through various experiments based on implemented system in practice.

Acknowledgments. This work was supported by 'Electrically phase-controlled beamforming lighting device based on 2D nano-photonic phased array for lidar' grant from Civil Military Technology Cooperation, Korea and Institute for Information (No. 14-BR-SS-02), and Communications Technology Promotion (IITP) grant funded by the Korea government (MSIP) (No. B0101-15-0104, The Development of Supercomputing System for the Genome Analysis).

References

1. International Data Center Corporation. http://www.idc.com
2. Lin, M., Wierman, A., Andrew, L.L.H., Thereska, E.: Dynamic right-sizing for power-proportional data centers. IEEE/ACM Trans. Networking **21**(5), 1378–1391 (2013)
3. Xiao, Z., Song, W., Chen, Q.: Dynamic resource allocation using virtual machines for cloud computing environment. IEEE Trans. Parallel Distrib. Syst. **24**(6), 1107–1117 (2013)
4. Beloglazov, A., Buyya, R.: Optimal online deterministic algorithms and adaptive heuristics for energy and performance efficient dynamic consolidation of virtual machines in cloud data centers. Concurrency Comput. Pract. Experience **24**, 1397–1420 (2012). doi:10.1002/cpe.1867
5. Openstack. http://www.openstack.org
6. A-Eldin, A., Tordsson, J., Elmroth, E., Kihl, M.: Workload Classification for Efficient Auto-Scaling of Cloud Resources. Umea University, Sweden (2013)
7. Deb, K., Pratap, A., Agarwal, S., Meyarivan, T.: A fast and elitist multiobjective genetic algorithm NSGA-II. IEEE Trans. Evol. Comput. **6**(2), 182–197 (2002)
8. YOCTO-WATT. http://www.yoctopuce.com/EN/products/usb-electrical-sensors/yocto-watt
9. G-Technology. http://www.g-technology.com/products/g-drive
10. PowerWake. http://manpages.ubuntu.com/manpages/utopic/man1/powerwake.1.html
11. Montage. http://montage.ipac.caltech.edu/

Resource Management, Models and Performance

A New Framework
for Cloud Business Process Management

Mohamed K. Watfa$^{(\boxtimes)}$, Nafez A.L. Najjar,
Jad Cheikha, and Nayef Buali

University of Wollongong in Dubai, Knowledge Village, Dubai, UAE
MohamedWatfa@uowdubai.ac.ae,
{nan926,jcc693}@uowmail.edu.au, nayefbuali@gmail.com

Abstract. Cloud BPM is a technology that utilizes Cloud computing offerings
for running a Business Process Management System (BPMS). Both technologies are of high interest to business and technology domains and it is understood
that the combination of both Business Process Management and Cloud computing will result in a higher level of business efficiency. This research paper
uses both quantitative and qualitative analysis in order to have an in depth
details on the Cloud Business Process Management adoption rate and the
benefits it offers for end users. Since Cloud Business Process Management is a
new technology trend, we propose a standard Cloud Business Process Management model which focuses on business efficiency. We were able to identify
the reasons behind the lack of Cloud BPM adoption in the local market and
gathered sufficient evidence to prove that there is a relation between Cloud BPM
and business efficiency.

Keywords: Cloud computing · Business Process Management (BPM) · Cloud
Business Process Management (CBPM) · Business efficiency · Cloud Business
Process Management adoption

1 Introduction

Business Process Management (BPM) is a holistic management approach focused on
aligning organizational objectives and other aspects to continuously improve business
processes; i.e., is referred to as a "process improvement" process. The aim of Business
Process Management is to improve the business performance of an enterprise by
changing business operations to perform more effectively and efficiently. BPM as a
management discipline, has its origins in previous management disciplines such as
business process reengineering (BPR), as developed in the seminal works of Hammer
in the 1990s [1]. Organizations are continuously subjected to internal and external
challenges and threats; hence the ability to adapt to new opportunity and change in
business processes is mandatory to stand out among rivals. The core advantage of BPM
is to achieve efficiency by continuously improving business processes. BPM also helps
organizations in being customer oriented as this is one of the most demanding goals
and targets in achieving business goals. Furthermore, BPM plays a key role in product
and services improvement, quality and innovation.

© ICST Institute for Computer Sciences, Social Informatics and Telecommunications Engineering 2016
Y. Zhang et al. (Eds.): CloudComp 2015, LNICST 167, pp. 83–92, 2016.
DOI: 10.1007/978-3-319-38904-2_9

BPM is sometimes wrongly considered to be a means of software or application only, while in fact it consists of multiple steps and functionality within the BPM life-cycle; however a software or application is considered part of the BPM lifecycle which also includes process design, system configuration, process enactment, and diagnosis where analysis and monitoring tools, flow times, process bottlenecks, utilization are used. The Business Process Management is part of the enactment phase which consists of software suites used for process modeling, management, execution, and monitoring. The main components of a BPMS as summarized in Fig. 1 are divided into:

- The *Business Process Modeling* component aims to create a process models and is usually achieved by means of graphical notations.
- The *Business Process Environment* includes the components that trigger the initiation of the process.
- The *Business Process Model Repository* is a space where models are saved.
- The *Process Engine* is the core where the process models are executed and acts as a compiler in SW coordinating communication and interaction with service providers.
- *Service Providers* act as an Input/Output system and consists of computer systems and humans who interact with the process engine.

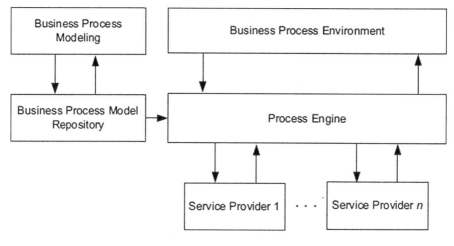

Fig. 1. BPMS components

According to Gartner [10], forty percent of Respondents with BPM Initiatives use Cloud Computing to Support at Least ten percent of BPM Business Processes. BPM is a proven technology with a paramount goal to improve business processes and a transformation to be cloud based is a solution already offered by many BPM providers. Cloud computing offers many advantages to the business and applications that have moved to the cloud inherit many of its wide range advantages and drawbacks as well. Cloud BPM is being implemented as PaaS or SaaS by most of the vendors. However, researches in this field indicate that Cloud BPM can be implemented as IaaS cloud offerings [2]. Furthermore most of the current vendors are offering Cloud BPM as a public cloud type of offering. On the other hand, according to the research by Han *et al.* in [3], Cloud BPM can be offered in any of the cloud deployment models. Furthermore, a combination that includes separating components of a BPM system between multiple types and that is offered as a hybrid cloud is also suggested. BPM and Cloud independent advantages are widely recognized among organizations however what's gaining attention more and more is the collective advantages of BMP in Cloud. The economic value of a BPM in the cloud eliminates the need for an upfront capital investment as it functions on a "Pay per use" model which decreases the overall cost of the solution. With BPM in the cloud, organizations no longer need to worry about scaling their system up or down and how this scaling might affect their systems since it will be completely handled by their BPM-C Vendor upon request. Some other BPM-C advantages include continuous operational efficiency improvement, high availability and performance, increased revenue, decreased overall cost, competitive advantage and many more. These benefits combined together will offer the organizations a dynamic responsive IT infrastructure which can be continuously improved or adjusted in order to meet the business needs and keep up with the rapid changes in the market.

In this research, we focus on the BPM being shifted to the cloud in order to address the how successful this move can be for organizations in the local market. On the other hand, we provide a detailed study of the current thoughts of this technology in terms of advantages, drawbacks and adoption rates to assist current and future vendors offering cloud based BPM systems adopt, innovate and change to satisfy markets need in this context. The rest of the paper is organized as follows: Sect. 2 states the research problem and its corresponding research questions highlighting the significance of this research work. Section 3 summarizes the related research work. Section 4 summarizes our research design and methodology and results. Section 5 concludes this work.

2   Research Questions

Addressing the concept, models, advantages and disadvantages of cloud BPM over non Cloud based BPM are to be studied, proposed and tested furthermore. Also, the adoption factor and adoption status according to both SMB and enterprises will be extracted and analyzed to address to what extent it is acceptable and seen as an added value to enhance and improve organizations business processes.

2.1   Research Questions

Our research question focuses on the analysis and justifications of the lack of Business Process Management in the Cloud (BPM-C) adoption among local Enterprises and SMEs and how cloud based BPM platforms can contribute to improve the efficiency of an organization through modeling and standardizing core business processes. In this research, we will be using a non-causal correlation methodology along with a cross sectional study setting. A non-contrived methodology will also be used in order to discuss rigorously our research question.

In a nutshell, our main objectives are listed below:

- Identify the differences between cloud based BPM and BPM.
- Identify cloud BPM models and frameworks.
- Understand if and how cloud BPM can enhance organizations' efficiency.
- Study the advantages and disadvantages of cloud BPM.
- Analyze future trends relating to cloud BPM.
- Analyze local adoption behavior compared to other regions.

3 Related Work in Cloud BPM

Whibley [4] discusses the business benefits of having a cloud BPM and how the BPM will integrate with the cloud architecture. Moreover, he discusses the challenges and how the future of cloud BPM will transform the delivery of business processes. The author argues that the cloud adoption in packaged apps is on the rise but on the other hand the adoption of BPM to cloud is slower because BPM applications do not have the same features of packaged apps. Multiple concerns and weakness come to mind in which the author did not discuss or mention. First, he mentions the BPM as a PaaS while in reality BPM can also be offered and supported through multiple other service models. A second concern includes the challenges besides data security, for example unknown reliability of the Infrastructure which is provided by the cloud vendor and the challenges of integrating the BPM system in house and legacy systems within an organization. Moreover, there is the issue of computation vs. non computational intensive activities that might lead into increasing the cost on the user side. It also seems that the author relied on theoretical information and did not provide any statistical data to support his analysis. This short coming was somehow addressed in the next research by Railton *et al.* [5]. Railton *et al.* performed a literature review and an online survey on Cloud based BPM to propose the definition and concept of cloud BPM, identify main benefits and drawbacks of cloud based BPM, its characteristics, market trends and adoption rates.

Existing research work on cloud BPM [4–7] primarily focused on the definition, characteristics, benefits, drawbacks and market trends. However, there was a small focus on the adoption rates of Cloud BPM. Since cloud BPM inherits many of its characteristics from cloud computing and the lack of literature studies that addresses the adoption of Cloud BPM, analyzing papers on the adoption of Cloud computing [8, 9] is presumed to facilitate our goal of studying and analyzing Cloud BPM adoption. Yeboah-Boateng et al. [8] evaluates the main factors and issues that are affecting the adoption of Cloud Computing technologies within SMEs in developing economies. Cloud adoption has recently increased however the interest in these kinds of services in the developing economies is still slow and not up to the speed. Due to this, the identification of enabling and constrain adoption features arises. Some of the main enabling features are low cost, business continuity, enhanced communications and scalability. On the other hand, some of the adoption constrains are security, unconventional internet connections and lack of trust for current systems.

Moreover, some of the factors that influence the adoption of cloud computing technologies are efficiency of cloud vendors, management support and trial periods. A survey of cloud-computing adoption studies can be found in [8, 9] where a noticeable part of the published research was conducted in well-developed countries. In addition, existing studies [8, 9, 11] focus on the acceptance of services and deployment models for cloud computing while disregarding the factors that drive adoption.

4 Research Methodology and Analysis

In this research, we used a mixed research method that includes both qualitative and quantitative methods. The qualitative method will aim to gather in-depth information and understanding on Cloud BPM and its impact on business process efficiency. On the other hand, the quantitative method will gather statistical information which will help us analyze the information gathered. Furthermore, the findings, relationships and assumptions will be studied and tested using hypotheses testing. We also study the relationship between Cloud BPM and Business Efficiency. For that we will be using a Non-Causal investigation type. This type will be used to study, analyze and answer the correlation between Cloud BPM and Business Efficiency. In order to achieve and accurate result, the study will be conducted on real life Cloud BPM systems that are currently running in local SMEs or Enterprises. This Non-Contrived study will consist of multiple interviews, surveys from different personnel in the BPM area and an analysis of archival data. A cross sectional methodology will be used where all the data will be collected at a certain point in time. In order to get an unbiased data sample, the unit of analysis for this research will be a mixture of individuals, groups, divisions and industries.

The target population for this research is divided in to three sections. The first are BPM providers and users, second are cloud providers and users and finally the third are cloud BPM providers and users. The reason behind targeting Cloud and BPM providers is in hopes of finding difficulties with providing Cloud BPM since they do not offer this kind of service and they will have an unbiased opinion about it. With respect to the above target population, the sampling frame will consist of the following: Local Enterprises such as IBM, Oracle, Microsoft, EMC; Telecommunications and Banking industries; and Government hospitals and local IT SMEs. The following sample units will be derived out of the above sampling frame: 30 samples from Enterprises, 30 samples from Telecommunications industry, 30 Samples from the banking industry and 30 samples from local IT SMBs and SMEs. We have chosen the probability sampling technique with multi-stage sampling consisting of two stages. The sampling methodology will start by randomly selecting two to three samples from the sampling frame and assigning them into clusters. Once this is done, we will again randomly select multiple clusters in order to acquire twenty to thirty samples from each selected cluster.

In order to have accurate measurements, survey and interview questions will be worded to focus on the Cloud BPM attributes that relate to the hypotheses and research questions. Mainly the questions and interviews will focus on the areas of adoption and business efficiency attributes with regards to Cloud BPM. After a successful literature review we concluded that the following will be the main Cloud BPM attributes that we will focus on: *Adoption, Implementation, Flexibility, Reliability, Security, and Functionality.*

The survey will consist of two to three questions on each of the above attributes and the style of the questions will contain a mixture of "Closed Questions" that will be answered using the Likert Scale, Multiple Choice, Tick Box, and Open Questions. Since reliability and accuracy of the collected data are of high importance to this research, part of the questions will concentrate on collecting the personal information of the respondents. This will assist us at a later point by measure the respondent's involvement in the Cloud BPM area. Also, hypotheses based on the literature review and the studies conducted on Cloud Business Process Management were analyzed.

4.1 Data Collection and Sampling

An online survey was used to collect data that addresses our research framework attributes with at least two questions per attribute. Furthermore, we conducted interviews with Cloud BPM vendors. The questions are a combination of knowledge, background, experience, opinion and feeling questions. The selection of our targeted respondents was carefully done by selecting local organizations that can be but in two classifications as shown in Tables 1 and 2.

Table 1. Sample classification based on company size.

Row variable	Cloud BPM	No cloud-BPM	Total
Enterprise	84	24	108
SMB	57	15	72
Total	141	39	180

Table 2. Sample classification based on adoption of cloud computing and adoption of Cloud BPM.

Row variable	Cloud BPM	No cloud-BPM	Total
Have cloud computing	138	15	153
Don't have cloud computing	3	24	27
Total	141	39	180

4.2 Research Analysis and Results

Some interesting results from our data analysis included the following;

- **Cloud computing characteristics and adoption behavior effect cloud BPM**: As expected Cloud BPM would inherit many characteristics and adoption factors from Cloud computing as the framework depends on including cloud computing as a key enabler to our suggested framework. 65 % of our respondents indicate that PaaS is the most deployed cloud computing delivery model, while 70 % indicated that PaaS is the most deployed Cloud BPM model. Furthermore, hybrid deployment model is the highest adopted model among private and public models with 42 % in companies that have Cloud Computing solutions, and 41 % among companies that have Cloud BPM implementations.

- **Company size effect on Cloud BPM adoption**: Respondents from both enterprises and SMBs would have the same interest in deploying Cloud BPM.
- **Cloud BPM key advantages**: We included six questions to uncover and validate key advantages and adoption enablers in our framework; five of the questions are Likert scale based while one allows the respondents to choose the 4 most important advantages among 10. Some results included:

  - 95 % agreed that Cloud BPM would enhance the efficiency of organization utilizing it, which indicates that organizations would more likely adopt Cloud BPM to achieve their overall goal of process improvement.
  - More than 95 % agreed that applying BPM in a cloud based approach would provide higher uptime and lower downtime. This could be due to the fact that one of the main Cloud Computing characteristics is availability of the service anywhere and anytime through means of network access and is built and constructed with this key feature in mind.
  - Almost all of the respondents agreed to the potential acceleration of cloud BPM adoption among local organizations.
  - The majority of the respondents with a proportion of more than 95 % agreed that Cloud BPM can support both simple and complex business processes, hence can replace the traditional BPM.
  - All of the respondents agreed that Cloud BPM is considered flexible and can scale up and down. This can be a consequence of inheriting this key feature from cloud computing offerings which support scaling the resources as needed by the underlying applications.

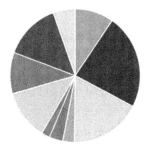

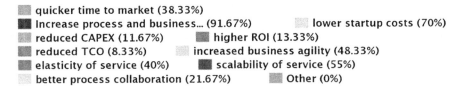

- quicker time to market (38.33%)
- Increase process and business... (91.67%)   lower startup costs (70%)
- reduced CAPEX (11.67%)   higher ROI (13.33%)
- reduced TCO (8.33%)   increased business agility (48.33%)
- elasticity of service (40%)   scalability of service (55%)
- better process collaboration (21.67%)   Other (0%)

Fig. 2. A pie chart depicting the different perceived advantages of cloud BPM.

- **Perceived Advantages of cloud BPM**: To analyze the advantages, a question offered the respondents to choose the most four important advantages of adopting a Cloud based BPM among a total of ten advantages extracted from our literature review. Figure 2 describes the respondents' answers. Increase process and business efficiencies was the highest selected advantages with a percentage of 91.7 %, while the second highly selected advantage was lower startup costs with almost two third of the respondents.
- Also, almost half of the organizations indicated that lower startup costs and increased business agility were evident advantages of cloud BPM.
- **Cloud Based BPM vs. On Premise Solution**: The last set of charts gathered information on the Advantages and Disadvantages of Cloud BPM. Most of the respondents consider the security is the main disadvantage of a Cloud BPM even though most of them don't consider it a show stopper if implemented correctly with the proper Cloud Models. As for the advantages of a Cloud BPM, the two options that received the most selection and stand out are the "Increase process and business efficiency" and "Lower startup cost" as depicted in Fig. 3.

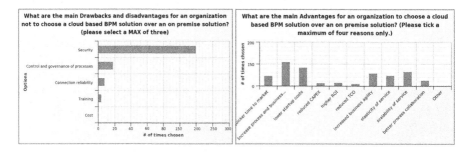

Fig. 3. Charts comparing cloud based BPM and on premise solutions.

Also, hypotheses based on the literature review and the data collected on Cloud Business Process Management were analyzed and associated conclusions were derived as shown below:

H_1: The majority of local organizations are using Platform as a service (PaaS) as their main Cloud BPM service model rather than (IaaS, SaaS) service models.

Conclusion 1: At 95 % confidence level, using a single population hypothesis t-test, there was sufficient evidence to conclude that the majority of local organizations are using Platform as a service (PaaS) as their main Cloud BPM service model rather than (IaaS, SaaS) service models.

H_2: The majority of local organizations use Hybrid Cloud model for their Cloud BPM deployments compared to the international adoption rate of the same model.

Conclusion 2: At 95 % confidence level, using a single population hypothesis t-test, there was sufficient evidence to say that the majority of local organizations are using Hybrid Cloud model for their Cloud BPM deployments compared to the international adoption rate of the same model (58 %).

H_3: There is a relation between company size and the adoption behavior of Cloud BPM. Local Enterprises are more interested in deploying Cloud BPM Services compared to Local SMBs.

Conclusion 3: Using a Chi-Square Test Statistic for dependency, we failed to reject the Null Hypothesis and conclude that we do not reject H0 and conclude that there is no sufficient evidence that the two proportions are different at $\alpha = 0.05$, hence "Company size" and the "Adoption rate of Cloud based BPM" are independent.

5 Conclusions

Our Cloud BPM research is considered the first of its kind in the local market that provides insightful information on the lack of Cloud BPM adoption reasons and the relationship between Cloud BPM and business efficiency according to the local market. Furthermore, our survey results provide statistical information on the current state and market maturity level when it comes to Cloud BPM. Other studies conducted on Cloud BPM do not apply to the local market due to the difference in the IT maturity level between the two regions. Moreover, previous researches focus mainly on the technical aspect of cloud models and BPM components. Concisely, we were able to identify the reasons behind the lack of Cloud BPM adoption in the local market and gathered sufficient evidence to prove that there is a relation between Cloud BPM and business efficiency. We were also able to identify the advantages and disadvantages of Cloud BPM according to the local market.

Moreover, we identified the most commonly used Cloud BPM components. Extended hypothesis testing and inferential regression analysis will be provided in an extended version of this work.

References

1. Hammer, M.: Reengineering work: don't automate, obliterate. Harvard Bus. Rev. **68**(4), 104–112 (1990)
2. Illustration of Cloud Taxonomy. http://www.cloudcontrols.org/cloud-standard-information/cloud-definitions/
3. Han, Y.-B., Sun, J.-Y., Wang, G.-L., Li, H.-F.: A cloud-based BPM architecture with user-end distribution of non-compute-intensive activities and sensitive data. Cloud Comput. 11 (2010)
4. Whibley, P.: Transforming the business case for process improvement. BPM Cloud 8 (2012)
5. Railton, J., Karakostas, B.: Cloud based Business Process Management systems. Cloud BPM 126 (2011)

6. Fang, Z., Yin, C.: BPM architecture design based on cloud computing. Intell. Inf. Manage. **2**(5), 329–333 (2010)
7. Duipmans, E.F., Pires, L.F., da Silva Santos, L.O.B.: A transformation-based approach to Business Process Management in the cloud. J. Grid Comput. 29 (2013)
8. Yeboah-Boateng, E.O., Essandoh, K.A.: Factors influencing the adoption of cloud computing by small and medium enterprises in developing economies. Cloud Comput. Adoption **2**(4), 8 (2014)
9. Rath, A., Mohapatra, S., Kumar, S., Thakurta, R.: Decision points for adoption cloud computing in Small, Medium Enterprises (SMEs). Cloud Comput. Adoption 22 (2012)
10. Market, 2011, Gartner, 2011. http://www.gartner.com/newsroom/id/1550514
11. Cloud Computing Trends: 2014 State of the Cloud Survey (2014). http://www.rightscale. com/blog/cloud-industry-insights/cloud-computing-trends-2014-state-cloud-survey

On Increasing Resource Utilization of a High-Performance Computing System

Lung-Pin Chen[(✉)] and Yu-Shan Cheng

Computer Science and Information Science, Tunghai University, Taichung, Taiwan
{lbchen,g01350061}@thu.edu.tw

Abstract. In a render farm, a render host usually requires high I/O bandwidth for reading scene files and writing rendering results. A multi-core render host may only activate partial cores in order to restrict its total throughput to the bandwidth limitations. This paper investigates feasible ways for using resource fragments formed by inactivated cores. We develop a parallel application consisting of single-core malleable tasks with small input/output data, and demonstrate that it can be scheduled to adaptive to the unstable resource fragments of the render farm. We develop a broker to collect idle processor cores and control the execution of the malleable tasks in background mode. The experimental results show a significantly increasing on resource utilization of the render farm without interfering with the original rendering tasks.

Keywords: High performance computing · Parallel task scheduling · Render farm

1 Introduction

High-performance computing (HPC) refers to the techniques featuring a large number of computing nodes, *e.g.* supercomputers or computer clusters, to solve complex computational problems. It has been used in many areas including biosciences, climate modeling, computer games, *etc*. The parallel jobs supported by HPC systems are usually classified into the following four categories [1]: (1) rigid, (2) moldable, (3) evolving, and (4) malleable. A rigid job has to designate a fixed number of cores before scheduling. In contrast, both moldable and evolving job can designate a flexible range of core number. The difference is that evolving jobs can reconfigure the resources during execution, while moldable jobs cannot. Malleable jobs can change their processor requirements during execution by an *external* job scheduler.

A render farm is a high performance computer cluster that is built to render computer graphics. The input data of a computer graphic rendering task can be divided into a sequence of frames that can be rendered independently. Since computer graphic rendering is both compute and I/O intensive, parallelism has become a crucial tool to building a high performance computer graphic system.

When handling parallel jobs that require multiple simultaneous cores, unused computing resources called *fragments* often occur. For example, many rendering tasks require high I/O bandwidth for reading scene files and writing result data. For this sort

© ICST Institute for Computer Sciences, Social Informatics and Telecommunications Engineering 2016
Y. Zhang et al. (Eds.): CloudComp 2015, LNICST 167, pp. 93–101, 2016.
DOI: 10.1007/978-3-319-38904-2_10

of applications, the worker computer only activates partial cores in order to restrict their total throughput to the I/O bandwidth.

Although a render farm can monitor and collect resource fragments, sharing unused resource to other HPC systems seems intractable. This paper demonstrates that the single-core malleable tasks with small input/output data size, such as heuristic search or game tree search applications, are suitable to be executed on the resource fragments of a render farm.

We implement a resource broker in the Qube render management system which can collects idle resources and make use of them to execute the malleable tasks. Our implementation work demonstrates a significantly increasing on resource utilization without interfering with the original rendering tasks.

In Sect. 2, we will introduce the application and the environment we used in the experiments. Section 3 will introduce the system architecture. Section 4 will discuss the scheduling methods for the malleable job scheduling system. Section 5 is the experiments section, which shows the resource utilization of the improved system. Finally, concluding remarks and future work are given in Sect. 6.

2   Background

Formosa 3 is a high performance render farm built by the National Center of High-Performance Computing (NCHC) in 2011, which is Taiwan's primary organization supporting supercomputing and high speed networking. Formosa 3 features a cluster of 76-node, each equipped with dual six-core hyperthreaded Intel Xeon 2.8 GHz processors and 48 GB memory. The InfiniBand 40 GB/s fabric serves as the interconnecting backbone of the cluster. Formosa 3 achieves a peak performance of 9 teraflops so far.

Formosa 3 employs Qube [15] as the render farm management system. Figure 1 depicts the architecture of the render farm management system. There are three main components in a Qube system:

- The *Worker* which is a program runs on every computer (called a "host" or a "worker host") on which users execute jobs. There are render daemons run on every worker host to receive instructions from the supervisor.
- The *Supervisor* which runs on a dedicated machine and uses a collection of Render Queues to keep track tasks. It decides when a job runs, and which job runs on which worker.
- The *Client* which is a computer let a user submit jobs via various interfaces, *e.g.* command line, standalone GUI, or in-application submission GUIs.

When rendering, the user first need to upload the scene files and all the necessary data to the NAS (network attached storage) server. After the job starts, the supervisor controls the execution of the tasks according to the *agenda* which specifies the sequence numbers of the frames and the number of cores required for parallel rendering. Upon receiving the job from the supervisor, the worker renders out individual frames. The rendering results are sent and stored to the NAS server.

Desktop grid is a network computing model that can harvest unused computational power from desktop level computers. In this paper we employ the CGDG which is a desktop grid platform designed for parallel game tree search applications [5].

3   System Design

3.1   Architecture

In this paper, the *resource stealing* approach is developed intended to fully utilize idle cores in the render farm without not interfering the rendering tasks. That is, the render farm will not sense the existence of the extra foreign tasks.

The proposed system involves a render farm (RF), a desktop grid (DG) and a component named ResourceMonitor, as illustrated in Fig. 1. In the system architecture, the ResourceMonitor is a process that continually monitors the resource usage of the render farm and then notifies the desktop grid server.

To avoid confusing, the workers of the desktop grid and the render farm are called *DG-worker* and *RF-workers*, respectively. To achieve resource stealing, the client-side software of the desktop grid have to be installed in the render host in order to turn it to be a DG-worker. A DG-worker that run in a render host is called a *"RFDG-workers"* hereinafter. We assume that the desktop grid establishes connection-oriented control links between the desktop grid servers and the workers, enabling direct control to the workers in a timely manner.

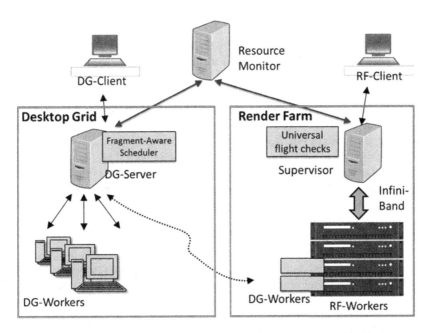

Fig. 1. The architecture of the fragment-aware scheduler ("RF" refers to render farm; "DG" refers to desktop grid).

It is possible that a render host can execute tasks sent from render farm and desktop grid at the same time. In this case, both DG-task and RF-task share the same resources (such as CPU, storage space, and I/O bandwidth) on a same computer that are managed by the multitasking operating system.

However, in the system architecture shown in Fig. 1, a render host runs desktop grid tasks only when the Qube rendering system have not allocate tasks. When receiving a new rendering task, an RFDG-worker directly aborts and preempts the running desktop grid task without coordination to the desktop grid server. This abort operation can be done via the connection-oriented TCP/IP links between the DG-server and the workers.

3.2   Establishing Workers

The architecture shown in Fig. 1 provides a loosely coupled integration between the render farm and the computer game desktop grid. There are no direct communication between two systems. All communications are done via ResourceMonitor. This approach takes the advantages that no costly modification is required for both systems.

An important issue is establishing RFDG-workers. Since a render farm can contain dozens or even hundreds of render hosts, installing desktop grid software to all render hosts one by one is apparently intractable. We simply use a batch script to copy and install the software in the render hosts. Automatically deploying the software packages to a large number of render hosts is considered beyond the scope of this paper.

3.3   Resource Fragment Monitoring

This subsection discusses a new scheduling algorithm that tries to maximize the effect of using the high-capability RF-workers. In the new Fragment-aware scheduling algorithm, the Result tasks of the same workunit are grouped and assigned to either the render farm or the desktop grid.

In our system, there is a server named ResourceMonitor which continually detects the resource fragments on the Qube and tries to notify the DG server when useful idle resources are detected. ResourceMonitor can be implemented in polling mode or event-driven mode, as shown in Fig. 2.

The most up-to-date version of Qube supports the universal *preflight* and *postflight* events (called *universal flight checks* in Fig. 1) which are triggered immediately before and after a collection of render hosts is allocated or deallocated for a rendering task. The preflight and postflight events are developed intended to monitoring resource changes for the render system. For old versions of Qube system, a polling mode, also inefficient, can be adopted.

The event-driven ResourceMonitor works as follows. Qube system triggers the pre-flight and post-flight events before and after a task execution. Upon receiving a pre-flight message, ResourceMonitor notifies the DG-server that the render farm worker is going to be activated for some rendering task. The DG-server then immediately aborts the current tasks and release the resources.

On the other hand, upon receiving a post-flight message, ResourceMonitor knows that the render farm releases some computing resources. ResourceMonitor has to wait

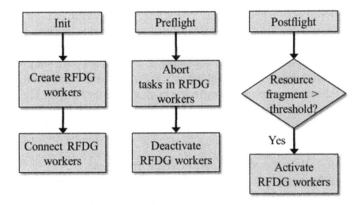

Fig. 2. Workflows of task executions in the MJS system.

for a period of time (*e.g.* 60 s) to ensure that there are no upcoming rendering tasks. After detecting idle resources, ResourceMonitor notifies the DG-server, which in turn activates the RFDG-worker via the connection-oriented control link. Note that the DG-server does not push tasks to a worker; instead, it passively waits for the worker to issue the task request.

4   Fragment-Aware Scheduling Algorithm

In the parallel game tree search applications, a tree node is implemented as a lightweight, single-code and malleable task. Unlike traditional parallel programs, such malleable task can be interrupted without server coordination. The server will simply discard or redispatch a task when it expires. Owing to this property, the game tree application can generate enough number of tree nodes to adaptive to the unstable idle resources in the render farm.

The DG-server relies on the inherently unstable computer CPU cycles that are stolen from the render farm. In this way, the resource availability must be taken into consideration before operating on these resources. In the DG platform, a task, also called a *Workunit* (WU), is replicated to several instances, called *Results*. A scheduled workunit is complete when its Results are reported and a certain agreement policy, such as majority voting threshold, is reached. For a same Workunit, its Result tasks are called in the same *group*. Based on the statistics principle, the Result tasks in a same group should be assigned to different unrelated workers in order to mitigate the effects of unstable and malicious workers.

In the above Result-based mechanism, the Result tasks in a same group may be assigned to different systems (*i.e.* the render farm and the desktop grid). For example, for a same WU, the replica Result 1 is assigned to an RF-worker, while replica Result 2 is assigned to some DG-worker. However, often a DG-worker disconnects with unsolved Result tasks, halting them until timeout and getting rescheduled. Therefore, although the high capability RF-worker can speeding up the

Result 1, the global performance of the WU it may not be improved since the WU's completion time is determined by the Result instance that finishes last.

The traditional scheduler of DG-server does not distinguish DG-workers and RFDG-workers. Restated, Result tasks, even belonging to a same WU, are simply treated as individual tasks. In this paper, we develop a new *fragment-aware scheduling* algorithm that improves the task response times by trying to maximize the effect of high capability RF-workers.

The fragment-aware scheduling algorithm uses three priority queues to store Work-units:

- Qinit: Initially, all the Result tasks, are placed in this queue.
- QDG: stores the Result tasks that are going to assign to DG-workers.
- QRF: stores the Result tasks that are going to assign to RF-workers.

Each Workunit w partitions its redundant instances into three lists:

- w.waitResults: records the Result tasks waiting for scheduling.
- w.pendResults: records the Result tasks that are assigned to some worker but not reported yet.
- w.completeResults: records the completed Result tasks.

The order of workunits in the priority queues is determined by the property
w.key = (|w.waitResults| + |w.pendResults|)/replication_factor,

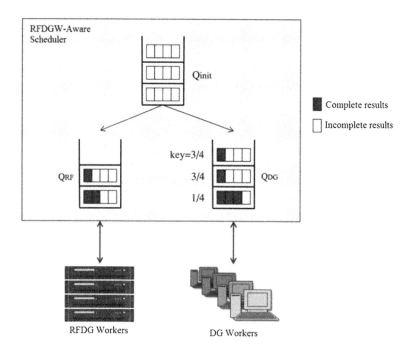

Fig. 3. Fragment-aware scheduler.

where the denominator (i.e. replication_factor) is the number of total number of Results of a workunit and the numerator is the number of incomplete tasks. In this paper, we set replication_factor to 4 for all the experiments.

Workunit with less key has higher priority. Thus, performing an extract-min operation on the queues will extract the workunit with the higher ratio of completed tasks. For example, in Fig. 3, the workunit in the front of queue QDG has the key 1/4 and the workunit in the front of queue QRF has the key 2/4.

Algorithm 1 Fragment_Aware_Scheduler in DG-server:

A: When generating a new workunit *w*:

(1) Generate four copies of replicas (*i.e.* Result tasks) of *w*;

(2) Add all the Result tasks to list w.waitResults;

(3) Add w to Qinit using w.key;

B: When receiving a task request from a worker:

(1) If the worker is a DG-worker then

. Q ← QDG;

else //(the worker is an RF-worker)

. Q ← QRF;

End if

(2) If Q is empty then move a Workunit (and the list of its Results) from Qinit to Q ;

(3) w ← extractMin(Q); //get the workunit with highest priority

(4) If w is not null then

. *r* ← pop(w.waitResults);

. Move *r* from *w*.waitResults to *w*.pendResults;

. Send task *r* to the worker;

End if

➤ **C:** When receiving a report of task *r* :

(1) Find the workunit w containing *r* ;

(2) Move r from w.pendResults to w.completeResults;

(3) Update w.key and the queue order;

(4) Delete w from the queue if w is completed;

In Algorithm 1, after the first allocation (Step B(2)), a workunit and all of its Result tasks are stored in either QDG or QRF. Also, in Step B(1), the DG-server always assign tasks in QDG (or QRF) to a DG-worker (or an RF-worker). This strategy ensures that the Result tasks in the same workunit are assigned to the workers in the same system. We design this strategy to make tasks in a same group finish within the near time period, since the recorded execution time of a workunit group is determined by the member finishes last.

In Step B(2), the server moves tasks from Qinit to QDG or QRF according to the job consumption rate of the DG-workers and the RF-workers. Furthermore, in Step B(3), when selecting workunits from QDG (or QRF), the scheduling algorithm tends to select workunits with the higher progress ratio in order to complete workunits as earlier as possible.

In Step C, when the DG-server receives a completion report of a Result task, it updates the workunit progress status. The workunit is recorded as completed and is deleted from the queue if its Result tasks confirm a majority agreement on the execution results.

5   Experiments

In this work, we ran a series of simulated jobs on a Qube render management system in Formosa 3 and a Computer Game Desktop Grid (CGDG) as described above. Hereinafter, we will refer to the desktop grid system as the malleable job system and the render farm as the rigid job system. The experimental results are average of 100 runs that are conducted in two different experimental configurations. The first kind of short jobs use 1 core for 10 min, while the second kind long jobs use 1 core for 60 min. Note that in the render farm the computing resources may be unused because, when the system swaps, there will often be a delay, during which there will be unused resources.

Figure 4 demonstrates the effect of resource stealing on the render farm. In this figure, the normal resource utilization of the render farm is about 46 %. That is, in average, more than half resources are unused. Figure 4 (Left) shows that, when the malleable tasks are added to the render farm system, the system resources can be fully utilized. Since the malleable tasks are lightweight single-core tasks that ca be adapted to the fractured idle resources in the render farm, the system resources can be fully utilized by involving malleable tasks.

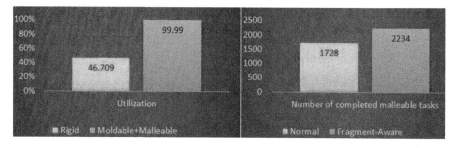

Fig. 4. (Left) System utilization of the high performance cluster: without malleable tasks (only rigid tasks) and with malleable tasks. (Right) Average number of task completion rate using the normal scheduler and the fragment-aware scheduler.

In Fig. 4 (Right), we conduct the experiment for completion rate of using the fragment-aware scheduler presented in the previous section. As mentioned earlier, the malleable jobs running on the stolen render farm resources can be aborted when rendering tasks arrive. That is, an malleable job may be aborted and the computation will be discarded. In this experiment, the completion rate can be improved by 30 % when using the fragment-aware scheduler.

6 Conclusion

In this paper, we propose a malleable job scheduling system for sharing resource between a high-performance render farm and a desktop grid. The proposed system maximizes the resource utilization by allocating unused resource fragments for the lightweight single-core malleable jobs. Our work demonstrates a successful integration of the two systems in which the desktop grid tasks gain significant resources without interfering with the original rendering tasks.

Acknowledgments. This study was supported by grant MOST-103-2221-E-029-027 from Ministry of Science and Technology, ROC.

References

1. Kalé, L.V., Kumar, S., Jayant, D.: A malleable-job system for timeshared parallel machines. In: 2nd IEEE/ACM International Symposium on Cluster Computing and the Grid, 2002, p. 230. IEEE (2002)
2. Anderson, D.P.: BOINC: a system for public-resource computing and storage. In: Proceedings of Fifth IEEE/ACM International Workshop on Grid Computing, 2004, pp. 4–10. IEEE (2004)
3. BOINC website. http://boinc.berkeley.edu/
4. Wu, I.-C., et al.: Job-level proof number search. IEEE Trans. Comput. Intell. AI Games 5(1), 44–56 (2013)
5. Chen, Y.-W.: The study of the broker in a volunteer computing system for computer games. Master thesis, Department of Computer Science, NCTU (2011)
6. Han, S.-Y.: the study of the worker in a volunteer computing system for computer games. Master thesis, Department of Computer Science, NCTU (2011)
7. Zhou, S.: LSF: load sharing in large heterogeneous distributed systems. In: Workshop on Cluster Computing (1992)
8. Le Boudec, J.-Y.: Rate adaptation, congestion control and fairness: a tutorial. Web page, November 2005
9. Ali, G., et al.: Choosy: max-min fair sharing for datacenter jobs with constraints. In: Proceedings of the 8th ACM European Conference on Computer Systems. ACM (2013)
10. Qube Render Farm: (2015). http://www.pipelinefx.com

A Game Theory Based Automated SLA Negotiation Model for Confined Federated Clouds

Asma Al Falasi$^{(\boxtimes)}$, Mohammed Adel Serhani,
and Younes Hamdouch

UAE University, Al Ain, UAE
{asma.alfalasi, serhanim, younes.hamdouch}@uaeu.ac.ae

Abstract. Federation of Cloud services is notably landing interests from both Cloud providers and consumers. Cloud providers nowadays are required to form federations to remain competitive, and sustain their market share. Cloud consumers however seek optimized services from Clouds federation. They strive to maximize their satisfaction level, which is often measured by Quality of Service (QoS). Federations are governed by a mutual contract known as Service Level Agreement (SLA), which both consumers and providers must negotiate, so as to reach an agreement. The focus of this paper is to address issues related to SLA negotiation for the purpose of QoS assurance within federation of Clouds. We define, and specify an automated SLA negotiation model based on *Fair Division Game*. We evaluate our model using different use cases, and the obtained results proved fairness, and efficiency of the proposed SLA negotiation model in *CloudLend*.

Keywords: Clouds · Federation · SLA negotiation · Game theory

1 Introduction

The aggregation of several Cloud services provided by different vendors, in order to achieve a specified goal is known as Clouds federation. The notion of federation of Clouds is not commonly adopted by Cloud vendors yet, although it is variably present in confined environments; such us governments and enterprises where distributed data centers are expected to collaborate and integrate. Nevertheless, at any federated environment, it is essential for consumers to receive guarantees on service delivery from Cloud providers. Such guarantees are provided through Service Level Agreements (SLAs). SLAs govern, and control service provisioning between consumers and Cloud providers. SLA negotiation takes place prior to federation establishment. It is a mutual decision making process for the purpose of resolving providers and consumers conflicting objectives [1]. Many recent research efforts in SLA negotiation in Clouds have invested in the adoption of SLA negotiation approaches of Grid computing, Web services, and SOA. Some others opted for intelligent software agent, and game theory. The SLA negotiation model we are proposing employs the principals of game theory in order to achieve efficient SLA negotiation. Game theory began with the work of

© ICST Institute for Computer Sciences, Social Informatics and Telecommunications Engineering 2016
Y. Zhang et al. (Eds.): CloudComp 2015, LNICST 167, pp. 102–113, 2016.
DOI: 10.1007/978-3-319-38904-2_11

Neumann and Morgenstren [2]. It supports understanding, and resolving situations; where two or more individuals make decisions that will affect one another's welfare, through general mathematical techniques.

To feature our SLA negotiation model we use a federated Cloud network named *CloudLend*. Which we described in a previous work that was formerly known as *The Sky* [3]. *CloudLend* is a social-based Clouds federation network. It provides several functions including Cloud services provisioning, QoS specification, and monitoring. It enables Cloud services discovery, interaction, and collaboration. Connections among services within *CloudLend* are bounded by SLAs. As services are supposed to extend their social ties, multi-level SLAs are required to manage, and maintain these relationships. We have previously introduced an SLA management model for federated Cloud environments in [4]. We studied the life cycle of SLA in our *CloudLend* network as an example of a federated Cloud environment. This encompasses; SLA specifications, and monitoring schemes. In this work we extend the SLA management model to cover SLA negotiation phase. This paper is organized as follows: the next section describes the problem, and introduces the motivation of this work. Section 3 summarizes research efforts on the adoption of game theory for SLA negotiation in service computing. Section 4 introduces our automated SLA negotiation model based on the *Fair Division Game,* while Sect. 5 provides a formal description of the proposed SLA negotiation model. Section 6 highlights the results of our model's evaluation. Finally, Sect. 7 concludes the paper and points out planned future work.

2 Problem and Motivation

Typically in Cloud computing, Cloud providers define their SLAs, and publish them for consumers in a *take-it-or-leave-it* manner. Consumers are not privileged with an adequate SLA negotiation opportunity that enables them to impose their QoS requirements on Cloud providers. Besides, the problem of enabling Cloud federation through portable APIs, in order to provide value-added services is considered a dynamic and complex problem. Selecting the most appropriate Cloud service, considering a set of properties to participate in a federation is multi-criteria, and a multi-decision complex problem. A federation is required to match consumer's requirements, through an aggregated selection of Cloud services from different providers, having different interests. Thus in a federated environment, such as *CloudLend;* SLA negotiation requires specific considerations because of specific characteristics exhibited by the network. Namely, Cloud services interconnect with other services in order to fulfill QoS-aware consumers' requests. Such interconnections can extend to reach further services in order to carry out minor subtasks. Additionally, a Cloud service can maintain connections with one or more other Cloud services at the same time. This results in a chain of interconnected services that are bounded by multi-level SLAs.

Henceforth, there exist a need for an automated negotiation model that fairly enables federated Cloud services to review SLAs, respond to SLA offers, and eventually sign an SLA contract. A negotiation model is required to facilitate the negotiation process while considering the complexity of services interconnections within the *CloudLend* network. Assuring that negotiation on multiple levels does not burden the federated network, and does not impede resources utilization of Cloud providers, nor overlooks consumers' QoS requirements. There upon, motivated by the lack of automated SLA negotiation models in federated Clouds, we aim to achieve the following research objectives:

(1) Propose a game theory-based automated SLA negotiation model in *CloudLend* network, which is capable of:

  (a) Balancing the trade-offs among consumers' various QoS requirements, as well as providers' resources utilization.
  (b) Prioritizing SLA terms, which are more important to both Cloud consumer, and provider.
  (c) Supporting both consumers, and providers in negotiating SLA terms, and guiding them towards signing a contract.
  (d) Assisting consumers in service selection, by enabling evaluation of different service alternatives based on a computed utility gain.

(2) Evaluate the efficiency of the proposed SLA negotiation model in a federated Cloud environment, *CloudLend.*

3   Related Work

Game theory is intended to optimize negotiation outcome using various initiation conditions [5]. Researches on this area are not concerned with the characteristics of the negotiation process itself, nor with the interaction between involved parties. Conversely, the emphasis is mainly on the outcome of the negotiation process. Hence, game theory outcomes are utilized to evaluate the satisfaction level of different notions of an optimal solution, to any given negotiation game. This section reviews research efforts on the adoption of game theory for SLA negotiation in service computing.

A bargaining game approach in [6] describes an automated one-to-one web services SLA negotiation mechanism. While [7] applies another bargaining game for an automated SLA negotiation in Cloud computing. Both approaches consider a game of only two players, and assume that players have complete information on the possible strategies, in addition to corresponding outcomes of their opponents. In reality, such assumption is not always true. [8] introduces a mathematical negotiation model for high-performance computing (HPC). Their approach is based on signaling game in two rounds. Unlike our strictly competitive Fair division approach, signaling is either competitive or cooperative. [9] addresses the problem of resource allocation in competitive grids. Their negotiation strategy can achieve a fair resource allocation. Nevertheless, SLA negotiation in grid, and HPC is not the same as SLA negotiation in Clouds. Its is less complicated, as it involves specific users interested in some resource. Whereas in Cloud environments, complexity of negotiation is driven by market competition. [10] describes a generic SLA negotiation platform for the SLA@SOI [11], a framework for service-oriented environments. Yet, they address enabling SLA negotiation protocols. In this work we focus on SLA negotiation strategies.

To the best of our knowledge, there is no automated SLA negotiation model that assures fairness and efficiency of SLA negotiation in a federated Cloud services environment. Our approach is based on the *Fair Division* game [12], which is a sequential game, that allows multiple players, and assumes perfect information of all previous events that have occurred prior to a player's decision. The properties of this game makes it very appropriate to be implemented in a dynamic, and complex environment such as *CloudLend*.

4 Automated SLA Negotiation Model Based on Game Theory

In this section we describe, and illustrate the game of SLA negotiation in *CloudLend*.

4.1 Model Description

In *CloudLend*, Cloud services participate in the SLA negotiation game not to ultimately win the game. Conversely, they aim to reach the best collection of SLA terms, that would satisfy all players' requirements. The outcome of the game is basically a measure of the value; a Cloud service gains by establishing a relationship with other players. In game theory, this outcome is known as *utility*. Players negotiate SLAs to evaluate the expected utility from the anticipated relationships, which is used then to make the decision of relationship establishment. We introduce an SLA negotiation model that considers the SLA contract as a whole entity that consists of several SLA terms. Therefore, during negotiation, players bargain over the value of SLA terms, that make up the utility gain of the whole SLA contract. Every player values each individual SLA term differently. Eventually, both players need to decide on the impact every SLA term has on the total value of the SLA contract.

We look at the SLA negotiation problem in *CloudLend* as a *Fair Division* game [12]. Such games involve players in a sequential game, where they need to decide on how to divide an item. Every player value the item to be shared among them differently. An example of a *Fair Division* game is called Fair Cake-cutting [12]. A cake with different toppings must be divided among many players, who have different preferences over different parts of the cake. The division needs to be fair to every player. In this case, each player receives a slice that he believes to be a fair share. In our case, the SLA contract is a resource that is compiled of several different SLA terms. During negotiation, players will evaluate every SLA term differently. Each player knows the value of a single SLA term to him. Eventually, players need to reach a consensus on how much of a value is assigned to every single SLA term, out of the overall value of the SLA contract. In such situation, where a set of items is to be divided among players, yet these items themselves need to be kept as a whole; a proportional and envy-free division procedure is used [12]. The Adjusted Winner procedure (AW) [13] is one of the proportional and envy-free division procedures. Once played out, the outcome is proven to exhibit three important properties:

(1) *Pareto optimal:* any alternative allocation of items that improves one player's outcome will worsen the others.
(2) *Envy-free:* each player is allocated a share of items that is at least as large, or at least as desirable as that received by any other player.
(3) *Equitable:* every player believes that his allocation is valued the same as the other player's (based on their declared ratings).

The AW procedure describes a fair division of a set of n items that can be shared between two players. Each player examines the n items, and assigns a rate for each individual item, out of a total of 100 points among them all. These points are a relative preference of the players for the various rated items. We adopt the Adjusted Winner procedure as the most appropriate model of SLA negotiation in *CloudLend*. A list of essential elements of such SLA negotiation game is described as follows:

(1) **Players:** are the decision makers. Each has a goal to maximize its utility by choice of actions. In *CloudLend* players are: Cloud consumers, and Cloud providers.
(2) **Actions:** are choices available for players to make. In *CloudLend* players' possible set of actions includes: place an SLA offer, accept an SLA offer, reject an SLA offer, place an SLA counter-offer, and end an SLA negotiation.
(3) **Strategy:** of a player is a rule that tells him which action to choose at each instant of the game, given his information set about the game and other players. In *CloudLend* a player's strategy is represented by: ratings of SLA terms.
(4) **Outcome:** the result of a player deciding to settle on a particular strategy, measured numerically. In *CloudLend* the outcome of the negotiation game is: allocation of SLA terms.

4.2   Illustrative Example of SLA Negotiation using Fair Division Game

The following example explains how the AW procedure works when implemented in the SLA negotiation process within *CloudLend*. Let two Cloud services S_1, and S_2 be negotiating an SLA contract. The contract specifies 6 different SLA terms $T_{SLA} = \{t_1, t_2, t_3, t_4, t_5, t_6\}$. The game goes as follows:

(1) Both services S_1, and S_2 rate every term in T_{SLA} out of 100 score among them all. As described in Table 1.

Table 1. Services' ratings of SLA terms

Term	S1 rating	S2 rating
t_1	25	37
t_2	12	15
t_3	30	8
t_4	6	21
t_5	7	9
t_6	20	10

(2) Let T_1 be the set of all SLA terms that S_1 rated more than S_2. $T_1 = \{t3, t6\}$. Sum up all of S_1 scores for all SLA terms $\in T_1$. Total S_1 score is 50.

(3) Let T_2 be the set of all SLA terms that S_2 rated more than S_1. $T_2 = \{t_1, t_2, t_4, t_5\}$. Sum up all of S_2 scores for all SLA terms $\in T_2$. Total S_2 score is 82.

(4) S_2 is assigned all SLA terms $\in T_2$. And S_1 is assigned all SLA terms $\in T_1$. Order SLA terms assigned to the S_2 as follows:

- Create a ratio for each SLA term i, of S_2's score to S_1's score. Calculated ratios are listed in Table 2.

Table 2. $\frac{S_2}{S_1}$ Ratio for all SLA terms

Term	$\frac{S_2}{S_1}$ Ratio
t_1	$\frac{37}{25} = 1.48$
t_2	$\frac{15}{12} = 1.25$
t_3	$\frac{8}{30} = 0.25$
t_4	$\frac{21}{6} = 3.5$
t_5	$\frac{9}{7} = 1.28$
t_6	$\frac{10}{20} = 0.5$

- Since S2 has a greater total score. T2 is rearranged so that SLA terms with the smallest ratio are first, followed by the one with the second smallest ratio, and so on. $T2 = \{t_2, t_5, t_1, t_4\}$.

(5) To make the assignment more equitable, transfer SLA terms from S_2 to S_1; starting with terms with the smallest ratio.

(6) We reassign t_2 to S_1. and recalculate totals of S_2 and S_2 as follows:
$T_1 = \{t_2, t_3, t_6\}$. Total S_1 score is 62.
$T_2 = \{t_5, t_1, t_4\}$. Total S_2 score is 67.

(7) We might need to transfer a fraction of an SLA term. An appropriate fraction is the one that brings both player's total score to the same level. We must transfer part of t_5 to T_1. Let x be the portion of t_5 that will be transferred to T_1. We must solve the following equation for x: $67 - 9x = 62 + 7x$ $x = 0.31$
Thus we transfer 31 % of t_5 from T_2 to T_1
T_1 calculated rating for t_5 is: $7 \times \frac{31}{100} = 2.19$
T_2 calculated rating for t_5 is: $9 - \left(9 \times \frac{31}{1000}\right) = 6.19$
Total score assigned to each player is: 64.19

(8) The final division:
S_1: wins all of SLA terms t_2, t_3, t_6 all the time, and is allocated t_5 for 31 % of the time of the contract.
S_2: wins all of SLA terms t_1, t_4 all the time, and is allocated t_5 for 69 % of the time of the contract.

The final allocation of terms is the outcome of the SLA negotiation game. This outcome is satisfactory for both players; since it is proven to be Pareto optimal.

5 SLA Negotiation Model Formulation

This section provides a formal representation of the SLA negotiation game in *Clou-dLend*. The *CloudLend* network is composed of a set of federations $F_i(i = 1, 2, \ldots, I)$. Each federation F_i is composed of a set of Cloud providers $P_{ij}(j = 1, 2, \ldots, J_i)$. Each Cloud provider P_{ij} can offer a subset of services $S_{ij} \subset S$, where $S = \{s_1, s_2, \ldots, s_N\}$ is the set of all service types that can be offered within *CloudLend*. A service consumer $C_i(i = 1, 2, \ldots, I)$, can be a Cloud customer, or another Cloud provider. The *Clou-dLend* network can be seen as a global network of networks in which each node S_{ijm} represents the mth service offered by $P_{ij}(1 \leq m \leq M_{ij})$, where M_{ij} is the number of service types offered by P_{ij}. Each link between two cloud services $\left(s_{ijm}, s_{i'j'm'}\right)$ describes a relationship r, where $s_{ijm} = s_n, s_{i'j'm'} = s_n l$ with $n \neq n'$ A relationship r can be established only if both services involved in the relationship are available. Each relationship $r\left(s_{ijm}, s_{i'j'm'}\right)$ between two services is bounded by an SLA contract. Which describes one or more QoS properties, and their attributes. $q^{ijm, i'j'm'}$ represent a single SLA term of the SLA contract, concerned with a single QoS property of service $s_{i'j'm'}$.

SLA negotiation in *CloudLend* is regarded as an exchange of bids between the Cloud service provider, and the consumer up to the final agreement on the provided SLA terms. Both parties involved in the negotiation process exchange their bids during negotiation rounds. A negotiation round is the period of time, through which one party offers a bid, while the other reviews that bid to either accept or place a counter offer. Hence, starting another negotiation round. In *CloudLend* negotiation usually occurs on the following cases: (1) Between a consumer C, and a Cloud provider P;(*one− to − one*). (2) Between a Cloud provider Px, and another Cloud provider(s) $Py, \ldots Pz$ when forming a federation; (*one − to − many*). (3) Between service Sx, and other services $Sy, \ldots Sz$ within a Clouds federation; (*one − to − many*).

For each class of consumer requests with the same root service, the objective of the service provider is to maximize his profit with the minimum possible number of SLA negotiation rounds N_r. Where $N_{min} \leq N_r \leq N_{max} \cdot N_{min}$ and, N_{max} are the minimum, and the maximum number of SLA negotiation rounds set by the network. While the objective of a service consumer is to maximize his satisfaction of the service's QoS. At any given negotiation round, P_{ij} aims at having minimum changes made to the offered ratings of SLA terms. While C_i aims at winning SLA terms that are of high importance to him. The level of Ci's and P_{ij}'s satisfaction is measured by the utility gained of the *Fair Division* game played at every negotiation round. This gained utility represents the payoff a *CloudLend* member gains by establishing a link with another member. *CloudLend* members negotiate SLAs to evaluate the expected utility from the antici-pated relationships. Utility is used then to make the decision of relationship establishment.

6 SLA Negotiation Model Evaluation

The evaluation of our proposed SLA negotiation model aims to measure its fairness, and efficiency. Which is indicted by the satisfaction level of both Cloud providers, and consumers; when the model is applied to various SLA negotiation situations within *CloudLend.* To achieve this objective we ran the AW procedure with several number of SLA terms, and different SLA terms' ratings. Figure 1 illustrates our evaluation process for the proposed SLA negotiation model. To begin with, we run k-means algorithm to find a player's expected SLA terms allocations using Weka [14]. k-means is a widely used clustering algorithm that enables prior set of clusters number. Which works well for our small data set. We set the number of clusters to two; indicating important and unimportant SLA terms. At the same time we find the actual SLA terms allocation after running the AW procedure, using an AW tool [15]. Comparing both; the expected, and actual SLA terms' allocations yields satisfaction level for both players, Cloud provider, and consumer (1).

$$\text{Satisfaction level for Player}_i = \frac{\text{No. of allocated SLA terms}}{\text{No. of expected SLA terms}} \times 100 \qquad (1)$$

6.1 Test Scenarios

Assuming a single negotiation round is initiated between a Cloud provider, and a consumer. There is a number of SLA terms to be included in the SLA contract. In this test we apply the AW procedure, considering various number of SLA terms; 5, 10 and 20 terms. The SLA terms ratings provided by the two players; provider, and consumer shall be experimented as follow: **Scenario 1**: Each player provides different and

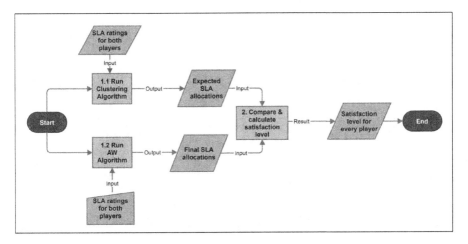

Fig. 1. SLA negotiation model evaluation process

independent ratings of all SLA terms. **Scenario 2:** Both players provide identical ratings for all SLA terms. **Scenario 3:** Each player favors a single different SLA term and neglect the others. **Scenario 4:** Players provide disparate ratings for every SLA term.

6.2   Results and Discussion

Figure 2 illustrates the satisfaction level when players provide different and independent ratings. The negotiation model provides %92–%93 satisfaction level for both consumer, and provider when the number of SLA terms = 5. When the number of SLA terms = 10; the model's satisfaction level drops to %87–%85 for both consumer, and provider. The satisfaction level for both consumer, and provider is also %87–%86, when the number of SLA terms = 20. Figure 3 illustrates the satisfaction level when players provide identical ratings. The negotiation model provides %100 satisfaction level for both consumer, and provider when the number of SLA terms = 5.

However, the model's satisfaction level drops as the number of SLA terms increases. Figure 4 illustrates the satisfaction level when players independently favor a single term, and neglect the rest of the SLA terms.

While Fig. 5 illustrates the satisfaction level when players show conflicting interests, and provide disparate ratings for all SLA terms. When running the two scenarios; the negotiation model provides %100 satisfaction level for both consumer, and provider regardless of the number of SLA terms.

As a result, we can see that the AW procedure provides a fair an efficient SLA allocations, when submitted ratings are disparate. Since the AW procedure will obviously identify the most important terms for every player. And the more the rating of terms differ, the more points each player will gain. Additionally, the model provides an accepted efficiency when submitted ratings are different and independent. This is related to the fact that; the more the terms, the less the points available for ratings out of

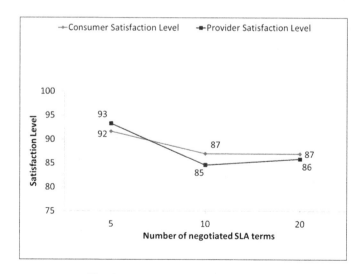

Fig. 2. Satisfaction level for Scenario 1

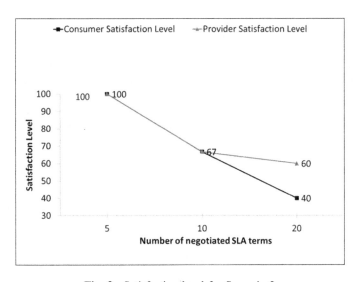

Fig. 3. Satisfaction level for Scenario 2

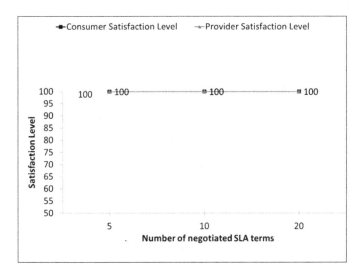

Fig. 4. Satisfaction level for Scenario 3

the total of 100 points. Which reduces the proximity between submitted ratings, and increases the error rate when calculating the expected terms allocation.

However, the model is not well defined when the submitted ratings are identical. This is owing to the tie-breaking method used by the AW procedure; it starts by allocating all terms to one player, then starts transferring terms of lower ratings to the other player, until equality attained. Consequently, as the number of SLA terms increases, chances are one player is assigned more important terms, and the other is assigned more unimportant terms. Hence decreasing the satisfaction level.

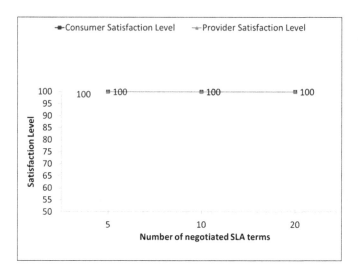

Fig. 5. Satisfaction level for Scenario 4

7 Conclusion

In this paper, we proposed an automated SLA negotiation model for federated Cloud services, based on Game theory. The model applies a *Fair Division* game for SLA terms allocations between Cloud services within a network of federated Cloud services called *CloudLend*. We illustrated the Adjusted Winner procedure, and described how it performs within *CloudLend*. Finally, we executed several experiments that evaluated our SLA negotiation model, and demonstrated its ability to allocate SLA terms fairly, and efficiently in most test cases. We aim to further improve our SLA negotiation model to show enhanced results in situations where both a consumer, and a provider equally strive for the same SLA terms. As well as when the number of negotiated SLA terms increases.

References

1. Dastjerdi, A.V.: Qos-aware and semantic-based service coordination for multi-cloud environments. Ph.D. Dissertation, The University of Melbourne, March 2013
2. Neuman, J.V., Morgenstern, O.: Theory of Games and Economic Behavior. Princeton University Press, Princeton (1944)
3. Falasi, A.A., Serhani, M.A., Elnaffar, S.: The sky: a social approach to clouds federation. Procedia Comput. Sci. **19**, 131–138 (2013)
4. Falasi, A.A., Serhani, M.A., Dssouli, R.: A model for multi-levels SLA monitoring in federated cloud environment. In: 10th International Conference on Ubiquitous Intelligence and Computing and 10th International Conference on Autonomic and Trusted Computing (UIC/ATC), pp. 363–370. IEEE (2013)

5. Binmore, K., Vulkan, N.: Applying game theory to automated negotiation. Netnomics **1**(1), 1–9 (1999)
6. Zheng, X., Martin, P., Powley, W., Brohman, K.: Applying bargaining game theory to web services negotiation. In: 2010 IEEE International Conference on Services Computing (SCC), pp. 218–225. IEEE (2010)
7. Alsrheed, F., El Rhalibi, A., Randles, M., Merabti, M.: Rubinstein's alternating offers protocol for automated cloud computing negotiation. In: Proceedings of the 14th Annual PG Symposium on the Convergence of Telecommunications, Networking, and Broadcasting (2013)
8. Figueroa, C., Figueroa, N., Jofre, A., Sahai, A., Chen, Y., Iyer, S.: A game theoretic framework for SLA negotiation. HP Laboratories Palo Alto, Technical report HPL-2008-5 (2008)
9. Silaghi, G.C.: A time-constrained SLA negotiation strategy in competitive computational grids. Future Gener. Comput. Syst. **28**(8), 1303–1315 (2012)
10. Yaqub, E., Wieder, P., Kotsokalis, C., Mazza, V., Pasquale, L., Rueda, J.L., Gómez, S.G., Chimeno, A.E.: A generic platform for conducting SLA negotiations. In: Wieder, P., Butler, J.M., Theilmann, W., Yahyapou, R. (eds.) Service Level Agreements for Cloud Computing, pp. 187–206. Springer, New York (2011)
11. Wieder, P., Butler, J.M., Theilmann, W., Yahyapour, R.: Service Level Agreements for Cloud Computing. Springer Science & Business Media, New York (2011)
12. Brams, S.J., Taylor, A.D.: Fair Division: From cake-Cutting to Dispute Resolution. Cambridge University Press, New York (1996)
13. Brams, S.J., Taylor, A.D.: The Win-Win Solution: Guaranteeing Fair Shares to Everybody. WW Norton & Company, New York (2000)
14. University of Waikato: "Weka 3"
15. New York University: Adjusted winner website

Experiences on Setting up On-Premise Enterprise Cloud Using OpenStack

R. Ananthalakshmi Ammal$^{(\boxtimes)}$, K.B. Aneesh Kumar, Beniwal Alka, and B. Renjith

Broadcast and Communications Group,
Centre for Development of Advanced Computing (CDAC), Thiruvananthapuram, India
{lakshmi,aneesh_kb,alkab,renjithb}@cdac.in

Abstract. Cloud Computing allows users to access a shared pool of computing resources which include networks, servers, storage, applications and services. One of the major advantages of cloud is that the resources can be rapidly provisioned. However, many enterprises are still unwilling to move their IT infrastructure to cloud. Major concerns of enterprises are the initial expenditure on capital and the cost of maintenance of the cloud infrastructure which requires a new set of expertise. The huge licensing cost of proprietary cloud solutions is also a major concern. Hence open source cloud solutions are gaining popularity. In this paper we discuss major challenges faced while implementing an on-premise cloud using OpenStack and the solutions developed to overcome the same. The source code availability and strong support from a wide community made us choose OpenStack. The cloud usage model, introduced for better ROI (Return on Investment), which is capable of providing both Infrastructure as a Service (IaaS) and Platform as a Service (PaaS) is also discussed. Our experience proved that irrespective of all the challenges enterprise can save both time and money with the adoption of an on-premise open source cloud with a suitable service model.

Keywords: OpenStack · ROI · IaaS · Cloud usage model · Experience with OpenStack

1 Introduction

Efficient and fair provisioning of resources for achieving optimal resource utilization is a challenging task for organizations. Ensuring on-time availability of resources for development teams is yet another issue faced by management. Traditional resource allocation and management is time consuming and fails in timely allocation. In contrast to the traditional approach, cloud based solutions provide many benefits in terms of virtualization, scalability, flexibility and provisioning. The advantages of using cloud in resource provisioning and how it differs from the traditional approach is discussed by Kepes [1]. Cloud computing provides primarily three service models, namely Infrastructure as a Service (IaaS), Platform as a Service (PaaS) and Software as a Service (SaaS) [2]. There are primarily three deployment models which are public cloud, private cloud and hybrid cloud [3]. Public cloud offers scalability, elasticity and a pay-per-use model on shared infrastructure. Private Cloud is owned by an organization, hosted and

© ICST Institute for Computer Sciences, Social Informatics and Telecommunications Engineering 2016
Y. Zhang et al. (Eds.): CloudComp 2015, LNICST 167, pp. 114–125, 2016.
DOI: 10.1007/978-3-319-38904-2_12

operated internally. Hybrid cloud is a mixture of private cloud and public cloud services with orchestration between the two. Private cloud and public cloud offer similar benefits, but in public cloud there is a concern of data security and compliance. Amid these choices, the decision for a suitable service and deployment model, that is best suited for an organization, is very difficult and depends on the analysis of multitude of factors and requirements.

Cloud Computing frameworks are available from commercial vendors as well as open source community. Some of the popular commercial offerings include 'vCloud' from VMWare and Azure from Microsoft. Open source cloud platforms include Eucalyptus, Nimbus, OpenStack, OpenNebula and CloudStack. Many tradeoff parameters such as price, documentation, features, expertise, etc. have to be considered before finalizing an open source cloud framework compared to commercial offerings. Several studies compare the cloud- frameworks in terms of these factors [3–7]. Studies on open source platforms conclude that OpenStack provides powerful features, especially the support for a wide array of hypervisors. The architecture and features of OpenStack show that it is ideal for large-scale private cloud deployments [8, 9]. Moreover, the support community behind OpenStack is very wide and strong. As a result of the analysis and in consideration of the comparative studies [2–7], we have chosen IaaS deployment model using OpenStack. It also allows leveraging our existing infrastructure to provide PaaS services.

Even though the use cases initially considered for the deployment of cloud system were generic in nature, the cost savings on the infrastructure was one of the prime objectives. In fact, dedicated hardware resources were chosen for the implementation on account of performance [10]. During the deployment we faced multiple challenges to fulfill some of the requirements. However we could overcome those challenges and came up with a successful deployment which is characterized by improved utilization, legitimate provisioning and greater availability of resources. A service portal for users to request specific software and services was introduced and software platform with custom applications were built as part of the cloud image itself. In cloud-networking, we extended existing VLANs (Virtual Local Area Network) of departments as multiple external networks, a feature which was not available by default in OpenStack. As a result of these, a better usage model for the cloud which is acceptable for all users was introduced. This was based on efficient sharing of services and software, which could generate significant ROI for the organization.

The paper is structured as follows: Sect. 2 gives related work and requirements are explained in Sect. 3. The Challenges faced are described in Sect. 4 and solutions developed are explained in Sect. 5. The implementation details are explained in Sect. 6 and results are presented in Sect. 7. Conclusion is given in Sect. 8.

2 Related Work

The main studies on OpenStack are focused on its architecture, components, characteristics and comparison with other cloud solutions, but only a few are focused on the challenges that enterprises have to face during deployment of an open cloud solution.

Keshavarzi et al. [11] discussed six challenges about cloud computing, which include security, Autonomic Resource Management (ARM), adoption, development, benchmarking and big data, in detail but no solutions are developed so far. Huang et al. [12] pointed out several key security problems. The study aims to identify the most vulnerable security threats in cloud computing with emphasis on security of cloud data storage. It also discuss security issues regarding data integrity, data confidentiality, access control and data manipulation to encourage the researchers to come up with some techniques and solutions so that the whole cloud storage system is reliable and trustworthy.

Cloud computing always tries to maximize the utilization of its resources. Private cloud setup requires a lot of investment in hardware implementation. Kashyap et al. [13] proposed a solution of Virtual Machine migration that minimizes the total energy consumption of cloud infrastructure. In cloud, a number of VMs (Virtual machine) are spawn and are destroyed every single minute, resulting in underutilization of physical servers. To solve this problem, cloud-providers use VM migration, in which active VMs are fused to a single physical machine to save energy. Thenceforth, underutilized servers are switched off and the consolidated servers ensure a power efficient green cloud. Raiyani Kashyap has also proposed a VM placement algorithm to migrate VMs based on system load.

Ristov et al. [14] estimated security vulnerabilities of OpenStack cloud framework. They used Nessus 5, the vulnerability and configuration assessment scanner, to exploit OpenStack server node and tenant and Acunetix Web Vulnerability Scanner for OpenStack-dashboard. The study warns about some security issues on deploying an open source cloud. Since intruders can access the cloud source code they can exploit its vulnerabilities. However these vulnerabilities can be mitigated, with software patches. As far as our knowledge, a study that addresses the challenges during and after the deployment of a private OpenStack cloud is not available.

3 Requirements

Embracing the cloud in an organization is a significant step even for mature IT organizations. The first step is identifying the requirements for the cloud. There are some generic advantages of private cloud namely monitoring of resources, flexibility of customization, ability to recover from failure and the ability to scale up or down based on demand.

Each department in our Organisation has their own subnets, IP schemes, network gateway and VLAN. The network configuration has to remain unchanged while migrating to cloud. To achieve the same, extension of existing VLANs into OpenStack network is required. In other words, the objective is to seamlessly integrate the cloud with the existing network without causing any disruption to the existing workflows.

Each department is managing its own hardware and software resources. Many of the servers and storage in each department are underutilized. Moreover these resources are not shared among departments because of physical location, security and authorization constraints. In order to achieve optimal utilization of resources, sharing of resources among departments, without compromising on security, is a requirement that is to be fulfilled.

Security is the biggest concern when it comes to cloud computing. Data security is one of the major concerns today due to which organizations are not fully adopting this technology. Even in private cloud which is built and managed in-house, there are some security issues. Data stored by a department in the cloud should be visible to that department only, denying access even to the cloud administrator.

The demand for resources is always dynamic based on application development needs and most of the time short-lived. So allocation of resources is a complex task affecting the productivity of the Organisation. In many cases provisioning of resources with different operating systems or their variants is a time consuming task which cripples the productivity. There is a strong need to manage the dynamic allocation of resources to various projects.

Organization wants to remove unnecessary overhead, minimize operational cost, maximize resource utilization, and an infrastructure with better ROI. Some of these requirements can be satisfied by the default features of OpenStack while others demand customization. Since the OpenStack code is openly distributed, it can be modified and adapted according to the requirements.

4 Challenges

As discussed, we selected OpenStack, in the light of thorough comparison of multiple cloud platforms. Moving an organization infrastructure from traditional system to cloud is not an easy task. It requires changes in the mindset of people, process and technology. There should be convincing use cases that can rationalize the upfront investment in the cloud and shall be ready to rebut questions like "Is cloud suitable for us? Does the cloud coexist with our existing IT infrastructure and able to meet our performance requirements? Is my data secure in the cloud?" In addition to the above, there are technical challenges to meet specific organization requirements. In this section, we discuss the challenges faced during the implementation, operation and management of a multi-node enterprise OpenStack cloud.

4.1 Selection of Hypervisor

OpenStack is compatible with many hypervisor such as KVM, Xen, LXC, QEMU, UML, Hyper-V etc., which makes difficult to choose from [15]. Selection of hypervisor is always a critical task as it affects the cloud performance and features. Studies were conducted to evaluate performance of different Hypervisors i.e. VMWare ESXi Server, XenServer and KVM in the private cloud using CloudStack and proved that XenServer and ESXi hypervisors exhibit impressive performance in comparison with KVM [16]. It was also proved that there is no perfect hypervisor among Hyper-V, KVM, vSphere and Xen since overheads incurred by each hypervisor can vary significantly depending on the type of application and the resources assigned to it [17]. Different workloads may be best suited for different hypervisors. Our challenge is to find a Hypervisor that is best suited for OpenStack which meets our organization requirements.

4.2 Develop a Cloud Service Usage Model

Although cloud service models and cloud deployment models are well defined, we could not find any best practices or usage models that can be suited for a private cloud deployment. In a highly abstract way, we can say that a usage model based on effective sharing of resource will work for any organization, but to concretize the concept, it requires serious thoughts. It has specific dependency on the service environment of the cloud as well as on the unique requirements of the organization. Hence to build a cloud usage model that adheres to the requirements of an organization is not an easy task and the success of the deployment is much dependent on this model. The main focus of ours was maximizing resource sharing and reducing CAPEX (Capital expenditure), there by maximizing the ROI while maintaining the resource allocation time in its least minimum. Major challenge was to device a usage model for the cloud to address these specific requirements.

4.3 Extension of External VLANs to GRE Based Tenant Network

Departments require individual tenants in cloud and complete isolation in terms of networks and resource. Additionally, the same VLAN network configuration has to be retained in cloud as well. To achieve the same, there should be a mechanism to extend the departmental VLANs to OpenStack Cloud VMs. Although OpenStack provides GRE (Generic Routing Encapsulation)/VLAN based tenant-network isolation, there is no default mechanism to extend existing external VLAN networks to these tenant networks.

4.4 Image Creation for OpenStack

To create instances in OpenStack, Operating System (OS) image has to be built and updated to the image store. There are two ways to obtain a cloud virtual machine image. The simplest way is to download pre-built images. But pre-built images are available only for open-source operating systems. Second way is to create the image manually outside of OpenStack and then upload those images to cloud. There are some drawbacks associated with the former method. Firstly, the pre-built images are not customized according to our needs. Second they have their default administrator username and password. For some OS images, there is no provision to change the administrator username. The most important is the security concern as these pre-built images are uploaded by random users and we cannot trust them. The latter method requires so many steps to be followed to make an image and has to take care of the drivers required for OpenStack environment. This is one of the major challenges faced during the operation of cloud.

4.5 Data Security

The security of data has consistently been cited as the primary barrier to cloud adoption [18]. Storage functionality is provided by three components in OpenStack i.e. Cinder, Swift and Glance. One of the primary concerns is about the security of the data stored in Cinder volumes. There is no provision to encrypt the Cinder volumes for a virtual machine. Encryption of volume can be done in two ways. The users can encrypt it themselves or rely on the cloud provider to do so. On one hand, there is significant security, but high-complexity. On the other, we have ease of use, but limited protection. As per requirement, we require user configurable data encryption.

5 Solution

5.1 Selection of Hypervisor

XenServer and KVM support almost equal features that can be controlled through compute [19]. XenServer is a bare metal Hypervisor whereas KVM is hosted hypervisor. KVM has strong guest isolation with an extra layer of protection against guest breakouts. KVM is rigorously implemented and tested. It is open source software so developers are continuously inspect KVM for flaws. It has the advantage over other x86 hypervisors in terms of lower total cost of ownership and greater flexibility than competing hypervisors [20]. It is part of Linux and uses the regular Linux scheduler and memory management. It makes KVM much smaller and simpler to use; it is also more feature rich. From user's perspective, there is almost no difference in running a Linux OS with KVM disabled and running a Linux OS with KVM enabled, except the speed difference. A user having fair knowledge of Linux can manage KVM Hypervisor. KVM is most widely used hypervisor in OpenStack. Most OpenStack development is done with the KVM hypervisor for which more community support is available Moreover, bugs associated with KVM hypervisor is negligible as compared to other hypervisors [21–23].

5.2 Develop a Cloud Service Usage Model

For generating better ROI, a cloud usage model has been developed. Licensing cost of software components is a big issue for organizations. For efficient utilization of these licenses, a service sharing mechanism is introduced without violating terms and conditions of license providers. A self-service portal that enables users to request infrastructure and platforms as a service is introduced. It contains a service catalog that lists the categories and the services available. The service portal enables reserving as well as requesting the services on demand. Cloud administrator will service the request if enough resources are available and users will be provided with credentials and IP address of the allocated instance. In addition to that, separate storage volumes will be maintained for each of the users and this storage will be attached to the instance based on the request. Users have to use the credentials provided by the administrator to access the system. One VM instance will be shared across multiple users but the volume associated with the instance varies with the user.

5.3   Extension of External VLANs to the GRE Based Tenant Network

Tenant-network provides internal connectivity for its instances (VMs) as well as isolation from other tenant networks. OpenStack supports both GRE and VLAN based tenant networks. Out of which, VLAN based isolation requires the configuration of physical switches to trunk the required VLANs. On the other hand, GRE is an overlay network which uses encapsulation for network traffic. VLAN based tenant network limit the maximum networks to 4096 but GRE has no hard limit on this number. In view of these facts we used GRE for tenant networking with soft-routers provided by OpenStack for external network connectivity. These soft-routers use NAT (Network Address Translation) for linking the IPs of both external and tenant-network. OpenStack generally uses a single flat external network but we require multiple VLANs as external networks.

Available configuration options of OpenStack were insufficient to achieve the above requirement. As a solution, we adopted custom scripting in addition to OpenStack configuration scripts. Figure 1 illustrates the architecture for exposing multiple VLANs as external networks in the cloud. As in the diagram, 'eth1', the physical interface, connected to the trunk-port of the physical switch which is trunked to allow all departmental VLANs. For each of the external VLAN, which has to be extended to the tenant network, a bridge interface 'br-ex*' is created (* represents the network number). These bridge ports (br-ex* and br-eth1) are interlinked through a Linux 'veth-pair' (virtual link) and 'br-eth1' is configured in promiscuous mode so as to allow all network traffic through it. Custom scripting is used to achieve these configurations at the Neutron-node of the OpenStack implementation. OpenStack creates a set of 'veth-pairs' (int-br-ex*, phy-br-ex*) for each of the external networks to the 'br-int' port. For each of these 'veth-pairs' the phy-br-ex* is tagged with the ID of the corresponding external VLAN. Soft-router of the OpenStack uses these virtual links to forward the external network traffic based on the external network to which it is associated. In effect this configuration enables to extend any number of VLANs in the external network to the cloud.

5.4   Image Creation

There is no specific tool to create images for OpenStack cloud. We created images manually since we require customized images that can be directly deployed to OpenStack. Virtual machine images come in different formats. Out of which we selected qcow2 (QEMU copy-on-write version 2) because it supports snapshots and use sparse representation which results in smaller size of the image. Smaller images mean faster uploads. The qcow2 format is commonly used with the KVM hypervisor [24]. We installed KVM hypervisor to create customized images. We have created images for various operating systems along with required software. For Windows images creation, hypervisor specific drivers and tools are required; for example: VirtIO for KVM and XenServer tools for XenServer/XCP. The image created consists of software and applications required by users along with the Operating System. In other words, the image created is all encompassing and the instances which are created using the images are ready to be used with all the required software, tools and frameworks for end users.

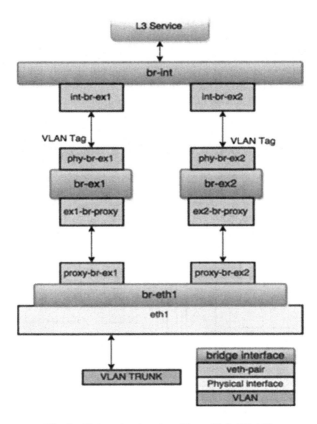

Fig. 1. External networks with multiple VLANs

5.5 Data Security

Encryption of the VM's data prior to writing to disk is provided by the latest release of OpenStack which is Kilo, as of this writing. Still, it is vulnerable for attack since this implementation uses a single, fixed key. It does not provide protection if that key is compromised [25]. Moreover, the fixed key is configured by cloud administrator and users always may not trust cloud administrators. Hence our challenge to allow the cloud user to encrypt their data before sending to the cloud storage remains as an open problem.

6 Implementation

Based on the requirements, we sized cloud infrastructure and used five PMs (Physical Machine). Four of them (PM1, PM2, PM3, PM4) are Dell PowerEdge -C6220 Sled servers, while the fifth one (PM5) is a PowerEdge -R720 server. The corresponding hardware configuration is shown in Fig. 2. On all PMs, we have installed Ubuntu 12.04.4 LTS server. On PM1 we installed an OpenStack controller with Keystone, Glance, Swift,

Nova (but without Nova-Compute), MySQL and Horizon services. PM2, PM3 and PM4 are compute nodes (CN). PM5 is configured as a storage node as well as network node. The Compute nodes run KVM, the native Linux VM Hypervisor. All PMs are equipped with 2 Intel Xeon processors with 8 cores each, which are enabled for hyper-threading, resulting in 32 VCPUs (Virtual CPU). On compute nodes, the Nova-Compute service was installed in order to be able to instantiate VMs on top of it.

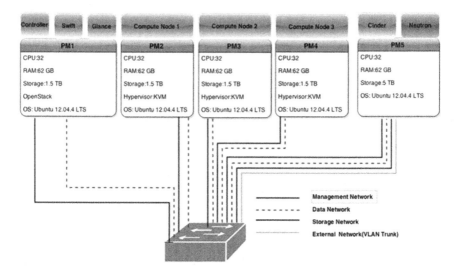

Fig. 2. Cloud infrastructure setup with PMs and hardware/software configuration

We used the management network as 10.176.46.0/24 and data network as 192.168.0.0/16. External networks were multiple VLANs in the range 10.176.1.0/23-10.176.44.0/23. All Compute nodes had two physical NICs (Network Interface Card). One attached to the management network and the other one to data network.

Storage functionality is provided by three components. Swift is the sub-project that delivers object storage. Cinder is the block-storage component that uses standard protocols such as iSCSI. Glance provides a repository for VM images and can use storage from basic file systems or Swift. Using a dedicated storage node or storage subsystem to host, Cinder volumes can be provided. We have used a dedicated storage node of 5 TB.

6.1 Service Request Portal

A user service portal request is also developed which is running outside the cloud framework, and is used by end users to request for any specific platform for a period of time. The service portal is integrated with OpenStack controller using API.

7   Result

Every year we find an increase on demand in the required resources from end users and the computing nodes are increased based on this demand. With the introduction of cloud, currently about 70 % of the physical infrastructure requirement is being met with cloud. Moreover, the time required to fulfill these ever increasing demands either for the initiation of new projects or commissioning of new departments, has been reduced substantially by avoiding delays in procurement and provisioning. In effect, the cloud platform helped the organization to improve utilization, productivity and early adoption of open source technologies with minimal financial overhead. It is also proven that by proper strategy and planning for shared use of software, systems and other services can generate greater cost-saving for organizations. If such a strategy and a cloud usage model are in place, it will have huge impact on the ROI of organizations.

8   Conclusion and Future Work

Successful implementation of cloud computing in an enterprise requires proper planning and understanding of emerging risks, threats, and vulnerabilities and possible countermeasures. We were able to deploy fully operational OpenStack Cloud environment in our enterprise infrastructure successfully with best practices for operating a cloud. There were many challenges to implement a community driven cloud solution but we could successfully overcome those challenges either through customization of OpenStack or introduction of agile models for the cloud usage. Our experience proved that even though a private cloud implementation entails substantial cost from hardware acquisition, deployment, on-going maintenance, management and monitoring, there are corresponding benefits as well. It has reasonably reduced the cost of investment in physical resources and created a noticeable ROI. OpenStack is found to be promising for private cloud implementation and can be adopted by even small organizations.

Overall we feel that, OpenStack's security solution on volume-storage is still in its infancy. Although a few solutions have been developed recently like volume-encryption, all are configurable by cloud service provider only. Therefore a solution, which allows the tenants to configure their encryption mechanism, is highly desirable. This will pose additional challenge on volume-encryption. Hence this research paper will hopefully motivate future researchers to come up with secure user configurable volume encryption algorithms and framework to strengthen the cloud computing security.

Acknowledgements.   This work is sponsored by Department of Electronics and Information Technology (DeitY) of the Government of India. We greatly acknowledge Mr. B.M Bhaveja, Group Coordinator, R&D in CC&BT for providing funding support for this project.

References

1. Kepes, B.: Revolution Not Evolution: How Cloud Computing Differs from Traditional IT and Why it Matters. http://broadcast.rackspace.com/hosting_knowledge/whitepapers/Revolution_Not_Evolution-Whitepaper.pdf. Accessed June 2015

2. Gibson, J., Eveleigh, D., Rondeau, R., Tan, Q.: Benefits and challenges of three cloud computing service models. In: Proceedings of 2012 Fourth International Conference on Computational Aspects of Social Networks (CASoN), Sao Carlos, pp. 198–205 (2012)
3. Yadav, S.: Comparative study on open source software for cloud computing platform: Eucalyptus, OpenStack and OpenNebula. Int. J. Eng. Sci. **3** (2013)
4. Thilagavathi, M.: Cloud platforms – a comparison. Int. J. Adv. Res. Comput. Sci. Softw. Eng. **3**, 275–279 (2013)
5. Cloud platform comparison-Comparison of CloudStack, Eucalyptus, vCloud Director and OpenStack. http://www.networkworld.com/article/2189981/tech-primers/cloud-platform-comparison–cloudstack–eucalyptus–vcloud-director-and-openstack.html. Accessed May 2015
6. von Laszewski, G., Diaz, J., Wang, F., Fox, G.C.: Comparison of multiple cloud frameworks. In: Proceedings of 2012 IEEE 5th International Conference on Cloud Computing (CLOUD), Honolulu, HI, pp. 734–741 (2012)
7. Buyyaa, R., Yeoa, C.S., Venugopala, S., Broberga, J., Brandic, I.: Cloud computing and emerging IT platforms: vision, hype, and reality for delivering computing as the 5th utility. Future Gener. Comput. Syst. **5**, 599–616 (2009)
8. Kamboj, R., Arya, A.: OpenStack: open source cloud computing IaaS platform, **4**, 1200–1202 (2014)
9. Sefraoui, O., Aissaoui, M., Eleuldj, M.: OpenStack: toward an open-source solution for cloud computing. Int. J. Comput. Appl. **55**(03), 38–43 (2012). (0975 – 8887)
10. Nasim, R., Kassler, A.J.: Deploying OpenStack: virtual infrastructure or dedicated hardware. In: Proceedings of 2014 IEEE 38th International Conference on Computer Software and Applications Conference Workshops (COMPSACW), Vasteras, pp. 84–89 (2014)
11. Keshavarzi, A., Haghighat, A.T., Bohlouli, M.: Research challenges and prospective business impacts of cloud computing: a survey. In: Proceedings of 2013 IEEE 7th International Conference on Intelligent Data Acquisition and Advanced Computing Systems (IDAACS), Berlin, pp. 731–736 (2013)
12. Huang, C., Qin, Z., Kuo, C.J.: Multimedia storage security in cloud computing: an overview. In: Proceedings of 2011 IEEE 13th International Workshop on Multimedia Signal Processing (MMSP), Hangzhou, pp. 1–6 (2011)
13. Kashyap, R., Chaudhary, S., Jat, P.M.: Virtual machine migration for back-end mashup application deployed on OpenStack environment. In: Proceedings of 2014 International Conference on Parallel, Distributed and Grid Computing (PDGC), Solan, pp. 214–218 (2014)
14. Ristov, S., Gusev, M., Donevski, A.: Security vulnerability assessment of OpenStack cloud. In: Proceedings of 2014 Sixth International Conference on Computational Intelligence, Communication Systems and Networks (CICSyN), Tetova, pp. 95–100 (2014)
15. Hypervisors-OpenStack Hypervisors. http://docs.openstack.org/icehouse/config-reference/content/section_compute-hypervisors.html. Accessed May 2015
16. Reddy, P.V.V., Rajamani, L.: Evaluation of different hypervisors performance in the private cloud with SIGAR framework. Int. J. Adv. Comput. Sci. Appl. (IJACSA) **5**, 60–66 (2014)
17. Hwang, J., Zeng, S., Wu, F., Wood, T.: A component-based performance comparison of four hypervisors. In: Proceedings of 2013 IFIP/IEEE International Symposium on Integrated Network Management (IM 2013), Ghent, pp. 269–276 (2013)
18. Bajwa, M.S., Himani: A concern towards data security in cloud computing. Int. J. Comput. Appl. **114**, 17–19 (2015)
19. Hypervisor Support Matrix. http://docs.openstack.org/developer/nova/support-matrix.html#guest_setup_inject_networking. Accessed May 2015
20. Wilson, G., Day, M., Taylor, B.: KVM hypervisor security you can

21. OpenStack Compute (Nova)-Compute bugs associated with XenServer. https://bugs.launchpad.net/nova/+bugs?field.tag=xenserver,xen. Accessed May 2015
22. OpenStack Compute (Nova)-Compute bugs associated with KVM. https://bugs.launchpad.net/nova/+bugs?field.tag=kvm. Accessed May 2015
23. OpenStack Compute (Nova)-Compute bugs associated with VMware. https://bugs.launchpad.net/nova/+bugs?field.tag=vmware. Accessed May 2015
24. Image guide-OpenStack Image guide. http://docs.openstack.org/image-guide/content/ch_introduction.html. Accessed May 2015
25. Volume Encryption-Volume Encryption with Static Key. http://docs.openstack.org/kilo/config-reference/content/section_volume-encryption.html. Accessed May 2015

Performance Evaluation of Scientific Workflow on OpenStack and OpenVZ

Amol Jaikar[1,2]($\boxtimes$), Syed Asif Raza Shah[1,2], Sangwook Bae[2],
and Seo-Young Noh[1,2]

[1] Grid and Supercomputing Department,
Korea University of Science and Technology, Daejeon 305-350, South Korea
{amol,asif,rsyoung}@kisti.re.kr
[2] National Institute of Supercomputing and Networking,
Korea Institute of Science and Technology Information, Daejeon
305-804, South Korea
wookie@kisti.re.kr

Abstract. Cloud computing is capturing attention of the market by providing infrastructure, platform and software as a services. Using virtualization technology, resources are shared among multiple users to improve the resource utilization. By leasing the infrastructure from public cloud, users can save money and time to maintain the expensive computing facility. Therefore, it gives an option for cluster and grid computing technology which is used for industrial application or scientific workflow. Virtual machine enables more flexibility for consolidation of the underutilized servers. However, containers are also competing with virtual machine to improve the resource utilization. Therefore, to adopt cloud computing for scientific workflow, scientist needs to understand the performance of virtual machine and container. We have used cloud computing with different virtualization technologies like KVM and container to test the performance of scientific workflow. In this work, we analyze the performance of scientific workflow on OpenStack's virtual machine and OpenVZ's container. Our result shows that container gives better and stable performance than virtual machine.

Keywords: Performance · Scientific workflow · OpenStack · OpenVZ

1 Introduction

Cloud computing is a new flexible model of loosely coupled distributed system. Cloud computing technology provides infrastructure, platform and software as a service to the users [1]. Software and hardware techniques for virtualization enable cloud computing technology [2] to create virtual infrastructure. Moreover, hardware companies are also looking forward to support the virtualization [3]. Due to the flexible nature of cloud computing, server consolidation technique is used to reduce the power consumption of a data center. Peak clustering based placement technique gives better performance than correction based placement

© ICST Institute for Computer Sciences, Social Informatics and Telecommunications Engineering 2016
Y. Zhang et al. (Eds.): CloudComp 2015, LNICST 167, pp. 126–135, 2016.
DOI: 10.1007/978-3-319-38904-2_13

technique for server consolidation [4]. Because of these advantages, research organizations and industries are trying to adopt cloud computing technology.

Research organization requires considerable amount of computing infrastructure to calculate scientific experiment's results. This requirement varies frequently depending on the scientific project. Therefore, flexible infrastructure is more suitable for scientific world. In order to adopt cloud computing, it is compulsory to understand the performance difference between physical and virtual infrastructure. Virtual machines and containers are available options to adopt cloud computing for scientific workflow.

In terms of virtual machines, there are different type of hypervisors like KVM [5], Xen [6] and VMware [7]. We have used KVM for our implementation. To manage the virtual machines, we have used OpenStack [8] as a middleware. In case of containers, we have used OpenVZ [9].

The paper is organized as follows. Section 2 gives the background information including virtualization and batch processing software. Furthermore, Sect. 3 describes the related work. Section 4 covers the implementation part of this paper which include the execution of jobs. Section 5 discusses about suitability for scientific workflow. Lastly, Sect. 6 concludes the paper.

2 Background

This section gives the background information of technologies used in this experiment which includes virtualization and batch processing software.

2.1 Virtualization

Virtualization technology enables to creation of virtual machine on physical machine with CPU, memory, network, operating system for providing different types of services. There are three types of virtualization; full, para and operating system level (OS-level) virtualization [10].

Full virtualization technology provides environment to run virtual machine with unmodified operating system. It includes the simulation of all features of hardware to run the virtual machine. Complete full virtualization is based on hardware support provided by *AMD* and *Intel* by storing guest virtual machine state into VT-x or AMD-V [11]. KVM is an example of full virtualization. We have used KVM as a hypervisor for OpenStack. In case of para-virtualization, the guest operating system needs to modify to run on hypervisor. This technology gives better performance than full virtualization [12]. Xen is an example of para-virtualization technology.

In OS-level virtualization, the kernel of host operating system provides the isolated user space to run different environment like containers, virtualization engines or virtual private servers. Container is a lightweight virtualization technology which enables to run many isolated instances of same host operating system. This technology does not simulate all hardware environment. It also requires fewer CPU and memory to run the virtual environment (container) [13]. We have used OpenVZ as a container technology for testing scientific workflow.

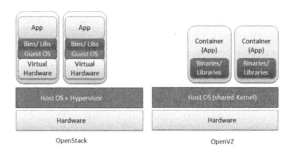

Fig. 1. OpenStack and OpenVZ Architecture

Virtual Machine. In case of virtual machine, hypervisor runs along with host operating system. This hypervisor simulates the virtual hardware including CPU, memory and network. The virtual machine runs on this hypervisor with its own operating system called as guest operating system. Therefore, instruction execution must pass through guest operating system as well as hypervisor which lead to an overhead. Nested page table technique has huge overhead for memory access [14]. We have used KVM as a hypervisor for OpenStack middleware. OpenStack is responsible for management of the virtual infrastructure including creation, deletion, migration and many more operations of virtual machine. It provides simple interface for user to interact with the virtual infrastructure. OpenStack is scalable, flexible and compatible for most of the hypervisors [15].

Container. Virtual machine comes with an overhead. In order to avoid this overhead, container-based virtualization technology provides lightweight alternative [16]. Hypervisor works at hardware level while container-based virtualization isolates the user space running at operating system level. Containers run at operating system level by sharing the host operating system kernel. Therefore, container-based virtualization has comparatively less isolation than hypervisor. Restriction of resource usage feature is available in containers which enables the fair usage of resources among all containers. Figure 1 refers the OpenVZ container architecture. OpenVZ system uses process ID (PID) and inter process communication (IPC) namespace to isolated the process contexts. OpenVZ also provides the network namespace for better network performance [17].

2.2 HTCondor

HTCondor is a non-interactive high throughput computing batch processing software which is developed by University of Wisconsin [18]. It has master-slave architecture where master is responsible for management of jobs and slave is responsible for execution of jobs. Figure 2 shows the logical view of HTcondor environment. HTCondor is used in this experiment for scientific job submission. The jobs, which are submitted by different user, are executed by slaves (OpenStack's virtual machine and OpenVZ's container).

3   Related Work

Jianhua Che et al. described the performance evaluation on different virtualization technologies by using standard benchmarks with the consideration of high performance computing [19]. Nathan Regola et al. also showed the performance comparison for high performance system [20]. Igli Tafa et al. have evaluated the transfer time, CPU consumption and memory utilization using FTP and HTTP protocol [21]. Igli Tafa et al. have also showed the virtual machine migration performance [22] for different virtualization technology. Our contribution is to evaluate the performance of high throughput computing scientific workflow on virtual infrastructure.

4   Implementation

This section gives the description of not only experimental setup but also scientific jobs.

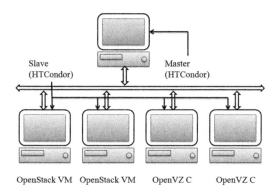

Fig. 2. Cloud System Architecture

4.1   Setup

In this testing environment, we used four servers of the same configuration of 6 cores with 2660 MHz of frequency and 24 GB of RAM with Scientific Linux distribution. Two among four servers are OpenStack controller and compute. We have used two-node architecture for OpenStack. Third server is used for OpenVZ and last server is for HTCondor master. To test the performance, we have used OpenStack virtual machine with HTCondor installed on Scientific Linux image. In case of OpenVZ, we have used containers with HTCondor installed on Scientific Linux template. Figure 2 shows the logical view of the HTCondor virtual cluster where OpenStack virtual machines and OpenVZ containers are working as a slave.

In order to test the performance of the scientific jobs, we characterized them into CPU, I/O, memory and network intensive jobs. Figure 3 shows the performance of scientific jobs using *top* command. Process id (PID) 3204 is a CPU intensive job while PID 3277 is a I/O intensive job. In case of PID 3080, it consumes more memory while PID 3254 is a network intensive job. Virtual machine and container are of the size 1 vCPU, 2 GB RAM and 20 GB HDD. In this experiment, we have executed 10 jobs on 2, 6 and 10 virtual machines and containers to analyze the performance of scientific workflow. These virtual machines and containers are on two different physical machines.

OpenStack(2VM) means OpenStack's 2 virtual machines are executing these 10 jobs to calculate the result. In case of *OpenVZ(2C)*, OpenVZ's 2 containers are executing these 10 jobs simultaneously. Number of jobs completed per unit time is the main attribute of high throughput computing.

PID	USER	PR	NI	VIRT	RES	SHR	S	%CPU	%MEM	TIME+	COMMAND
3204	xyz	20	0	459m	315m	2800	R	99.4	17.0	0:37.98	python

PID	USER	PR	NI	VIRT	RES	SHR	S	%CPU	%MEM	TIME+	COMMAND
3277	xyz	20	0	425m	314m	1668	R	99.1	16.9	0:26.46	python

PID	USER	PR	NI	VIRT	RES	SHR	S	%CPU	%MEM	TIME+	COMMAND
3080	xyz	20	0	3510m	1.5g	556	R	98.7	85.0	3:36.99	python

PID	USER	PR	NI	VIRT	RES	SHR	S	%CPU	%MEM	TIME+	COMMAND
3254	xyz	20	0	181m	12m	3156	R	2.0	0.7	0:00.60	python

Fig. 3. Scientific job's performance

4.2   CPU Intensive Job

This job does the matrix multiplication and consumes more CPU cycles. As per Fig. 3, it(PID 3204) consumes around 100 % of CPU. We executed 10 CPU intensive jobs on multiple virtual machines and containers. Figure 4 shows execution time of these jobs. X-axis shows the number of the job and Y-axis shows the execution time. When we tested on 2 virtual machines of OpenStack and 2 containers of OpenVZ , the performance is almost identical to the physical host. But OpenStack virtual machine gives non-stable results. In case of 6 virtual machines and 6 containers, OpenVZ containers perform better than OpenStack virtual machines. Same results occur when testing on 10 virtual machines and 10 containers. But in this case, the execution time gets double than physical host which is considerable overhead. From the Fig. 4, we can analyze that OpenVZ gives better and stable performance than OpenStack.

4.3   I/O Intensive Job

This job creates the file on the HDD and writes data into the file. This job creates around 1 GB file. Figure 3 shows that it(PID 3277) consumes around 100 % of CPU and 16 % of memory. This job is to test the I/O performance of virtual machine as well as container. Figure 5 shows the execution time of these jobs. X-axis shows the number of the job and Y-axis shows the execution time in

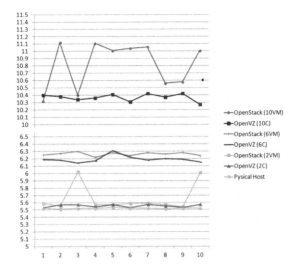

Fig. 4. CPU performance

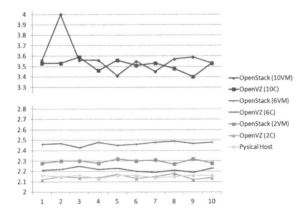

Fig. 5. I/O performance

minutes of that job. OpenVZ container always takes less time than OpenStack virtual machine, to execute the I/O intensive job. In case of 10 virtual machines and containers, container gives stable performance than virtual machine.

4.4 Memory Intensive Job

Memory intensive job consumes more memory to calculate the results. This job creates the string and append it with number of other strings continuously. Figure 3 shows that, it(PID 3080) consumes 85 % of the memory to get the result. Figure 6 shows the execution time of the memory intensive jobs. In this

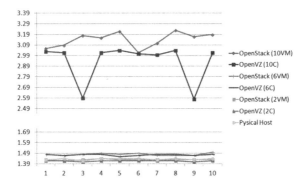

Fig. 6. Memory performance

case also, container performs better than virtual machine. But in case of 10 virtual machines and 10 container, execution time gets double than physical host which is also considerable.

4.5 Network Intensive Job

In this network intensive jobs, it continuously download the file from server and writes on the hard disk. Figure 3 shows that it(PID 3254) consumes less memory and CPU. Figure 7 shows the execution time of the network intensive jobs. The results are scattered around the numbers from 13 to 23 min, it may be because of network traffic. In case of virtual machines and containers, execution time is surprisingly less than physical host's execution time. It may be because of cache.

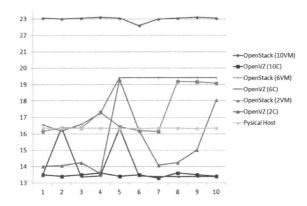

Fig. 7. Network performance

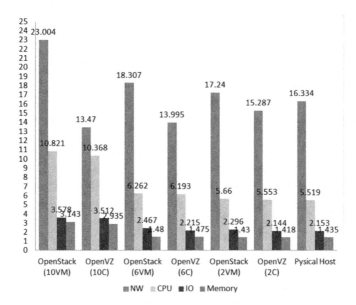

Fig. 8. Average execution time

5   Discussion

In order to understand the exact difference between OpenStack's virtual machine and OpenVZ's container, we took an average of 10 job's execution time. Figure 8 shows the average execution of network, CPU, I/O and memory intensive jobs. This graph clearly shows that containers gives better performance than virtual machine. Therefore, containers give better throughput than virtual machine.

In the scientific world, every user is authenticated by set of processes. Therefore, only authorized person can use this computing infrastructure of scientific world. Most of the computing infrastructure uses Scientific Linux as an operating system. Moreover, the scientific data is also accessible to all these authorized scientists. Therefore, containers are more suitable for scientific world than virtual machine. Moreover, containers are faster and stable in performance than virtual machines. The advantage of virtual machine is, different operating system virtual machines can reside on single physical machine. But in case of scientific world, most of them are using Scientific Linux distribution.

6   Conclusion

Cloud computing enables more opportunities for the scientific workflow. Resources can be leased from the public cloud when needed. This feature empowers more flexibility for the users to save money and time to maintain the computing infrastructure. There are two options for scientific community to adopt cloud computing technology for scientific workflow; virtual machine and containers. Thus, in this paper we tried to understand the performance of scientific workflow on virtual machine and container. To investigate, we first characterized the scientific workflow into CPU, I/O, memory and network intensive jobs. Then, we executed and captured the performance of these jobs on virtual machines and containers. We found that container gives better and stable performance than virtual machine. As per our discussion, containers are more suitable for scientific workflow.

Acknowledgment. This work was supported by the program of the Construction and Operation for Large-scale Science Data Center (K-15-L01-C05) and by National Research Foundation (NRF) of Korea (N-15-NM-IR01).

References

1. Armbrust, M., Armando, F., Rean, G., Joseph, A.D., Randy, K., Andy, K., Gunho, L., et al.: A view of cloud computing. Commun. ACM **53**(4), 50–58 (2010)
2. Adams, K., Agesen, O.: A comparison of software and hardware techniques for x86 virtualization. ACM Sigplan Not. **41**(11), 2–13 (2006)
3. Uhlig, R., Gil, N., Dion, R., Santoni, A.L., Fernando, M., Anderson, A.V., Bennett, S.M., Alain, K., Leung, F.H., Larry, S.: Intel virtualization technology. Computer **38**(5), 48–56 (2005)
4. Verma, A., Dasgupta, G., Nayak, T.K., De, P., Kothari, R.: Server workload analysis for power minimization using consolidation. In: Proceedings of the Conference on USENIX Annual Technical Conference, p. 28. USENIX Association (2009)
5. http://www.linux-kvm.org/page/Main_Page. Accessed June 2015
6. http://www.vmware.com/. Accessed June 2015
7. http://www.xenproject.org/. Accessed June 2015
8. https://www.openstack.org/. Accessed June 2015
9. https://openvz.org/Main_Page. Accessed June 2015
10. Matthews, J.N., Wenjin, H., Hapuarachchi, M., Deshane, T., Dimatos, D., Hamilton, G., McCabe, M., Owens, J.: Quantifying the performance isolation properties of virtualization systems. In: Proceedings of the 2007 Workshop on Experimental Computer Science, p. 6. ACM (2007)
11. Walters, J.P., Chaudhary, V., Cha, M., Guercio Jr., S., Gallo, S.: A comparison of virtualization technologies for HPC. In: 22nd International Conference on Advanced Information Networking and Applications, AINA 2008. pp. 861–868. IEEE (2008)
12. Deshane, T., Zachary Shepherd, J., Matthews, M.B.-Y., Shah, A., Rao, B.: Quantitative comparison of Xen and KVM. In: Xen Summit, Boston, MA, USA, pp. 1–2 (2008)
13. Vaughan-Nichols, S.J.: New approach to virtualization is a lightweight. Computer **39**(11), 12–14 (2006)
14. Kivity, A., Kamay, Y., Laor, D., Lublin, U., Liguori, A.: kvm: the Linux virtual machine monitor. In: Proceedings of the Linux Symposium, vol. 1, pp. 225–230 (2007)
15. Sefraoui, O., Aissaoui, M., Eleuldj, M.: Openstack: toward an open-source solution for cloud computing. Int. J. Comput. Appl. **55**(3), 38–42 (2012)

16. Soltesz, S., Ptzl, H., Fiuczynski, M.E., Bavier, A., Peterson, L.: Container-based operating system virtualization: a scalable, high-performance alternative to hypervisors. In: ACM SIGOPS Operating Systems Review, vol. 41, no. 3, pp. 275–287. ACM (2007)
17. Xavier, G., Miguel, M.V., Neves, F., de Rose, C., Augusto.: A performance comparison of container-based virtualization systems for mapreduce clusters. In: 2014 22nd Euromicro International Conference on Parallel, Distributed and Network-Based Processing (PDP), pp. 299–306. IEEE (2014)
18. http://research.cs.wisc.edu/htcondor/. Accessed June 2015
19. Che, J., Yong, Y., Shi, C., Lin, W.: A synthetical performance evaluation of openvz, xen, kvm. In: Services Computing Conference (APSCC), 2010 IEEE Asia-Pacific, pp. 587–594. IEEE (2010)
20. Regola, N., Ducom, J.-C.: Recommendations for virtualization technologies in high performance computing. In: 2010 IEEE Second International Conference on Cloud Computing Technology and Science (CloudCom), pp. 409–416. IEEE (2010)
21. Tafa, I., Beqiri, E., Paci, H., Kajo, E., Xhuvani, A.: The evaluation of transfer time, cpu consumption and memory utilization in XEN-PV, XEN-HVM, OPENVZ, KVM-FV and KVM-PV hypervisors using ftp and http approaches. In: 2011 Third International Conference on Intelligent Networking and Collaborative Systems (INCoS), pp. 502–507. IEEE (2011)
22. Tafa, I., Zanaj, E., Kajo, E., Bejleri, A., Xhuvani, A.: The comparison of virtual machine migration performance between XEN-HVM, XEN-PV, Open-VZ, KVM-FV, KVM-PV. IJCSMS Int. J. Comput. Sci.: Manag. Stud. 11(2), 65–75 (2011)

An Science Gateway with Cost Adaptive Resource Management Schemes

Woojoong Kim$^{(\boxtimes)}$, Seung-Hwan Kim, and Chan-Hyun Youn

Department of Electrical Engineering, KAIST, Daejeon, Korea
{w.j.kim, s.h_kim, chyoun}@kaist.ac.kr

Abstract. In order to process heavy data and computation applications such as scientific application in cloud computing environment, it is important to do an efficient resource schedule that decrease the resource usage cost while guaranteeing users' Service Level Agreement. To resolve this issue, we propose and implement Science Gateway, which execute the scientific application efficiently on heterogeneous cloud service providers instead of users. Especially, we propose a cost-adaptive resource management schemes (i.e. VM pool management scheme that decreases the resource management cost significantly based on the long-term payment plans of cloud resource providers and VM placement management scheme that guarantee the performance of communication between VMs). Finally, we demonstrate that our proposed system improves the performance of existing cloud systems through some experimental and simulation results.

Keywords: Cloud computing · Scientific workflow application · Cloud broker

1 Introduction

Heavy data and computation applications usually require the huge amount of computing and storage resource. With the emergence of cloud computing, users can utilize the resource as a cloud service based on pay-per-usage base to execute their own heavy applications [1]. However, it is still difficult for users to decide how much cloud service should be leased in order to minimize the amount of cloud resource while guaranteeing the certain performance of the application. In addition, there are a lot of cloud services from various cloud providers and they have various policies on cloud service and service charge. In this case, users can make non-optimal decision with the limited information on cloud services and waste the execution time and cost because of the inefficient decision. Thus, third party entity (i.e. cloud broker) presented between user and Cloud Service Provider (CSP) is defined to make an optimal decision with rich information on cloud services instead of users.

The key issue of the cloud broker is to decrease the resource usage cost from cloud environment in order to increase the profit while guaranteeing the certain performance of cloud service required by user. In this paper, to resolve this problem, we propose and implement the cloud broker called Science Gateway with the cost adaptive resource schemes including VM pool management scheme and VM placement management scheme.

© ICST Institute for Computer Sciences, Social Informatics and Telecommunications Engineering 2016
Y. Zhang et al. (Eds.): CloudComp 2015, LNICST 167, pp. 136–144, 2016.
DOI: 10.1007/978-3-319-38904-2_14

The VM pool management scheme utilizes the reserved VM payment policy(RVM) which reserve some virtual machines(VM) on long-term in a discount price. Organizing a RVM pool by estimating the amount of resource demand on the future with this scheme, the cloud broker decreases the resource usage cost by providing the available RVM in the RVM pool instead of On-demand VM(OVM).

The VM placement management scheme decides a certain physical node within the cloud server structure to lease new VM instance in order to guarantee the network capacity between leased VMs and decrease the data transmission delay between VMs.

2   A Model Description of the Science Gateway

The object of science gateway is to minimize a resource usage cost while satisfying user's SLA for cloud resource providers instead of users. In our model, the science gateway concentrates on scientific applications and users only request for their application execution with their SLA to the science gateway.

The scientific application can be represented as a workflow $A(T, E, D)$ where A is the set of tasks, E is the set of edges and D is deadline. We assume that the total execution time of each tasks in A are known. By the science gateway, each task is allocated to their proper VM instance and processed in order of their starting time decided by SLA constraints such as deadline D.

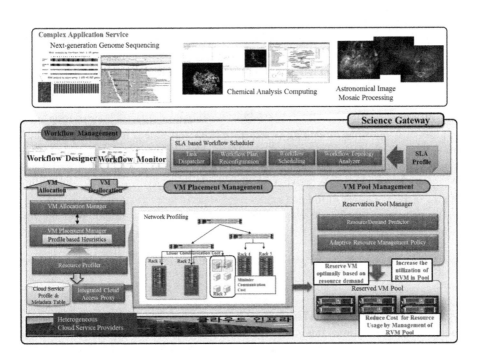

Fig. 1. Architecture of the proposed science gateway

Different types of VM instances have the different computing performance. We assume that CSP provides only three types of cloud resource service: small, medium, large. Each type of VM is charged in proportion to their capacity with Billing Time Unit (BTU). BTU is the base time unit to charge for resource usage time and partial-BTU resource usage time is rounded up to one BTU. A VM type is represented as $VT_i = \{VT_{c_i}, VT_{m_i}, VT_{s_i}\}, i \in \{1, 2, \ldots, K\}$: *number of VCPU (#) VT_{c_i}, memory size (GBs) VT_{m_i}, storage space (GBs) VT_{s_i}.* CSP provides OVM and RVM payment plans [2]. By RVM plan, VM instance can be leased for long BTU (e.g., monthly or yearly) with the discount price.

The science gateway is described in Fig. 1. It receives the scientific application request from users through GUI based workflow designer. Workflow management schedules the resource plan for each task within the requested application and processes all tasks on the VM instances provided by VM Placement Management Scheme and VM Pool Management Scheme.

3   Cost Adaptive Cloud Resource Management Schemes

VM Pool Management Scheme is shown in Algorithm 1. This scheme decides the appropriate amount of RVMs to be leased in the heuristic way in order to decrease the resource usage cost. This scheme works in the period of time interval T. The amount of RVMs is dependent on the resource demand. The historical data on all the executed tasks and their allocated VM types during the previous time interval T' is used for this scheme. We assume that the request trend in the current time interval T will be similar with the one in T'. As a result, we can decide the appropriate amount of i-type RVM, N_i for current time interval T. First, we organize clusters for each task within A based on their assigned VM instance type VT_i. Eventually, all the tasks within A are classified into some clusters Cl_{VT_i}. On each cluster Cl_{VT_i}, we organize groups g_m. It is a batch of non-overlapped tasks. After the tasks of Cl_{VT_i} are sorted in order of their starting time, each task of Cl_{VT_i} is picked into g_m in sequence if its start time st is later than the finish time ft of last task in g_m. This procedure is repeated until there is no available task in Cl_{VT_i} anymore. Finally, with $gct(g_m)$ total execution time of g_m and $VT(g_m)$ allocated VM instance type of g_m, we derive a RVM lease duration $RVM_{VT(g_m),gct(g_m)}$ by finding the size of BTU closest to the $gct(g_m)$.

We determine whether to lease $RVM_{VT(g_m),gct(g_m)}$ from CSP or not with the following condition.

$$\frac{C\left(RVM_{VT(g_m),gct(g_m)}\right)}{\sum_{\forall t \in g_m} et(t) \cdot C\left(OVM_{VT(t)}\right)} < 1 \qquad (1)$$

The denominator of Eq. (1) is the total resource usage cost on OVMs for the tasks having the execution time et in g_m. The numerator of Eq. (1) is the total resource usage cost of RVM for g_m. If Eq. (1) is satisfied, it means that RVM is more efficient on cost than OVMs for g_m. As the value of Eq. (1) is decreased, leasing RVM is more efficient.

Algorithm 1. VM Pool Management Scheme

Input: historical data including $A = \{ \forall t_{i,j} \}$ and $\forall VT(t_{i,j})$ during previous time interval T'

Output: N_i during current time interval T

01:   **For** $VT_i, \forall i \in \{1,2,...,K\}$.

02:     **For** $\forall t \in S$

03:       $Cl_{VT_i} = Cl_{VT_i} \cup \leftarrow t \in S$ if $VT(t) = VT_i$

04:     **End for**

05:   **End for**

06:   $m = 0$

07:   **For** $Cl_{VT_i} \; \forall i \in \{1,2,...,K\}$.

08:     sort $tasks$ in Cl_{VT_i} in order of their starting time

09:     **While** available $tasks$ exists in Cl_{VT_i} **do**

10:       **For** $\forall t' \in Cl_{VT_i}$

11:         **If** $st(t') \geq ft(t'')$, $t'' = $ last task in g_m

12:           $g_m = g_m \cup t'$

13:         **End If**

14:       **End For**

15:       remove tasks in g_m from Cl_{VT_i}

16:       $m = m + 1$

17:     **End while**

18:   **End for**

19:   **For** $\forall g_m$

20:     $gct(g_m) = ft(g_m) - st(g_m)$

21:     **If** $\dfrac{c\left(RVM_{VT(g_m),gct(g_m)} \right)}{\sum_{\forall t \in g_m} et(t) \cdot c\left(OVM_{VT(t)} \right)} < 1$ **then**

22:     lease $RVM_{VT(g_m),gct(g_m)}$
                                  from cloud resource provider

23:     **End if**

24:   **End for**

VM Placement Management Scheme guarantees the network capacity for the continuous created VM considering the network interference occurred between co-location VMs, so that reduce the occurred data transmission delay between VMs for executing the scientific application efficiently. To do this, the science gateway manages the last used resource table *LastUsedResourceTable* for each user in order to save the physical node used lastly to create the VM. When a user requests a VM in the first time, there is no available last used resource information. In this case, the VM is created in a physical node *maxCapacityPN* having maximum free resource capacity within cloud server structure in order to increase the probability that the physical node keep a free resource capacity for the next VM creation of the user. After creating the VM, the information on the physical node of the created VM with the user id *uid* are saved to the last used resource table. When the user requests again, the last used resource information is available in the last used resource table. Therefore, a VM is created in the same physical node with the last used resource if possible in order to guarantee the maximum network bandwidth. In the case that the resource capacity of this physical node is not enough for the flavor type *f* requested by the user, available physical nodes *availablePNs* are sorted in the closest order from the physical node of the last used resource. The new physical node close to the physical node of the last used resource while having enough free resource capacity for flavor type *f* and having the smallest network traffic is chosen to reduce the network interference with other VMs on the physical node. The network traffic of each physical node is monitored in real-time. After finding the new physical node and creating the VM, the resource information on the new physical node is updated to the last used resource table for the corresponding user. Algorithm 2 shows the procedure of the proposed network aware VM placement algorithm.

Algorithm 2. VM Placement Management Scheme

Input : uid^k, f (uid^k : *request id*, f : *flavor type*)

Output : *created VM*

```
01: if LastUsedResource of uid^k is available
02:      physicalNode p^k ← get LastUsedResource of uid^k
03:      if physicalNode p^k is available for flavor type f
04:          createdVM = createNewVM(p^k, f)
05:          return createdVM
06:      else
07:          sort availablePNs in closest order from p^k
                 and split availablePNs into sameLevelPNs (∈ availablePNs )
08:          for sameLevelPNs ∈ availablePNs
                 sort sameLevelPNs in smallest traffic order
                 for p^i ∈ sameLevelPNs
09:                  if p^i is available for flavor type f
10:                      createdVM = createNewVM(p^i, f)
11:                      record {uid^k, p^k} into LastUsedResource
12:                      return createdVM
13:                  end if
                 end for
14:          end for
15:          return null
16:      end if
17:  else
18:      maxCapacityPN ← max( remainCapacity(p^j) )    ⋯  ( p^j ∈ PNSet )
19:      if maxCapacityPN is available for flavor type f
20:          createdVM = createNewVM(maxCapacityPN, f)
21:          record {uid^k, p^k} into LastUsedResource
22:          return createdVM
23:      else
24:          return null
25:      end if
26: end if
```

---

4   Test Environments and Performance Evaluation

For the evaluation, we built a science gateway, which is a solution platform to execute workflow typed scientific applications for solving complicated scientific problems by organizing the distributed heterogeneous cloud resources in this paper. The request from the user is dealt through the workflow designer as scientific application service provider. The workflow engine demands cloud resources to resource provisioning manager and process the scientific application. We applied a phased workflow scheduling scheme with division policy [3] as scheduler. Also, we organized Next Generation Sequencing (NGS) with Burrows-Wheeler Aligner (BWA) as a scientific application [4].

To evaluate the performance of the proposed schemes, we built the test environment with the science gateway as shown in Fig. 2 with the specific configuration on

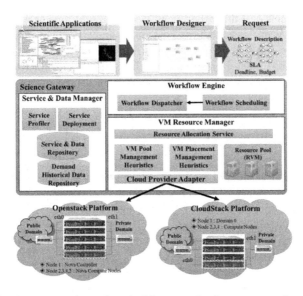

Fig. 2. An experimental testbed for cost adaptive resource schemes

Table 1. Specific configurations on testbed environment

		OpenStack Platform	CloudStack Platform
Hypervisor		KVM	XEN
H/W Specification		Intel Xeon E5620 2.40GHz, Core 16, MEM 16G, HDD 1T, 5 Node	Intel Core i7-3770 CPU 3.40GHz, Core 8, MEM 16G, HDD 1T, 4 Node
S/W Specification		OS: Ubuntu 14.04	OS: CentOS 6.0
VM Types	small	Spec: 1 VCPU, 2 GB MEM, 80GB Disk On-demand VM Unit Time Cost: 2 RC per second Reserved VM Unit Time Cost: 1,209,600 RC per week	
	medium	Spec: 2 VCPU, 4 GB MEM, 80GB Disk On-demand VM Unit Time Cost: 4 RC per second Reserved VM Unit Time Cost: 2,419,200 RC per week	
	large	Spec: 4 VCPU, 8 GB MEM, 80GB Disk On-demand VM Unit Time Cost: 8 RC per second Reserved VM Unit Time Cost: 4,838,400 RC per week	
	c4.small	Spec: 4 VCPU, 1 GB MEM, 80GB Disk Unit Time Cost: 4 RC per second Reserved VM Unit Time Cost: 2,419,200 RC per week	
	m8.small	Spec: 1 VCPU, 8 GB MEM, 80GB Disk Unit Time Cost: 4 RC per second Reserved VM Unit Time Cost: 2,419,200 RC per week	

testbed platform shown in Table 1. We organize the cloud platforms with 5 computing nodes on the OpenStack and 4 computing nodes on the CloudStack respectively [5, 6] to compose the heterogeneous resource.

We applied relative cost in order to evaluate the proposed scheme on cost performance in cloud environment. The definition of relative cost on the ith cloud service is described as Eq. (2) where c_u^i is unit time cost and t_u^i is resource usage time.

For the convenience of this experiment, we assign unit time as a second for OVM and a week for RVM. The unit time cost on resource contract c_{ur}^i is calculated as Eq. (3) where the weight vector $\vec{w} = [w_c, w_m]$ means the effectiveness of each element such as CPU core and memory respectively. The weight vector for RVM is applied to half of OVM's with the reference of CSP GoGrid (on annual case) [7].

$$RC^i = c_u^i \cdot t_u^i \tag{2}$$

$$c_{ur}^i = w_c \cdot r_c^i + w_m \cdot r_m^i \tag{3}$$

In the experiment of the VM pool management scheme, we measured relative cost on the sum of OVM leasing cost and RVM leasing cost between the case without VM pool management, the case of the VM pool management scheme with static number of RVM (1, 2 respectively) and the case of the proposed scheme on various average interarrival time of workflow request in exponential distribution. This experiment is executed in scale-downed 4 weeks.

As shown in Fig. 3, the measured VM leasing costs for three cases are expressed in log scale. Our proposed scheme shows good adaptivity and cost efficiency on the resource management compared to the static pool management for all environment case. Therefore, we can decrease the VM leasing cost by the proposed scheme.

In the experiment of the VM placement management scheme, we evaluate the performance of proposed scheme compared to the existing VM placement scheme proposed by Alicherry and Lakshman [8].

The proposed scheme has the smaller total data transmission delay over the entire request interarrival time compared to the existing scheme as shown in Fig. 4. The existing scheme cannot guarantees the network capacity for the continuous created VM on BWA

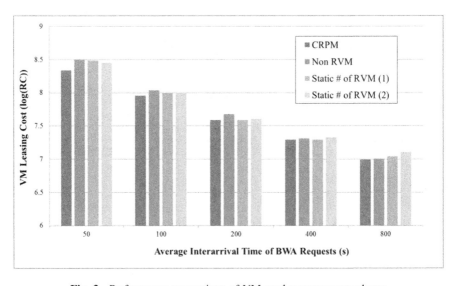

Fig. 3. Performance comparison of VM pool management scheme

service compared to the proposed scheme because it is only focused on the placement for a VM creation request and not considers the interference occurred by the traffic congestion.

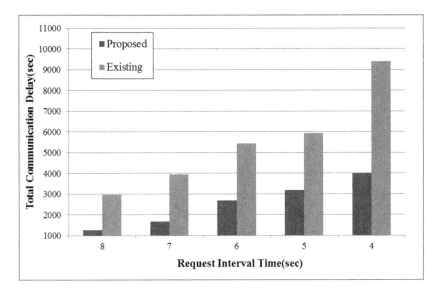

Fig. 4. The total data transmission delay of proposed scheme and existing scheme

5   Conclusion

In this paper, to decrease the resource usage cost while guaranteeing user's SLA on executing the scientific application in cloud environment, we propose and implement the science gateway with the cost adaptive resource management schemes. Experiment shows the proposed schemes decrease the expenditure of leasing VM instances and also guarantee the good performance. Finally, we demonstrate that our proposed schemes shows good adaptivity and cost efficiency compared to the existing schemes.

Acknowledgments. This work was supported by 'The Cross-Ministry Giga KOREA Project' grant from the Ministry of Science, ICT and Future Planning, Korea and the MSIP (Ministry of Science, ICT & Future Planning), Korea in the ICT R&D Program 2014.

References

1. Zhang, Q., Cheng, L., Boutaba, R.: Cloud computing: state-of-the art and research challenges. J. Internet Serv. Appl. **1**(1) (2010)
2. Chaisiri, S., Lee, B.S., Niyato, D.: Optimization of resource provisioning cost in cloud computing. IEEE Trans. Serv. Comput. **5**(2), 164–177 (2012)

3. Kim, S.-H., Joo, K.-N., Ha, Y.-G., Choi, G.-B., Youn, C.-H.: A phased workflow scheduling scheme with task division policy in cloud broker. In: Leung, V.C.M., Lai, R., Chen, M., Wan, J. (eds.) CloudComp 2014. LNICST, vol. 142, pp. 76–86. Springer, Heidelberg (2015)
4. BWA. http://bio-bwa.sourceforge.net
5. Openstack. http://www.openstack.org
6. Cloudstack. http://cloudstack.apache.org
7. GoGrid. http://www.gogrid.com/
8. Mansoor, A., Lakshman. T.V.: Network aware resource allocation in distributed clouds. In: 2012 Proceedings IEEE, INFOCOM. IEEE (2012)

Hybrid Workflow Management in Cloud Broker System

Dongsik Yoon[✉], Seong-Hwan Kim, Dong-Ki Kang,
and Chan-Hyun Youn

School of Electrical Engineering, KAIST, Daejeon 305-701, Korea
{dongsik.yoon,s.h_kim,dkkang,chyoun}@kaist.ac.kr

Abstract. In Cloud broker system, workflow application requests from different users are managed through workflow scheduling and resource provisioning. In workflow scheduling phase, most existing algorithms allocate each task on certain VM in serial. In general, single task does not fully utilize allocated resource such as CPU, memory, and so on. When multiple tasks are processed with same resource in parallel, the resource utilization is improved that leads to saving the cost. In order to solve this problem, the Parallel Task Merging scheme in the same VM is proposed, which saves the cost of execution while satisfying SLA deadline. After workflow scheduling, VM resource provisioning is required. Auto-scaling VM resources approach is proposed, which adjusts the number of VMs while the number of requests varies. In this paper, we do experiment the parallel task merging and auto-scaling approaches on different environments to observe on which conditions these two approaches are working well or not.

Keywords: Workflow scheduling · Virtual machine allocation · Cloud resource provisioning

1 Introduction

In Cloud system, various scientific workflow applications can be processed with different goals. In general, lowering the total execution time of workflow requires higher cost, while saving the total execution cost of workflow results in longer execution time. Moreover, there are many other things to consider such as selection of resource (including CPU cores, memory, storage, and so on) types, ordering tasks in workflow to execute and Virtual Machine (VM) allocation of each task. To support these whole procedures, Cloud broker system was proposed to mediate between service users and resource providers. In Cloud broker system, guaranteeing the fairness between many users is additional challenge [1].

Workflow management by Cloud broker system can be categorized into two main parts; workflow scheduling and resource provisioning [1]. When users submit workflow applications with their Service Level Agreement (SLA) such as deadline or budget to the broker system, the workflow application is parsed into tasks connected with dependencies, which is represented as Directed Acyclic Graph (DAG). In workflow scheduling phase, the information of each task such as earliest start time, latest finish time, historically earliest execution time or estimated execution time on each VM type should be obtained. Furthermore, each task should be ordered and VM type should be decided to be allocated to the task, while SLA is not violated. When the scheduling of each workflow is executed, available VM resource with proper type should be allocated to each task. However, in heterogeneous distributed computing system environment, such workflow task scheduling is generally NP-complete problem [2]. Since the arrival of each task is random and the status of resource is changing, dynamic scheduling is required. Furthermore, in resource allocation process, task affinity obtained by profiling should be used, which refers to the degree of suitability to certain computing resource. Such task ordering and allocating resource problems constitute the workflow scheduling, which is difficult to solve.

Scheduling of single workflow application has been studied by many researches. The main goal of the workflow scheduling is to reduce total execution time using limited resource or budget. One of the workflow scheduling algorithms is Heterogeneous Earliest-Finish Time (HEFT) algorithm [3]. It considers critical path to minimize makespan which is actual execution time on the distributed computing environment. The critical path means the longest path in the workflow. However, HEFT algorithm is a single objective scheduling considering only makespan, not the execution cost. Furthermore, this algorithm is a static scheduling that is hard to cope with unexpected results. Another workflow scheduling algorithm is IaaS Cloud Partial Critical Path (IC-PCP) algorithm [4]. It is multiple objective scheduling which considers both cost and time, but static scheduling algorithm. Additionally, Time Distribution (TD) Heuristics [5] is dynamic scheduling and multiple objective scheduling. It has a goal to minimize the cost while satisfying the deadline given by user. On task division phase, it classifies simple tasks and synchronization tasks which have multiple parent nodes or child nodes. On planning phase, all workflow tasks are allocated to proper resources based on Markov Decision Process (MDP) [6].

In addition, GAIN/LOSS approach [7] is the heuristic based workflow scheduling. All tasks are allocated on resources that minimize the makespan, then re-allocated by using GAIN/LOSS weight value. This approach does not guarantee the best optimization, however it has low time complexity and easiness to implement.

With the existing workflow scheduling algorithms, each request from users is isolated and allocated to separate VMs. In result, each task in a certain VM is executed in serial, not in parallel. However, in general, single task does not use full allocated resources such as CPU, memory and so on, which means that the resource on processing each task is not maximally utilized [8].

In this paper, we propose the Parallel Task Merging approach to improve the resource utilization in processing workflow applications, for saving the total execution cost. In our proposed scheme, multiple tasks are simultaneously processed on the same VM instance when certain conditions are satisfied. With this parallel task merging scheme, the utilization of resources can be increased, which results in saving the cost of VM resources.

When the workflow scheduling is completed, Cloud broker system should allocate each task to VM type decided in scheduling phase. To support this, Cloud broker system should monitor resource utilization and adjust the number of VMs. In this paper, we propose and utilize dynamic Auto-scaling cloud resource scheme. This scheme adjusts the number of VM resources according to workflow application requests.

The rest of the paper is organized as follows. Section 2 describes the details of the Parallel Task Merging approach in workflow scheduling phase and Auto-scaling approach in VM resource provisioning phase. Section 3 presents and evaluates the experimental results. Section 4 concludes the paper.

2 A Hybrid Model of the Parallel Task Merging and Auto-Scaling Algorithms in Cloud Broker System

2.1 Problem Description

When the workflow applications are executed in Cloud environment, the workflow scheduling and resource provisioning constitutes two main parts. Since the whole procedure of workflow management is considerably complicated for ordinary users, Cloud broker system was suggested as an intermediary [1]. The relationships between workflow service users, Cloud broker system and resource providers are presented as shown in Fig. 1.

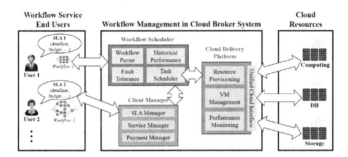

Fig. 1. An architecture of workflow management system in Cloud service [1]

At the beginning, a user submits tasks to be scheduled to Cloud resource broker with SLA constraints. The received workflow is parsed to individual tasks and dependencies between tasks in Workflow Management Module. The parsed workflow is then scheduled by VM allocator using workflow scheduling algorithm. When the workflow scheduling process is executed, the actual allocation of VMs to the given workflow is conducted by Cloud computing resource adaptor.

However, the existing workflow scheduling algorithms isolate each request from users and allocate tasks to separate VMs, while each single task usually does not maximally utilize allocated resources such as CPU, memory, and so on. Moreover, the resource pool management could be more efficient if VM requests are predicted and the number of VMs is adjusted, while keeping backup idle VMs to save the startup time.

2.2 The Parallel Task Merging and Auto-Scaling Scheme

To increase the utilization of VMs in a compact way, we propose the Parallel Task Merging algorithm. This approach merges multiple tasks on the same VM instance for running simultaneously, if the VM cost is reduced and possibly increased execution time does not violate SLA deadline. To adopt this approach, it is essential to acquire the execution time of merged tasks on the same VM instance prior to the workflow scheduling processes. Despite such parallel task merging would result in increasing execution time of each task, it is worthy only if SLA deadline is still not violated because the VM cost would be saved. In reality, many tasks are not fully utilizing given resources such as CPU and memory, which makes parallel-task-merging possible.

A workflow application is represented as a directed acyclic graph $G(Q, E)$, where Q is a set of n tasks $(q_1, q_2, \ldots, q_n)$ and E is a set of m edges $(e_1, e_2, \ldots, e_m)$ [1, 4, 5, 8]. Each edge represents dependency between two tasks. The task which does not have any parent task is q_{start} and the task which does not have any child task is q_{end}. To adapt our approach, SLA deadline should be submitted with workflow $G(Q, E)$ to be scheduled. When the scheduling is executed, the VM type among the set of VM flavor types *FlavorSet* to be allocated on each task q_i is decided, and each task q_i is allocated on proper VM instance, which is represented as VM_{q_i}. Such task scheduling and resource allocation is a hard problem, because of data dependencies between tasks according to constraint of the workflow topology.

To adapt parallel task merging approach, the workflow should be initially scheduled by some existing approach. In this paper, we use GAIN/LOSS which is heuristic based resource allocating algorithm [7]. In GAIN approach, all tasks are allocated to resources that minimize the execution cost, then re-allocated to the machine where the largest makespan benefit is obtained by the smallest cost. This is repeated until the whole budgets are exceed. On the other hand, in LOSS approach, tasks that are initially scheduled by existing scheduling algorithm are re-allocated to cheaper machine, until the cost becomes equal or less than budget.

Once the workflow is scheduled, the parallel task merging approach shown in Fig. 2 is executed. If two tasks are overlapped and satisfies all conditions to be merged, then two tasks are allocated to the same VM and executed in parallel. Although the execution time of each task could be increased, it does not affect the total execution time of workflow much, because the tasks on the critical path, which represents the longest path in workflow and decides the total execution time, is not considered to be merged.

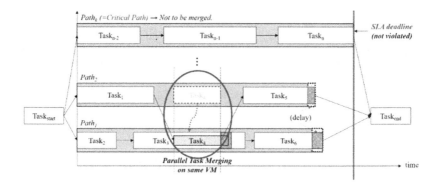

Fig. 2. Parallel task merging approach

The pseudo code of the parallel task merging is shown in Fig. 3. Input is the initially scheduled workflow $G_1(Q,E)$ and SLA deadline from the user. Q_{merged} is the set which contains the task pairs to be merged, and initially set to null. For all task pairs (q_i, q_j) in the workflow which are not in Q_{merged} and $CriticalPath$, merge q_i into q_j in VM_{q_j} if they are overlapped. $ST(q_i)$ is the start time of task q_i and $ET(q_i)$ is the end time of task q_i. Tasks on $CriticalPath$ are not considered to be merged, because parallel task merging increases the execution time of each task and $CriticalPath$ decides the total execution time of whole workflow. If the total execution time of workflow is increased, then SLA deadline could be violated. The execution time of q_i and q_j after merging is calculated as follows,

$$XT(q_i)_{aftermerging.VM_{q_j}} = (XT(q_i)_{alone.VM_{q_j}} - OT(q_i,q_j)_{alone.VM_{q_j}}) + \frac{OT(q_i,q_j)_{alone.VM_{q_j}}}{XT(q_i)_{alone.VM_{q_j}}} \cdot XT(q_i)_{merged.VM_{q_j}}$$

(1)

$$XT(q_j)_{aftermerging.VM_{q_j}} = (XT(q_j)_{alone.VM_{q_j}} - OT(q_i,q_j)_{alone.VM_{q_j}}) + \frac{OT(q_i,q_j)_{alone.VM_{q_j}}}{XT(q_j)_{alone.VM_{q_j}}} \cdot XT(q_j)_{merged.VM_{q_j}}$$

(2)

where $XT(q_i)_{aftermerging.VM_{q_j}}$ is the execution time of q_i when (q_i, q_j) are merged on VM_j. Additionally, $XT(q_i)_{alone.VM_{q_j}}$ is the execution time of q_i on VM_{q_j} without merging and $OT(q_i,q_j)_{alone.VM_{q_j}}$ is the overlapped execution time of (q_i, q_j) on VM_{q_j} without merging. Using the execution time after merging, check whether $XT(q_i)_{aftermerging.VM_{q_j}} + XT(q_j)_{aftermerging.VM_{q_j}} - OT(q_i,q_j)_{afteremerging.VM_{q_j}}$ is shorter than $XT(q_i) + XT(q_j)$, which means execution time before merging of q_i and q_j, respectively. With the changed information of VMs, the total cost of the workflow $TotalCost(G_2(Q,E))$ is also calculated. If the first condition is satisfied and the total cost of the workflow after merging is less than the original total cost of the workflow, then put (q_i, q_j) task pair into Q_{merged} set. After all these recursive procedures, the re-scheduled workflow $G_2(Q,E)$ is output.

When the workflow scheduling is executed, the Cloud broker system should manage resource provisioning. In this paper, we propose Auto-scaling scheme which adjusts VM resource provision according to varying workflow application requests. The pseudo code of the auto-scaling scheme is shown in Fig. 4. This scheme predicts VM requests in each VM type using the autoregressive integrated moving average (ARIMA) model [9–11] and is conducted every period T. The number of predicted VM requests in each VM type is calculated as follows,

---

Algorithm 1. Parallel Task Merging
Input: Initially scheduled workflow $G_1(Q, E)$, SLA deadline
Output: Workflow $G_2(Q, E)$ with parallel task merging

Q_{merged} ←null
for all ($q_i \in Q$ and $q_i \notin Q_{merged}$ and $q_i \in CriticalPath$) **do**
  for all ($q_j \neq q_i$ and $q_j \in Q$ and $q_j \notin Q_{merged}$ and $q_j \in CriticalPath$) **do**
    if ($ST(q_j) \leq ST(q_i)$ and $ET(q_j) > ST(q_i)$) **then**
      $G_2(Q, E)$ ←apply task merging of (q_i, q_j) to VM_{q_j} for $G_1(Q, E)$
      calculate $XT(q_i)_{afteremerging.VM_{q_j}}$ and $XT(q_j)_{aftermerging.VM_{q_j}}$ (using
Eqs. (1) and (2))
      calculate $OT(q_i, q_j)_{afteremerging.VM_{q_j}}$
      if ($XT(q_i)_{afteremerging.VM_{q_j}} + XT(q_j)_{aftermerging.VM_{q_j}} - OT(q_i,q_j)_{afteremerging.VM_{q_j}} \leq$
$XT(q_i) + XT(q_j)$ and $TotalCost(G_2(Q,E)) < TotalCost(G_1(Q,E))$) **then**
        Q_{merged} ←add (q_i, q_j)
      end if
    end if
  end for
end for
$G_2(Q, E)$ ←$G_1(Q, E)$
for all ($(q_i, q_j) \in Q_{merged}$) **do**
  $G_2(Q, E)$ ←apply task merging of (q_i, q_j) to VM_{q_j} for $G_1(Q, E)$
end for

Fig. 3. The algorithm of parallel task merging scheme

$$N_{instance,k}^{predicted}(t) = \left\lfloor \frac{1}{T} \sum_{i=t}^{t+T} R_{p,k}(i) - N_{instance,k}^{processing}(i) \right\rfloor \qquad (3)$$

where $N_{instance,k}^{predicted}(t)$ is the number of predicted VM requests in VM type k, $R_{p,k}(t)$ is the predicted requests in VM type k during $[t, t+1]$ and $N_{instance,k}^{processing}$ is the number of VM instances in VM type k which is processing some jobs. If obtained $N_{instance,k}^{predicted}(t)$ is greater than zero, then add $N_{instance,k}^{predicted}(t) + N_{instance,k}^{backup}$ VM instances in VM type k. Otherwise, remove $N_{instance,k}^{predicted}(t) - N_{instance,k}^{backup}$ VM instances in VM type k. $N_{instance,k}^{backup}$ is the number of backup idle VM in VM type k. With this scheme, there are always $N_{instance,k}^{backup}$ backup VMs in each VM type which process nothing to save some time in generating new VM instance. The goal of this approach is to keep low number of VMs leading to better cost efficiency, while keeping backup idle VMs in each VM type to save VM instance startup time.

Algorithm 2. Auto-scaling VM resources
Input:
historical VM requests in each VM type during $[t - T, t - 1]$, where T is a VM requests prediction period
set VMTYPE: each component of set is VM flavor type

for all $(k \in \text{VMTYPE})$ **do**
   predict VM requests during $[t, t + T]$
   calculate $N_{instance,k}^{predicted}(t)$ (using Eq. (3))
   if $(N_{instance,k}^{predicted}(t) > 0)$ **then**
      add $N_{instance,k}^{predicted}(t) + N_{instance,k}^{backup}$ VM instances in VM type k
   else
      remove $N_{instance,k}^{predicted}(t) - N_{instance,k}^{backup}$ VM instances in VM type k
   end if
end for

Fig. 4. The algorithm of auto-scaling VM resources scheme

In Sect. 3, we test the workflow management process to evaluate our two proposed schemes. The parallel task merging approach is adopted in workflow scheduling phase, and the auto-scaling scheme is adopted in resource provisioning phase. Through the experiment, we discuss how much cost could be saved through increasing the utilization of resources with the proposed approaches, while satisfying SLA deadlines.

3 Experimental Environment and Performance Evaluation

In order to evaluate the performance of the parallel task merging scheme with auto-scaling resource provisioning, we establish and execute Cloud resource broker system on the Cloud environment using OpenStack [12], which is the open source Cloud platform. In addition, we utilize one of the OpenStack component called Nova, which support VM resource managements such as VM instance allocation, VM image enrollment, VM flavor type management, and so on. The details of the experimental configuration is shown in Fig. 5. In our experiment, we use 5 HP Xeon (2.4 GHz) machines consisting of 4 Nova compute nodes for actual computing works, and one Nova controller node which manages the entire operations between compute nodes. Each machine has 8 CPU cores, 16 GB Memory, 1 TB storage and two wired Network Interface Cards (NIC) which generate private and public network. OpenStack Cloud platform in our experiment is based on Ubuntu 15.04.

In our experiment, we adopt open-source based scientific workflow application called Montage [13]. Montage is a toolkit, which is designed to assemble Flexible Image Transport System (FITS) images into custom mosaics. In our experiment, we use M105, M106 and M108 FITS images to be processed by Montage application. During the Montage workflow process, each FITS image is processed by several tasks in workflow, which are called mImgtbl, mMakeHdr, mProjExec, mAdd and MJPEG.

OpenStack

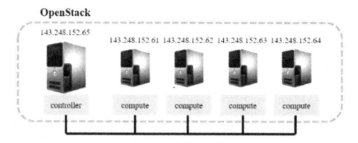

	Node 1	Node 2	Node 3	Node 4	Node 5
Function	Cloud Controller node Network, Volume, API, Scheduler and Image Services Nova compute	Nova Compute	Nova Compute	Nova Compute	Nova Compute
Specification	H/W: HP, Intel Xeon E5620 2.4GHz, 8 cores, Mem 16GB, HDD 1TB, Wired NIC 2EA OS: Ubuntu 15.04				
IP addresses	Eth0 (143.248.152.65)	Eth0 (143.248.152.61)	Eth0 (143.248.152.62)	Eth0 (143.248.152.63)	Eth0 (143.248.152.64)
	Eth1 (192.168.3.5)	Eth1 (192.168.3.1)	Eth1 (192.168.3.2)	Eth1 (192.168.3.3)	Eth1 (192.168.3.4)

Fig. 5. OpenStack-based experimental environment

Among these tasks in Montage application, we only consider mProjExec, mAdd and MJPEG tasks, because other tasks have negligibly small processing time. Therefore, we totally have 9 tasks by using three FITS images. With these tasks, we compose three virtual workflow models shown in Fig. 6, which are to be processed by Cloud broker system for evaluating the performance our approaches.

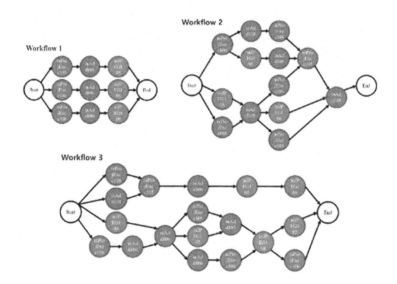

Fig. 6. Three test workflows composed of Montage application tasks [13]

In addition, in order to mimic the real VM type model of Cloud provider, we adopt GoGrid [14] provider model. The configuration of each VM flavor type and cost is shown in Table 1. In this paper, we suppose that the cost is charged based on the exact resource using time, unlike commercial pricing model that charges based on fixed time unit, such as hour, month or year.

In our experiment, we utilize three workflow types shown in Fig. 6. Each workflow type with its own deadline and budget forms each service user type. Accordingly, there are three user types. These user types have deadlines of 300, 700 and 800 s and budgets of 33.33, 60 and 66.67 dollars, respectively. The inter arrival time of requests from users conforms to exponential distribution with mean 500 s and request type is randomly selected each time. Since our parallel task merging scheme requires initial workflow scheduling with resource allocation, we adopt GAIN and LOSS algorithms [7] as an initial scheduling. Prior to adopt our approach on workflow scheduling process, we acquire the execution time of merged tasks on same VM instance from many experimental results.

Figure 7 shows the execution time and cost of each workflow scheduled by GAIN algorithm without and with our parallel task merging scheme. When parallel task merging scheme is adapted on GAIN scheduling algorithm, the total execution cost of

Table 1. VM pricing model corresponding to each flavor type [14]

VM type	CPU core(s)	RAM	Storage	Cost per hour
Small	1	1 GB	50 GB	$0.08
Medium	2	2 GB	100 GB	$0.16
Large	4	4 GB	200 GB	$0.32
X-large	8	8 GB	400 GB	$0.64

each workflow is decreased by 12.7 %, 2.5 %, 2.2 % respectively, compared to original GAIN algorithm. On the other hand, the total execution time of each workflow is increased by 1.3 %, 0.6 %, 2.8 % respectively, however, it does not violate each SLA deadline.

Similarly, Fig. 8 shows the execution results of each workflow scheduled by LOSS algorithm without and with our proposed scheme. When parallel task merging scheme

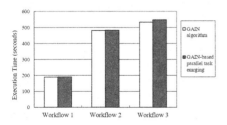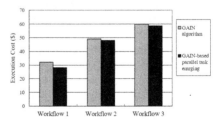

Fig. 7. Execution time and cost of GAIN and the proposed algorithms

is adapted on LOSS scheduling algorithm, the total execution cost of each workflow is decreased by 11.5 %, 20.4 %, 0.9 % respectively, compared to LOSS algorithm

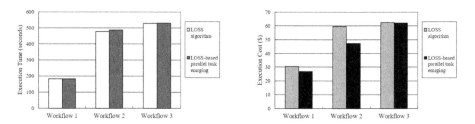

Fig. 8. Execution time and cost of LOSS and the proposed algorithms

without our approach. The total execution time of each workflow is increased by 0.1 %, 1.9 %, 0.5 % respectively, however, it still satisfies each SLA deadline.

Since the goal of our parallel task merging approach is to increase the resource utilization, the execution cost is decreased while the total execution time is increased. However, the increased execution time is not huge to violate SLA deadline, because when we choose the tasks to be executed in parallel, tasks in the critical path are not selected. Therefore, the increased time caused by parallel execution of tasks has a few influence to affect the whole execution time of workflow. Moreover, if total increased time of tasks does not make the each corresponding path to reach the time length of critical path, then the execution time of workflow would be totally unrelated to our parallel task merging scheme. Additionally, the auto-scaling approach also contributes to saving the cost of resources, since this approach allocates many requests on each VM as long as the number of requests does not exceed upper limit.

4   Conclusion

In this paper, we proposed two algorithms in Cloud broker system that consists of workflow scheduling phase and resource provisioning phase. In workflow scheduling part, most traditional approaches have allocated each task on certain resource in serial, not in parallel. However, generally single task does not maximize the utilization of given resource, which led us to propose the parallel task merging approach that allocate overlapped multiple tasks on the same resource, simultaneously. In resource provisioning part, we proposed auto-scaling approach, which adjust the number of VMs according to changing the number of requests.

Through the experimental performance evaluation, we showed that our proposed approaches decreased the total execution cost of each workflow compared to conventional GAIN and LOSS algorithms [7], while the SLA deadline was still satisfied. Generally, single task does not maximally utilize allocated resource such as CPU, memory, and so on. With our parallel task merging scheme, the multiple tasks were processed on the same resource simultaneously, which led to the improved resource utilization and the decreased cost. Additionally, in the resource provisioning phase, the proposed auto-scaling algorithm made the efficient resource pool management through adjusting the number of VMs and maximizing the utilization of VMs.

Acknowledgments. This work was supported by 'The Cross-Ministry Giga KOREA Project' grant from the Ministry of Science, ICT and Future Planning, Korea.

References

1. Ren, Y.: A cloud collaboration system with active application control scheme and its experimental performance analysis. Master's thesis, KAIST (2012)
2. Gary, M.R., Johnson, D.S.: Computers and Intractability: A Guide to the Theory of NP-Completeness. W.H. Freeman and Co., New York (1979)
3. Topcuoglu, H., Hariri, S., Wu, M.Y.: Performance-effective and low-complexity task scheduling for heterogeneous computing. IEEE Trans. Parallel Distrib. Syst. (2002)
4. Abrishami, S., Naghibzadeh, M., Epema, D.H.J.: Deadline-constrained workflow scheduling algorithms for infrastructure as a service clouds. Future Gener. Comput. Syst. (2013). (Elsevier)
5. Yu, J., Buyya, R., Tham, C.K.: Cost-based scheduling of scientific workflow applications on utility grids. In: International Conference on e-Science and Grid Computing (2005)
6. Howard, R.A.: Dynamic Programming and Markov Processes. The Massachusetts Institute of Technology Press, Cambridge (1960)
7. Sakellariou, R., Zhao, H.: Scheduling workflows with budget constraints. In: Gorlatch, S., Danelutto, M. (eds.) Integrated Research in GRID Computing. CoreGRID Series. Springer, Heidelberg (2007)
8. Kang, D.K., Kim, S.H., Youn, C.H., Chen, M.: Cost adaptive workflow scheduling in cloud computing. In: ICUIMC. ACM (2014)
9. Brockwell, P.J., Davis, R.A.: Introduction to Time Series and Forecasting. Springer, New York (2002)
10. Fang, W., Lu, Z., Wu, J., Cao, Z.: RPPS: a novel resource prediction and provisioning scheme in cloud data center. In: IEEE Ninth International Conference on Services Computing (2012)
11. Kim, H., Ha, Y., Kim, Y., Joo, K.-N., Youn, C.-H.: A VM reservation-based cloud service broker and its performance evaluation. In: Leung, V.C.M., Lai, R., Chen, M., Wan, J. (eds.) CloudComp 2014. LNICST, vol. 142, pp. 43–52. Springer, Heidelberg (2015)
12. OpenStack. https://www.openstack.org/
13. Montage, An Astronomical Image Mosaic Engine. http://montage.ipac.caltech.edu/
14. GoGrid. https://www.datapipe.com/gogrid/

Mobile Cloud and Media Services

Mobile Cloud Computing System Components Composition Formal Verification Method Based on Space-Time Pi-Calculus

Peng Wang[1,2(✉)], Ling Yang[2], and Guo Wen Li[3]

[1] School of Management Fudan University, Shanghai, China
wangpeng@shcloudvalley.com
[2] Shanghai Cloud Valley Development Co., Ltd., Shanghai, China
yangling@shcloudvalley.com
[3] Shanghai Yangpu Science and Technology Innovation Group Co., Ltd.,
Shanghai, China
liguowen@shcloudvalley.com

Abstract. To build different mobile cloud computing system (MCS) business applications, how to design open system architecture is essential. First, a service-oriented architecture is put forward. In this architecture, MCS components are expressed as the form of interoperable MCS services, which are combined to achieve complex business needs. Second, a formal method is proposed based on space-time (S-T) Pi-calculus, in order to verify validity of MCS service composition model. Finally, the case study shows that how to apply the model and method. The experiment result shows that they are feasible.

Keywords: Mobile cloud computing · Service composition · Service-oriented architecture · Pi-calculus

1 Introduction

Mobile Cloud Computing is the combination of cloud computing, mobile computing and wireless networks to bring rich computational resources to mobile users, network operators, as well as cloud computing providers [1]. As the evolution of cloud computing, mobile cloud computing network resources are virtualized and allocated a set number of distributed computers rather than in the traditional local computer or servers. And they are assigned to the mobile devices such as intelligent mobile phone, smart terminal, etc. [2, 3]. On account of mobile cloud computing system (MCS) includes physical device, it is complex to design the architecture of MCS. Sat. M. proposed a system architecture, which uses virtual platform to offer personalized services to mobile device, but it doesn't resolve latent WAN latency issues [4]. Zhang X. put forward a flexible application programming model which constructed by CloneCloud, forever it's difficult to provide middleware to storage data mechanisms at terminal and cloud side [5].

This work is supported by China Postdoctoral Science Foundation funded project (No. 2014M 551334), special fund for Shanghai Zhangjiang National Innovation Demonstration Zone (No. ZJ2015ZD006).

© ICST Institute for Computer Sciences, Social Informatics and Telecommunications Engineering 2016
Y. Zhang et al. (Eds.): CloudComp 2015, LNICST 167, pp. 159–167, 2016.
DOI: 10.1007/978-3-319-38904-2_16

In this paper, we proposed a novel SOA [6] architecture, in which hardware and software of MCS are integrated together in the form of compatible services. And these services can be combined to implement complex operational requirements.

Formal validation method is indispensable to verify the stability MCS service composition model, and the researches on it have achieved the rapid development, such as Finite State Machines [7] and Petri Net [8]. However, state-space-explosion of using charts is brought a big challenge. Pi-calculus [9] is able to represent concurrent computations as a formal analysis tool, although it's bound by space and time constraints, which is included in MCS [10]. In this paper, S-T Pi-calculus is presented by bring space and time operator into Pi-calculus, and a formal verification for MCS components composition is proposed based upon.

The remainder of this paper is organized as follows. The next section presents the conceptions of MCS service and S-T Pi-calculus. Section 3 devises a formal verification for verifying validity of MCS service composition. Section 4 presents a case study to show the applicability of model and formal verification. The paper concludes in Sect. 5.

2 Basic Conceptions

2.1 MCS Service View

We regard MCS as a combination of encapsulated MCS services, which includes units of mobile terminal, cloud computing and communications, as shown in Fig. 1. Mobile terminal unit is composed of computing terminals, sensors, and actuators. Communications unit offers communicative mechanism by utilizing mobile communication network. Cloud computing unit realizes functions of computation, control and storage, and it implements temporal and spatial management. Discrete domain blends with continuous domain in this unit.

MCS service interfaces' implementation details are hidden, which can be realized by different technologies from any service provider. There are characteristics, operation guide, access protocol, parameters and data types in interfaces description. The interfaces are provided to receipt and transmit messages, and it would take time to finish the receipt-transmit acts. As described above, we define MCS service view as follows.

Definition 1 (MCS Service View). $\equiv MCSV = (R, r_0, S, U, W, E, f, g)$. A brief description of each element is listed below.

$R = \{r_0, r_1, \ldots\}$: finite states set of MCS service.
r_0: initial state.
S: final states set, $S \subseteq R$.
$U = Act \cup \overline{Act} \cup \{\tau\}$: act set. $Act = \{a | a \in \Sigma\}$ is receipting act set (Σ is alphabet); $\overline{Act} = \{\overline{a} | a \in \Sigma\}$ is transmitting act set; τ is internal act.
$W \subseteq R \times U \times R$: relation of state transformation.
E: MCS service messages set.
$f: U \to E$ act-message function. $\forall x \in U$, $f(x)$ represent receipting or transmitting messages of x.
$g: U \to R^+$ act-time function. $\forall x \in U$, $g(x)$ represent the time spending in finishing x.

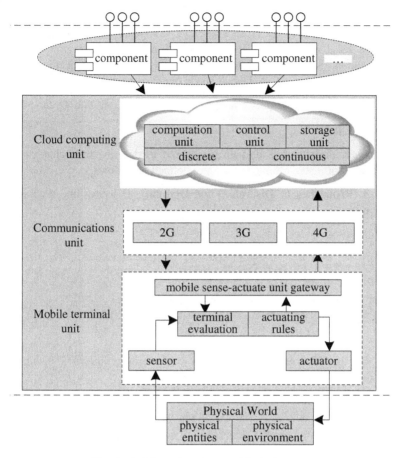

Fig. 1. MCS service structure block diagram

2.2 S-T Pi-Calculus

By definition, there is a tight correspondence between process of Pi-calculus and MCS service. Concretely speaking, channel corresponds to act; transmitting and receipting variable corresponds to transmitting and receipting message of act; composition, process, summation, replication in Pi-calculus correspond to structures of parallel, sequence, case and iterative. Nevertheless, there are no syntaxes representing temporal and spatial features. In this paper, we propose space and time operators, and define what syntaxes and operational semantics of S-T Pi-calculus are.

Physical modules of MCS are abstracted to spatial objects based on topological relation theory of spatial database [11]. Topological relations between two spatial objects, which are regarded as point sets, are expressed by a quaternion formed by boundary and interior of point set. Let M and N indicate two geospatial objects, and let $\partial M, M^0, \partial N, N^0$ represent interior and boundary. The quaternion is $\mathbf{R}(M,N) = \begin{pmatrix} \partial M \cap \partial N & \partial M \cap N^0 \\ M^0 \cap \partial N & M^0 \cap N^0 \end{pmatrix}$. There are eight kinds of topology models i.e., inside, disjoint, contain, meet, overlap, equal, covered, and cover by, and they are indicated by $S_{loc} = \{s_{in}, s_{ct}, s_d, s_m, s_o, s_e, s_c, s_{cb}\}$. Supposing Q includes m physical modules, and let d_i represents relationship between benchmark region and the i-th module's location. $\exists\ S_i \subseteq S_{loc}$, this module could work properly meeting criteria of $d_i \in S_i$. Let $S = \{S_1, S_2, \ldots, S_m\}$. Define space operator below.

Definition 2 (Space Operator). $\equiv Loc[S]$. $Loc[S]Q$ expresses that Q can start only when $\prod\limits_{i=1}^{n} d_i \in S_i$ is true.

In this paper, discrete time domain is adopted to describe time characteristic of MCS. Properties of discrete time domain are defined as follows.

Definition 3 (Properties of Discrete Time Domain). Discrete time domain T has following properties.

(1) $\forall t \in T,\ t \neq \infty \Rightarrow \infty > t$;
(2) $\forall t \in T,\ t \neq 0 \Rightarrow t > 0$;
(3) $\forall t \in T,\ t + 0 = t,\ t + \infty = \infty$;
(4) $\forall t, t' \in T,\ t > t' \Leftrightarrow \exists \Delta t > 0,\ t' + \Delta t = t$;
(5) $\forall t, t' \in T,\ (t > 0) \wedge (t' \neq \infty) \Rightarrow t' + t > t'$;
(6) $\forall t_2, t_3 \in T,\ \forall [t_1, t_4],\ \exists t', t' \in T,\ t_2 \leq t' \leq t_4$, then $t' \in [t_1, t_2]$;
(7) $\forall t_1, t_2 \in T,\ t_1 > t_2,\ \{t | t_1 \leq t \leq t_2\}$ is represented as $[t_1, t_2]$.

Definition 4 (Time Operator). $\equiv Int(t_r, \Delta t)$, t_r is reference time, $\Delta t \geq 0$. $Int(t_r, \Delta t)Q$ represents Q can start only when it meets $t \in [t_r, t_r + \Delta t]$.

Definition 5 (Syntax of S-T Pi-Calculus).

$$Q ::= 0 | \bar{a}\langle x \rangle.Q | a(x).Q | \tau.Q | Q + P | Q | P | (x)Q | [x = y]Q | !Q | \\ Loc[S]Q | Int(t_r, \Delta t)Q \qquad (1)$$

See reference [10] for concrete meanings of the above expressions.

Definition 6 (Operational Semantics of S-T Pi-Calculus).

(1) Space operator.

$$\frac{Q \xrightarrow{\alpha} Q'}{Loc[S]Q \xrightarrow{\alpha} Q'},\ c_i \in S_i;$$

$$\frac{Q \xrightarrow{\alpha} Q'}{Loc[S]Q \xrightarrow{\alpha} 0},\ c_i \notin S_i;$$

(2) Time operator ($\alpha \in \{\tau,\ a(x),\ \bar{a}\langle x \rangle\}$).

$$\frac{Q \xrightarrow{\alpha} Q'}{Int(t_r, \Delta t)Q \xrightarrow{\alpha} Q'}, \ t \in [t_r, t_r + \Delta t];$$

$$\frac{Q \xrightarrow{\alpha} Q'}{Int(t_r, \Delta t)Q \xrightarrow{\alpha} 0}, \ t \notin [t_r, t_r + \Delta t];$$

See reference [10] for other operational semantics.

3 A Formal Verification for MCS Components Composition

Basic MCS service portfolio modes include sequence structure, selection structure, parallel structure and recursive structure. They can be expressed as S-T Pi–calculus process expressions as follows.

(1) Sequence structure

$MCSV_1$ sends a message *msg* to $MCSV_2$ from port a, and then $MCSV_2$ receives this message from port b, as shown in Fig. 2.

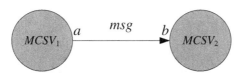

Fig. 2. Sequence structure

This structure can be expressed as following process expressions.

$$\bar{a}\langle msg \rangle.MCSV_1 \text{ and } b(msg).MCSV_2$$

(2) Selection structure

$MCSV_1$ selects to send one message from port a. If it sends msg_1, $MCSV_2$ would receive this message from port b. If it sends msg_2, $MCSV_3$ would receive this message from port c, as shown in Fig. 3.

This structure can be expressed as following process expressions.

$$(\bar{a}\langle msg_1 \rangle.MCSV_1) + (\bar{a}\langle msg_2 \rangle.MCSV_1),$$
$$b(msg_1).MCSV_2 \text{ and } c(msg_2).MCSV_3$$

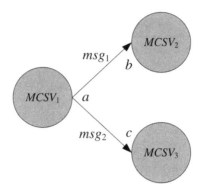

Fig. 3. Selection structure

(3) Parallel structure

$MCSV_1$ sends a message msg_1 to $MCSV_2$ from port a, and then $MCSV_2$ receives this message from port c. Meanwhile, $MCSV_1$ also sends a message msg_2 to $MCSV_2$ from port b, and then $MCSV_2$ receives this message from port d, as shown in Fig. 4.

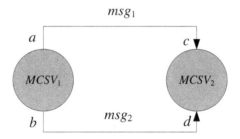

Fig. 4. Parallel structure

This structure can be expressed as following process expressions.

$$(\bar{a}\langle msg_1\rangle.MCSV_1)|(\bar{b}\langle msg_2\rangle.MCSV_1) \text{ and } (c(msg_1).MCSV_2)|(d(msg_2).MCSV_2)$$

(4) Recursive structure

$MCSV_1$ sends the same message msg to $MCSV_2$ repeatedly from port a, and $MCSV_2$ receives this message constantly from port b, as shown in Fig. 5.

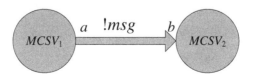

Fig. 5. Recursive structure

This structure can be expressed as following process expressions.

$$!(\bar{a}\langle msg\rangle.MCSV_1)\ \text{and}\ !(b(msg).MCSV_2)$$

A formal verification is put forward for MCS service composition as the following three steps. First, a S-T Pi–calculus model is constructed based on MCS service portfolio modes. Secondly, temporal and spatial attributes of actual MCS services are introduced into the Pi–calculus model. Thirdly, from the process expression being deadlock or not, we can judge whether this MCS service composition can reach the final state. Then, the validity of MCS service composition can be verified.

4 Experiments and Results

In this section, We take Parking Electric Fence in Shanghai YangPu center business circle for example, to demonstrate the formal verification about building and validating a MCS components composition. Business case is described below. If a owner wants to stop, his request from intelligent terminal will be sent to vehicle dispatch center. In case there are no spaces available, the dispatch center would set electric fence. Meanwhile all cars inside the virtual fence would receive early warnings periodically.

Parking electric fence is designed to four MCS services as shown in Fig. 6. Let $P_{pr}, P_{vs}, P_{vf}, P_{ew}$ denote Parking Request, Vehicle Scheduling, Virtual Fence, and Early Warning, respectively. We make virtual fence benchmark region. Early Warning is inside i.e., $S_{ew} = \{\{s_{in}\}, \{s_{in}\}, \ldots, \{s_{in}\}\}$. The other ones are unconstrained i.e., $S_{pr} = S_{vs} = S_{vf} = \{S_{loc}, S_{loc}, \ldots, S_{loc}\}$. There are four process expressions modeling as below.

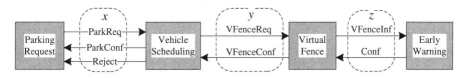

Fig. 6. Business process of the Parking Electric Fence

(1) Parking Request

When a parking request message is sent in t_0, answer must received in $t_0 + 3$ seconds (unit below the same).

$$P_{pr} = Int(t_0, 0)Loc[S_{pr}]\bar{x}\langle ParkReq\rangle.(Int(t_0, 3)Loc[S_{pr}]x(ParkConf) + \\ Int(t_0, 3)Loc[S_{pr}]x(Reject)) \tag{2}$$

(2) Vehicle Scheduling

Within $t_1 + 2$, this MCS service must react to parking request in time. Once the congestion level reaches a certain one, virtual fence request should be sent within $t_2 + 1$. Then virtual fence confirmation has to be received in $t_3 + 1$.

$$
\begin{aligned}
P_{vs} =& Loc[S_{vs}]x(ParkReq).(Int(t_1, 2)Loc[S_{vs}]\bar{x}\langle ParkConf \rangle \\
&+ Int(t_1, 2)Loc[S_{vs}]\bar{x}\langle Reject \rangle). \\
&[msg = ParkConf](Int(t_2, 1)Loc[S_{vs}]\bar{y}\langle VFenceReq \rangle. \\
&Int(t_3, 1)Loc[S_{vs}]y(VFenceConf))
\end{aligned}
\tag{3}
$$

(3) Virtual Fence

Within $t_4 + 1$ of receiving virtual fence request, electric fence will be set up. After that, each car in benchmark region would receive early warning messages in $[t_5, t_5 + 30]$ ($t_5 = t_5 + 30$, increasing constantly). Let us take *CarA* inside of benchmark region for example. Confirmation message from CarA has to be got in $t_{Ae} + 30$ (t_{Ae} is virtual fence information sending time).

$$
\begin{aligned}
P_{vf} =& Loc[S_{vf}]y(VFenceReq).Int(t_4, 1)Loc[S_{vf}]\bar{y}\langle VFenceConf \rangle. \\
&!\ (Int(t_5, 30)Loc[S_{vf}]\bar{z}\langle VFenceInf \rangle.Int(t_{Ae}, 30)Loc[S_{vf}]z(Conf))
\end{aligned}
\tag{4}
$$

(4) Early Warning

Within $t_{Ar} + 10$ (t_{Ar} isvirtualfence information receiving time) is virtual fence information receiving time), early warnings would be sent to CarA.

$$
P_{ew} =!\ (Loc[S_{ew}]z\langle VFenceInf \rangle.Int(t_{Ar}, 10)Loc[S_{ew}]\bar{z}(Conf))
\tag{5}
$$

We express Parking Electric Fence MCS service composition as W. $W = P_{pr}|P_{vs}|P_{vf}|P_{ew}$. On the basis of formal verification of Sect. 3, temporal and spatial attributes of actual MCS components are introduced into W. Then from W being deadlock or not, we can judge whether this MCS service composition can reach final state. After that, the validity can be verified, and errors could be recognized early.

In practice, park electric fence runs normally in six months' test, which validates the correctness of analysis results. So this case study shows that the formal verification for MCS components composition is reasonable.

5 Conclusion

In this paper, a service-oriented architecture and a formal verification method are proposed for MCS components composition. The case study demonstrates that they are of innovative and practical. The future works will focus on two aspects as follows. (1) Achieve reusing by adding process adapter for MCS services which can't meet space and time constraints. (2) Make optimal decision by taking further study on action-time function and construct time state space.

References

1. Olaleye, S.B., Ishan, R.: A review on enhancing storage space of smartphone using virtualization. In: 2015 International Conference on Futuristic Trends on Computational Analysis and Knowledge Management, pp. 739–743. IEEE Press, Noida (2015)
2. Fernando, N., Loke, S.W., Rahayu, W.: Mobile cloud computing: a survey. J. Future Gener. Comput. Syst. **29**, 84–106 (2013)
3. Dinh, H.T., Lee, C., Niyato, D., Wang, P.: A survey of mobile cloud computing: architecture, applications, and approaches. J. Wirel. Commun. Mob. Comput. **13**, 1587–1611 (2013)
4. Satyanarayanan, M., Bahl, P., Caceres, R., Davies, N.: The case for VM-based cloudlets in mobile computing. J. Pervasive Comput. **8**, 14–23 (2009)
5. Zhang, X., Kunjithapatham, A., Jeong, S., Gibbs, S.: Towards an elastic application model for augmenting the computing capabilities of mobile devices with cloud computing. J. Mob. Netw. Appl. **16**, 270–284 (2011)
6. Erl, T.: Service-Oriented Architecture: Concepts, Technology, and Design. Prentice Hall PTR, New Jersey (2005)
7. Tan, J.Q., Kavulya, S., Gandhi, R., Narasimhan, P.: Visual, log-based causal tracing for performance debugging of mapreduce systems. In: 30th International Conference on Distributed Computing Systems, pp. 795–806. IEEE Press, Genoa (2010)
8. Gutierrez-Garcia, J.O, Sim, K.-M.: Agent-based service composition in cloud computing. In: Kim, T.-H., Yau, S.S., Gervasi, O., Kang, B.-H., Stoica, A., Ślęzak, D. (eds.) GDC/CA 2010. CCIS, vol. 121, pp. 1–10. Springer, Heidelberg (2010)
9. Milner, R.: Communicating and Mobile Systems: The π-Calculus. Cambridge University, Cambridge (1999)
10. Wang, P., Yang, L., Li, G.W., Gao, X.: A novel substitution judgment method for mobile cloud computing application system components. In: 6th International Conference on Cloud Computing Technology and Science, pp. 911–916. IEEE Press, Singapore (2014)
11. Egenhofer, M.J., Herring, J.R.,: A mathematical framework for the definition of topological relationships. In: 4th International Symposium on Spatial Data Handling, Zurich, pp. 803–813 (1990)

Monitoring Prayer Using Mobile Phone Accelerometer

Reem Al-Ghannam[1(✉)], Eiman Kanjo[2], and Hmood Al-Dossari[1]

[1] King Saud University, Riyadh, Saudi Arabia
r.g.alghannam@gmail.com
[2] Nottingham Trent University, Nottingham, UK

Abstract. The ever-increasing ability of smartphones for sensing paves the way for a new form of human-computer interaction which wasn't possible before. One of these possibilities is monitoring Muslims' prayers which consist of a set of physical activities that must be conducted in a correct way, i.e. ordered and complete. In this paper, we introduce a novel method to monitor and detect prayer activities using mobile phone accelerometers in order to evaluate the correctness of prayer. The method involves four stages: data collection, signal pre-processing, features extraction and classification.

Keywords: Mobile sensing · Accelerometer · Activity recognition · Prayer monitoring

1 Introduction

Prayer is the second most important pillar of Islam and the most regular compulsory action in a Muslim's life. If a person's prayer is accepted, then other acts of worship are accepted. Thus, Muslims must carefully perform their prayers in order to be accepted by Allah. The ability to concentrate in prayer may be improved by undertaking adequate psychological, mental and physical preparation before the prayer and by utilizing certain techniques during the prayer [1, 2]. To improve prayer performance, current technology may help to monitor and track the prayer's activities (i.e. the Muslim's body movements).

Among the huge amount of technology available nowadays, smartphones are among the most widely used devices. The success of smartphones is leading to an increasing amount of sensors in mobile phones to provide new features and services to end-users, to reduce costs through more integration or to improve hardware performance. Significant interest in smartphone sensing [3] in recent years can be attributed to several factors, including their ubiquitous nature, rapid evolution toward smartphones with several built-in sensors and their portability making them easy to use for "mobile sensing".

Not surprisingly then, mobile sensing has been used in a very creative way to produce interactive and interesting applications which have been realized or envisioned in diverse domains (e.g., transportation, social networking, health monitoring) [4].

Mobile sensing has a wide variety of types classified by their purposes. For example, accelerometers that detect translational motion, gyroscopes that detect

Y. Zhang et al. (Eds.): CloudComp 2015, LNICST 167, pp. 168–175, 2016.
DOI: 10.1007/978-3-319-38904-2_17

rotational motion, digital compasses, barometers and proximities. The aim of this study is to utilize mobile phone accelerometers to monitor Muslims' body positions and movements in order to determine their prayer quality. To do so, the accelerometer data will be collected and analyzed to detect and discover the prayer's activities: standing, bowing, prostration and sitting.

In this paper we present a novel method for detecting prayer activities based on the mobile phone accelerometer. We discuss the related work in Sect. 2. Then in Sect. 3, we describe our activity model and the process for addressing the activity recognition task. Next, in Sect. 4, we go on to evaluation techniques that we have used to assess our system. Toward the end, in Sect. 5, we discuss our conclusion.

2   Related Work

Recent advances in computers have given rise to a large number of technologies that can be used for various purposes. For example, mobile sensors are now widely used by people to record data while they move. These sensors range from specific sensors that can be embedded in systems such as location-based sensors (e.g. GPS) to stand-alone systems such as physiological sensors that can be used to detect emotions or vital signs (e.g. Galvanic skin response), or mobile sensor accelerometers used in our study that can be embedded to devices (e.g. wearable device or mobile phone) to monitor human activities.

Mobile accelerometer sensors have been used in a wide variety of applications. They are currently the most widely used sensors in human physical activity monitoring in clinical and free-living settings [5]. For example, Ravi et al. [6] have used accelerometer data to recognize user activity and by formulating as a classification problem. In addition, accelerometer sensors could be used in fall detection and health monitoring as [7] has implemented wireless acceleration sensor module and algorithm to detect the wearer's posture, activity and fall. This system can be applied to patients, elders and sports athletes' exercise measurement and pattern analysis.

The convergence of pervasive and sensing technologies and signal processing, provides a platform for a wide range of innovative applications based on a more refined understanding of the users' context; wherever they are, whatever they might be doing and why. These applications can range from environment monitoring [3], emotion mapping [8] to religious application [9]. Nowadays, with the increase in technologies' popularities among Muslims, many developers resort to program Islamic applications to meet their religious needs. Islamic-focused mobile phone applications are not a new phenomenon. Several of these applications were available over the past few years; however most of them have focused on verses of the *Quran* such as *iQuran*, Qibla: the direction that should be faced when a Muslim prays, such as *"Find Mecca"* and other instructional applications like Athkar, Islamic Pocket Guide etc. [10].

Other important aspects should be covered in worship, besides verbal aspects. Physical movements play an important role in Muslims' lives which needs more research to be conducted technically. Indeed, many applications have monitored physical worship but they are still limited. For example, Ravi et al. [11] and Alnizari [12] have proposed an architecture using radio frequency identification (RFID) technology to track and monitor individuals during Hajj pilgrimage. Mohandes et al. [13] have outlined a system for tracking and monitoring pilgrims during Hajj in the Holy area, consisting of a mobile phone equipped with a Global Positioning System (GPS) used by pilgrims and wireless sensor networks (WSNs) installed in the surrounding environment to observe the locations of pilgrims. Mantoro et al. [14] have also proposed a HajjLocator framework for Hajj Pilgrim tracking based on mobile phone environments as it is reasonably affordable and is widely used by people. Amro et al. [15] have put together a plan for assisting the pilgrimage leader (Mutawwif) to perform his/her duties and add new capabilities and solutions for the most significant challenges such as finding lost pilgrims, predicting where they are and avoiding losing them.

As well as the studies conducted into the potential of technology in assisting pilgrimages, a small range of projects have been developed regarding prayer practice. El-Hoseiny et al. [16] have worked on a system capable of recognizing major postures and actions performed by a Muslim normally during the prayer. The core of their scheme was based on video-processing which contained a basic module known as the *front end*. The action recognition phase was implemented as a customized module using a special model developed specifically to fit this purpose. Muaremi et al. [17] have also presented their work to differentiate, in the first case, between congregational prayers and individual prayers, and in another case, between silent prayers and loud prayers by using two wearable sensors namely chest belts and wrist-worn devices. They collected data from bio-physiological responses of people performing different types of prayers during an Umrah pilgrimage. Nonetheless, none of the previous works have monitored physical activities during prayers. Using the technology in the Islamic applications is still in the stages of early development and there is a space to utilize the technology to support Islamic worships. The focus of this work is on investigating the use of mobile phone accelerometers to monitor and recognize the prayer's activities in order to assess its correctness.

3 Prayer Activities Detection System

In this section, we present a novel method for detecting prayer activities. The work presented in this paper comprises six components as illustrated in Fig. 1.

For further illustration, in this work, different techniques have been manipulated to analyze and detect prayer movements' patterns in collected data. Mobile phones are commonly used as a sensor for a wide range of applications. Most of off-the-shelf smartphones offer built-in sensors including accelerometer, gyroscopes and vibration monitoring. These sensing capabilities can provide a rich source of information about body movements and physical behavior. This study utilizes mobile phones as a means of data collecting and analysis of body movement during prayer (i.e. prayer here refers to Muslim prayer). In order to record the sequence of movements, a mobile phone application needs to be used to capture the data. A number of applications have been reviewed and the application with the best performance has been adopted for this study. Android has been adopted as the main platform for data collection, since Android applications are easy to access and easy to use and does not require the application to have special permission to use it [18]. In order to monitor prayer activities the mobile phone is attached

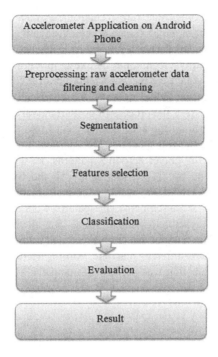

Fig. 1. System components.

to the worshipper before the start of the prayer in a convenient and comfortable fashion. A preliminary set of experiments have been conducted in order to figure out the best place to locate the mobile (e.g. on the chest, the hip, the back or the arm). The upper back was the best location we have selected because it provided a clear pattern of movement and usability combined with comfort. The best position was chosen for the rest of the experiments and data collection stages. During the prayer activity, the body of a person will change between six possible positions, as illustrated in Fig. 2, from the person standing still (No. 1), to the person's forehead touching the ground (No. 6). For this task, we examined the posture and acceleration data of the mobile phone. The application monitors the body movements by collecting data using some methods to analyze it followed by measuring the correctness of each activity in every round.

Fig. 2. A sequence of the prayer covering all the possible positions of the subject's body.

Based on vibration readings, the raw accelerometer data has the following attributes: timestamp, acceleration along x axis, acceleration along y axis and acceleration along z axis [19]. All collected data was subject to inspection and analysis to remove any corrupted data using various techniques including moving average filter in order to obtain only higher values which are the most representative for movements. Thus, we obtained smoother acceleration values to work on, which allow more accurate results compared to just raw data. After the process of noise removal, further processing of the data was carried out to partition the acceleration values into small segments based on their approach for visual pattern inspection. The segmentation of acceleration signals made it easy to highlight the prayer activities patterns, as shown in Fig. 3 (Standing tagged with no. 1, Bowing no. 2, Prostrating no. 3 and Sitting no. 4). Also, this segmentation helps to understand and identify the main features in the collected data for classification. For each of the segments, the features were extracted which made the signal distinct. We have generated average values for all three axes (x average, y average and z average). The features selection process is followed by feature reduction in order to run and compare different machine learning techniques to classify prayer activities. After that, the labeling was performed manually, choosing from one of the four prayer activities available.

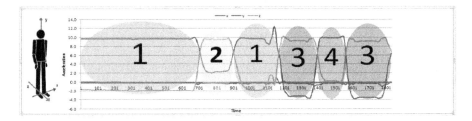

Fig. 3. Prayer activities patterns in one round of prayer.

Regarding the classification step, many different approaches have been used in the literature in the context of activity recognition [20]. In our study, we have applied supervised classification methods and training phases because of the nature of prayer activities. Previously, various classification models have been adopted in order to detect physical activities. Here, appropriate classification algorithms have been exploited to classify body movements into different categories e.g. standing, bowing, prostrating and sitting, as shown in Fig. 3. Classification of acceleration segments into a given number of classes using the segments' features can be achieved by various statistical and predictive methods. Naïve Bayes, K-Nearest Neighbor or IBL and J48 Decision Trees algorithms were chosen due to their good performance and high accuracy to detect prayer activities. There is no universally accepted method of detecting a particular range of activities and all techniques have associated benefits and limitations [21].

4   Evaluation and Results

To evaluate our system, we have used two groups of datasets in our experiments: training and testing datasets. The training set was implemented to build a model, while a test (or validation) set is to validate the model built. For the training model, the data has been collected from thirty rounds; each round consists of eight stages with the following order: long standing, bowing, and short standing, first prostrating, first sitting, second prostrating and second sitting. During the classification stage, we have implemented Naïve Bayes, IB1 and J48 Decision Tree algorithms available in Weka, which is a machine learning workbench that supports many activities of machine learning practitioners. After the feature reduction process, the dataset used 10 Cross-Validation evaluation technique provided by Weka and achieved a mean classification accuracy of $\bar{x} = 100\,\%$ using Naïve Bayes. The IB1 algorithm was tested and achieved a mean classification accuracy ($\bar{x} = 100\,\%$). The J48 Decision Trees algorithm was also tested and achieved the lowest mean classification accuracy ($\bar{x} = 94.9153\,\%$). This suggests that the prayer activities can be classified relatively accurately. By observing the results, it appears much more difficult to recognize the standing and sitting patterns; we find that this is because those two similar activities are often confused with one another. After applying different machine learning algorithms to the prayer activities dataset, another dataset containing the prayer activities (testing dataset) was tested using an evaluation technique known as a "Supplied Test Set". In this evaluation technique, we test the learning model using a dataset that has not been seen previously. To evaluate our learning models, we have used ten subjects. Table 1 shows the mean classification accuracies to classify prayer activities for all testing subjects using all three algorithms.

Table 1. Mean classification accuracies for testing subject using all three algorithms.

Classification algorithm	Classification accuracy
Naïve Bayes	91.8462 %
IB1	87.7692 %
J48 Decision Tree	89.8462 %

By comparing the classification accuracies that resulted from the three algorithms, we notice that Naïve Bayes performs better than both the IB1 and J48 algorithms since the Naive Bayes algorithm is based on conditional probabilities that might be more suitable given the nature of our data. However, the results presented here are optimized after several trials were made to enhance the classifiers' performance.

5   Conclusion

Our preliminary experiments and results showed a noticeable pattern in accelerometer signals in relation to different prayer activities. The prayer activities sensed are a rich source of information and could be used in monitoring prayers in order to determine prayer quality regarding its order and completeness of different prayer positions. Moreover, it could also be used to develop learning and educational applications to advise people praying on the accuracy of their prayers.

References

1. The Importance of Prayer: http://islamicpamphlets.com/the-importance-of-prayer/. Accessed 5 Mar 2015
2. Murad, K.: Salah Tips. http://www.islamtomorrow.com/salah_tips.asp. Accessed 5 Mar 2015
3. Kanjo, E., Bacon, J., Landshoff, P., Roberts, D.: Mobsense: making smart phones smarter. IEEE Pervasive Comput. **8**(4), 50–57 (2009)
4. Radu, V., Kriara, L., Marina, M.K.: Pazl: a mobile crowdsensing based indoor WiFi. In: Network and Service Management (CNSM), Zurich (2013)
5. Chen, K.Y., Janz, K.F., Zhu, W., Brychta, R.J.: Redefining the roles of sensors in objective physical activity monitoring. Official J. Am. Coll. Sports Med. **44**(1), 13–23 (2012)
6. Ravi, N., Dandekar, N., Mysore, P., Littman, M.L.: Activity recognition from accelerometer data. In: IAAI 2005, Proceedings of the 17th Conference on Innovative Applications of Artificial Intelligence (2005)
7. Lee, Y., Lee, M.: Implementation of Accelerometer Sensor Module and Fall Detection Monitoring System Based on Wireless Sensor Network, p. 342. InTech, Rijeka (2011)
8. Al-Husain, L., Kanjo, E., Chamberlain, A.: Sense of space: mapping physiological emotion response in urban space. In: UbiComp 2013 Adjunct, Proceedings of the 2013 ACM Conference on Pervasive and Ubiquitous Computing Adjunct Publication, New york (2013)
9. Campbell, H.A., Altenhofen, B., Bellar, W., Cho, K.J.: There's a religious app for that! a framework for studying religious mobile applications. Mob. Media Commun. **2**(2), 154–172 (2014)
10. Hackner, M.: Islam Goes Mobile, 25 August 2011. http://forumone.com/insights/islam-goes-mobile/. Accessed 5 Mar 2015
11. Ravi, K.S., Abdul Aziz, M., Ramana, B.V.: Pilgrims tracking and identification using RFID technology. Adv. Electr. Eng. Syst. (AEES) **1**(2), 96–105 (2012)
12. Alnizari, N.A.: A real-time tracking system using RFID in Mecca. Massey Unirversity (2011)
13. Mohandes, M.A., Haleem, M.A., Kousa, M., Balakrishnan, K.: Pilgrim tracking and identification using wireless sensor networks and GPS in a mobile phone. Arab. J. Sci. Eng. **38**(8), 2135–2141 (2013)
14. Mantoro, T., Ayu, M.A., Mahmud, M.: Hajj crowd tracking system in a pervasive environment. Int. J. Mob. Comput. Multimedia Commun. **4**(2), 11–29 (2012)
15. Amro, A.: Pilgrims "Hajj" tracking system (e-Mutawwif). Contemp. Eng. Sci. **5**(9), 437–446 (2012)
16. El-Hoseiny, M.H., Sabhan, E.: Muslim prayer actions recognition. In: Second International Conference on Computer and Electrical Engineering, ICCEE 2009 (2009)
17. Muaremi, A., Seiter, J., Bexheti, A., Arnrich, B.: Monitor pilgrims: prayer activity recognition using wearable sensors. In: Proceedings of the 8th International Conference on Body Area Networks (2013)

18. Das, S., Green, L., Perez, B., Murphy, M., Perrig, A.: Detecting user activities using the accelerometer on android smartphones. The Team for Research in Ubiquitous Secure Technology, TRUST-REU Carnefie Mellon University (2010)
19. Gjoreski1, H., Gams, M., Chorbev, I.: 3-axial accelerometers activity recognition. In: ICT Innovations 2010 Web Proceedings, Ohrid, Macedonia (2010)
20. Kanjo, E., Bacon, J., Landshoff, P., Roberts, D.: MobSense: making smart phones smarter. IEEE Pervasive Comput. **8**(4), 50–57 (2009)
21. Cleland, I., Kikhia, B., Nugent, C., Boytsov, A., Hollberg, J., Synnes, K., McClean, S., Finlay, D.: Optimal placement of accelerometers for the detection of everyday activities. Sensors **13**(7), 9183–9200 (2013)

A Prospective Cloud-Connected Vehicle Information System for C-ITS Application Services in Connected Vehicle Environment

SeongMin Song$^{(\boxtimes)}$, Woojoong Kim, Seong-Hwan Kim, GyuBeom Choi, Heejae Kim, and Chan-Hyun Youn

School of Electrical Engineering, KAIST, Daejeon, South Korea
{songsm87,w.j.kim,s.h_kim,mosfetlkg, kim881019,chyoun}@kaist.ac.kr

Abstract. In the era of the Internet of Things (IoT), various applications providing people with utilities are rapidly emerging by the needs for people. Recently, combining cloud computing, IoT technologies, and vehicular applications promotes Intelligent Transportation System (ITS). In other words, this is for safety of vehicles and drivers as well as convenience of the drivers. Vehicular Ad-hoc Network (VANET) is an application of Mobile Ad-hoc Network (MANET), which is a networking technology including vehicle-to-vehicle (V2V) and vehicle-to-infrastructure (V2I) using wireless communications. In real life, vehicles and infrastructures which have a lot of sensors generate various data for Cooperative-Intelligent Transportation System (C-ITS) application services according to each sensor type. Therefore, collecting, processing, and storing a number of data generated from various sensors built in vehicles and infrastructures require a great computing capacity and storage resources. In this paper, we propose an architecture of prospective cloud-connected vehicle information system for C-ITS application services in connected vehicle environment and describe the procedure of our local and global vehicle information system concerned with case scenario.

Keywords: IoT · ITS · C-ITS · Vehicular network · VANET · V2V · V2I · Cloud computing · Connected car · LDM

1 Introduction

With advanced IT technologies in the cloud computing era, Internet of Things (IoT) allows to design and devise a wide range of applications in a number of different ways. Recently, this flow meets increasing interests in amazing future vehicle system so that a wide variety of vehicular applications is used for Intelligent Transportation System (ITS) such as automatic driving. This allows ITS to guarantee safety for vehicles and drivers or convenience on driving for drivers, ease traffic congestion, and mitigate environmental pollution, which can be realized by implementing IoT framework in the vehicular cloud environments [1].

© ICST Institute for Computer Sciences, Social Informatics and Telecommunications Engineering 2016
Y. Zhang et al. (Eds.): CloudComp 2015, LNICST 167, pp. 176–183, 2016.
DOI: 10.1007/978-3-319-38904-2_18

Various sensors mounted in vehicles show the characteristics of the dynamic node topology in accordance with the movement of the vehicles on road, which is different from traditional static Wireless Sensor Network (WSN). Very dynamic changing topology of sensors in the circumstance of rapidly moving vehicle nodes creates a network topology that cannot be predicted. This can cause data loss and deliver distorted information while the data packets are passing between network nodes [2]. VANET which is an application of MANET is a networking technology that provides wireless communications between a plurality of rapidly moving vehicles and with Infrastructures (e.g. RodeSide Unit) such as V2V or V2I respectively. Saif Al-Sultan [3] describes a comprehensive VANET communication. Li [4] classifies and summarizes the most well-known routing protocols for VANET as follow: Topology-based, Position-based, Cluster-based, Infrastructure-based, and broadcast [4]. A vehicle information system is really needed in local automotive environment as well as global cloud environment through this network.

Cooperative-Intelligent Transportation System (C-ITS) application services relating to traffic safety and efficiency use the meaningful information of the data obtained from the ego-vehicle, other vehicles, and infrastructures on roads. One of characteristics of vehicles in C-ITS applications is to have a huge chuck of sensors that are pouring so much data, which have much interest in even field with big data as the automotive industry. Precise analysis of vehicle information on driving and vehicle behaviors provide objective information on vehicles or roads and help to make data-driven decisions. Therefore, we need appropriate vehicle information system for C-ITS application services to realize amazing future vehicle system for storing, managing and transmitting data used for the C-ITS application services in connected vehicle environment and computing resource or storage capacity to handle a large scale information for realizing actual models in the real world. It means that cloud-connected vehicle information system can be one solution.

Ericssion [5] proposes open Connected Vehicle Cloud (CVC) which supports various business models and application development needed in automotive ecosystem providing vehicle and device data connector, cloud management functions as open API. T-System [6] also proposes open CVC supporting development and deployment of C-ITS application services on OEM, Telco Provider, and 3rd party with Embedded Connected Car Platform (ECCP), M2M Platform, and Central Connected Car Platform (CCCP). However, many automotive platforms and systems still are static on cloud resource management operation in accordance with the application requirements.

In this paper, we propose an architecture of prospective cloud-connected vehicle information system for C-ITS application services in connected vehicle environment and describe the procedure of our local and global vehicle information system concerned with case scenario (Fig. 1).

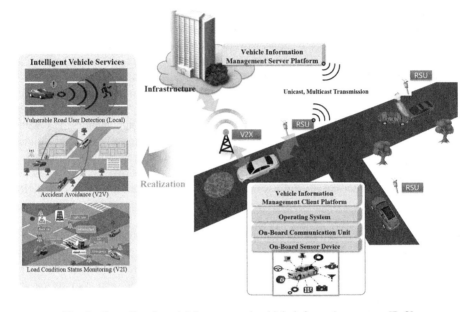

Fig. 1. Overall real model for proposed vehicle information system [7, 8]

2 Proposed Architecture of Prospective Cloud-Connected Vehicle Information System for C-ITS Application Services in Connected Vehicle Environment

We propose an architecture of prospective cloud-connected vehicle information system for C-ITS application services in connected vehicle environment. Advanced Driver Assistance System (ADAS) which is an application of our proposing system recognizes or judges the set of circumstances of ego-vehicle or road state, and provides drivers with analysis contents on surroundings area through visualization. This information used for applications such as ADAS is not limited to a single-node. A vehicle information system generates a real-time traffic information through crowdsourcing method. In other words, it is utilized to multiple-node for a wide range of applications through V2X based communications to perform the exchange of information between our local vehicle information systems in mobile devices and our global vehicle information systems in cloud infrastructures. The architecture of the vehicle information system we propose in mobile devices and cloud infrastructures is as follows (Fig. 2).

Proposed our mobile vehicle information system is composed of next-generation high-speed wireless networks based V2X communication units between other vehicles and roadside infrastructures. Our mobile vehicle information system in mobile devices analyzes the status of the vehicles in real time using a built-in sensor data collected in the mobile vehicle information database. When an accident of driver's vehicle occurs, the system can automatically provide C-ITS application services such as sending the current position and state information of the vehicle to the vehicle information system

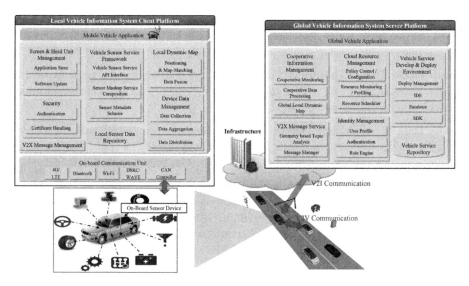

Fig. 2. Overall architecture of prospective cloud-connected vehicle information system for C-ITS application services in connected vehicle environment

of other mobile terminals in other vehicles and the central control center in cloud. Our mobile system continuously shares and exchanges useful information between roadside infrastructures and the other vehicles, but not limited to information acquired form a single node. The drivers who are linked to a central control center of the vehicle information system through the networks provide an integrated information and utilize C-ITS application services such as a critical alarm and safety precaution. Functions of our mobile vehicle information system in a mobile terminal of a vehicle are as follows.

On-Board Communication Unit: Integrated communication network management of the automotive environment of connected vehicle within the mobile devices. It constitutes In-vehicle network, V2V, and V2I and determines to use what on-board communication unit such as Bluetooth, Controller Area Network (CAN), DSRC/WAVE, Wi-Fi, and 4G/LTE by configuration to scenario.

Screen & Head Unit Management: Deployment of developed C-ITS application services via application store and management of the application services via software update function.

Security: Security manager of the personalized system using authentication by login interface of an individual user who uses the vehicle application services and management of certificate repository of the user.

V2X Message Management: Message manager of management, transition, and reception of collected, processed, and managed data to apply for various application services using V2X Message Interface.

Vehicle Sensor Service Framework: Framework on processing the sensor data generated in the vehicle, which objectifies sensors in vehicles based on metadata of sensors and provides sensor mashup composition and vehicle sensor service API interface.

Local Sensor Data Repository: Central repository for holding the contents of the local vehicles such as ego-vehicle and others in the vicinity for particular application services using V2X communication.

Device Data Management: General device data management, which actually collect, aggregate, and distribute sensor data the system will use for C-ITS application services.

Local Dynamic Map (LDM): Conceptual data storage for information relating to operate Cooperative-ITS (C-ITS) applications for road traffic safety and efficiency. The LDM database reflects the road traffic information and the road status information around vehicles on a fixed map information. This idea helps communicate among various applications via LDM, which shortens the response time on the request for information in the database and improves C-ITS application performance, as well as reduces the data traffic.

Vehicle Application: Mobile application services provided by the in-vehicle mobile devices.

The large amounts of data collected by infrastructures and vehicles is transmitted to the central control center of big data processing system to process it. The central control center provides comprehensive information for smooth traffic flow and safe driving to the driver of each vehicle generating information after various data processing. Our global vehicle information system in cloud environment performs complex processing by the event by combining data from multiple sources. The global traffic information being produced continuously over the cloud computing resources in real-time is collected and processed. Our system can construct the environment for analysis of big data by extracting meaningful information from it, which ensures the reliability of data, seeks the scalability of the data analysis, and makes the effect of reducing the time and costs for traffic analysis through a distributed application such as Hadoop running on secure computer clusters. Functions of the vehicle information system of the physical infrastructure in the cloud is shown below.

Global Vehicle Application: Global C-ITS application services provided by global cloud environment.

Cooperative Information Management: Global integrated information management by monitoring, processing, and storing information as global LDM in global cloud environment.

V2X Message Service: V2X message service management as a mobile vehicle information system as well as topic analysis interested in particular local area based on geometry.

Cloud Resource Management: Cloud resource management, which controls policy for using cloud resource dynamically, monitors, profiles, and schedules the cloud resources.

Identity Management: Security manager which is linked security in mobile vehicle information system giving functions such as profiling user information, authentication determined by rule engine.

Vehicle Service Repository: Storage for the global vehicle application services.

Vehicle Service Develop & Deploy Environment: Development environment which allows to develop global and local vehicle application services in cloud and deploys the application linking Screen & Head Unit Management in client vehicle system.

3 Scenario Case: Procedure of Local and Global Vehicle Information System

The mobile vehicle information system in mobile terminals collects and analyzes sensor data from in-vehicle and surrounding other vehicles or infrastructures in real-time using V2X communication units within the vehicle on-board communication unit. Objectifying sensor devices is to make a variety of things such as devices objects using profile which is information of a variety of things and devices in order to provide the web service of the vehicle environment, which is a phase as sensor metadata scheme. A combination of sensor objects using a sensor mashup composition makes it possible to provide a newly-configured service. Collected data from sensor devices is managed as object catalog, meta-database, local area database, and global area database. This managed data is used in various applications through networks via V2X message management which has V2X message manager, message transmitter, and message receiver functions, and these data builds and constitutes LDM environment through the positioning of the vehicle and map-matching in a fixed map information database via the data fusion. LDM includes information of the real world which comprise a conceptual information on objects that affects with respect to the traffic flow. Data depicting objects in the real world is defined by layering and expressing in the flowing categories (permanent static data, transient static data, transient dynamic data, and highly dynamic data) [9]. Monitoring road traffic information and road status information in real time to detect and diagnose a particular event occurring for each event is set to enforce action decided by established automation of analysis of the big data collected from sensors using a machine learning. C-ITS application services such as detection of vulnerable road user and accident avoidance guarantee the safety and convenience of the driver by recognizing the road conditions or circumstances such as roadside. C-ITS application is determined whether it exercise in local mobile devices or global cloud resources according to requirements of application services. The collected data through the cloud resource-linked offloading via a network which contains the information of the node by using a global LDM vehicle cloud-based collection, storage, through a process step to the relational information for the entire single road conditions processing to build a databases. Through Complex Event Processing (CEP) analysis with the resource pattern matching and filtering on provided cloud computing resources linked to a central control center, when we build an integrated environment of the vehicle information system that responds to detect changes, implementing C-ITS in the real world can be operated more easily and efficiently (Fig. 3).

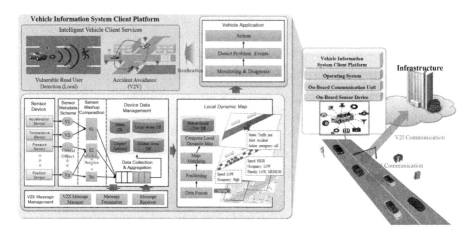

Fig. 3. Procedure of proposed local and global system concerned with case scenario

4 Conclusion

In this paper, we propose an architecture of prospective cloud-connected vehicle information system for C-ITS application services in connected vehicle environment and describe the procedure of our local and global vehicle information system concerned with case scenario. Data generated from a variety of sensors in infrastructure on road or vehicles in the real world is the big data requiring more computing resources to process it efficiently. Processing a number of data generated from various sensors built in vehicles and infrastructures requires a great computing capacity and storage resources. The information by the respective vehicle nodes using the VANET network access is aggregated in global vehicle information system of central control center to manage the data acquisition process according to the definition of the data type of LDM. Therefore our local and global vehicle information system to process or manage efficiently transportation relational big data enhance a quality of C-ITS application services using various functions. In addition, we need to study more related-research on greater access to vehicle information in cloud which can improve C-ITS application service such as autonomous driving [10].

Acknowledgments. This work was supported by 'Electrically phase-controlled beamforming lighting device based on 2D nano-photonic phased array for lidar' grant from Civil Military Technology Cooperation, Korea.

References

1. He, W., Yan, G., Da Xu, L.: Developing vehicular data cloud service in the IoT environment. IEEE Trans. Ind. Inform. **10**, 1587–1595 (2014)

2. Yu, X., Zhao, H., Zhao, L., Wu, S., Krishnamachari, B., Li, V.O.K.: Cooperative sensing and compression in vehicular sensor networks for urban monitoring. In: IEEE International Conference on Communications (2010)
3. Al-Sultan, S., Al-Doori, M.M., Al-Bayatti, A.H., Zedan, H.: A comprehensive survey on vehicular Ad Hoc network. J. Netw. Comput. Appl. **37**, 380–392 (2014)
4. Li, F., Wang, Y.: Routing in vehicular Ad Hoc networks: a survey. IEEE Veh. Technol. Mag. **2**, 12–22 (2007)
5. Ericsson: http://www.ericsson.com/
6. T-System: http://www.t-systems.com/
7. Vehicle-to-Vehicle Communications: Readiness of V2V Technology for Application, NHTSA (2014)
8. Office of the Assistant Secretary for Research and Technology: http://www.its.dot.gov/
9. ETSI TR 102 863 (v.1.1.1): Intelligent Transport System (ITS); Vehicular Communications; Basic Set of Applications; Local Dynamic Map (LDM); Rationale for and guidance on standardization (2011)
10. Kumar, S., Gollakota, S., Katabi, D.: A cloud-assisted design for autonomous driving. In: MCC 2012 (2012)

Video and USB Transmission Devices for Cloud Desktop Service

Chanho Park$^{(\boxtimes)}$ and Hagyoung Kim

Cloud Computing Research Department,
Electronics and Telecommunications Research Institute (ETRI),
218 Gajeong-ro, Yuseong-gu, Daejeon, Korea
{jangddaeng,h0kim}@etri.re.kr

Abstract. This paper shows a video and USB transmission device for high-quality cloud desktop service. In a general software-based desktop service, an application such as a game cannot be serviced normally due to a long latency. To solve this problem, a passthrough virtualization system which assigns a graphic card to each user is used and hardware devices which transfer video and USB signals to the network are developed. In the hardware device, a simplified switch is adopted to support multi-user. A cloud desktop service using these devices can provide a satisfactory service in an application where the latency becomes a problem.

Keywords: Video · USB · Latency · Simplified switch

1 Introduction

Cloud Services can be divided largely into SaaS, PaaS and IaaS. The service ordinary users often encounter is the SaaS. DaaS (Desktop as a Service) is similar to SaaS and this service provide a personal desktop virtually to a user. These services (SaaS and DaaS) can support many users on a single server, but has limitations on the application which they can provide. For a high-resolution multimedia service, as concurrent users increase, it becomes more difficult to provide the service. Indeed, for an application such as a game which requires low response time, it is almost impossible to provide the service. This is mostly because of the long delay time of graphic processing.

There are several methods for graphic virtualization in a server. Typical examples are full virtualization, mediated passthrough [1], and direct passthrough [2, 3]. Additionally, hybrid styles such as gVirt are also possible [4]. Among them, direct passthrough method shows good performance close to the non-virtualized system, even though it can support fewer users because one GPU has to be assigned to every VM. And it has advantage that chipper video cards can be used.

Passthrough feature is not only applicable to GPUs but also to other peripheral devices. DaaS user can directly interface to the VM without emulation if the passthrough feature is applied to USB devices. A system called "green PC solution" which applies passthrough feature to graphic cards and USB ports is developed. In this system, a graphic card and a USB port are assigned to each VM and output of graphic card and

USB port is connected to the user with a direct cable. In this paper, to substitute the direct cable with an IP network, an add-in card for a server and a client device for a user are proposed. Additionally, a switch structure in the add-in card is described.

2   Video and USB Transmission Devices

In a common cloud service, software based solution is installed in a server and a service user uses a device called "Thin client" or "Zero client". The proposed system is equipped with multiple graphic cards and a server card which transmit the graphic card output port and USB port signals to a network. For a service user, a dedicated "Zero client" is used for short response time, even though a common "Thin client" can work. Figure 1 shows the difference between the common cloud and the proposed cloud service systems. The server card can be implemented in several ways.

Fig. 1. Comparison of the common cloud system and the proposed system

Figure 2 shows an example of a server card using commercial chips which convert video and USB signals into network packets. This example is a server card which supports 4 users. Each "video & USB processor" receives video and USB signal from the port and convert them into network packets. It also receives network packets which contains USB information, convert the packets into USB signals, and sent the signal to the USB ports. Because this card has only one network port, each "video & USB processor" has different IP address and the network packets are routed by the switch chip. Video transmission chip and USB over IP chip can be separately implemented. The client device is implemented with the same chip of the server card without a switch because it is only for one user. FPGA can be used instead of commercial chips [5]. In this case, switch can be implemented in the FPGA together. In some case, a commercial chip has the function of a graphic card. Then, graphic cards are not required and the chips communicate with the server using PCI-express interfaces. However, these chips cannot be used for an application requiring GPU with high performance, so these chips are used as BMC in the server management system or as a processor for KVM over IP system.

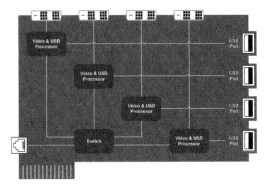

Fig. 2. An example of a server card

3   Simplified Switch Structure

Since the server card has to support multiple users, it must include a switch. Generally, a common switch chipset is used. However, switch chip becomes expensive as the number of port increases. And, in this case, it is not necessary for the chip to act as a general switch. Because video and USB signals of VM are only required by a user in an external network, communications between inner ports are not necessary. In the switch, all packets from inner ports should go to the external port and packets from the external port should be distributed to the inner ports. Therefore, the simplified form of switch can be used instead of a general switch chip.

Figure 3 shows a simplified model of a switch chip. All packets from inner ports are delivered to external port without any processing (or with simple congestion control algorithm). All packets from external port are distributed to inner ports according to the destination IP address. For this, the IP information of "video & USB processors" connected to the inner ports must be recorded in the registers. If a received packet does not have a unicast IP as a destination, this packet is broadcasted to every inner port.

To simplify the structure of switch further, all packets from external port can be broadcasted to every inner port. It is shown in Fig. 3(b). Whether packets are received or dropped is the responsibility of the chips which are connected to the inner ports. By this approach, the switch function can be implemented very easily, but has some disadvantage of power consumption due to unnecessary packet delivery.

As mentioned before, if the server card is implemented with FPGA instead of commercial chips, switch function can be implemented in FPGA together. Because there are no separated chips, only one MAC is enough to accomplish the switch function. Not only the MAC address, IP address can be shared among VMs (the IP to send and receive video and USB signals, not the IP of VM itself). In this case, received packets from external port can be distributed according to the port number.

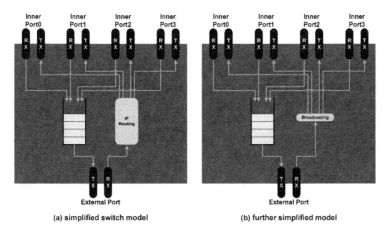

Fig. 3. Simplified switch model

4   Implemented Results

Figure 4 shows server cards supporting two users and client devices, each of which consists of a commercial chips and FPGAs. With these devices, the delay time of DaaS service on a LAN is tested. Each represent the delay time of 40 ms and 70 ms. The difference between the two delay times is mostly due to hardware codec implementation. In both cases, there is no problem to service an application which requires fast response time such as a game.

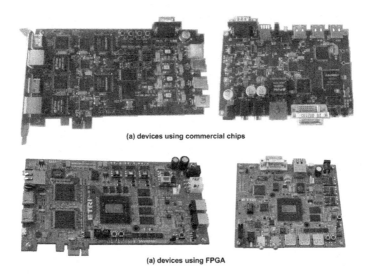

Fig. 4. Implemented server cards and client devices

5   Conclusion

This paper shows a video and USB transmission device for high-quality cloud desktop service. A passthrough virtualization system which assigns a graphic card to each user is used and hardware devices which transfer video and USB signals to the network are developed. In the hardware device, a simplified switch is adopted to support multi-user and to reduce design complexity and cost. A cloud desktop service using these devices has delay time less than 70 ms on the LAN and provides a satisfactory service in an application where the latency becomes a problem.

Acknowledgement.   This work was supported by the ICT R&D program of MSIP/IITP. [B0101-15-0548, Low-power and High-density Micro Server System Development for Cloud Infrastructure].

References

1. Xia, L., Lange, J., Dinda, P., Bae, C.: Investigating virtual passthrough I/O on commodity devices. In: Proceedings of ACM SIGOPS, pp. 83–94 (2012)
2. Abramson, D., Jackson, J., Muthrasanallur, S., Neiger, G., Regnier, G., Sankaran, R., Schoinas, I., Uhlig, R., Bembu, B., Wiegert, J.: Intel virtualization technology for directed I/O. Intel Technol. J. **10** (2006)
3. Dong, Y., Dai, J., Huang, Z., Guan, H., Tian, K., Jiang, Y.: Toward high-quality I/O virtualization. In: SYSTOR (2009)
4. Tian, K., Dong, Y., Cowperthwaite, D.: A full GPU virtualization solution with mediated passthrough. In: Proceedings of USENIX Annual Technical Conference, pp. 121–132 (2014)
5. Park, C., Kim, H.: Low latency video transmission device. In: Proceedings of International Conference on Information Science and Application, pp. 217–222 (2015), International Conference (2014)

A Feature-Oriented Mobile Software Development Framework to Resolve the Device Fragmentation Phenomenon for Application Developers in the Mobile Software Ecosystem

Younghun Han[1](✉), Gyeongmin Go[1],
Sungwon Kang[1], and Heuijin Lee[2]

[1] Department of Computer Science, KAIST, Deajeon, Republic of Korea
{younghun.han, imarch, sungwon.kang}@kaist.ac.kr
[2] Samsung Electronics, Suwon, Republic of Korea
koslee@kaist.ac.kr

Abstract. In the current mobile software environment, the device fragmentation phenomenon causes a serious problem to the mobile software ecosystem stakeholders. Since mobile manufacturers make various differentiated hardware components for product differentiation around strategically selected open platforms, a huge number of devices are produced each year. Since the application developers have to verify manually whether the developed application is compatible with specific devices, a tremendous burden is put on the application developers. To solve this problem, we propose a feature-oriented mobile software development framework and implement as part of it an automated tool for compatibility verification. To evaluate our framework, we conduct a case study with 10 devices and 21 features from the real world. The result of the case study indicates that a significant effort reduction can be achieved by using our framework.

Keywords: Mobile software ecosystem · Device fragmentation phenomenon · Feature model · Android

1 Introduction

"A Software ECOsystem (SECO) is the interaction of a set of actors on top of a common technological platform that results in a number of software solutions or services" [1]. A Mobile Software ECOsystem (MSECO) is a software ecosystem that consists of a set of actors where the actors interact with each other through a common technological platform that enables a number of mobile applications to simultaneously run on mobile devices such as smart phone, tablet and smart watch [2].

In the past, the mobile manufacturers developed mobile software using in-house platforms whereas today the majority of manufacturers develop mobile software using open platforms such as Android. Since mobile manufacturers develop various differentiated hardware components for device differentiation around strategically selected open platforms, there are a huge number of devices [3] in the current mobile software environment. This is called the *device fragmentation phenomenon* [4].

© ICST Institute for Computer Sciences, Social Informatics and Telecommunications Engineering 2016
Y. Zhang et al. (Eds.): CloudComp 2015, LNICST 167, pp. 189–199, 2016.
DOI: 10.1007/978-3-319-38904-2_20

According to the survey in [3], conducted by Open Signal, as of 2013, there exist approximately 682,000 Android devices. These devices are classified into 11,868 species by various criteria, such as manufacturer, version of API, display resolution etc. Moreover, since the number of mobile devices increase steadily every year, devices fragmentation phenomenon will be worse in 2015. The device fragmentation phenomenon affects four stakeholders in the software ecosystem: the platform providers, the end-users, the application developers, and the market service providers. Among them, especially, the application developers will have difficulty in verifying compatibility whether developed application will run on specific devices.

To relieve the application developers of the burden arising from the device fragmentation phenomenon, we propose the *Feature-Oriented Mobile Software (FOMS) development framework* and implement as part of the framework a tool that automates compatibility verification. Our framework is the result of viewing the device fragmentation phenomenon from the perspective of application developers. It is composed of the domain part and the application part. In the domain part, domain experts collect the features of devices and analyze it using the software product line approach. In the application part, developers take advantage of the artifacts constructed by domain experts for application development. To evaluate our framework, we conducted a case study with 10 devices and 21 features used in real world. It shows that a significant efforts reduction is possible by using our framework rather than the traditional approach.

This paper is organized as follows. In Sect. 2, we introduce background for understanding our framework. In Sect. 3, we describe the FOMS development framework for resolving the device fragmentation phenomenon from the perspective of application developers. In Sect. 4, we introduce our tool for automation of compatibility verification. In Sect. 5, we conduct a case study. In Sect. 6, we discuss related works dealing with the device fragmentation phenomenon. Lastly, we conclude with our contributions and future works in Sect. 7.

2   Background

In this section, we introduce the device fragmentation phenomenon, the concept of feature model and a classification of mobile device features.

2.1   The Device Fragmentation Phenomenon

The stakeholders of the mobile software ecosystem are the platform provider, the end-user, the application developer and the market service provider. To these stakeholders the device fragmentation phenomenon causes the following problems. First, the platform provider has difficulty in managing platform evolution since various versions of a platform exist. Second, the end-user has difficulty in finding an application that is compatible with the user device. Third, the application developer has difficulty in testing developed software because they do not know the compatible target devices. Lastly, the market service provider has difficulty in providing exact application since they do not know precisely what features each device has.

2.2   Feature Model

Feature model was first introduced in the feature oriented domain analysis (FODA) [5] method in 1990 by Kang et al. Since then, feature model has been widely used to model relationships between features including commonality and variability of features by many Software Product Line Engineering [6] researchers. In the early stage of software product line development, the feature modeling technique is very instrumental in identifying and analyzing reusable parts. There are many kinds of feature models including FODA, FORM [7], Cardinality-based FM [8], etc. Among them, we will use the basic feature model in [9], which includes mandatory, optional, OR and alternative feature and constraints (i.e. the require constraint and the exclude constraint).

2.3   Classification of Mobile Device Features

Lee and Kang [2] classified features in mobile devices into four groups: platform features, manufacturer features, regional features and differentiated features. A platform feature is a feature distributed by a platform vendor. Examples of a platform feature are GPS, Bluetooth and LTE. A manufacturer feature is a feature made by the mobile manufacturer to compete with other mobile companies. A regional feature is a feature used for a specific country or a network operator. Lastly, a differentiated feature is a unique feature for product differentiation. Examples of a differentiated feature are IrDA, S-pen and Finger scan. In this paper, the domain experts will construct a feature model using a classification method and the basic feature model technique.

3   A Feature-Oriented Mobile Software (FOMS) Development Framework

In this section, Sect. 3.1 describes our FOMS development framework for resolving the device fragmentation phenomenon and Sect. 3.2 explains the process of the framework with a simple example.

3.1   Methodology

Figure 1 shows our FOMS development framework. It consists of two parts: the domain part and the application part. In the domain part, the domain experts such as software product line experts and platform vendors are in charge of data collections and construction of a feature model. In the application part, the application developers derive useful information for application development from the constructed feature model.

The FOMS development framework has six steps. In steps (1) and (2), device information is gathered from a specific source such as a description file, which describes device information in a format specified by the market service provider.

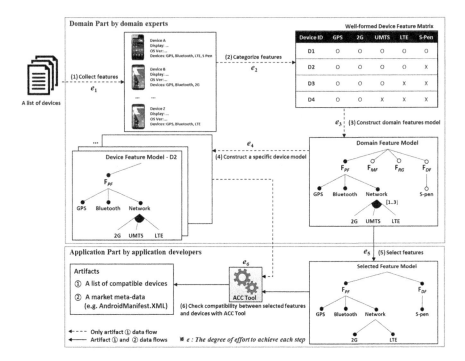

Fig. 1. The procedure of the FOMS development framework

To extract the features of a device, the domain experts can take advantage of description file. Each piece of device information should be given in a well-organized form, such as matrix, table or database.

In steps (3) and (4), the domain experts construct the feature model from the Device Feature Matrix. Since the feature model has a hierarchical tree structure, the domain expert should know the characteristics of each feature of a device. All of the features are categorized into the four groups using the classification method explained in Sect. 2.3. As a result, two feature models are constructed: Domain Feature Model and Device Feature Model. The domain feature model represents all device information while the device feature model represents feature information of a specific device.

In step (5), the application developers can select various features in the domain feature model following the application specification of what the developer should develop.

In step (6), compatibility between the selected feature model and each device feature model should be checked. To that end, the application developer can use the ACC (Automated Compatibility Calculation) tool that we developed as part of the FOMS development framework, which automatically check compatibility between them.

At the end of the process, the framework generates two artifacts: a list of compatible devices and a market meta-data. The market meta-data will take advantage of the fragments of AndroidManifest.xml for checking compatibility between developed application and specific devices in Google Play Store.

3.2 A Conceptual Example for the FOMS Development Framework

An example of a well-organized device feature matrix is given in Fig. 2(1). Since GPS is a kind of geographical sensor, the parent feature of GPS can be named as "Geo-sensor". In addition, since all devices have the GPS feature, it should be a mandatory feature. The features 2G, UMTS, and LTE are network features. So their parent feature can be named as "Networks", which can have at least one and at most three sub-features.

The domain feature model in Fig. 2(2) shows the feature model constructed from Fig. 2(1). To model the observations in the previous paragraph that the "Networks" feature is made up of three features (i.e. 2G, UMTS and LTE), Fig. 2(2) uses the *inclusive_or* constraint, in this case with the cardinality of *inclusive-or* of "from 1 to 3". The categories "Geo-sensor" and "Networks" can be classified into Platform Feature by [2]. On the other hand, since S-Pen is a feature for product differentiation by a Company S, it can also be classified into Differentiated Feature by [2]. The domain experts should name the parent feature of S-Pen as Company S and this feature is an optional feature.

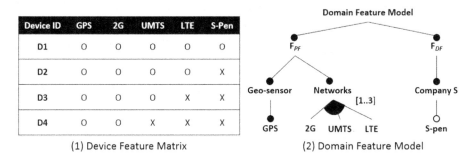

(1) Device Feature Matrix   (2) Domain Feature Model

Fig. 2. Device feature matrix and domain feature model

After the domain feature model is constructed, the developers can select the features in Fig. 2(2). In our example, if a developer selects four features, for example GPS, 2G, UMTS, and LTE, which can be described as:

Table 1. Compatibility calculation for the example in Table 1 and C_e

Devices	Platform feature				Differentiated feature	Compatibility calculation with C_e
	GPS	2G	UMTS	LTE	S-Pen	
D1	O	O	O	O	O	O
D2	O	O	O	O	X	O
D3	O	O	O	X	X	X^*
D4	O	O	X	X	X	X^{**}

[*]LTE is not supported by D3
[**]UMTS and LTE are not supported by D4

$$C_e = \{GPS,\ 2G,\ UMTS,\ LTE\}$$

To support development, the framework produces two pieces of information: a list of compatible devices and a market meta-data. Table 1 shows that D1 and D2 are compatible while D3 and D4 are not. In addition, we will describe a detailed description of the market meta-data in Sect. 5.

4   The Automation of Compatibility Calculation

As part of the FOMS development framework, we implemented a tool ACC and posted it at http://salab-intra.kaist.ac.kr/FOMS. The language used for the server side of ACC is PHP. ACC consists of two components: one for domain feature model configuration and the other for application development support. Developers can get application development support by making a device configuration for an application in the former component after pressing 'submit' button. The application development support component consists of three sections: a list of compatible devices, a list of incompatible devices and auto-generated market meta-data, which is applied to AndroidMenifest. xml. With the result component, the developers can notify which devices are compatible with the application. Moreover, the developers can paste auto-generated XML code fragments directly into the development asset, i.e. AndroidManifest.xml.

The ACC tool uses the set operation *union* ($\cup$) for implementing compatibility calculation as in the formula F1. As an example for using ACC, if a set of features in device D (i.e. Device Feature Model) is compatible for given selected features C (i.e. Selected Feature Model), then C must be subset of D and F1 should be satisfied.

$$D \cup C = D \tag{F1}$$

To implement the compatibility calculation, the feature set of device information is represented as a binary scheme as exemplified in Fig. 3. A bit location represents a feature. The value indicates existence or non-existence of a feature, with "1" representing that the device or configuration have the feature and "0" representing that the device or configuration does not have the feature. For example, in Fig. 3, ①, ②, ③ and ④ each represents a feature. The value 1001 means that features 1 and 4 exist but features 2 and 3 do not.

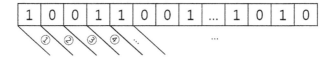

Fig. 3. A binary scheme for representing device information

For compatibility calculation, the condition whether the given configuration satisfies a compatibility F1 or not, can be defined as F2.

$$(d + c) \oplus d = 0 \tag{F2}$$

where **d** is a binary scheme for a specific device **D**, and **c** is the configuration for device **C** given by the developer.

When OR operation is applied to **d** and **c**, if **C** is subset of **D**, then it will produce value **d**. Since XOR gives 0, if two given operands have the same value, the result is 0. The meaning of the result with 0 from this calculation is that the device and given configuration is compatible. Table 2 shows an example of compatibility calculation. Suppose that the domain has four features, each named as "Feature n". Then if the developer gives device configuration with the value 1101 (Features 1, 2, and 4), the compatibility calculation results become as in Table 2, which shows that devices A and B are compatible with the configuration that comes from the user. However, it also shows that C and D are incompatible.

Table 2. Device compatibility calculation

Device name	Device A	Device B	Device C	Device D
d	0xF (1111)	0xD (1101)	0x9 (1001)	0x2 (0010)
c	0xD (1101)	0xD (1101)	0xD (1101)	0xD (1101)
Calculation	1111 + 1101 $\oplus$ 1111 0000	1101 + 1101 $\oplus$ 1101 0000	1001 + 1101 $\oplus$ 1101 0100	0010 + 1101 $\oplus$ 1111 0010
Result	Compatible	Compatible	Incompatible	Incompatible

5 A Case Study

For the device feature tree, we used a well-formed table, the appendix table in [2], as an input. We classified 21 features and represented its actual values in binary. The identified features were 21, and we limited the number of devices to 10. Table 3 shows the result of classifications.

There are 21 identified features, and we limited the number of devices to 10. There are three identified categories: Platform Feature (PF), Manufacturer Feature (MF), and Differentiated Feature (DF). PF is further classified into four categories: Graphic Resolution with five features, Geographic Devices with 2 features, Network with three features and Wireless Network with three features. MF is classified into one category, touch panel. Since we identified the touch panels that are included in all devices but the type of touch panel differs from manufacturer to manufacturer, those features are

Table 3. Classification of 21 features and their binary values

Category	Classification	Features	V: hex value (true)	S: count of shift
Development information	API version	Version 4	0x4	19
		Version 3	0x2	
		Version 2	0x1	
Platform feature	Graphic resolution	HD	0x10	14
		WXGA	0x8	
		WVGA	0x4	
		WQVGA	0x2	
		QVGA	0x1	
	Geo-sensor devices	GPS	0x2	12
		Accelerometer	0x1	
	Networks	2G	0x4	9
		UMTS	0x2	
		LTE	0x1	
	Wireless network	NFC	0x0	2
		IrDa	0x4	
		Bluetooth	0x2	
Manufacturer feature	Touch	Common touch	0x1	5
		TouchWiz	0x4	
		Optimus UI	0x2	
		Sense UI	0x1	
Differentiated feature	Company S	S Pen	0x2	0
	Company L	Back hold	0x1	

Table 4. Device binary code for compatibility verification

Device ID	D1	D2	D3	D4	D5
Code	0x1FFF14	0x1FFF1C	0x1FFF9E	0x1FFF9A	0x1FFF55
Device ID	D6	D7	D8	D9	D10
Code	0x1FFF90	0x1FFF14	0x046404	0x04FC30	0x1FF29E

classified into Manufacturer Feature. DF is classified into 2 company names with 1 feature for each. Furthermore, for the market meta-data auto-generation, we added a new category "Development Information".

For convenience, we divided features by category and added the count of shift to left that is required to represent the actual value. The formula for getting actual decimal value is as follows:

$$R = V \cdot 2^S$$

In the case of the HD graphic resolution feature, the hex value for it is as follows:

$$0x10 \cdot 2^{14} = 0x10 \ll 14 = 0x40000$$

With this feature value, we represented 10 devices as a sequence of 21 bits as shown in Table 4. We named each device with alphabet D and a number, i.e. D1 through D10. One of the data we used is bit representation for D1, which is 0x1FFF14. This means that API versions are compatible with $2 \sim 4$ (first three bits from left is 111) and all graphic resolutions are covered. However, it also says that the "S-Pen" feature and the "Back hold" feature are unusable on this device because the last two bits are 00.

We configured the domain feature model with the following feature set:

$$E = \{ \text{API Version 4, HD, WVGA, GPS,} \\ \text{Accelerometer, Common touch panel, Bluetooth} \}.$$

The result showed that compatible devices for this configuration are D1, D2, D3, D5 and D7. In addition, the auto-generated *SDK version* tag and set of *permission* tags of device usage for a market meta-data, AndroidManifest.xml. Developer should copy & paste to the AndroidManifest.XML which belongs to developing application. To evaluate our approach, the required efforts for both the traditional approach and the FOMS development framework should be measured quantitatively for comparison.

The traditional approach requires developers to verify compatibility and write market meta-data in manual. If changes occur to an application, developers should verify it with n devices. Also they should verify compatibility and apply changes to market meta-data n times. Let define the required efforts for verifying compatibility to be v and those for giving changes on market meta-data to be δw. Moreover, if there are m comparisons, the overall efforts become m times bigger. The total required efforts are as in F3.

$$E_t = m \cdot \sum_{i=1}^{n} (v_i + \delta w_i) \tag{F3}$$

To measure the performance of our FOMS development framework, let us define the efforts required for step n as e_n. Steps $1 \sim 4$ are required only once even if there are many devices. Therefore, they are independent from m. For step 5, there can be m configurations. In the case of step 6, the compatibility verification work is automated to ACC. Therefore, e_6 is ignored. Thus, the formula for the overall required efforts becomes F4.

$$E_{FOMS} = \sum_{i=1}^{4} e_i + m \cdot e_5 \tag{F4}$$

To show the usefulness of our approach, the result of F4 should be smaller than F3. F5 shows the interaction formula between the traditional approach and FOMS.

$$\sum_{i=1}^{4} e_i + m \cdot e_5 < m \cdot \sum_{j=1}^{n} (v_j + \delta w_j) \tag{F5}$$

However, in the perspective of application developers, the required efforts for steps $1 \sim 4$ are constants. Therefore, e_5 are independent from the number of devices n. F6 shows F5 in the big-O notation.

$$O(m) < O(m \cdot n) \tag{F6}$$

6   Related Works

As the works that address the device fragmentation phenomenon, there are only a few methods developed in the past and they all approached it from the perspectives of the platform provider and the market service provider.

Google Android is an open source platform that is based on the embedded Linux and a modified JAVA virtual machine [10]. In the case of open platform, due to the features arbitrarily appended by the device manufacturer, it is hard to avoid device fragmentation [2]. Therefore, to solve this problem, Google distributes both the device compatibility policy [11] and the application filtering policy [12]. However, the traditional platform-centric method handles only the features of platform vendors without considering unique features of devices, such as a device-manufacturer's feature and a device-differential feature [2]. To solve this problem, [2] proposed a device-centric method that considers all features of existing devices. The above methods tried to solve device fragmentation phenomenon from the market service perspective. However, in order to eliminate the problem of device fragmentation phenomenon in a fundamental way, its solution should be considered from the development perspective, as was done in this paper, since application developers do not know target devices and will develop software that runs on the reference terminal such as Google Nexus 5, Nexus 7 and Nexus S.

7   Conclusion

The FOMS development framework relieves the application developers of the burden of manually verifying device compatibility that arises from the device fragmentation phenomenon by providing a systematic process and the automated compatibility calculation tool ACC. According to the process, a domain feature model is first constructed and device feature models that can be commonly used by all application developers are constructed from it. Then the developer of a specific application can efficiently select from the domain feature model a feature model corresponding to the application and use the tool to produce a list of compatible devices automatically from the selected feature model and the device feature models.

To evaluate our approach, we conducted a case study with 10 devices and 21 features. We also presented evaluation formulas and showed the proposed framework is more efficient for mobile application development than the traditional approach by resolving device fragmentation phenomenon from the perspective of application developers.

For future works, we plan to integrate our framework into an existing IDE such as Eclipse and RmCRC IDE [13]. Furthermore, we are going to resolve device fragmentation phenomenon also from the viewpoints of the end-user and the platform provider.

Acknowledgments. This research was supported by the MSIP (Ministry of Science, ICT and Future Planning), Korea, under the ITRC (Information Technology Research Center) support program (IITP-2015-H8501-15-1015) supervised by the IITP (Institute for Information & communications Technology Promotion).

References

1. Manikas, K., Hansen, K.M.: Software ecosystems–a systematic literature review. J. Syst. Softw. **86**, 1294–1306 (2013)
2. Lee, H., Kang, S.W.: An efficient application-device matching method for the mobile software ecosystem. In: 2014 21st Asia-Pacific Software Engineering Conference (APSEC), pp. 175–182. IEEE (2014)
3. Android Fragmentation Report, July 2013. http://opensignal.com/reports/fragmentation-2013/
4. Park, J.-H., Park, Y.B., Ham, H.K.: Fragmentation problem in android. In: 2013 International Conference on Information Science and Applications (ICISA), pp. 1–4. IEEE (2013)
5. Kang, K.C., Cohen, S.G., Hess, J.A., Novak, W.E., Peterson, A.S.: Feature-oriented domain analysis (FODA) feasibility study. DTIC Document (1990)
6. Böckle, G., van der Linden, F.J., Pohl, K.: Software Product Line Engineering: Foundations. Principles and Techniques. Springer Science & Business Media, Heidelberg (2005)
7. Kang, K.C., Kim, S., Lee, J., Kim, K., Shin, E., Huh, M.: FORM: a feature-oriented reuse method with domain-specific reference architectures. Ann. Softw. Eng. **5**, 143–168 (1998)
8. Czarnecki, K., Kim, C.H.P.: Cardinality-based feature modeling and constraints: a progress report. In: International Workshop on Software Factories, pp. 16–20 (2005)
9. Benavides, D., Segura, S., Ruiz-Cortés, A.: Automated analysis of feature models 20 years later: a literature review. Inf. Syst. **35**, 615–636 (2010)
10. Butler, M.: Android: changing the mobile landscape. IEEE Pervasive Comput. **10**, 4–7 (2011)
11. Device Compatibility. http://developer.android.com/guide/practices/compatibility.html
12. Filters on Google Play. http://developer.android.com/google/play/filters.html
13. Nguyen, H.-Q., Nguyen, T.-D., Pham, P.-H., Pham, X.-Q., Alsaffar, A.A., Huh, E.-N.: An efficient platform for mobile application development on cloud environments. In: International Conference on Computer Applications and Information Processing Technology (2015)

Improving Data Access for Smart World

Tariq Lasloum[✉] and Ahmad S. Almogren

Computer Science Department, College of Computer and Information Sciences,
King Saud University, Riyadh, Saudi Arabia
lisloom@hotmail.com, ahalmogren@ksu.edu.sa

Abstract. Devices are becoming increasingly interconnected and increasingly linked to humans beings. The Internet of Things (IoT) concept was developed from the following technologies: the internet, wireless networks, and micro-electromechanical systems (MEMS). It is currently employed for home and industrial applications. Because of differing requirements, different protocols are used. It works on IP, TCP, and HTTP on TCP protocols through the MQTT, XMPP, DDS, and AMQP protocols. IoT evolved from the convergence of MEMS wireless technologies (like RFID and NFC) and the internet. The IoT concept is used in M2M applications like power, gas, and oil utilities' transmission and transport. In this paper, we use OPNET simulation to look at two scenarios and gather traffic data - received and average - for DB query, FTP and Email. We propose an optional addressing method for smart-things to make up the smart world enabling the transmission and analysis of data automatically.

Keywords: The Internet of Things · Sensors · RFID · OPNET

1 Introduction

As technology moves forward, probably the most important advances are in its applications to business and everyday life; information and communication are fields in which innovation has proceeded in a very short time - totally changing how people communicate, interact and do business. Within most organizations, and in everyday living, information travels through familiar routes and pathways. Proprietary data and information is stored in databases and can be analyzed and then shared with other parties, also data and information may be sourced from outside. Medical data, for example, is stored in medical records and can be shared through a secure network with authorised personnel - e.g. doctors.

In some instances, the physical world has become a form of information system: with physical objects taking part via their sensors and their ability to communicate; thus, creating a new kind of information network. These new information networks have the potential to improve communications, create new business models, and improve business processes. They also have the potential to increase convenience and reduce communications costs.

In the IoT, actuators, sensors, and data transmitters are components of physical objects. These physical objects range from pacemakers, to fridges, to roadways, and are connected through a series of wireless and wired networks. These networks often use the Internet protocol (IP) which connects the World Wide Web (www). The physical objects have the

© ICST Institute for Computer Sciences, Social Informatics and Telecommunications Engineering 2016
Y. Zhang et al. (Eds.): CloudComp 2015, LNICST 167, pp. 200–210, 2016.
DOI: 10.1007/978-3-319-38904-2_21

ability to sense the environment around them and to communicate - generating huge volumes of data to be analysed by computers. The IoT holds great promise for the future and will no doubt have many applications. This paper evaluates the concept of IoT: looking at its evolution, history, protocols, its simulation, and via this its capacity for throughput. After that, conclusions are presented. Relevant peer-reviewed and/or otherwise credible sources of literature are used as sources of information.

The Internet of Things is made up of Internet-linked devices: at any time, and in any place - as shown in Fig. 1. Examples of 'things' are: your mobile, or a device which remotely starts your car or turns on or off your air-conditioner.

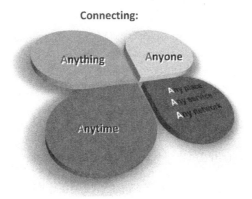

Fig. 1. Connected anything, anytime and anyplace.

The IoT is a phenomenon in which uniquely identifiable objects, including human 'objects' are represented in a virtual internet-like structure. The participants in this network are able to communicate and transfer data and information over a network automatically without human or computer mediation. A 'Thing' in the IoT framework refers to any physical object, even a human being, which has been allocated a unique identifier: a human being, for instance, might have a tiny monitor in their blood intestinal tract which scans and transmits data. In general, a 'thing' is any device or entity with a unique identifier to which an IP address can be assigned and which can transmit information over a network. Entities or devices with component parts which are chips that can automatically transmit information and have IP addresses are termed 'smart devices' [1].

At present, very many places have wireless networks and are thus available to the internet - therefore it is possible to include these in the Internet of Things. Clearly, the internet is not only a network for people to communicate with each other using computer but also to connect with those around you from the devices over wireless networks. An IoT is a network that connects all devices with the existing IT infrastructure, that uses sensor technologies, that includes Radio-Frequency Identification (RFID), wireless sensor networks, and also mobile telephony. The IoT concept can help in more than one area. One of these is domestic energy management. As shown in Fig. 2.

In this paper, we first introduce the IoT. In Sect. 2, we describe some related work; Sect. 3 shows a typical IoT architecture. Simulations of the different application environments which can use the IoT are presented in Sect. 4. Finally, our conclusions are discussed in Sect. 5.

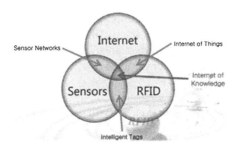

Fig. 2. The internet, sensors and RFID.

2   Related Work

The IoT is sometimes referred to the IoO (The Internet of Objects), and it already affects human life and how animals, humans, and machines interact. The IoT has huge potential for data and information gathering, also for analysis and distribution and thus for turning data into knowledge. IoT projects are being undertaken which will narrow the gap between the rich and poor, and which have the potential to better distribute resources amongst people. With an IoT involving sensors planted in many places and connected to computers/software, it will be possible to improve our understanding of the universe and how humans interact with it.

At the present the IoT can be looked on as a 'network of networks'. For example, the cars that we drive today have many sensors which control functions from fuel injection, to engine speed, to braking and in-car temperature. Homes have control systems that handle heating, air conditioning, and indoor humidity. These separate networks will in future be connected, with resultant increased management functionalities - due to the IoT [2].

The IoT has many current applications, and many more potential applications that have the capacity to revolutionize the world. Mobile phones presently account for the highest connected segment, but industries like healthcare, security, financial services, and the car industry hold great potential for further inter connectivity. It is projected that the number of connected devices will be approximately 24 billion by 2020: creating a global new business impact of $ 4.5 trillion [3].

The majority of device source code is based on specific operating systems (for example TinyOS2 and Contiki3) which were developed for resource-controlled platforms. Furthermore, in the wireless sensor networks (WSNs) area, the application source code is conventionally developed directly over the Operating System OS. Mainly the source code is developed in the same language as the OS, statically associated to it, and not, in any effective way, isolated from it. This leads to an efficient application, although also it may increase the level of errors and make the code more complex, - requiring the developers to understand both the specifics of the OS and the platform [4].

The top ten applications of IoT include connected cars, remote clinical monitoring, assisted living, building and home security, and pay as you drive car insurance. Other areas are smart meters, traffic management applications, charging electric vehicles, and building automation. Home energy monitoring and car sensors are areas with extensive IoT applications. Energy is today a sensitive topic with concerted efforts being made to reduce consumption, use renewable sources, and also use clean energy. Energy monitoring IoT applications exist which use an open network platform working over a wireless system with sensors [5].

The term 'internet of things' was coined in 1999; the development of the IoT has progressed through a number of stages due to the convergence of MEMS (micro-electromechanical systems), wireless technologies, and the internet. RFID (radio frequency identification) is also something which falls within the scope of the modern day IoT. The concept was developed from the principle of uniquely identifying objects and people – thus making the network manageable by computers [6].

The development of IoT was, in particular, due to the requirements of critical operations such as oil and gas drilling, and also manufacturing. For instance, drilling a geothermal well requires the use of a constant stream of information which cannot effectively be managed by a human agency. The need for an automatic and reliable method for collecting and transmitting information thus became important [7].

Other applications, for instance tracking and loading passenger luggage, required an automated process as human intervention was tedious and cumbersome. The situation also required occasional human intervention (for managing and identifying items quickly and automatically). These needs have led to the development of RFID and other technologies - including NFC (near field communication), QR codes, barcode, and digital watermarks. In general though, the IoT has been associated more closely with M2M (machine to machine) communications - mainly in power, gas, and oil utilities, and with manufacturing. The IoT can be traced to the early automated devices with internet capability such as the coke machine. Programmers had the ability to check if a cold drink would be available to them if they went to the vending machine. A similar system was developed in relation to a coffee machine that would let people know whether there was coffee available in the machine - remotely. Such initiatives increased interest in enabling devices and humans to communicate more seamlessly in various other application areas including health and industry. The internet is playing a key role in the evolution and development of the IoT as it allows data and information transmission over wired or wireless devices [7].

The recent development of more unique addressing capability courtesy of the internet protocol version 6 (IPv6) will greatly enhance the development of the IoT. The address space expansion courtesy of IPv6 implies an almost unlimited number of IP addresses that can be assigned - so IP addresses can be assigned to many more things. For example, a credit card with a smart chip can have an IP address assigned to it. With, in addition, fingerprint sensing, this means that the card could alert the user and the credit card company of any unauthorized use - even before a transaction took place. Such a transaction could then be stopped before it happened, and the card deactivated.

Presently over 5 billion devices have been interconnected. These devices range from home appliances to devices used in manufacturing. Homes now have automated lighting, sprinkler systems, and security systems – all possibly linked to the internet. Industry's needs have led to the requirement for horizontal and vertical balance in making interconnections.

Future developments will require a challenge like multi connectivity, power management, security, rapid evolution and complexity [8].

One of the most important attributes of the IOT is the use of sensors. These are increasing in number and reducing in cost. Sensors can now provide data on almost any physical variable: movement, sound, light, temperature, moisture, location. Some sensors are used only for a few days and then discarded.

Traditional Wi-Fi systems allow the network to be setup by the sensor. Normally, networks are made up of a number of Wi-Fi transceivers that allow actuators and sensors to be linked to the Access Point (AP). Of course, the Access point may be connected to Internet - as shown in Fig. 3.

Fig. 3. Sensors and actuators linked directly to an Access Point (AP).

3   System Architecture

The IoT protocol works on a series of rules including D2D (device to device communication) where devices must communicate with each other. This communication and movement of data uses protocols which include MQTT, XMPP, DDS, and AMQP.

Data from devices must be collected and sent to a server infrastructure (D2S- device to server) which then shares the data from the devices with other servers (S2S – server to server). The data and information can then be sent back to the devices, shared with people, or analysed using programs [6].

We have, so far, identified the high level components needed for the Internet of Things. Each of these components may also be found outside of the IoT. The following are IoT components:

(a) **Hardware** - actuators, embedded communication hardware, and sensors.
(b) **Middleware** - storage and computing utilities for information analytics that are on demand.

(c) **Presentation** - visualization that is clear to understand and implemented in such a way that it can be accessed across different platforms. In addition, these tools may be considered for diverse applications as shown in Fig. 4.

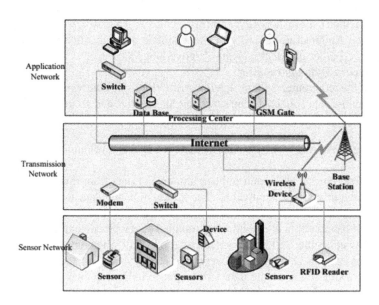

Fig. 4. Typical architecture of IoT.

Radio Frequency Identification (RFID). Important components in embedded communications are represented by RFID technology. This allows the development of microprocessor systems which record data about wireless communications. Passive RFID tags do not need batteries to operate. In addition, the RFID reader can receive an ID by operating on the power of the signal. There are a number of places where such systems can be found: e.g. transportation (instead of tickets, registration labels) and admin/control applications. Furthermore the tags can be used in bank credit cards and on toll roads.

Wireless Sensor Networks (WSN). Autonomous sensors distributed by a wireless sensor network (WSN) of spatially to control the physical and environmental terms, and to cooperatively maintain data flow on a network to a core location.

Wireless communications have made available well-organized, low cost, low power, and very small devices which can be used in remote recognition applications. The components that create the WSN monitoring network contain:

(a) **WSN hardware**
A node (WSN core hardware) which uses processers, sensor interfaces, power source, and transceiver units. They are, in effect, a series of several converters for the sensor interface.

(b) **WSN communication stack**

The communication stack at the node needs to link with the external world via the Internet, and to work as an entry to the Internet and the WSN subnet.

(c) **Middleware**

It is a method used to merge cyber infrastructure with a sensor networks and Service Oriented Architecture (SOA) to make available administration to heterogeneous sensor resources in a deployment self-governing.

(d) **The secure Data aggregation**

One of the requirements for prolonging the lifetime of the network and making sure that reliable data collected from sensors is an effective and secure data aggregation method [6].

Data storage. An important element in this area is the development of an unprecedented.

The IoT revolution will result in huge amounts of data from different sources and devices, all requiring huge bandwidths. The information and data are same to be transmitted through the WAN (wide area networks) which already suffers from a bandwidth gap. Limited bandwidth will result in the strangled development and wider adoption of the IoT. New endpoints will be introduced by the IoT, of which endpoints will also be different from what is being used. However, the strategy was adopted for the provision of low bandwidth, high volume data throughput to help keep costs low. This can be achieved through cellular networks using high speed technologies like 3G that will offer higher data rates. Wireless systems that use very low data throughputs as well as low power were developed. Other means for connectivity include satellite M2M that has unique capabilities as it can work nearly everywhere in the world. Satellite M2M can be rolled out fast and on a universal scale without the need for local connectivity for instance, using SIM cards.

Satellite M2M is very scalable with the ability to recover quickly from natural disasters and outages. It can be applied in dual mode devices that have terrestrial and satellite networks. Because of the multi device nature, IoT will require low cost and low power ubiquitous systems to work efficiently. Because of the different protocols and requirements at different stages, the IoT system uses integrated communication links incorporating radio, cable, and fibre optic. Future developments will require fibre connection between servers, satellite M2M and cable or radio between devices and servers.

4 Simulation

The IoT will result in connecting billions of 'things', and this requires prior simulation before it can be implemented in real world situations. Simulation will be necessary in order to understand the IoTs various components and operating principles, especially with regard to scale. Simulating the IoT will require the integration of an accurate OS (Operating System) simulation into a generic simulation environment as a first step.

OMNeT++ and Contiki can provide a suitably integrated OS. Contiki has wide support for sensors and hardware actuators embedded into devices, making it suitable for IoT. OMNeT++ is a simulation library that has been used widely and has a large set of available extension frameworks and simulation models.

For this paper, we use the OPNET program for the simulation of two scenarios in order to deduce traffic - received and average - for DB query, FTP and Email. In scenario 1 we used 30 nodes and in scenario2 we used 40 nodes. This is shown in Fig. 5.

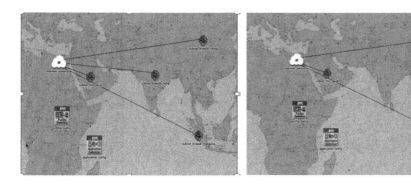

Fig. 5. Two scenarios.

In Fig. 6, we show FTP in terms of packets rate from 30 nodes in the chart (a) and from 40 nodes in the chart (b). In Fig. 7, we show DB query in terms of packets rate from 30 nodes in the chart (a) and from 40 nodes in the chart (b). In Fig. 8, we show the Email in terms of packets rate from 30 nodes in the chart (a) and from 40 nodes in the chart (b).

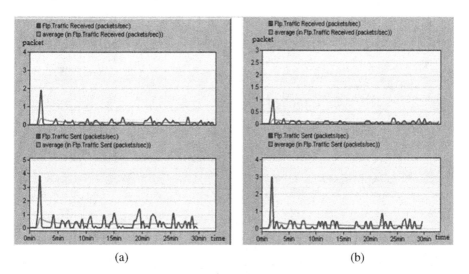

(a)   (b)

Fig. 6. (a) Simulation for FTP application, traffic received, sent and average in scenario1, (b) simulation for FTP application, traffic received, sent and average in scenario2 (Color figure online).

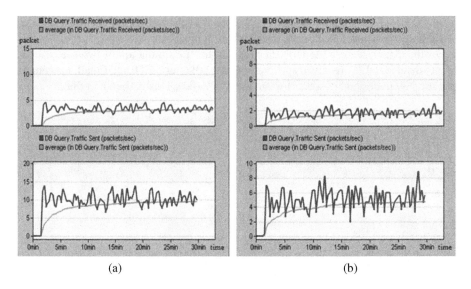

Fig. 7. (a) Simulation for DB query application, traffic received, sent and average in scenario1, (b) simulation for FTP application, traffic received, sent and average in scenario2 (Color figure online).

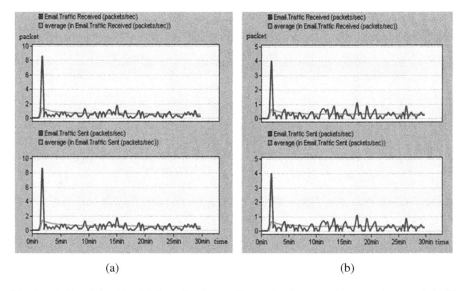

Fig. 8. (a) Simulation for eMail application, traffic received, sent and average in scenario1, (b) simulation for FTP application, traffic received, sent and average in scenario2 (Color figure online).

The second step in the simulation is the accurate presentation of the various protocols from the different-used network stack layers. Low layer protocols such as ZigBee can be used for protocol representation since it can be modelled accurately in OMNeT++.

By using the actual protocol implementation, we will give better and more accurate results for instance using the NSC (network simulation cradle). Moreover, using real protocols during IoT simulation enable designers and stakeholders unearth concepts not yet understood about IoT.

5   Conclusion

The IoT is a promising phenomenon. Many things are interconnected through networks, and communicate by using various network protocols. IoT is a concept which uniquely addresses 'things', inanimate or human, which are able to gather and transmit information and data automatically. IoT evolved from the convergence of MEMS wireless technologies like RFID and NFC, and the internet. IoT has been used in M2M applications like power, gas, and oil utilities transmission and transport. IoT uses the IP, TCP and HTTP over TCP protocols as its communications backbone. Because of differing requirements, different protocols are used. For this paper, we used OPNET to look at two scenarios and gather traffic data - received and average - for DB query, FTP and Email.

IoT has a bright future and will revolutionize how people do business, communicate, and interact with 'things' - it is a network of networks.

References

1. Castro, D., Misra, J.: The Internet of Things, November 2013
2. Evans, D.: The Internet of Things, How the Next Evolution of the Internet is Changing Everything, April 2011
3. Royer, M.: The Internet of Things (IoT). Ph.D., August 2013
4. Kovatsch, M., Lanter, M., Duquennoy, S.: Actinium: a RESTful runtime container for scriptable Internet of Things applications. In: Proceedings of the 3rd International Conference on the Internet of Things (IoT 2012), Wuxi, China, October 2012
5. Bouhafs, F., Rajabi, D.: Open sensing platform for HomeEnergy monitoring in the Internet of Things. Int. J. Eng. Sci. 2(1), 53–61 (2013)
6. Gubbi, J., Marusic, S., Buyya, R., Palaniswami, M.: Internet of Things (IoT): a vision, architectural elements, and future directions. Future Gener. Comput. Syst. 29(7), 1645–1660 (2013)
7. Chase, J.: The Evolution of the Internet of Things, September 2013
8. Links, C.: Sentrollers and The Internet of Things. GreenPeak Technologies, Utrecht, May 2013
9. Guinard, D., Ion, I., Mayer, S.: In search of an Internet of Things service architecture: REST or WS-*? A developers' perspective. In: Proceedings of Mobiquitous 2011 (8th International ICST Conference on Mobile and Ubiquitous Systems), pp. 326–337, Copenhagen, Denmark, December 2011
10. Brown, M., Coughlan, T., Lawson, G., Goulden, M., Houghton, R.J., Mortier, R.: Exploring interpretations of data from the Internet of Things in the home. Interact. Comput. 25(3), 204–217 (2013)
11. Carretero, J.: The Internet of Things: connecting the world. Pers. Ubiquit. Comput. 18(2), 445–447. Springer, London (2013)

12. Khriyenko, O., Terziyan, V., Kaikova, O.: End-user facilitated interoperability in Internet of Things. Int. J. Adv. Internet Technol. **6**(1&2), 90–100 (2013)
13. Mattern, F., Floerkemeier, C.: From the internet of computers to the Internet of Things. In: Sachs, K., Petrov, I., Guerrero, P. (eds.) Buchmann Festschrift. LNCS, vol. 6462, pp. 242–259. Springer, Heidelberg (2010)
14. Bin, S., Yuan, L., Xiaoyi, W.: Research on Data Mining Models for the Internet of things (2010)
15. Uckelmann, D., Harrison, M., Michahelles, F.: An architectural approach towards the future Internet of Things. In: Uckelmann, D., Harrison, M., Michahelles, F. (eds.) Architecting the Internet of Things, pp. 1–24. Springer, Berlin Heidelberg (2010)
16. Fleisch, E.: (ETH Zurich/University of St. Gallen) what is the internet of things, January 2010

Pervasive Cloud Applications, Services and Testbeds

Implications of Integration and Interoperability for Enterprise Cloud-Based Applications

Justice Opara-Martins[✉], Reza Sahandi, and Feng Tian

Faculty of Science and Technology, Bournemouth University, Bournemouth, UK
{joparamartins,rsahandi,ftian}@bournemouth.ac.uk

Abstract. Enterprise's adoption of cloud-based solutions is often hindered by problems associated with the integration of the cloud environment with on-premise systems. Currently, each cloud provider creates its proprietary application programming interfaces (APIs), which will complicate integration efforts for companies as they struggle to understand and manage these unique application interfaces in an interoperable way. This paper aims to address this challenge by providing recommendations to enterprises. The presented work is based on a quantitative study of 114 companies, which discuss current issues and future trends of integration and interoperability requirements for enterprise cloud application adoption and migration. The outcome of the discussion provides a guideline applicable to support decision makers, software architects and developers when considering to design and develop interoperable applications in order to avoid lock-in and integrate seamlessly into other cloud and on-premise systems.

Keywords: Enterprise cloud · Integration · Cloud-to-cloud integration · SaaS integration · Distributed applications · Business process transformation

1 Introduction

Cloud computing has emerged as a strong factor driving companies to remarkable business success [1]. The cloud paradigm is an attractive deployment option for many enterprises as they continuously strive to reduce business complexity and improve user productivity through process standardization [2]. The scalability, multitenancy, elasticity and on-demand access of the cloud, etc. removes many barriers to enterprise deployment. While cloud applications offer outstanding value in terms of multitenant features and functionalities, they introduce several integration and interoperability challenges that hinder enterprises' decisions for or against cloud adoption. The first challenge is that, many organisations have different systems and applications that might use different technologies, protocols, applications and devices distributed across a network [2, 3]. In such heterogeneous environments, information can come from many places — such as transactions, operational, document repositories and external information sources in many formats, including data, content and streaming information [3]. In this aspect, lost, inaccurate or incomplete information also can generate high costs and the loss of productivity when having to search for information or synchronize data. Moreover, poor data quality can lead to failure of business processes and erroneous decision-making. The second challenge is that most core enterprise applications (such as Customer Relationship Management or CRM, Supply Chain Management or SCM and Enterprise Resource Planning or ERP systems) are being packaged to the cloud in a Software-as-a-Service (SaaS) model, and delivered to companies as point solutions that service only one Line of Business (LoB). As a result, organisations without a means of synchronizing data between multiple LoBs are at a serious disadvantage in terms of maintaining accurate data, inability to make real-time and information-backed decisions, and difficulty in realizing complete business process automation. Real-time sharing of data and functionality becomes difficult in such distributed computing environment. Finally, since each vendor that provides a cloud solution creates its own application programming interfaces (APIs) to the application, this will complicate integration efforts for companies of all sizes (small or large) and locations as they struggle to understand and then manage these unique application interfaces in an interoperable way, and integrate applications from cloud to cloud and cloud to on-premise systems.

Therefore, as enterprise environments are becoming increasingly distributed and heterogeneous, there is a need to integrate between disparate systems to satisfy business requirements and needs. In this paper, we argue that interoperability is one of the means by which enterprises can achieve such integration. Interoperability enables the exchange of data between two or more systems by adhering to common standards and protocols, whereas integration contends with the software and implementation details for interoperations. This includes exchange of data via interface standards, the use of middleware, mapping to common information exchange models etc. [4]. Integration in a general sense deals with technical connections between systems. In the absence of shared standards between systems, enabling seamless interaction between business processes in a heterogeneous environment becomes intricate. Since integration and interoperability both build upon standards, standardization should be considered as the key to achieve them in a distributed cloud environment. This argument is further substantiated with our survey findings reported at a later point in this paper.

The rest of the paper is structured as follows. Section 2 provides an overview of integration, evolving enterprise concerns and challenges, key survey findings and analysis, and the cloud integration imperatives. Current methods for enabling cloud integration are also discussed herein. Section 3 describes interoperability, highlights core enterprise requirements, and discusses how standards can be used to enable interoperability and seamless integration. Finally Sect. 4 presents conclusion and future research direction.

2   Cloud Integration

In the past, enterprise applications and data were linked within corporate Intranet through one or more standards-compliant integration platforms, brokers, and backbones such as, Enterprise Architecture Integration (EAI), Enterprise Service Bus (ESB), and Enterprise Information Integration (EII). Over the past few decades, there has been an evolution in integration architecture across the industry, with progressively greater degrees of exposure for a business function in a standardized way, enabled via "web APIs". In the current era, enterprises require capabilities that can be more easily sourced from cloud-based providers. Thus, exposing an interface offered by cloud providers or re-exposing an existing enterprise service via web API management is an efficient way of monetizing prior investment in integration.

Currently, with the advent of cloud computing, enterprise IT service delivery has moved from a single provider mode. This shift is increasingly based on the composition of multiple other services and assets (technological, human, or process) that may be supplied by one or more service providers distributed across the enterprise network in the cloud [5]. A consequence of this development is that consumers (i.e. enterprises and end-users) now have more choices of service provider that they can choose from. But as pointed out by [6], service consumers with global operations require faster response time, and thus save time by distributing workload requests to multiple clouds at the same time. Often, the onus is on the consumer to procure these web services individually and then integrate them per requirement [7]. To further complicate the situation, many companies are not (only) building on public clouds for their cloud computing needs, but combining public offerings with their own on-premise (private) IT infrastructure, leading to so-called hybrid cloud setups [8]. Management challenges also arise, due to privacy and compliance issues around data and existing investments in IT infrastructure, middleware, and business applications, which tend to provide opposing forces to hosting with the cloud. However, considering distributed cloud-based applications may be developed or provided by different vendors with varying programming languages, data formats and protocols, a significant integration effort is required to enhance and increase interoperability of these applications.

In such scenarios, the challenging question for enterprises' now is how to create seamless data flow between disparate applications hosted in the cloud environment so that they work together with other cloud products or with their on-premise counterparts. While a new generation of cloud-based integration tools has made this process less complex and expensive, contending with the explosive growth in APIs, software as a service (SaaS) applications etc. exponentially compounds the integration challenge. The required integration mechanism must federate between existing on-premise systems and new cloud applications, platform, and infrastructure, providing a rapid and easy-to-use method of setting up integrations [9]. The promise of cloud-based services is to reduce cost, simplify IT management, and improve productivity via automation and standardization [10]. However, the reality for consumers and IT managers is that to benefit from current cloud offerings, often they must adopt to cloud service provider specific interfaces that are incompatible with one another and with on-premise management services. Due to this beneficial extension, integration tasks have increased the complexity of decision-making in respect of enterprise cloud migration. The more enterprises adopt the cloud to host their business processes, equally there is a stronger need of a powerful tool to integrate their on-premise systems to the cloud. Therefore, as organisations struggle with the complexities of integrating cloud services with other critical systems residing on-premise, the ability to share data across these hybrid environments is critical.

2.1 Survey Findings and Analysis

This study seeks to identify interoperability requirements and integration implications for enterprise cloud-based application adoption. The research method used is based on Survey Monkey, a quantitative online survey questionnaire tool [11]. A total of 200 companies were invited to participate in the survey. Overall, 114 participants completed the online survey, which constituted an acceptable total response rate of 63 %. Participants in the survey varied between IT professionals, managers and decision-makers within their respective business enterprise. Prior to discussing the key findings, it should be pointed out that the questionnaire comprised of several questions, however only those which revealed crucial issues of integration and interoperability are presented and discussed in context.

The research reported in this paper reveals that over 50 % of businesses are already using cloud services, while a greater majority (69 %) utilise a combination of cloud services and internally owned applications (hybrid IT) for organisation needs. To explore the business rationale for migrating on-premise IT services to the cloud, this study raised the question "are you considering moving business critical systems (or applications) to the cloud?" The findings reveals that about 54 % of organisations have planned to move one or more business critical systems, while 20 % have expected to host critical systems in the cloud. However, only 10 % of organisations have actually implemented critical systems in the cloud environment.

Underestimating the difficulty associated with integrating between cloud and on-premise is a common pitfall with migrating enterprise systems to the cloud. Cloud adoption will be hampered if there is not a good way to integrate data and applications across clouds [12]. Moreover in [13], it is argued that the cost and complexity of developing and maintaining integrations between heterogeneous platforms with disparate interfaces and protocols can easily erase the economic and efficiency gains the cloud delivers. In agreement with the aforesaid, the survey by [14] of business managers around the world on their experiences with cloud-based applications, revealed that companies have abandoned the use of roughly one departmental cloud application a year due to integration problems. In the same study, 54 % of respondents acknowledge they have experienced staff downtime due to integration problems, and 75 % have had their ability to innovate impaired by poor integration of their cloud applications. This is further sustained with a more recent study by [15], which shows that 43 % of companies, with revenues greater than $500 million, noted integration challenges as primary barrier to enterprise cloud application adoption in 2015. Nevertheless, the survey conducted in this paper paints a clear picture on the importance of integrating cloud solutions with on-premise systems. As illustrated in Fig. 1, a vast majority (56 %) of respondents indicated that it is very important for their organisations to integrate on-premise IT assets with cloud-based services. This finding suggests organisations with a unique portfolio of IT investments migrating to cloud-based solutions require a mechanism that can easily, quickly and efficiently connect their critical systems to the cloud. It is anticipated that standardization of APIs will significantly help resolve this integration imperative, because it will facilitate development as well as the deployment process – eliminating the necessity of factoring applications to comply with other cloud providers APIs (as discussed further in Sect. 3). In fact, this means the integration solution must intersect somewhere between the corporate firewall. To look further at the figure below, the result also suggests most organisations are unlikely to have in place the in-house skills to support a major organization change in the near future. In this case, cloud providers are better placed to assist enterprises for their integration implementation, business process transformation, and strategic guidance (Fig. 1).

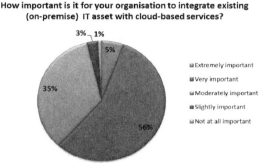

How important is it for your organisation to integrate existing (on-premise) IT asset with cloud-based services?

- Extremely important
- Very important
- Moderately important
- Slightly important
- Not at all important

Fig. 1. Imperative of Cloud Integration.

2.2 Cloud Integration Imperative

In today's contemporary business environment, immediate access to timely information is essential to quickly respond to changing customer needs, widening competitive threats, and new market openings. A major challenge in this aspect is the ability to capture the data being generated in this rapidly evolving environment and synchronize the data to optimize business operations while capitalizing on new market opportunities. This integration imperative is briefly discussed below to illustrate the emerging data and application challenges associated with utilizing proprietary cloud-based solutions.

Data Management: With the proliferation of cloud-based applications, platforms and infrastructure, the potential for data fragmentation and disconnected data silos has grown exponentially [16]. Only a decade ago, five million records would have been considered a large volume of data. However, at present, the volume of data stored by enterprises is often in the Petabyte, or even Exabyte [3]. Consequently, as the volume of data increases at a faster rate than the ability to absorb and manage, it creates a data management problem for both consumers and businesses. This situation raises issues related with data portability, interoperability, and inability to ensure enterprise data privacy and security – considering information multiplies and is shared even more widely in the cloud. Moreover, if data is properly managed and maintained, data integration and data quality can actually become critical enablers (and not inhibitors) for successfully deploying enterprise cloud computing services.

Application Management: Enterprise applications are progressively becoming more decoupled, service-oriented and composed of multiple layers [17]. However, their composition and integration is hindered by the fact that legacy code needs to be re-written to take advantage of elasticity [18]. In consequence, cloud computing has been fast adopted by start-ups developing from scratch new applications and less by large organisations owning legacy systems [ibid]. Therefore, when selecting the right inte-gration approach to connect cloud applications (i.e. SaaS) to on-premise systems, it is critical that the solution is able to seamlessly bridge the source and target systems within the enterprise network. This means that cloud integration solution will share a common codebase, runtime engine and overall architectural integrity with the on-premise data integration platform. Understanding this relationship early in the integration process will offer immediate insight into interoperability, security, scalability and performance concerns [16].

2.3   Approaches for Cloud Integration

A report published by [19] suggests that businesses currently have the following four primary choices for integrating cloud-based applications with on-premise systems: (a) building a custom-based solution based on the cloud vendor's API, (b) purchasing integration software, (c) subscribing to an integration-as-a-service (IaaS) solution, and (d) engaging professional services or a system integrator. Once a choice has been made, the integration process can be instantiated and implemented in four promi-nent layers and levels as briefly discussed below.

Data Integration: Data integration deals with moving or federating data between different type of data sources [20, 21]. The main drawback of data integration between cloud and on-premise environment is that the developer will have to understand and maintain the underlying schemas regularly to address any changes [16]. This approach is complex for SaaS applications since the consumers neither have access rights nor control to manipulate the underlying database. The data formats and contents are handled by the service provider, so major data portability considerations are needed. Further, as communication between clouds and on-premise typically has a high latency, this makes synchronization difficult. Also, the two environments may have different access control regimes, complicating the task of moving and integrating data between them. Therefore it is critical that organisations ensure the chosen integration solution is able to synchronize data bidirectional from SaaS to on-premise systems securely without opening the firewalls.

Business Logic Integration: To facilitate integration at this level, the development of a middleware technology is required. Middleware technologies help developers by making the design of distributed cloud solutions less challenging [22, 23]. As an impor-tant integration technology, middleware is often used by enterprises to integrate new applications, emerging technologies, and legacy applications. In order for cloud appli-cations to offer the maximum value to users they must provide simple mechanism to import or load external data, export or replicate data for reporting or analysis purposes, and also keep enterprise data synchronized with on-premise applications [20].

Communication Layer Integration: This layer connects the service requestor to the service provider and its underlying solutions platforms realizing the requested service [24]. For example, an enterprise procures a cloud-based application (e.g. SalesForce customer relationship management service) and need to synchronize their master list of customers and other business critical data with on-premise enterprise resource planning (e.g. SAP software) systems in order to meet certain business objectives. Typically, protocols such as HTTP and Internet Inter-ORB Protocol (IIOP) are used to facilitate information exchange among different distributed applications [25].

Presentation Layer Integration: The integration in this layer mainly focuses on user interface (UI) integration [26]. Further work on effective standardization at the presentation layer is required for effective user interface integration to take place. Furthermore, as cloud computing enables new technologies and devices to be introduced into enterprise systems, UI integration poses new challenges associated with various interface types, standards, definitions, and service interfaces. All of these mean that presentation layer integration requires a good understanding of various applications, devices, and enterprise-wide integration requirements.

3   Interoperability Considerations

Interoperability is a critical enabler for broad adoption of cloud computing by enterprises [27]. Lack of interoperability makes it difficult to consolidate enterprise IT systems in the cloud. The term interoperability has many definitions from different viewpoints, and is often misused to include the term portability. A single comprehensive definition of interoperability would not provide much information. Instead, independent groups such as NIST [28] and Open Group [24] consortium have provided definitions for interoperability in three different cloud domains: (a) service interoperability, (b) application interoperability and (c) platform interoperability. Service interoperability is defined as the ability of customers to use services across multiple cloud platforms through a unified management interface. Application interoperability is the ability of cloud-enabled applications to collaborate, across different platforms, in order to deliver their functionalities or create new ones. In contrast, platform interoperability is the ability of platform components to interoperate. Generally, both service and platform interoperability is required to enable application interoperability.

Due to a number of variables that come into play in a complex cloud solution that involves interoperability capabilities, several case scenarios have been discussed by [5, 30, 31]. In a scenario selected, enterprise links in-house capabilities with cloud services. This is done in an effort to highlight key aspects of cloud computing interoperability and current methods for enabling seamless interoperation. This scenario is motivated by the case of a hybrid cloud solution in which the business processes are offered by a public cloud, while other business critical components, and are internally managed by the organization following a private cloud model. In such hybrid environments, enterprises are susceptible to challenges such as maintaining uniform control and transparency over all resources in the distributed environment, whether they are part of public or private cloud resources. However, in spite of how similar a public and private cloud is built, design and implementation differences will inevitably exist, thus triggering interoperability and data portability issues which further complicate the initial integration task [29].

In the scenarios above, the main obstacle to achieving a seamless integration is the poor interoperability, since several application components need to interoperate to achieve the business goal. Interoperability challenges come into play when such application components are distributed among clouds. To avoid rewriting the entire application, the cloud services hosting the components must share a compatible API. In this connection, a proper analysis of available APIs of both the in-house system and cloud services is highly required to clearly understand how the integrated system will function and perform during execution. An important aspect to also consider is the migration to and portability among clouds. Suppose an application of an enterprise is built in a particular cloud service or an in-house system, and for cost, performance or security reasons, the enterprise decides to shift the application and data to a new provider. The question is what happens if the new provider does not support the same export and import formats? An even more, there is no guarantee that the initial provider will offer an export mechanism, considering presently there is no legal provision that mandates cloud providers to provide data export functionality, in the first place. Assuming that portability among clouds is feasible and that the application is distributed among several clouds, there is still no guarantee that various parts of the application are able to interoperate due to lack of shared data formats, communication interface, security requirements etc. In a fully interoperable heterogeneous environment, the application can access data from both in-house and cloud databases through a common API thereby simplifying the overall integration tasks. In reality, current differences in cloud providers API, data, and message formats or communication protocols represent a major obstacle to the ubiquitous cloud realization. Tackling is often dependent on the usage of one or more business standards.

Standard initiatives have emerged as the most proposed method to tackle the interoperability challenge in cloud computing. Standardization strives to support applications by different service vendors to interoperate with one another, exchange traffic, and cooperatively interact with data as well as protocols for joint coordination and control [3]. However, cloud computing still suffers from widely accepted standards. In the absence of widely accepted standards for cloud APIs and data models, organisations willing to outsource and combine range of services from different providers and on-premise systems (Hybrid IT) to achieve maximum operational efficiency will experience technical difficulties when trying to get their in-house systems to interact with cloud services. Likewise the lack of standards brings disadvantages when migration, integration, or exchange of resources is required [27]. As cloud systems are typically external components to the enterprises' overall IT system, the need to have seamless security integration calls for interoperable standard interfaces for authentication, authorization, and communication protections [7]. An identity and access management standard to support secure integration of cloud systems into existing enterprise security infrastructure is also required.

The more cloud computing evolves, the more complex will the integration of cloud services will become for cloud consumers to manage. Interoperability between clouds is vital for the further development of the cloud ecosystem and market. Interoperability challenges caused by lack of widely accepted standards are what enterprises should wary about when considering cloud integration. Architecting systems to be interoperable and integratable requires one to consider a wide set of standards to implement the solution. To this end, it is therefore important that organisations become aware of appropriate standards and protocols used by cloud providers to support data/application movability, as well as to ease the task of integration. In the light of the advantages of standards in increasing interoperation between cloud and on-premise systems, unfortunately the survey conducted in this paper suggests most enterprises lack a comprehensive understanding in this respect. As can be drawn from Fig. 2, a significant majority (76.6 %) of businesses were unsure of relevant standards to support interoperable cloud implementations. Standards are key to ensure requirements for interoperability, portability, and security, are fully met in the cloud environment. It is therefore important for organisations using cloud computing as an essential part of their business operations, to adopt standards-based products, processes and services. In summary, since integration and interoperability both build upon standards, standardization should be considered as the key to achieve seamless integration and interoperability in a distributed cloud environment.

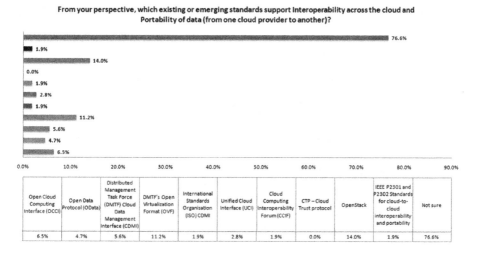

Fig. 2. Enterprises are unaware of interoperable standards

4   Conclusion

In this paper, we have discussed current issues and future trends of integrating with cloud-based services in respect of enterprise IT environments. We have also shown from an enterprise purview that integration and interoperability are seen the means of securing an enduring and compatible solution, while avoiding the pitfalls of multiple clouds. This is critical, as it guides software developers and architects to understand key barriers preventing companies from successfully combining cloud services with their on-premise IT infrastructure.

Today's dynamic business environment has made organisations to rely on the cloud for at least some of their capabilities. Unfortunately, the use of proprietary cloud-based, complicate and make integration critical. To tackle this issue, having a clear understanding of the commonalities among provider standard interfaces can help organisations identify the key interoperability requirements and features to effectively manage the integration process.

As a future work, we would like to develop a proof-of-concept (PoC) application, paying close attention to the use of open standards technologies, and test for integration between cloud-to-cloud and cloud-to-on-premise systems.

References

1. Ebneter, D., Grivas, S.G., Kumar, T.U., Wache, H.: Enterprise architecture frameworks for enabling cloud computing. In: 3rd IEEE International Conference on Cloud Computing, pp. 542–543. IEEE Press (2010)
2. Mahmood, Z., Hill, R.: Cloud Computing for Enterprise Architectures. Springer, London (2011)
3. IBM: Successful information governance through high-quality data. In: IBM Software White Paper, Information Management (2012)
4. Tolk, A.: Interoperability, composability, and their implications for distributed simulation. In: 17th IEEE/ACM International Symposium and Real Time Applications, pp. 3–9. IEEE Press (2013)
5. Joshi, K.P., Yesha, Y., Finin, T.: Automating cloud services life cycle through semantic technologies. J. IEEE Trans. Serv. Comput. **7**(1), 109–122 (2014)
6. Buyya, R.: Cloud computing: the next revolution in information technology. In: 1st International Conference on Parallel Distributed and Grid Computing (PDGC), pp. 2–3 (2010). doi:10.1109/PDGC.2010.5679963
7. Black, J., Draper, C., Lococo, T., Matar, F., Ward, C.: An integration model for organizing it service management. IBM Syst. J. **46**(3), 405–422 (2007). doi:10.1147/sj.463.0405
8. Satzger, B., Hummer, W., Inzinger, C., Leitner, P., Dustdar, S.: Winds of change: from vendor lock-in to the meta cloud. IEEE Internet Comput. **17**(1), 69–73 (2013). doi:10.1109/MIC.2013.19
9. IBM Redbooks: Integrating ERP and CRM applications with IBM WebSphere Cast Iron. In: IBM Redbooks Solution Guide (2013)
10. Breiter, G., Naik, V.: A framework for controlling and managing hybrid cloud service integration. In: IEEE International Conference on Cloud Engineering, pp. 217–224. IEEE Press (2013)
11. SurveyMonkey: Online Survey Development Tool. https://www.surveymonkey.com/
12. Buyya, R., Ranjan, R., Calheiros, R.N.: InterCloud: utility-oriented federation of cloud computing environments for scaling of application services. In: Hsu, C.-H., Yang, L.T., Park, J.H., Yeo, S.-S. (eds.) ICA3PP 2010, Part I. LNCS, vol. 6081, pp. 13–31. Springer, Heidelberg (2010)
13. Stravoskoufos, K., Preventis, A., Sotiriadis, S., Petrakis, E.G.M.: A survey on approaches for interoperability and portability of cloud computing services (2013)

14. Dynamic markets: cloud for business managers. In: Independent Market Research Commissioned by ORACLE (2013). http://www.qss.ba/doc/2014/?id=794
15. SnapLogic and TechValidate: Cloud Integration Drivers and Requirements (survey) in 2015. http://campaigns.snaplogic.com/rs/snaplogic/images/cloud-integration-drivers-and-requirements-in-2015.pdf
16. Informatica Whitepaper: Cloud Integration for Hybrid IT – Balancing Business Self-Service and IT Control, White Paper (2012)
17. Ellahi, T., Hudzia, B., Li, H., Robinson, P.: The Enterprise Cloud Computing Paradigm. Wiley, Hoboken (2011)
18. Petcu, D., Macariu, G., Panica, S., Crăciun, C.: Portable cloud applications from theory to practice. Future Gener. Comput. Syst. 29(6), 1417–1430 (2013). ISSN 0167-739X
19. Dell Boomi: The Quest for a Cloud Integration Strategy. http://www.boomi.com/files/boomi_whitepaper_the_quest_for_cloud_integration_strategy_final.pdf
20. Izza, S.: Integration of industrial information systems: from syntactic to semantic integration approaches. Enterp. Inform. Syst. 3(1), 1–57 (2009)
21. Chen, D., Doumeingtsb, G., Vernadatc, F.: Architectures for enterprise integration and interoperability: past, present and future. Comput. Ind. 59(7), 647–659 (2008)
22. Bernstein, P.: Middleware: a model for distributed systems services. Commun. ACM 39(2), 86–98 (1996)
23. Ooi, S.L., Su, M.T.: Integrating enterprise application using message-oriented middleware and J2EE technologies. In: Proceedings of the International Conference on Computing and Informatics, Kuala Lumpur, pp. 1–5 (2006)
24. The Open Group: SOA reference architecture technical standard: integration layer. In: SOA Source Book (2011)
25. Benatallah, B., Motahari Nezhad, H.R.: Service oriented architecture: overview and directions. In: Börger, E., Cisternino, A. (eds.) Advances in Software Engineering. LNCS, vol. 5316, pp. 116–130. Springer, Heidelberg (2008)
26. Daniel, F., Yu, J., Benatallah, B., Casati, F., Matera, M., Saint-Paul, R.: Understanding UI integration: a survey of problems, technologies, and opportunities. IEEE Internet Comput. 11(3), 59–66 (2007)
27. Opara-Martins, J.; Sahandi, R., Tian, F.: Critical review of vendor lock-in and its impact on adoption of cloud computing. In: 2014 International Conference on Information Society (i-Society), pp. 92–97, 10–12 November 2014
28. Mell, P., Grance, T.: The NIST definition of cloud computing: recommendations of the National Institute of Standards and Technology. Computer Security Division, NIST, Gaithersburg, MD (2011)
29. Baudion, C., Dekel, E., Edwards, M., et al.: Cloud standards customer council. In: Interoperability and Portability for Cloud Computing: A Guide (2014). http://www.cloud-council.org/CSCC-Cloud-Interoperability-and-Portability.pdf
30. Ahronovitz, M., Amrhein, D., Anderson, P., et al.: Cloud computing use cases-white paper. In: Discussion Group (Version 4.0). http://www.cloud-council.org/Cloud_Computing_Use_Cases_Whitepaper-4_0.pdf
31. Hogan, M., Liu, F., Sokol, A., Tong, J.: NIST cloud computing standards roadmap-special publication, 500-291 (2011). http://www.nist.gov/itl/cloud/upload/NIST_SP-500-291_Jul5A.pdf

Building and Operating Distributed SDN-Cloud Testbed with Hyper-Convergent SmartX Boxes

Aris Cahyadi Risdianto, Junsik Shin, and JongWon Kim[✉]

Gwangju Institute of Science and Technology (GIST), Gwangju, South Korea
{aris,jsshin,jongwon}@nm.gist.ac.kr

Abstract. In this paper, we describe our efforts for building and operating a distributed SDN-Cloud testbed by utilizing hyper-convergent SmartX Boxes that are distributed across multiple sites. Each SmartX Box consists of several virtualized functions that are categorized into SDN and cloud functions. Multiple SmartX Boxes are deployed and inter-connected to build a multi-regional distributed cloud infrastructure. The resulting deployment integrates both cloud multi-tenancy and SDN-based slicing, which allow developers to run experiments in a distributed SDN-Cloud testbed. It also offers enhanced troubleshooting capability by providing semi-automated resource configuration and tapping functionality.

Keywords: Hyper-convergent SmartX Box · Distributed and virtualized cloud · Software-defined networking · Future Internet testbed · DevOps automation

1 Introduction

Motivated by worldwide Future Internet testbed deployments (e.g., GENI [1], FIRE [2]), OF@TEIN project is started to build an OpenFlow SDN-enabled testbed over TEIN infrastructure in 2012 [3]. Several experimentation tools are developed to support both developers and operators in utilizing OF@TEIN testbed. Initially, a mixed combination of tools, ranging from simple web-/script-based to DevOps (Development and Operation) Chef-based automated tools, are deployed over SmartX Racks [4]. SmartX Rack consists of four devices: Management and Worker node, Capsulator node, OpenFlow switch, and Remote power device. Physically LAN-connected SmartX Racks are inter-connected by L2 (layer 2) tunnels, employed in Capsulator nodes. However, SmartX Racks with multiple devices are subject to physical remote reconfigurations, which are extremely hard to manage for distributed OF@TEIN testbed. Thus, from late 2013, a hyper-convergent SmartX Box is introduced to virtualize and merge the functionalities of four devices into a single box. In 2015, multiple hyper-convergent SmartX Boxes are deployed over 9 countries, as shown in Fig. 1.

SDN-based tools can assist developers and operators to prepare testing environment over OF@TEIN infrastructure, by enabling networking resources (e.g., switches and Flowspaces) preparation. Similarly, cloud management software is ready to cover computing resource (e.g., VMs) preparation. The combination for distributed SDN-Cloud testbed can provide scalable and flexible computing resources with enhanced

© ICST Institute for Computer Sciences, Social Informatics and Telecommunications Engineering 2016
Y. Zhang et al. (Eds.): CloudComp 2015, LNICST 167, pp. 224–233, 2016.
DOI: 10.1007/978-3-319-38904-2_23

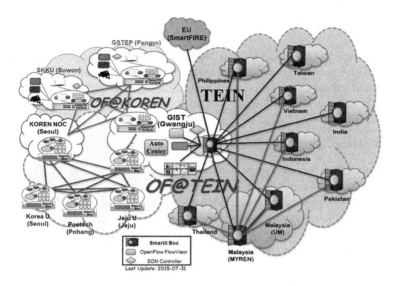

Fig. 1. OF@TEIN infrastructure.

networking capability. Thus, the seamless integration of SDN-enabled and cloud-leveraged infrastructure is a very challenging task, due to open and conflicting options in configuring and customizing resource pools together. That is, we should carefully provision all resource configuration aspects such as regional partitioning, virtualized resource slicing (i.e., isolation), and multi-tenancy support while considering hardware deployment for SDN-Cloud integrated.

As mentioned above, this paper introduces the hyper-convergent SmartX Boxes that can easily accommodate virtualized and programmable resources (i.e., OpenFlow-enabled virtual switches and OpenStack-leveraged cloud VMs) to build the OF@TEIN SDN-Cloud testbed. The collection of OpenFlow-enabled virtual switches is providing SDN capability, to-be-controlled by both developers and operators SDN controllers. At the same time, OpenStack-leveraged VMs (i.e., working as virtual Boxes) can be effectively managed by the OpenStack cloud management (i.e., OpenStack Keystone, Horizon, Nova, Glance, and others). The main contributions of this paper are:

1. Deploying OpenStack-leveraged computing/storage resources on top of SDN-enabled programmable networking resources for both developers and operators.
2. Providing OpenStack-leveraged multi-tenancy management interfaces as well as sliced network programming for multiple developers in multi-region distributed SDN-Cloud deployment.
3. Enhancing the semi-automated DevOps operation of OF@TEIN testbed by leveraging cloud deployment tools and OpenFlow-based SDN configuration tools with scaled-out hyper-convergent SmartX Boxes.
4. Prototyping and verifying the basic capability for resource-/flow-level visibility about hyper-convergent SmartX Boxes and their inter-connections.

2   Design of Distributed SDN-Cloud Testbed

There are several design aspects for distributed SDN-Cloud deployment: hyper-convergent SmartX Boxes, virtualized functions inside SmartX Boxes, automated provisioning tools for SmartX Boxes, and orchestrated control/management of the virtualize functions for SDN-Cloud integrated services.

2.1   Computing/Networking-Balanced Testbeds

It is well known that service-centric networking model to provide higher-level connectivity and policy abstraction is an integral part of cloud-leveraged applications. The emerging SDN paradigm can provide new opportunity to integrate cloud-leveraged services with enhanced networking capability through deeply-programmable interfaces and DevOps-style automation. A number of SDN solutions have been proposed to provide virtualized overlay networking for multi-tenancy cloud infrastructure. For example, Meridian has developed a SDN controller platform to support service-level networking for cloud infrastructure [5]. Also, CNG (Cloud Networking Gateway) attempts to address multi-tenancy networking for distributed cloud resources from multiple providers while providing flexibilities in deploying, configuring, and instantiating cloud networking services [6].

The large-scale deployment of GENI Racks over national R&E (research and education) backbone is also moving towards a programmable, virtualized, and distributed collection of networking/compute/storage resources, a global-scale "deeply programmable cloud". It will satisfy research needs in wide variety of areas including cloud-based applications. Moreover, GENI participates in significant international federations such as Trans-Cloud and the "Slice Around the world" efforts that include production (e.g., Amazon web services) cloud computing services for federations [1]. Another effort from EU, known as "BonFIRE" is a multi-site testbed that supports testing of cloud-based distributed applications, which offer a unique ease-to-use functionality in terms of configuration, visibility, and control of advanced cloud features for experimentation [7].

From these previous works for SDN-Cloud integration, there are several key requirements in integrating cloud services with SDN programmable infrastructure.

(1) The basic requirement is to provide cloud providers and tenant users to control and manage their own applications (functions for service chaining) as well as the connectivity among their applications on distributed cloud services.
(2) The connectivity requirements include the per-tenant creation and construction of virtual topology and network-layer information (i.e. switches, routers, subnets and access control lists).
(3) The fine-grained control over networking paths between distributed cloud services is required to provide fast failover and traffic prioritization, which utilizes Open-Flow-enabled SDN networking capabilities.
(4) The integration requirement to couple different APIs (application programming interfaces) is also needed to harmonize cloud-based resource/service orchestration and SDN-based virtual networking controllers.

2.2   Hyper-Convergent SmartX Box: Design

As mentioned above, the deployment conversion from SmartX Racks to SmartX Boxes are completed to better manage distributed cloud-leveraged services on the top of SDN-enabled inter-connect capabilities [8]. Thus, the design of hyper-convergent SmartX Boxes needs to carefully consider and balance both cloud and SDN aspects. The open-source OpenStack [9] cloud management software provides VM instances and basic networking options for diverse tenants. For SDN, several instances of virtual switches (derived from open-source Open vSwitch [10]) are installed and configured while allowing users/developers to share them simultaneously. Note that, to support the flexible remote configuration, each hyper-convergent SmartX Box requires dedicated P/M/C/D (power, management, control, and data) connections, which will be explained later [8].

However, besides the flexible dedicated connections, there are no specific hardware requirements for hyper-convergent SmartX Boxes. Therefore any commodity hardware with reasonable computing, storage, and networking resources can be utilized. The total amount of hardware resources will affect the capacity (e.g., total number of VM instances per flavor types) in specific boxes, sites, and regions. It is also important to consider the hardware acceleration support for virtualization and networking.

By merging all the required functionalities into the hyper-convergent SmartX Box, it is easier to realize the scale-out capability of SDN-Cloud testbed by simply adding hyper-convergent SmartX Boxes to increase the resource capacity of OF@TEIN infrastructure.

2.3   Virtualized SDN-Enabled Switches and Cloud-Leveraged VMs

In order to provide the integration of SDN-Cloud functions inside a single hyper-convergent SmartX Box, we arrange relevant functions as shown in Fig. 2. SDN-related virtual functions consist of several virtual switches with different roles, e.g., creating developer's networking topology, inter-connecting OpenFlow-based overlay networking, and tapping flows for troubleshooting. Also, cloud-related functions are placed to include VM instances for cloud-based applications and to support external connections to VMs.

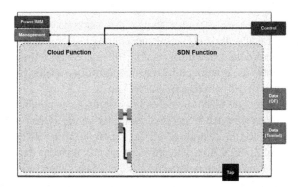

Fig. 2. Hyper-convergent SmartX Box: SDN-Cloud integration (top-level view).

The inside view of SDN-/Cloud-related functions are depicted in Fig. 3. First, SDN virtual switches are placed to cover named functionalities: *brcap* for capsulator (encapsulate OpenFlow packets through an overlay tunnel), *br1* and *br2* for users/developers switches, and *brtap* for tapping (capturing packets for troubleshooting [11]). Cloud-related VM instances (a.k.a., virtual Boxes: vBoxes) are managed by KVM hypervisors, which is controlled by OpenStack *Nova* with specific flavors and images. Additionally, virtual switches (i.e., *br-int, br-ex,* and *br-vlan*) and user-space virtual router are configured by OpenStack *Neutron* to provide required connectivity to cloud VM instances.

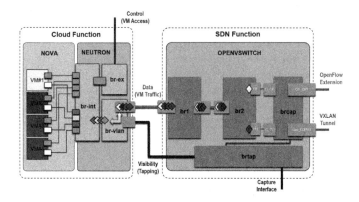

Fig. 3. Hyper-convergent SmartX Box: cloud-related (left) and SDN-related (right) functions.

2.4 Automated Provisioning

Deploying hyper-convergent SmartX Boxes in heterogeneous physical (i.e., network topology) environments is quite challenging, since it is subject to different performance parameters and independent network administrative domains. As a consequence, it is very hard to sustain the operation of all hyper-convergent SmartX Boxes. Thus, a set of automated provisioning tools is developed to minimize the consumed time for installing and configuring hyper-convergent SmartX Boxes with pre-arranged P/M/C/D connections. The P (Power) connection is used for power up/down SmartX Boxes. The M (Management) connection is mainly used for managing SmartX Box as the operator. Also, the C (Control) connection is used to access and control the SDN-/Cloud-related functions (i.e., virtual switches and VMs). Finally, the D (Data) connection is used for any kind of data-plane traffic that includes inter-connection traffic among multiple SmartX Boxes. Also, the automated provisioning tools are controlled by a centralized Coordinator Box, which has full access to all distributed hyper-convergent SmartX Boxes.

First, in order to automate SDN vSwitches provisioning, *ovs-vsctl* high-level programming interface for Open vSwitch is utilized. Note that *ovsdb* (Open vSwitch database) protocol is also utilized for the centralized configuration of Open vSwitch database inside each hyper-convergent SmartX Box. The provisioning task includes the creation of virtual switches, the configuration of virtual ports/links and overlay tunnels, and the connection of virtual switches and SDN controllers. Next, open-source OpenStack cloud software has special installation and configuration tools, called as *"DevStack"* that can support several modes of OpenStack configurations with selected OS (e.g., Ubuntu, Redhat Enterprise Linux, and CentOS) [12]. For OF@TEIN SDN-Cloud testbed, we customize DevStack-based installation and configuration to facilitate multi-regional OpenStack cloud deployment with centralized management and authentication.

2.5 SDN-Cloud Centralized Management

SDN-/Cloud-related virtual functions are inter-connected to provide the end-to-end communication for cloud-leveraged applications. The Cloud-related virtual functions are managed centrally by open-source OpenStack cloud management and orchestration software [9]. The SDN-related virtual functions are also centrally controlled by the ODL (Open Daylight) SDN Controller [13]. OpenStack *Keystone* is used for centralized user authentication. OpenStack *Nova* and OpenStack *Neutron* is utilized to create VM instances and to provide enhanced connectivity, respectively. The ODL SDN controller manipulates the flowtable entries of SDN-enabled virtual switches to enable the flexible steering of inter-connection flows among various functions located in different cloud regions (sites). Both cloud management software and SDN control software are required to mix and match the configurations so that we can ensure the consistent connections between cloud VM instances. Remember that the main challenge is how to accommodate cloud-based multi-tenancy virtual networks (e.g., flat, VLAN, or tunneled network) for OpenFlow-based network slicing (e.g., IP subnets, VLAN IDs, and TCP/UDP ports). Eventually VLAN-based multi-tenancy traffic control (e.g., tagging, steering, and mapping) is chosen to integrate tenant-based and slicing-based SDN-Cloud networking.

3 Verification and Evaluation

We now explain the details of SDN-Cloud testbed deployment, verification steps, and preliminary measurement results.

3.1 Multi-Site Deployment for Distributed SDN-Cloud Testbed

As shown in Fig. 4, multiple hyper-convergent SmartX Boxes are deployed for OF@TEIN testbed. Current deployment is focusing on migrating from limited open-source XEN VM hypervisor to open-source OpenStack cloud management. The OF@TEIN testbed relies on the heterogeneous physical underlay networks across multiple administrative domains. Thus, the multi-regional OpenStack cloud deployment is currently investigated as the deployment option, because it gives simple and common configuration for all regions (i.e., SmartX Box sites), supports independent IP addressing scheme, and has less dependency on the overlay networking among regions. Despite of multi-regional independent cloud deployment, the OF@TEIN testbed supports an integrated cloud management interface by deploying web-based OpenStack *Horizon* UIs and the centralized account/token authentication from OpenStack *Keystone*. The resulting OpenStack multi-regional cloud deployment is illustrated in Fig. 5 for OF@TEIN testbed.

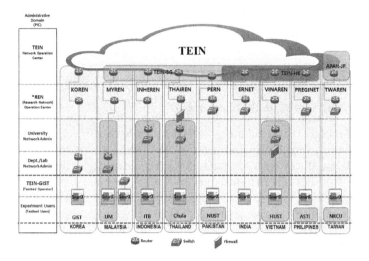

Fig. 4. OF@TEIN deployment over multi-domain R&E networks.

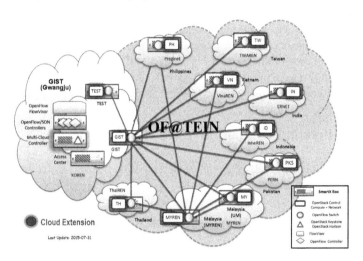

Fig. 5. OF@TEIN multi-regional cloud deployment.

Next, the OF@TEIN testbed is enhanced with multiple mesh-style inter-connections of NVGRE/VXLAN overlay tunnels, along with the special flow-tapping virtual switch [11]. The OpenStack multi-region deployment is modified to build a SDN-Cloud integrated testbed where inter-VM connectivity between cloud VMs is utilized by leveraging OpenFlow-enabled data planes. The data planes are programmed and controlled by the centralized SDN controller, co-located with the centralized cloud management.

3.2   Semi-Automated Provision: Verifications and Evaluations

In order to facilitate the agile deployment of OF@TEIN testbed, both SDN-/Cloud-related tools are utilized for automated provisioning of hyper-convergent SmartX Boxes. This is aligned with the recent employment of DevOps automation, since the OF@TEIN testbed is operated by a limited number of operators and becomes easily uncontrollable as it spans across multi-domain inter-connected networks beyond the privileges of testbed operators. Thus, by utilizing *DevStack*-based OpenStack deployment and *ovs-vsctl* or *ovsdb* protocol for virtual switch provisioning, we can simplify the semi-automated provisioning of hyper-convergent SmartX Boxes. In addition, REST APIs of ODL SDN controller is utilized for automated flow insertion, flow modification, and flow deletion. In summary, most of provisioning steps are automated with the exception of manual handling of critical tasks such as *DevStack*-based OpenStack service restart and VXLAN tunnel checking/recovery.

The semi-automated deployment shows takes around 50 min for fully upgrading a SmartX Box with ~300 Mbps network connection. It takes around 6 h for the slowest network connection of <10 Mbps. However, it takes only around 20 min (including Box restart) for installation and configuration without cleaning up the previous installation and upgrading the operating system. Moreover, it takes less than 10 min to re-configure hyper-convergent SmartX Box with offline mode (i.e., no online copy from OpenStack repository) (Table 1).

Table 1.   Provisioning time comparison of sites with different network connection speed.

Site ID	Network connection speed (Mbps)	Installation time
GIST	~ 200	50 min
MY	~ 100	4 h
PH	~ 10	6 h

3.3   Example Experiments with SDN-Cloud Playground

By manipulating both OpenStack cloud management and OpenFlow-enabled SDN control, as depicted in Fig. 6, an experiment for deploying VLAN-based multi-tenancy traffic control is designed to verify the SDN-Cloud integration. First, we place VMs in two cloud regions and prepare the connectivity for these VMs. These VMs are tagged by OpenStack *Nova* with specific tag ID. Second, OpenStack *Neutron* automatically maps and matches VLAN IDs with SDN-based slice parameters. This allows inter-connection flows for VMs to be steered by the developer's SDN controller, supervised by FlowVisor [14]. The SDN-based flow steering inserts flowtable entries according to the particular incoming and outgoing ports in developer's virtual switches, where several ports are mapped to other cloud regions/sites. Finally, based on the destination site, it maps to a specific tunnel interface that is pre-configured by the SDN controller of operators. Eventually, the testing of end-to-end connections between VMs is required to verify the consistency of flow tagging, steering, and mapping for specific testing flows.

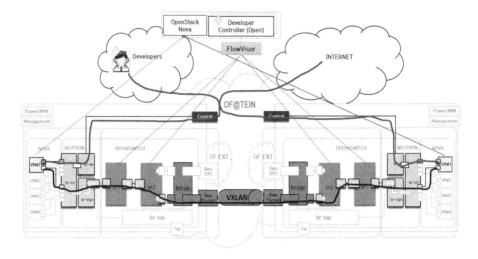

Fig. 6. An experiment example over OF@TEIN SDN-Cloud testbed.

Acknowledgements. This work makes use of results produced by the SmartFIRE project, which is supported by the International Research and Development Program of the National Research Foundation of Korea (NRF) funded by the Ministry of Science, ICT and Future Planning (MSIP, Korea) (Grant number: K2013078191) and the Seventh Framework Programme (FP7) funded by the European Commission (Grant number: 611165).

References

1. Berman, M., et al.: GENI: A federated testbed for innovative network experiments. Comput. Netw. **61**, 5–23 (2014). doi:10.1016/j.bjp.2013.12.037
2. FIRE: Future Internet Research and Experimentation, September 2015. http://www.ict-fire.eu/home.html
3. Risdianto, A.C., Na, T., Kim, J.: Running lifecycle experiments over SDN-enabled OF@TEIN testbed. In: Proceedings of the IEEE International Conference on Communications and Electronics, July–August 2014
4. Risdianto, A.C., Kim, J.: Prototyping media distribution experiments over OF@TEIN SDN-enabled testbed. In: Proceedings of the 40th Meeting of the Asia-Pacific Advanced Network, vol. 38, pp. 12–18 (2014). http://dx.doi.org/10.7125/APAN.38.2
5. Banikazemi, M., Olshefski, D., Shaikh, A., Tracey, J., Wang, G.: Meridian: an SDN platform for cloud network services. IEEE Commun. Mag. **51**(2), 120–127 (2013)
6. Mechtri, M., Houidi, I., Louati, W., Zeghlache, D.: SDN for inter cloud networking. In: IEEE SDN for Future Networks and Services (SDN4FNS), Trento, Italy, November 2013
7. Kavoussanakis, K., et al.: BonFIRE: The clouds and services testbed. In: IEEE 5th International Conference on Cloud Computing Technology and Science (CloudCom), vol. 2, pp. 321–326, December 2013
8. Risdianto, A.C., Shin, J., Ling, T.C., Kim, J.: Leveraging ONOS SDN controllers for OF@TEIN SD-WAN experiments. In: Proceedings of the 40th Meeting of the Asia-Pacific Advanced Network, vol. 40, pp. 1–6 (2015). http://dx.doi.org/10.7125/40.1

9. Sefraoui, O., Aissaoui, M., Eleuldj, M.: OpenStack: toward an open-source solution for cloud computing. Int. J. Comput. Appl. **55**(3), 38–42 (2012)
10. Pfaff, B., Pettit, J., Amidon, K., Casado, M., Koponen, T., Shenker, S.: Extending networking into the virtualization Layer. In: Proceedings of the HotNets, Chicago, IL, October 2009
11. Risdianto, A.C., Kim, J.: Flow-centric visibility tools for OF@TEIN OpenFlow-based SDN testbed. In: 10th International Conference on Future Internet (CFI 2015), Seoul, Korea, June 2015
12. DevStack - an OpenStack Community Production, July 2015. http://docs.openstack.org/developer/devstack/
13. Medved, J., Varga, R., Tkacik, A., Gray, K.: OpenDaylight: towards a model-driven SDN controller architecture. In: Proceedings of the IEEE International Symposium on a World of Wireless, Mobile and Multimedia Networks, June 2014
14. Sherwood, R., et al.: Flowvisor: a network virtualization layer. Technical report Openflow-tr-2009-1, Stanford University, July 2009

On Providing Response Time Guarantees to a Cloud-Hosted Telemedicine Web Service

Waqar Haider, Waheed Iqbal$^{(\boxtimes)}$, Fawaz S. Bokhari, and Faisal Bukhari

Punjab University College of Information Technology,
University of the Punjab, Lahore, Pakistan
{mscsf13m024,waheed.iqbal,fawaz,faisal.bukhari}@pucit.edu.pk.edu

Abstract. Traditionally healthcare services are deployed on dedicated physical systems and the functionalities are limited to the local network. Mostly, dedicated physical systems are either under-provisioned or over-provisioned. Cloud Computing technology addresses these limitations by dynamically allocating required resources to applications being hosted on such cloud platforms. In this paper, we study the viability of hosting a telemedicine service over Amazon Elastic Compute Cloud (EC2); a public cloud architecture. In particular, we study the performance of our telemedicine service under linearly increasing workloads by using multiple hosting options available in Amazon EC2. The performance analysis of our telemedicine service is based on fulfilling the specific number of requests per seconds under constraint response times. We find that dynamic resource provisioning on the web tier using medium type instances gives better results compared to static allocation using large and xlarge type instances without incurring any bottleneck issues, thereby, making it a feasible solution for telemedicine service providers.

Keywords: Cloud computing · Amazon EC2 · Telemedicine · Auto-scaling · Resource allocation · Web services

1 Introduction

Telemedicine is an enabling technology to facilitate the provision of health-care services based on information and communication technologies to serve a large population living in remote and underprivileged areas. In a typical telemedicine system, patients interact with the telemedicine server using Internet connection from a distant location by providing personal information, symptoms, and lab test reports. Once a patient's information reaches to the telemedicine server, an automated process assigns the patient to a doctor. Then the doctor provides the prescription or feedback to the patient from remote location. However, managing computing and storage resources to offer high availability and response time guarantees for a telemedicine service is quite challenging and an emerging research area. Traditionally, such healthcare services are deployed on dedicated physical systems which are mostly either under-provisioned or over-provisioned and their functionalities are limited to the local network. Since, a large number

© ICST Institute for Computer Sciences, Social Informatics and Telecommunications Engineering 2016
Y. Zhang et al. (Eds.): CloudComp 2015, LNICST 167, pp. 234–243, 2016.
DOI: 10.1007/978-3-319-38904-2_24

of users are accessing a particular telemedicine service concurrently from various locations, efficient resource utilization is a challenge to reduce operational cost and maintain specific application's response time.

Cloud computing technology has emerged as a promising technology for the provision of low cost, on-demand, high available, and dynamic resource provisioning services to enterprises and individual users [1]. With the increasing use of Internet applications, the demand for cloud computing services has seen an unprecedented rise recently. One of the motivating factor for the adoption of cloud platform for such applications is that, it provides high availability and better performance with a low operational cost to the hosted application. To offer these features, cloud computing model allows provisioning of resources dynamically on varying workloads [2–4]. Therefore, hosting a telemedicine service on a cloud provides better availability and response time guarantees to the end users.

There has been some research efforts in providing medical services over the cloud. For example, Shilin Lu et al. [5] have conducted several experiments to evaluate the performance of their custom designed medical service over the cloud and compared its performance with a traditional system. In another research by Jui-chien et al. [6], the authors have proposed a cloud based service which facilitates transmission and interpretation of ECG through mobile phones. Their contribution includes pre-hospital diagnosis and to enhance inter-operability of ECG results in rural and urban areas. The proposed service can be provided on running vehicles and it is claimed that the service is cheap, efficient and convenient. Charalampos et al. [7] has proposed a mobile health care system based on cloud computing. A mobile application was developed in Google's Android OS which provided patients data transmission and retrieval with the help of a mobile service. They have used Amazon's simple storage service (S3) in order to store and manage patients' data and presented a prototype of their proposed solution. Princy et al. [8] proposed a cloud based telemedicine health service in India in which the authors main focus were on providing real time video steaming by utilizing cloud services. Xiaoliang et al. [9] have presented a mobile based telemedicine service and unveiled some opportunities by which mobile cloud can be better optimized. Amitav et al. [10] proposed an implementation of a patient monitoring teledermatology system. However, none of these addresses the challenge of efficiently allocating cloud resources to minimize cost and maintain specific response time guarantees to the end users.

In this paper, we present our proposed telemedicine service and study its performance using different Amazon Elastic Compute Cloud (EC2) instance types namely medium, large, and xlarge to profile throughput and average response time on linearly increasing workloads. In addition to this, we also investigate the provisioning of dynamic resources to satisfy specific response time requirements of our telemedicine service. Our results show that dynamic provisioning helps to offer response time guarantees for the proposed telemedicine service using medium type instances on increasing workloads.

In the rest of this paper, we briefly explain our proposed telemedicine service, experimental design, and experimental results obtained using different deployment scenarios.

2   Design of Telemedicine Service

We have developed a telemedicine web service using Java Jersey [11] and MySQL database. We have deployed this service on Oracle WebLogic server. Figure 1 shows Entity Relationship Diagram (ERD) of our developed telemedicine service explaining main entities and their relationships. There are three main user roles; patient, doctor, and admin (administrator). The admin role is used to manage user accounts and access control. The doctor interacts with patient's visit and issues prescription. Each patient may have many visits and each visit may have multiple visitdata associated with it. A patient may optionally upload images and textual data with his/her visit. We also maintain audit logs of every interaction of users with the service.

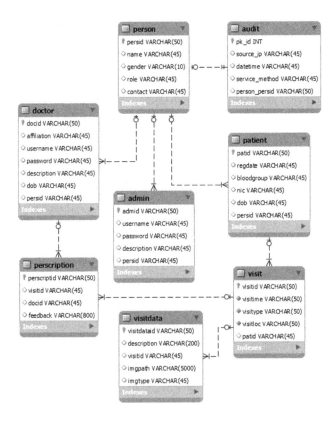

Fig. 1. *EERD of Telemedicine Web Service*

We have exposed our web service to be consumed in different client side implementations including mobile, desktop, and web applications through well defined URIs. For example, we provide specific end points in terms of URIs to perform create, read, update and delete (CRUD) operations for every entity explained in the ERD. Our proposed web service methods generate output in JSON format.

3   Experimental Setup

In this section, we describe our experimental cloud testbed, design of experiments to evaluate our proposed telemedicine web service, and workload generation method.

3.1   Cloud Testbed

We have used Amazon Web Services (AWS) to host and evaluate the performance of our telemedicine service using various different types of Elastic Compute Cloud (EC2) instances. An EC2 instance provides a virtual machine with a specific hardware resources. Table 1 shows the resource allocation and cost of EC2 instances used in our experimental evaluation. In each experiment, we have deployed web service tier and database tier on separate EC2 instances of a specific type.

Table 1. Resource allocation and cost of EC2 instances used in experiments.

Instance Type	vCPUs	Memory (GiB)	SSD Storage (GB)	Cost (USD/hour)
m3.medium	1	3.75	4	0.067
m3.large	2	7.5	32	$0.133
m3.xlarge	4	15	80	$0.266
m3.2xlarge	8	30	160	$0.532
c3.large	2	3.75	32	$0.105
c3.2xlarge	8	15	160	$0.42

3.2   Experimental Design

We have conducted five set of experiments to evaluate the performance of the telemedicine system. Table 2 provides details of the conducted experiments. In each experiment, we pre-allocate specific type of EC2 instance to web service tier and database tier and generate the synthetic workload to profile throughput (requests/second) and average response time of the application. However, in Experiment 5 we have enabled auto-scaling on web server tier using rule-based technique. We configure Amazon's auto-scale policy to increase one EC2 instance whenever average response time reaches to 1000 ms or CPU utilization of any instance allocated to web tier reaches to 70 %. We also configure Amazon's Elastic Load Balancing (ELB) service to load balance workload among allocated web tier instances.

Table 2. Experimental details.

Exp#	Experiment	Description
1	Static allocation using EC2 medium instance	Pre-allocated one EC2 instance of type `m3.medium` to web service tier and one EC2 instance of type `m3.2xlarge` to database tier
2	Static allocation using EC2 large instance	Pre-allocated one EC2 instance of type `m3.large` to web service tier and one EC2 instance of type `m3.2xlarge` to database tier
3	Static allocation using EC2 xlarge instance	Pre-allocated one EC2 instance of type `m3.xlarge` for web service tier and one EC2 instance of type `m3.2xlarge` to database tier
4	Static allocation with distributed workload generation	Pre-allocated one EC2 instance of type `m3.large` to web service tier and `c3.2xlarge` type of instance to database tier. For distributed workload generation, we used two instances of type `c3.large`
5	Dynamic allocation using EC2 medium instances	Horizontal auto-scaling enabled for web service tier using `m3.medium` EC2 instances and static allocation of `m3.2xlarge` instance type to database tier

3.3 Synthetic Workload Generation

We have used `httpef` [12] to generate a synthetic workload in linearly increasing fashion for the telemedicine service. We generate workload for 40 min emulating specific number of user session per second in a step-up fashion. A synthetic user session emulate a use case scenario to search a patient and then insert a new record of a patient. In each user session, we have two requests consisting of searching a patient which outputs a large number of patient's records from database and then issuing a put request to insert a new patient.

The workload generator is deployed on a separate EC2 instance of type `m3.2xlarge` to avoid any saturation at workload generator. However, we observe a bandwidth limitation in Experiment 2 and Experiment 3. In order to overcome this bandwidth limitation, we have distributed the workload generation using two instances in Experiment 4.

4 Experimental Results

In this section, we describe the results obtained in Experiment 1, 2, 3, 4, and 5 described in Table 2. For each experiment, we provide throughput (request/sec), average response time (milliseconds), and CPU utilization of allocated resources.

4.1   Experiment 1: Static Allocation Using EC2 Medium Instance

Figure 2 shows the throughput, average response time, and CPU utilization of EC2 instances allocated to web and database tiers during Experiment 1. It can be seen from the figure that by 16th min of the experiment, the throughput stops increasing linearly and response time of the application starts increasing exponentially. It can be clearly observed that the CPU utilization of web server tier reaches near to 100 % and shows the bottleneck here. By 32nd min, web server tier instance reaches to an unresponsive mode and we are unable to obtain throughput and response time metrics after this time lapse. However, we still obtain CPU utilization metrics for both instances from Amazon Cloud Watch service. The maximum throughput that we have observed in this experiment is 892 requests/second.

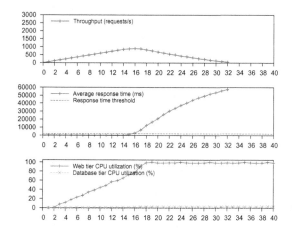

Fig. 2. Experiment 1: throughput (requests served/second), average response time, and CPU utilization of web server and database tier instances.

4.2   Experiment 2: Static Allocation Using EC2 Large Instance

Figure 3 shows the throughput, average response time, and CPU utilization of EC2 instances allocated to web and database tiers during Experiment 2. By 18th min of the experiment, the throughput stops increasing linearly, however, we do not observe any dramatic growth in the response time during this experiment. The average response time remains under 50 ms. Notice, that there is no dramatic increase of CPU utilization in the web server and database tier instances. The maximum throughput achieved in this experiment is 1020 requests/second. Ideally, the throughput should have continuously increased during this experiment, however, this is because the bandwidth became the bottleneck at 18th min of the experiment and web server tier instance is utilizing 201 MB/seconds and 416 MB/second in average respectively for network input and output.

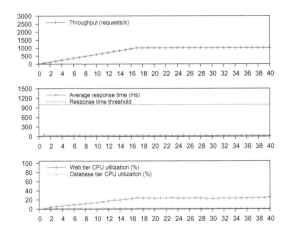

Fig. 3. Experiment 2: throughput (requests served/second), average response time, and CPU utilization of web server and database tier instances.

4.3 Experiment 3: Static Allocation Using EC2 Xlarge Instance

Figure 4 shows the throughput, average response time, and CPU utilization of EC2 instances allocated to web and database tiers during Experiment 3. It is shown in the figure that at 18th min, the throughput stops increasing linearly, however, there is no sign of any dramatic growth in response time during this experiment. The average response time remains under 50 ms. No saturation in CPU utilization of web and database tier instances has been observed. The maximum throughput we achieved in this experiment is 1020 requests/second. Notice, that the output of this experiment is similar to Experiment 2, mainly because, we observe the same bandwidth limitation in this experiment as existed in the previous one. It therefore, clearly shows that increasing resources to web tier instance does not help in overcoming bandwidth limitations.

4.4 Experiment 4: Static Allocation with Distributed Workload Generation

Figure 5 shows the throughput, average response time, and CPU utilization of EC2 instances allocated to web and database tiers during Experiment 4. It can be seen that at 25th min, the throughput stops increasing linearly and there is dramatic growth in average response time. It is also evident that the CPU utilization of web server tier reaches close to 100 % and turns to be the bottleneck in this experiment. The maximum throughput that we have achieved in this experiment is 2882 requests/second. By 31st min of the experiment, web server tier instance reaches to an unresponsive mode and we terminate the experiment at 33rd min of the experiment.

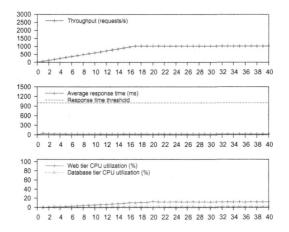

Fig. 4. Experiment 3: throughput (requests served/second), average response time, and CPU utilization of web server and database tier instances.

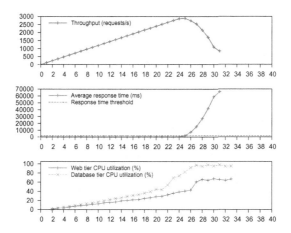

Fig. 5. Experiment 4: Throughput (requests served/second), average response time, and CPU utilization of web server and database tier instances.

4.5 Experiment 5: Dynamic Allocation Using EC2 Medium Instances

Figure 6 shows the throughput, average response time, dynamic addition of web tier instances, and CPU utilization of EC2 instances allocated to the web and database tiers during Experiment 5. It can be seen from the figure that at 17th min, the average response time crosses the acceptable response time threshold and our auto-scale policy kicks in, invokes another instance and adds it to the web tier. As soon as, the effect of the newly added instance is realized, the response time again reaches under acceptable threshold. However, at 37th min, CPU of the web tier instances cross the acceptable threshold of CPU utilization and then another instance is added to the web tier dynamically in order to cope up with the situation. Notice, that the throughput of our telemedicine application linearly increases in this experiment except at the times when response time violation occurred. The maximum throughput we have achieved in this experiment is 2398 requests/second. It is noteworthy to mention here, that in this experiment we have not observed any bottleneck resources. Therefore, we believe that using `m3.medium` instance with auto-scaling for web tier and `m3.2xlarge` type of instance for database tier would help us to offer response time guarantees to the users of our proposed telemedicine service without observing any bottleneck resources.

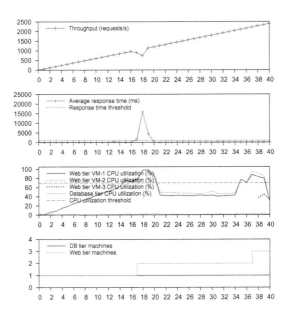

Fig. 6. Experiment 5: throughput (requests served/second), average response time, dynamic addition of web tier instances, and CPU utilization of web server and database tier instances.

5   Conclusion and Future Work

In this paper, we presented our developed telemedicine service and studied its performance using different Amazon EC2 instances on linearly increasing workloads. We found that dynamic resource provisioning on the web tier using medium type instances gives better results compared to static allocation using large and xlarge type instances without showing any bottleneck resources. We believe that this study would help the telemedicine service providers to use appropriate cloud resources in order to offer response time guarantees with minimal operational cost.

Currently, we are investigating the possibility of using NoSQL-based database to dynamically scale-out database tier instead of statically allocating over-provisioned resources to the database tier. It may greatly help to further reduce operational cost effectively.

Acknowledgments. We would like to thank Amazon Web Services (AWS) for providing us with a generous grant in terms of credits to use its cloud computing resources. The grant was part of its Amazon Educational Grant AWS Fund.

References

1. Buyya, R., Yeo, C.S., Venugopal, S.: Market-oriented cloud computing: vision, hype, and reality for delivering it services as computing utilities. In: Proceedings of the 2008 10th IEEE International Conference on High Performance Computing and Communications, Computer Society, HPCC 2008, pp. 5–13. IEEE, Washington, DC (2008)
2. Bodik, P., Griffith, R., Sutton, C., Fox, A., Jordan, M., Patterson, D.: Statistical machine learning makes automatic control practical for internet datacenters. In: Proceedings of the Workshop on Hot Topics in Cloud Computing, HotCloud 2009 (2009)
3. Iqbal, W., Dailey, M.N., Carrera, D., Janecek, P.: Adaptive resource provisioning for read intensive multi-tier applications in the cloud. Future Gener. Comput. Syst. **27**(6), 871–879 (2011)
4. Inc, A.: Amazon Web Services auto scaling (2009). http://aws.amazon.com/autoscaling/
5. Shilin, L., Ranjan, R., Strazdins, P.: Reporting an Experience on Design and Implementation of e-Health Systems on Azure Cloud (2013). http://arxiv.org/abs/1306.3624/
6. Hsieh, J.-c., Hsu, M.-W.: A cloud computing based 12-lead ECG telemedicine service (2012). http://www.biomedcentral.com/1472-6947/12/77/
7. Doukas, C., Pliakas, T., Maglogiannis, I.: Mobile healthcare information management utilizing Cloud Computing and Android OS (2010). http://www.ncbi.nlm.nih.gov/pubmed/21097207
8. Matlani, P., Londhe, N.D.: A cloud Computing Based Telemedicine Service (2013). http://www.biomedcentral.com/content/pdf/1472-6947-12-77.pdf
9. Wang, X., Gui, Q., Bingwei Liu, Y., Chen, Z.J.: Leveraging Mobile Cloud for Telemedicine: A Performance Study in Medical Monitoring (2013). http://harvey.binghamton.edu/ychen/NEBEC_2013.pdf
10. Mahapatra, A., Dash, M.: Design and Implementation of a Cloud based TeleDermatology System (2013). http://www.ijert.org/view-pdf/2269/design-and-implementation-of-a-cloud-based-teledermatology-system
11. Corporation, O.: Jersey: RESTful Web Services in Java (2010). https://jersey.java.net/
12. Mosberger, D., Jin, T.: httperf: A tool for measuring Web server performance. In: First Workshop on Internet Server Performance, pp. 59–67. ACM (1998)

Modeling Parallel Execution Policies of Web Services

Mai Xuan Trang[1]([✉]), Yohei Murakami[2], and Toru Ishida[1]

[1] Department of Social Informatics, Kyoto University, Kyoto, Japan
trangmx@ai.soc.i.kyoto-u.ac.jp, ishida@i.kyoto-u.ac.jp
[2] Unit of Design, Kyoto University, Kyoto, Japan
yohei@i.kyoto-u.ac.jp

Abstract. Cloud computing and high performance computing enable service providers to support parallel execution of provided services. Consider a client who invokes a web service to process a large dataset. The input data is split into independent partitions and multiple partitions are sent to the service concurrently. A typical customer would expect the service speedup to be directly proportional to the number of concurrent requests (or the degree of parallelism - DOP). However, we obtained that the achieved speedup is not always directly proportional to the DOP. This may because service providers employ parallel execution policies for their services based on arbitrary decisions. The goal of this paper is to analyse the performance improvement behavior of web services under parallel execution. We introduce a model of parallel execution policy of web services with three policies: Slow-down, Restriction and Penalty policies. We conduct analyses to evaluate our model. Interestingly, the results show that our model have a good accuracy in capturing parallel execution behavior of web services.

Keywords: Parallel execution · Service policy · Performance analysis

1 Introduction

Using the cloud environment to host web services offers numerous benefits. With cloud infrastructures, service providers are able to provide scalability for their services to support parallel execution. However, there are several factors that affect efficiency of parallel execution such as serial fractions in a task as pointed out in Amdahl's law [3,9], and parallel overhead [10]. Service providers may also make arbitrary decisions in selecting policies that control parallel execution of their services. In Service-Oriented Architecture (SOA), service users do not have control over computing resources or services' implementation, and so they need to know performance improvement behaviors of web services in order to configure the optimal parallel invocation to each web service.

In this paper we focus on analysing the effect of data parallelism, a technique often used to improve performance of tasks involving large-scale datasets. The data is split into small independent partitions that are executed in parallel by

© ICST Institute for Computer Sciences, Social Informatics and Telecommunications Engineering 2016
Y. Zhang et al. (Eds.): CloudComp 2015, LNICST 167, pp. 244–254, 2016.
DOI: 10.1007/978-3-319-38904-2_25

multiple task instances. This decreases the overall execution time of the task. In previous work [13] we used parallel execution policies of atomic web services to predict the optimal parallelism of composite services. However, the parallel execution policies of a variety of web services was not evaluated. To complement our previous work, this paper performs a series of experiments on real world web services. From the experiment results, we evaluate how well our policy model can capture parallel execution effects of different web services.

The rest of the paper is organised as follows. We begin with a motivating example in Sect. 2. Section 3 introduces parallel invocation of web services and elaborates our proposed policy model. Our testing methodology is described in Sect. 4. We show analysis results and evaluation in Sect. 5. We give some related works in Sect. 6. Finally, Sect. 7 concludes this paper.

2   Motivating Example

Consider a translation application that uses Google translation service to translate a document. In order to reduce the translation time, users configure the application to split the document into M independent partitions, and then send n multiple requests to Google translation service in parallel. Suppose that the method of splitting document is determined (M is fixed). Increasing n is expected to reduce the time taken to translate the whole document. Let *Speed-up* ($S(P)$) of the application be the ratio of the execution time of the application when $n = 1$ to the execution time of the application when $n = P$ ($S(P) = T(1)/T(P)$). A straightforward extrapolation to the higher number of concurrent requests would give the speed-up shown by the dashed line in Fig. 1.

This types of extrapolation is too common and unwarranted in our experience. As we will see, the actual speed-up of the application is more likely to follow the solid line in Fig. 1. The difference between these two predicted curves is significant. This example underscores the importance of obtaining a thorough understanding of the speed-up characteristics of a web service before invoking the services with parallel execution. One way to accomplish this is to assess speed-up patterns by analysing the parallel execution effects of different types of

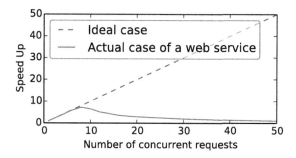

Fig. 1. Different speed-up patterns

web services. Once these patterns are determined we can define a model which can help users to better estimate service performance under parallel execution.

3   Parallel Invocation of a Web Service

We use *Data Parallelism* to perform parallel invocation to a web service as follows. Assume that a client wants to process a large dataset. At the client-side, the input data is split in to M partitions and n threads of the client are created to send n partitions to the service in parallel as shown in Fig. 2. At server-side the service needs to serve n requests in parallel. Execution time required for processing the input data depends on the number of concurrent requests, denoted by $f(n)$.

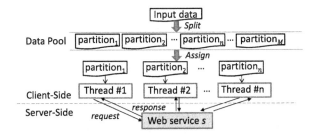

Fig. 2. Parallel invocations of a web service

3.1   Performance Speed-Up

We use *Speed-up* as a measure of the reduction in execution time taken to execute a fixed workload when increasing number of concurrent threads. Speed-up is calculated by the following equation: $S(n) = f(1)/f(n)$, where $f(1)$ is the execution time required to perform the work with a single thread and $f(n)$ is the time required to performance the same task with n concurrent threads.

Different web services may cause different speed-up behaviors. Such behaviors was examined in [1] and three categories were drawn:

- *Linear*–the speed-up ratio is equal to the number of concurrent processes, n, i.e., $S(n) = n$.
- *Sub-linear*–the speed-up ratio with n concurrent processes is lass than n, i.e., $S(n) < n$
- *Super-linear*–the speed-up ratio with n concurrent processes is greater than n, i.e., $S(n) > n$

Several models have been proposed to describe those speed-up behavior categories for parallel algorithms and architectures [9]. A well known and most cited model is Amdahl's law [3], which models the effect of the serial fraction of the task to the speed-up of the task as shown in Fig. 3. Different ratios of serial parts (F) yield different speed-up behaviors.

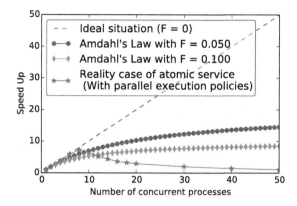

Fig. 3. Speed-up behaviors represented by Amdahl's Law model [13]

Most of existing models assume that the performance speed-up is determined chiefly by task limitations or computing resource limitations. The effect of service provider's arbitrary decision about how to implement parallel execution (parallel execution policies) on the performance speed-up (the solid line in Fig. 3) was not considered.

3.2   Parallel Execution Policy Model

In our previous work [13] we have proposed a model to capture parallel execution policies of web services. The model is defined by a tuple of parameters (α, $\alpha^\star$, α', P), with three policies as follows:

Slow-Down Policy. Performance improvement is throttled when the number of concurrent requests exceeds specified number (P_s) as showed in Fig. 4a. The execution time of the service is given by the following equation:

$$f(n) = \begin{cases} \alpha - \frac{\alpha-\alpha^\star}{P_s-1}(n-1), & \text{if } 1 \leq n < P_s \\ \alpha^\star - \frac{\alpha^\star-\alpha'}{M-P_s}(n-P_s), & \text{if } P_s \leq n \leq M \end{cases}$$

$$\text{with: } \alpha > \alpha^\star > \alpha', \text{ and } \frac{\alpha-\alpha^\star}{P_s-1} > \frac{\alpha^\star-\alpha'}{M-P_s}$$

Restriction Policy. Service performance statures when number of concurrent requests reaches to a specified number (P_r) as shown in Fig. 4b. The execution time of the service is given by the following equation:

$$f(n) = \begin{cases} \alpha - \frac{\alpha-\alpha^\star}{P_r-1}(n-1), & \text{if } 1 \leq n < P_r \\ \alpha^\star, & \text{if } P_r \leq n \leq M \end{cases}$$

$$\text{with: } \alpha^\star < \alpha, \text{ and } \alpha' \approx \alpha^\star$$

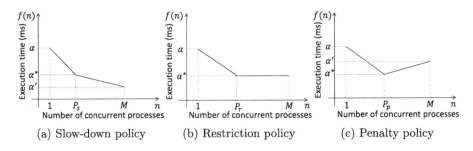

(a) Slow-down policy   (b) Restriction policy   (c) Penalty policy

Fig. 4. Performance improvement patterns of parallel execution policies

Penalty Policy. Service performance is reduced when number of concurrent requests exceeds a specified number (P_p) as shown in Fig. 4c. The execution time of the service is calculated by the following equation:

$$f(n) = \begin{cases} \alpha - \frac{\alpha - \alpha^\star}{P_p - 1}(n - 1), & \text{if } 1 \leq n < P_p \\ \alpha^\star + \frac{\alpha' - \alpha^\star}{M - P_p}(n - P_p), & \text{if } P_p \leq n \leq M \end{cases}$$

$$\text{with: } \alpha > \alpha^\star, \text{ and } \alpha' > \alpha^\star$$

4   Testing Methodology

We implement a testing system to evaluate our proposed model. A client is created to invoke web services with parallel execution. One challenge is to collect different web services provided by different providers for analysis. One of the most reliable sources we used is the Language Grid [5]. The Language Grid (LG) provides an infrastructure for sharing and combining language services. Different groups or providers can join and share language services on the Language Grid Platform[1]. Currently, more than 140 organizations have joined the Language Grid to share over 170 language services. We also assessed web services from outside the LG, such as from ProgrammableWeb[2].

Experiment Implementation. We implement a client using multi-threading technique to invoke web services. First, the input data is split into independent partitions. Then, n threads of the client are initialized to process n partitions in parallel. Therefore n requests are sent to the service concurrently. We also use pooling technique to stream data partitions to the client whenever a thread is available. We use the integration of the Language Grid and UIMA[3] [12] to realize our test system. First, we create a Document Splitter to split input document into independent partitions and store partitions to a queue. We create

---

[1] Web services on the LG: http://langrid.org/service_manager/language-services.
[2] ProgrammableWeb: http://www.programmableweb.com/.
[3] Apache UIMA: http://uima.apache.org/.

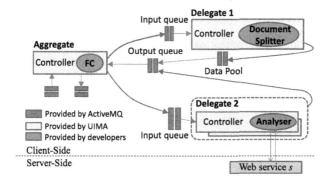

Fig. 5. Implementation concept of the test system

a client which invoke a web service to process data partitions from the queue. We implement a Follow Controller (FC) to connect the Document Splitter and the Client, and control the queues and number of threads of the Client. Figure 5 shows implementation concept of our experiment in the UIMA framework. With this implementation, all n threads of the client are running at all the time. This means that the service has to serve n concurrent requests at all the time.

5 Experiments

This section describes the results of testing the performance impact of parallel execution for web services provided by different providers. We observe that performance improvement patterns of different web services follow different parallel execution policies as defined in Sect. 3.2. Interestingly, from the analysis we observe that, a web service may employ a combination of parallel execution policies as shown in Fig. 6.

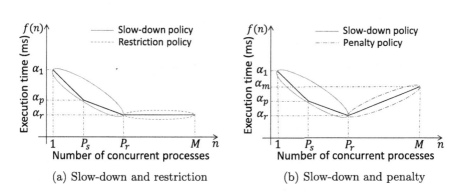

(a) Slow-down and restriction   (b) Slow-down and penalty

Fig. 6. Combination of policies

5.1   Combination of Slow-Down Policy and Restriction Policy

Figure 7 depicts different performance improvement behaviors of several web services. The results demonstrate that these services employ both the slow-down policy and the restriction policy as follows:

– Performance improvement of J-Server translation service follows slow-down and restriction policies with $P_s = 4$ and $P_r = 16$.
– Performance improvement of Mecab morphological analysis service follows slow-down and restriction policies with $P_s = 4$ and $P_r = 14$.
– Performance improvement of Google URL shorten service follows slow-down and restriction policies with $P_s = 2$ and $P_r = 12$
– Performance improvement of Amazon S3 service follows slow-down policy with $P_s = 14$. We have not observed restriction behavior of Amazon S3 when n increases until 50.

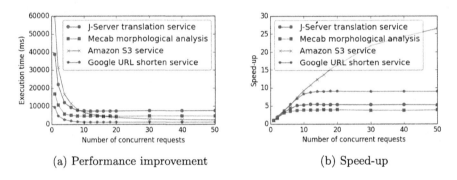

(a) Performance improvement   (b) Speed-up

Fig. 7. Web services with slow-down and restriction policy

5.2   Combination of Slow-Down Policy and Penalty Policy

Figure 8 depicts performance improvement behaviors of several other web services. The results demonstrate that the performance improvement of these services is combination of slow-down policy and penalty policy as follows:

– Performance improvement of TreeTagger service follows slow-down and penalty policies with $P_s = 4$ and $P_r = 8$.
– For Life science dictionary service, when number of concurrent requests larger than 6 some requests are blocked and error message are returned (the failed requests are resubmitted until corrected responses are returned). Eventually, the execution time of the service is increased. The performance improvement follows slow-down and penalty policies with $P_s = 6$ and $P_p = 8$.

- Performance improvement of Google translation service follows slow-down and penalty policies with $P_s = 4$ and $P_p = 8$.
- Performance improvement of Yandex translation service follows slow-down and penalty policies with $P_s = 10$ and $P_p = 12$

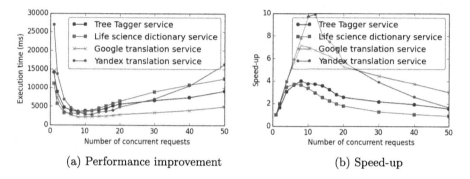

(a) Performance improvement   (b) Speed-up

Fig. 8. Web services with slow-down and penalty policy

In our analysis, we have analysed more than 50 web services, about two-thirds of them are registered in the Language Grid, the others are collected from outside the Language Grid. The experiment results show that, performance improvement of most of the collected web services can be categorized into the two categories listed above.

5.3 Evaluation

We evaluate our parallel execution policy model by using regression analysis. Our model is compared with two regression models: a linear fitting model and a curve fitting model with a quartic regression (curve fitting function: $y = ax^4 + bx^3 + cx^2 + dx + e$). Figure 9 shows comparison of our policy model and regression models of two different services: J-Server translation service and Google translation service.

We use standard error (S), and R-squared (R^2) to compare the models. S gives some idea of how much the model's prediction differs from the actual results. R^2 provides an index of the closeness of the actual results to the prediction. S and R^2 are calculated by the following equations:

$$S = \sqrt{\frac{\sum_{1}^{n}(Actual_i - Prediction_i)^2}{n - p}}, \text{ and } R^2 = 1 - \frac{\sum_{1}^{n}(Actual_i - Prediction_i)^2}{\sum_{1}^{n}(Actual_i - mean(Actual))^2}$$

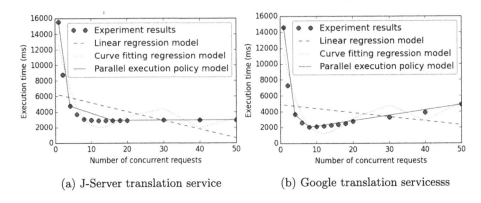

(a) J-Server translation service   (b) Google translation servicesss

Fig. 9. Evaluating policy model of different services

where n is number of observations, p is the number of regression parameters ($p = 2$ in the case of linear regression and our model, $p = 5$ in the case of the quartic regression model).

The F-test is used to calculate P-value for evaluating statistical significance of our policy model. Table 1 shows comparison of the policy model with the two regression models for different web services. The results show that, in all cases, the policy model has the lower standard error and higher R-Squared than either the linear regression model or the quartic regression model. The P-value of the policy model is significantly low (much less than 0.05). We repeated the evaluation with other web services, the results were similar. We conclude that our policy model has much better accuracy in capturing performance improvement behaviors of web services than the conventional regression models. The policy model is also highly statistically significant and can faithfully estimate the parallel execution effects of web services.

Table 1. Comparison of the proposed model with regression models

	S (milliseconds)			R-squared (%)			P-value
	Linear model	Quartic model	Policy model	Linear model	Quartic model	Policy model	Policy model
J-Server tran.	3287.94	1583.47	1049.75	21.3	86.3	92.0	1.23e-09
Google tran.	3415.02	1680.13	1075.34	4.9	82.73	90.6	2.55e-09
Mecab	3310.78	1634.90	764.73	19.9	85.3	95.7	3.71e-11
Amazon S3	13734.94	6264.98	4795.82	31.2	89.3	91.6	1.57e-09
Google URL	2080.93	1014.05	698.97	23.2	86.3	91.3	4.06e-09
Tree tagger	3078.94	1297.93	659.91	1.2	86.8	95.5	5.82e-11
LSD	2521.01	1267.16	885.72	4.5	89.5	93.2	1.56e-09

6   Related Work

Several papers have addressed the performance of web services. An optimization model for optimal resource allocation across a set of web service class running on the same physical server in virtual environment was proposed in [2]. Bonneta et al. [4] presented a service scripting language–S, together with its compiler and runtime system to efficiently exploit today's multi-core parallel architectures to scale the number of concurrent requests.

Some studies discuss about performance effect of deploying web services on the cloud. Ristov et al. [7] shown that migrating web service on the cloud reduces their performance compared to using the same hardware resources. Although the cloud can scale its resources, it does not guarantee that the performance will scale the same as the scaling factor. Virtualization is another layer that also produces performance discrepancy.

Other studies have introduced several parameters that impact web service performance such as the computation that the web service is performing [8], the CPU power and cores, the message size and the introduced security [11], and even the resource orchestration in the cloud virtual environment [6]. Most existing works do not consider the effect of services policies on performance improvement from the view of service users as we focus in this paper.

7   Conclusion

This paper analysed performance improvement behaviors of different web services under parallel execution. We provided analyses and evaluations of our parallel execution policy model which includes three types of policies: Slow-down policy, Restriction policy, and Penalty policy. By conducting a series experiments on more than 50 web services, we have experimentally confirmed our model well captures the effects of parallel execution policy. Our model has been proved to be superior to regression models in capturing the parallel execution effects of web services. The evaluation results also showed that our parallel execution policy model can well illustrate performance improvement behaviors of web services under parallel execution.

Our model introduced a new factor, which is service' policy, that affect parallel execution efficiency of the service. The model is useful for service users in understanding the parallel execution policies of web services. This will enable users to alter their parallel invocation of a web service to the service policy in order to attain the optimal speed-up. However, the three types of parallel execution policies may not correctly cover all types of web service policies. To make our model more rigorous, we will continue our analysis with larger number of web services and more parameters for parallel execution such as number of concurrent requests per second or the time when users invoke a web service.

Acknowledgments. This research was partly supported by a Grant-in-Aid for Scientific Research (S) (24220002, 2012-2016) from Japan Society for Promotion of Science (JSPS).

References

1. Alba, E.: Parallel evolutionary algorithms can achieve super-linear performance. Inf. Process. Lett. **82**(1), 7–13 (2002)
2. Almeida, J., Almeida, V., Ardagna, D., Cunha, Í., Francalanci, C., Trubian, M.: Joint admission control and resource allocation in virtualized servers. J. Parallel Distrib. Comput. **70**(4), 344–362 (2010)
3. Amdahl, G.M.: Validity of the single processor approach to achieving large scale computing capabilities. In: Proceedings of the Spring Joint Computer Conference, pp. 483–485. ACM (1967)
4. Bonetta, D., Peternier, A., Pautasso, C., Binder, W.: S: a scripting language for high-performance restful web services. ACM SIGPLAN Not. **47**(8), 97–106 (2012)
5. Ishida, T. (ed.): The Language Grid: Service-Oriented Collective Intelligence for Language Resource Interoperability. Cognitive Technologies. Springer, Heidelberg (2011)
6. Gusev, M., Ristov, S., Velkoski, G., Simjanoska, M.: Optimal resource allocation to host web services in cloud. In: Proceedings of the Sixth IEEE International Conference on Cloud Computing (CLOUD), pp. 948–949. IEEE (2013)
7. Ristov, S., Velkoski, G., Gusev, M., Kjiroski, K.: Compute and memory intensive web service performance in the cloud. In: Markovski, S., Gushev, M. (eds.) ICT Innovations 2012. AISC, vol. 207, pp. 215–224. Springer, Heidelberg (2013)
8. Ristov, S., Gusev, M., Velkoski, G.: Modeling the speedup for scalable web services. In: Bogdanova, A.M., Gjorgjevikj, D. (eds.) ICT Innovations 2014. AISC, vol. 311, pp. 177–186. Springer, Heidelberg (2015)
9. Sun, X.-H., Chen, Y.: Reevaluating amdahls law in the multicore era. J. Parallel Distrib. Comput. **70**(2), 183–188 (2010)
10. Tallent, N.R., Mellor-Crummey, J.M.: Effective performance measurement and analysis of multithreaded applications. In: ACM Sigplan Notices, vol. 44, no. 4, pp. 229–240. ACM (2009)
11. Tentov, A., et al.: Performance impact correlation of message size vs. concurrent users implementing web service security on linux platform. In: Kocarev, L. (ed.) ICT Innovations 2011. AISC, vol. 150, pp. 367–377. Springer, Heidelberg (2012)
12. Trang, M.X., Murakami, Y., Lin, D., Ishida, T.: Integration of workflow and pipeline for language service composition. In: Proceedings of the 9th edn. of the Language Resources and Evaluation Conference (LREC), pp. 3829–3836 (2014)
13. Trang, M.X., Murakami, Y., Ishida, T.: Policy-aware optimization of parallel execution of composite service. In: Proceedings of the 12th IEEE International Conference on Services Computing (SCC), pp. 106–113. IEEE (2015)

A Hybrid Cloud Computing Model for Higher Education Institutions in Saudi Arabia

Muhammad Asif Khan[(⊠)]

College of Computer Science and Engineering, Taibah University,
Madinah al Munawwarah, Saudi Arabia
asifkhan2k@yahoo.com

Abstract. Cloud computing is a new technology that has an increasing popularity among business enterprises especially small to medium enterprises. In educational institutions where information technology is backbone for conducting research and academic activities limited budget does not allow to acquire latest technology or upgrade the existing technology. Universities produce two different types of data i.e. intellectual data that needs to be shared among other institutions in order to keep updated each other and operational data that is used within a university for daily routine work. In this study a proposed hybrid cloud model is proposed for higher education institutions in Saudi Arabia in order to share intellectual data. The proposed hybrid model is viable under ministry of higher education in Saudi Arabia. Different aspects of the model have been discussed and efficacy of the model.

Keywords: Cloud computing · Cloud model · Cloud computing in Saudi Arabia

1 Introduction

Cloud computing is a new technology that has an increasing popularity among business enterprises especially small to medium enterprises. Since cloud computing is an evolving technology different people interpret cloud computing term in different ways and sometime they misinterpret the term in order to market their products. Cloud computing definitions have been reviewed by [1] and three main components were identified i.e. virtualization, scalability and pay-per-use service model that are the basics of cloud computing definition. In cloud computing framework computing resources are formed in a pool of resources on network and it allocates the required services dynamically to various applications based on user requirements. In cloud computing model users do not need to purchase any expensive hardware and just by paying the rental cost to the cloud provider all services can be availed. Since this model reduces cost and operational cost it is lucrative to organizations especially to small-scale enterprises [2]. Cloud computing model is comprised of two layers namely resource layer and service layer. Figure 1 shows the basic cloud model [4–6].

In the lowest layer of the service layer i.e. Infrastructure as a Service (IaaS) computing resources (memory allocation, processing time, disk based storage etc.) are provided to users. Users can run software of their choice using the resources and they

© ICST Institute for Computer Sciences, Social Informatics and Telecommunications Engineering 2016
Y. Zhang et al. (Eds.): CloudComp 2015, LNICST 167, pp. 255–259, 2016.
DOI: 10.1007/978-3-319-38904-2_26

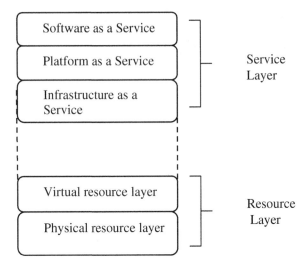

Fig. 1. A cloud computing layered model

are billed by their selection of choice [3]. The middle layer i.e. Platform as a Service (PaaS) provides personalized services in terms of software and hardware that enhance better performance. It provides to users a platform on which a user can develop and host their applications. This layer consists of an operating system and application development tools which are used to develop applications. The top layer of the service layer is Software as a Service (SaaS) that provides to users application environment such as email hosting where users have no control on the infrastructure.

The service layers are used by different users depending on their requirements; for example, IaaS service layer is used by large organizations that have resources to support applications and underlying platforms supplied by cloud service provider in order to save cost. The cloud computing framework can be used in educational environment in order to manage resources and keep updated with other institutions in the industry. Since private and public educational institutions work under financial constraints it is difficult to update with the latest information technology. It is almost impossible for organizations to be aligned with growing information technology. In order to have accessibility to latest IT tools and services and sharing research activities it is necessary to investigate cloud computing model and in the present study author strives to propose a cloud computing framework for educational institutions in Saudi Arabia.

2   Cloud Computing Model for Institutions

In many organizations cloud computing technology is being used due to its availability of virtualized resources [7]. Ministry of Higher Education (MOHE) in Saudi Arabia is responsible to dealing with higher education, creating higher education institutions, coordinating and supervising the post-secondary institutions. In Saudi Arabia there are 45 degree awarding universities/colleges (both public and private). Table 1 presents the details of the universities functioning in different regions of the Kingdom.

Table 1. Number of universities in Saudi Arabia

Province	Number of universities	
	Public	Private
Riyadh	7	8
Makkah	4	3
Madinah	4	1
Eastern Province	4	4
Asir	1	0
Hail	1	0
Najran	1	0
Tabuk	1	1
Al Jouf	1	0
Al Qassim	1	0
Al Baha	1	0
Northern Borders	1	0
Jazan	1	0

Universities produce intellectual capital data and the data that facilitate daily routine work. All educational material that includes course specifications, course reports, course material, curriculum, student's projects, assignments etc. are considered intellectual capital for an institute. When this capital is shared with other educational institutes a large number of people (teachers and students) would benefit them and cause reduction in duplication of efforts. If this capital is available to all universities under some authority and control then universities would extend their focus to innovative and creative ideas rather than re-inventing the wheel.

In addition to intellectual capital universities have their own data that they use internally to run business on daily routine basis. This data however cannot be shared with other universities and it is called as operational data.

Now the authors suggest a cloud computing model based on the above two types of data i.e. intellectual capital data and operational data. The proposed model can be called as a hybrid model that consists of two clouds i.e. public cloud (intellectual capital data) and private cloud (operational data).

In the proposed model it is suggested that a hybrid computing model would facilitate universities in Saudi Arabia to share knowledge and research activities. Since MOHE is responsible to coordinate and supervise higher education institutions in Saudi Arabia public cloud that consists of intellectual capital data generated by universities is owned by the ministry and it can be called as MOHE cloud. The operational data that is purely generated by the universities in order to running daily routine activities are placed in a private cloud and can be called as university cloud. Figure 2 shows the hybrid cloud model.

In the hybrid cloud model MOHE cloud is a public cloud that owns all the intellectual capital data generated by universities such as assessments, course specifications, course reports, course material, etc. that would be shared by any universities approved by the MOHE. However, MOHE would be responsible to place security and monitoring controls in order to prevent data from plagiarism. Universities which contribute in this cloud by supplying data are considered as source of information and those who receive data from the cloud are considered as sinks. A university can be considered a source and sink of the cloud at the same time.

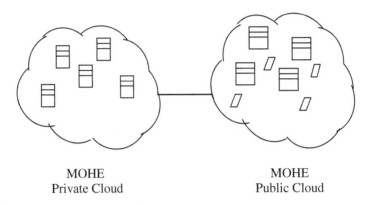

MOHE
Private Cloud

MOHE
Public Cloud

Fig. 2. A hybrid cloud model

University cloud is a private cloud where operational data of an individual university is placed. The data is sole propriety of the university and is inaccessible to other universities. Universities may grant access to the data to different users depending on their requirements. Students of a university may access their exams schedule or exam results without visiting university personally. However, security controls need to be more effectively implemented in the cloud as any breach of security may cause disastrous results.

3   Efficacy of Model

The hybrid cloud model will have great effects on educational institutions as well as on Saudi ministry of higher education which may develop and maintain a pool of knowledge and research material. This cloud however has great advantages such as a treasure of knowledge at one place and encouragement to other institutions to participate in increasing knowledge and research by using existing data and applying innovative ideas of their own. Another benefit of the cloud is to provide support in terms of assessment, projects and course material in order to improve effectiveness and quality of teaching. Since the MOHE owns the cloud a constant monitoring would help the ministry to identify and provide guidelines to improve quality of teaching at some universities that are found below the set criteria of quality.

The model will save huge budget of IT infrastructure spent in universities in order to provide and maintain IT services within universities. Universities are required to pay a usage fee to service provider since all IT infrastructure is maintained by the service provider. Hence, universities can utilize the latest technology without investing in acquisition of technology. The model provides information accessibility to its users with convenience and comfort any time and day they wish to access. Students may have access to a number of academic resources that may help them develop their knowledge and skills [8]. The private pool of universities facilitates students to access their exams schedule and results immediately they are announced without visiting universities. MOHE of Saudi Arabia would be in a position to monitor and align all higher education institutions to the required standards and guidelines provided by the ministry. This model will save heavy government investment that is required to purchasing hardware, software, networking and communication devices for research and higher education institutions.

4 Conclusion and Future Work

Cloud computing technology has helped business organizations especially small to medium business enterprises to benefit from the latest technology in order to manage their information. In the present study we have presented a hybrid cloud model that would facilitate business organizations to share and contribute knowledge and research in higher education in Saudi Arabia. The implementation of this model will save heavy investments in technology infrastructure in higher education and provide opportunities to sharing knowledge and research among universities. We intend to validate this framework in future and since strict security measures and controls are needed to implement the model; there is a need to investigate different security models and propose a viable security model that can be implemented in a hybrid cloud model for higher education.

References

1. Vaquero, L., Rodero-Merino, L.M., Caceres, J., Lindner, M.: A break in the clouds: towards a cloud definition. ACM SIGCOMM Comput. Commun. Rev. **39**, 50–55 (2008)
2. Michael, A., Armando, F., Rean, G.: Above the Cloud: A Berkeley View of Cloud Computing. Technical Report No.UCB/EECS-28 (2009)
3. Mell, P., Grance, T.: The NIST Definition of Cloud Computing. U.S. Department of Commerce (2009)
4. Cheng, Z., Bing, L.: Rearch on the stack model of cloud computing. Microelectron. Comput. **26**(8), 22–27 (2009)
5. Pallis, G.: Cloud computing: the new frontier of internet computing. IEEE Internet Comput. **14**, 70–73 (2010)
6. Fouquet, M., Niedermayer, H., Carle, G.: Cloud computing for the masses. In: Proceedings of the 1st ACM Workshop on User-provided Networking: Challenges and Opportunities at the International Conference On Emerging Networking Experiments and Technologies, Rome, Italy, pp. 31–36 (2009)
7. Ercan, T.: Effective use of cloud computing in educational institutions. Procedia Soc. Behav. Sci. **2**, 938–942 (2010)
8. Bai, X.: Affordance of ubiquitous learning through cloud computing. In: 5th International Conference on Fronteirs of Computer Science, pp. 78–82 (2010)

A Methodology to Select the Best Public Cloud Service for Media Focussed Enterprises

Subhranshu Banerjee[✉], Vikas Mathur, and Sreehari Narasipur

RightCloudz Technologies, Bangalore, India
{subhranshu.banerjee,vikas.mathur,
sreehari.narasipur}@rightcloudz.com

Abstract. With the advancement of cloud technologies, media focussed enterprises have started adopting cloud technologies to improve their offerings, to increase the reach and to gain competitive advantages. With the proliferation of public cloud services and the lack of standardisation in describing cloud services, it has become a very difficult task to identify the most suitable cloud service for an enterprise.

This paper discusses the methodologies that a media company can adopt while selecting a public cloud service to scientifically arrive at a purchasing decision. The model described herein has been successfully used by Right-Cloudz Technologies for their public cloud selection advisory services.

Keywords: Evaluation as a service · Compare clouds · Public cloud services for media companies · Public cloud selection

1 Introduction

There are three data center models that are commonly in use at most media focussed enterprises. Each of these models provide a different set of capabilities at varying degrees of efficiency[1].

(a) In-premise Data Center (Private or Outsourced to a Managed Services Provider)
(b) IaaS/PaaS/SaaS from Cloud Service Providers
(c) Hybrid model

This paper discusses a model and methodology that can readily be applied to compare Public IaaS/PaaS/SaaS services to be used by media focussed enterprises.

While working on this paper we looked into the challenges faced by media delivery companies, e.g., video-on-demand service providers, video conference service providers, news and publishing houses, etc. where the content is accessed through different types of devices and the peak load can not be easily anticipated. For example, a news item or a video clip may go viral for no apparent reason. Addressing the requirements of media production houses (viz. film/TV/animation/music industry) has been kept out of the scope of this paper.

---

[1] Efficiency has been defined as a function of timely completion of jobs with reduced average cost (one time cost, operating cost and both, as appropriate) for the resources.

© ICST Institute for Computer Sciences, Social Informatics and Telecommunications Engineering 2016
Y. Zhang et al. (Eds.): CloudComp 2015, LNICST 167, pp. 260–268, 2016.
DOI: 10.1007/978-3-319-38904-2_27

2   The Selection and Buying Processes in Vogue

Selecting a service provider by using the standard Request for Proposal (RFP) methodology is a well accepted method in the B2B sector. The RFP process generally works well
in situations where the number of vendors to select from is small or the vendors are
pre-selected/short-listed by using some other methodology prior to the RFP being
released.

3   A Paradigm Shift in the Buying Process

The era of cloud technologies, which has enabled enterprises to buy business critical
computing resources over the web, ironically has made it easier to skip the required due
diligence while buying computing resources in hurry.

With publicly available data and the data validated by 3rd parties about the quality
of services offered by a cloud service provider, many enterprises may prefer to do
online evaluation of cloud services before purchasing.

In the following sections we shall see how the commonly used techniques to select
a potential cloud service provider, may actually push the enterprises towards settling
down with a less than the best option available.

3.1   The Shortcomings of a Filter Based System

There are a few online services that help cloud customers identify the most suitable
cloud service for their business. Most of these services let the customer narrow down
the cloud vendor list based on simple feature filtering; e.g., if two vendors support SSD
as a storage option, both will get shortlisted if the customer's application requires SSD
type of storage. This kind of filtering mechanism does not provide an assessment of the
quality of the services provided and therefore the customer still has the difficult task of
picking the better of the two feature-equivalent services. Basically the filtering scheme
does not rank Cloud Service Providers on the basis of the quality of the service
provided. Also there is no way for the customer to specify relative priorities of the
requirements.

3.2   The Shortcomings of Research Reports

Research reports and whitepapers are good sources to get overall information about
cloud services provided by a set of Cloud Service Providers; some amount of company
profile is available part of the report. However, these reports are static in nature and the
data points used in them may not be very current – at best, the data points may be a
couple of months or a quarter older than the time the report was prepared. Also, these
reports are typically written for a large customer base and are not applicable to the
specific business needs of a particular enterprise.

Even with above mentioned shortcomings, an independent and unbiased cloud comparison report may help a media company to (i) prepare the list of requirements, (ii) short-list a set of vendors (for the required service).

3.3 The Dynamic Component in Ranking

A rating or ranking system is incomplete if it does not consider dynamic data in the evaluation process. Dynamic data may include several important pieces of information about a service provider's SLA adherence, performance and latency information, etc.

A good evaluation system should use static data about features and capabilities (as claimed by the Cloud Service Provider) and dynamic data (averaged out over a reasonably long period) for objective analysis and ranking.

4 A Path Breaking Evaluation Methodology[2]

This paper describes a path breaking evaluation methodology. There are three key players in this methodology: (1) Cloud Service Providers, (2) Consumer/user of cloud services, (3) "Cloud Evaluation as a Service" Provider.

To evaluate a cloud service provider for a set of services a few filters are used to prepare a shortlist of Cloud Service Providers. A list of all essential features for the required service is prepared. This is the list against which the customer requirements are compared to see which requirement is satisfied by which feature. Measurable parameters for all features are then identified, and raw data (both static and dynamic) are collected. While a major part of the data can be collected through an automated process, review of those data and other manually collected data are done. Then a score is assigned based on these raw data. The data refresh frequency should generally not be longer than two weeks. The task of keeping data current is one of the most important mantra of "Cloud Evaluation as a Service" providers.

Following diagram shows the interactions among the consumer (enterprises), Evaluation-as-a-Service provider, cloud service providers and 3rd party sites keeping track of performance of Cloud Service Providers (CSPs) (Fig. 1).

4.1 Defining the Meaning of a Priority Value

Each requirement (aggregation of related features of the service) in this system is defined by measurable parameters. A priority value from 0 to 10 is assigned to each requirement, where 10 is the highest priority value - for a requirement would call for satisfying particular threshold value of a certain group of parameters. A higher priority value would mean that all threshold values for lowers priorities are also to be satisfied for that requirement.

---

[2] Patent pending; for more information please visit www.rightcloudz.com.

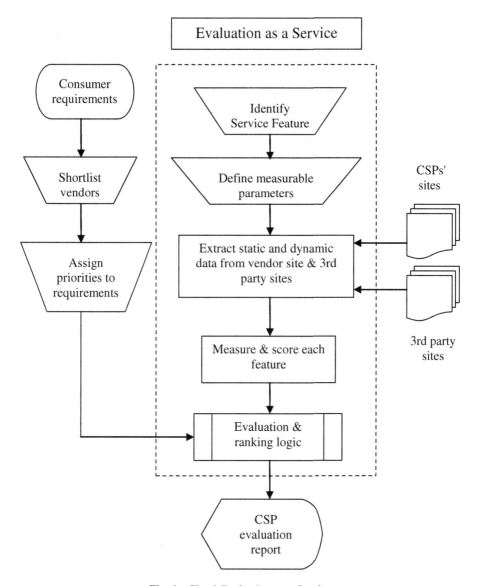

Fig. 1. Cloud Evaluation as a Service

By setting a priority value for a requirement, an enterprise communicates the importance of those parameters to be fulfilled. If a Cloud Service Provider does not fulfil one or more of those parameters, that will get a lesser score than the Cloud Service Provider which satisfies/does better for all those parameters.

The important points on assigning a priority value for a requirement by the customer are:

- The value for priorities are not absolute but rather a relative one with respect to other requirements.
- A priority value of zero means that the requirement has no value for the customer; e.g., media companies those who want to use transcoding as a service, may put a lower value for ease of use requirement.

4.2   Identifying Key Technology and Business Requirements ("Must Have") of Media Companies

Key requirements of media companies can broadly be grouped under following five kinds of services. One service may have dependency on/use part of services provided by another service.

(1) **Transcoding service** - both file based and streaming (for media companies providing video and audio services for a set of end-user-devices).
(2) **Network service** - ability to provision sufficient download bandwidth for satisfactory user experience.
(3) **Compute service** - the computing resource required to run transcoders and to meet the requirements of seasonal peaks.
(4) **Security service** - a secured channel for consumers to access subscribed services.
(5) **Storage service** - storage for accessing the media, on demand or in near future, and options for archival/cold storage of transcoded content/program.

4.3   Identifying Additional Technology and Business Requirements of Media Companies

While assessing cloud services, there are few common requirements which should also be satisfied for productivity and efficiency:

(6) **Operating cost** - cost of using various cloud infrastructure, support, data transfer, monitoring services and so on.
(7) **Ease of use** - how easy it is to use transcoding service and integrating those with the application.
(8) **Support** - kind and quality of support available to resolve any issue while using any of those cloud services.
(9) **SLA adherence** - how well the service level agreements for output transcoders, required bandwidth, etc. are provided.
(10) **Compliance** - Cloud Service Provider should have a clear policy and the ability to adhere to policies set by the government on streaming of video and other media.

The next step is to map each requirement to a group of measurable parameters which can be assigned a score. We shall discuss those in the coming sections.

4.4 Identifying Parameters Which Define Requirements

A requirement is best described by listing down the parameters which together give the meaning to that requirement. While some requirements may be defined by four to five parameters, other requirements may require ten parameters or more. As a thumb rule, a cloud usage scenario generally can be well defined with seventy to hundred quantifiable parameters spread across seven to fifteen requirements.

To illustrate the working of this model, we shall list down few parameters for the requirements identified above. For the sake of simplicity we have not listed all of the parameters for each requirement. One may want to add/remove one or more parameters and/or may have new requirements and parameters as required for his/her cloud usage scenario (Table 1).

Table 1. Measurable parameters for requirements of a Media Company

#	Requirements	Measurable parameters
1	Transcoding Service	(i) file based transcoding, (ii) max file size, (iii) stream transcoding, (iv) SDK support, (v) additional services to be used, etc.
2	Network Service	(i) bandwidth, (ii) baud rate, etc.
3	Compute Service	Compute resources: (i) memory, (ii) disk, (iii) vCPUs/cores, (iv) OS, (v) on demand/reserved instances, etc.
4	Security Service	(i) authentication and access control, (ii) configurable option when connected from multiple devices, (iii) encryption of sensitive data, etc.
5	Storage Service	(i) disk space, (ii) SSD, (iii) archival/cold storage, etc.
6	Operating cost	Cost of (i) compute, (ii) storage, (iii) network, (iv) transcoding (file/live) service, (v) support, (vi) data transfer, etc.
7	Ease of use	(i) how easy it is to integrate transcoding service, (ii) ease of using monitoring service, (iii) access to documentation, etc.
8	Support	(i) email/chat/phone based support, (ii) office hrs/24 h, (iii) account manager/escalation channel, etc.
9	SLA adherence	(i) unplanned downtime, (ii) time to restore services, etc.
10	Compliance	(i) certifications, (ii) tools to enforce policy, etc.

4.5 Setting Priorities for Each Requirement

Let us assume, following are the priorities set for each requirement. It is advisable to mark very important requirements with high priority value (>=8). It is better to assign high priority value to three to five requirements at maximum. The following table shows requirements (listed in alphabetical order) with assigned priority value (Table 2).

Table 2. Requirements with priority assigned

#	Requirement	Priority
1	Compliance	5
2	Compute	7
3	Ease of use	6
4	Network	9
5	Operating cost	6
6	Security	6
7	SLA adherence	7
8	Storage	8
9	Support	6
10	Transcoding	10

4.6   What to Look at to Zero in on a Cloud Service Provider

Once the scores for all parameters are available, these scores are normalized to bring them to comparable terms. Then these normalized scores for requirements are computed by weighted aggregation. One can decide either (i) to have equal weights for parameters of a requirement, or (ii) different weights for parameters of a requirement – this way the relative priorities of parameters within a requirement can be adjusted as per user needs.

Once the weighted normalized score of each requirement for the selected Cloud Service Providers is computed, we are ready to compare Cloud Service Providers against the requirements. The significance of comparing this way is equivalent to comparing an apple with an apple because the scores have been normalised at parameter level.

5   Vendor Scores and Sample Charts

To illustrate the concept we have used data of six cloud service providers/vendors for media companies; names of the companies have been masked intentionally and have been replaced by labels V1 through V6.

5.1   Top Vendors for User Assigned Priorities for Requirements

The chart and vendor scores with user assigned priorities are shown below (Fig. 2).

Looking at the total score, an enterprise may decide to choose cloud service provider V5 as that got the best overall score (Table 3).

5.2   Top Vendors for All Requirements with Equal Priorities

The chart below provides vendor ranking based on all relevant requirements but with all the priority levels set at the same level (10) (Fig. 3).

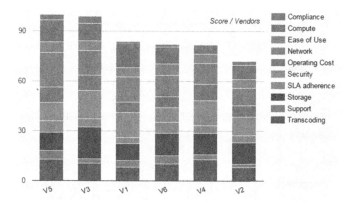

Fig. 2. Ranked Cloud Service Providers for user assigned priorities

Table 3. Scores of top five vendors with user assigned priorities for requirements

Requirement | Vendor	V5	V3	V1	V6	V4
Compliance	3.13	4.23	1.09	1.43	0.41
Compute	13.31	10.74	14.68	10.17	5.03
Ease of use	6.59	5.97	5.73	7.08	5.73
Network	20.69	14.52	15.18	12.90	12.31
Operating cost	9.38	9.46	6.16	6.60	10.13
Security	11.08	16.91	15.10	8.83	15.01
SLA adherence	6.98	5.01	3.77	6.38	4.48
Storage	10.81	19.12	10.03	13.75	12.81
Support	5.22	2.70	4.00	4.74	3.14
Transcoding	12.81	10.44	8.24	10.27	12.81
Total score	**100.00**	**99.10**	**83.98**	**82.15**	**81.86**

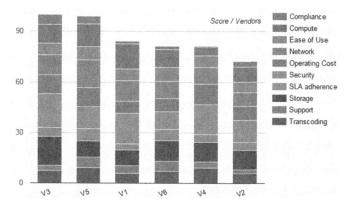

Fig. 3. Ranked Cloud Service Providers for equal priorities

Table 4. Scores of top five vendors with equal priorities for requirements

Requirement | Vendor	V3	V5	V1	V4	V6
Compliance	6.06	4.47	1.56	2.04	0.58
Compute	10.97	13.60	15.00	10.39	5.14
Ease of use	7.12	7.85	6.83	8.43	6.83
Network	11.53	16.44	12.06	10.25	9.78
Operating cost	11.27	11.18	7.35	7.86	12.07
Security	20.15	13.21	18.00	10.53	17.89
SLA adherence	5.12	7.14	3.85	6.51	4.58
Storage	17.09	9.66	8.96	12.29	11.45
Support	3.21	6.23	4.77	5.65	3.75
Transcoding	7.48	9.15	5.88	7.35	9.16
Total score =	**100.00**	**98.93**	**84.26**	**81.31**	**81.23**

It is important to note that when all requirements are considered to be of equal priority, cloud service provider V3 gets the best overall score, closely followed by cloud service provider V5 (Table 4).

In this particular illustration top two cloud service providers seem to have very close overall scores. However, for the given user priorities, cloud service provider V5 scores the best. Moreover, V5 scores better in two out of three high priority requirements as well (viz., Network and Transcoding services). So, cloud service provider V5 should ideally be selected by the enterprise.

6   Conclusion

Selecting a Cloud Service in a scientific manner is going to be as important if not more when compared with selecting data center servers or desktop machines for the enterprise. No two cloud platforms are identical. More over, the way the features are generally packaged by Cloud Service Providers makes it very difficult to do an apple to apple comparison.

One may tend to think that vendor lock-in is rare in cloud usage scenario. However, migrating back and forth and identifying the most suitable cloud service provider in that process is an expensive exercise. Also, the thought of using a cloud service which might have been used by many other enterprises successfully, even for a similar media business, may still turn out to be a bad idea if business priorities are different!

There is no shortcut to due diligence while selecting a cloud service provider for an enterprise. We believe that techniques described in this paper will definitely help media focussed enterprises in selecting the right Cloud Service Provider for their business. However this technique is not limited to selecting right media related service only. The technique is very flexible to help enterprises to make the right choice while selecting a Cloud Service Provider in any domain.

A Cloud Computing System Using Virtual Hyperbolic Coordinates for Services Distribution

Telesphore Tiendrebeogo[✉]

Polytechnic University of Bobo, Bobo-dioulasso, Burkina Faso
tetiendreb@gmail.com

Abstract. Cloud computing technologies have attracted considerable interest in recent years. Thus, these latters became inescapable in most part of the developments of applications. It constitutes a new mode of use and of offer of IT resources in general. Such resources can be used "on demand" by anybody who has access to the internet. Cloud architecture allows today to provide a number of services to the software and database developers among others remote. But for most of the existing systems, the quality of service in term of services' indexation is not present. Efforts are to be noted as for the search for the performance on the subject. In this paper, we define a new cloud computing architecture based on a Distributed Hash Table (DHT) and design a prototype system. Next, we perform and evaluate our cloud computing indexing structure based on a hyperbolic tree using virtual coordinates taken in the hyperbolic plane. We show through our experimental results that we compare with others clouds systems to show our solution ensures consistence and scalability for Cloud platform.

Keywords: Virtual coordinates · Cloud · Hyperbolic plane · Storage · Scalability · Consistency

1 Introduction

The deployment of Cloud Computing in our recent everyday life has strongly to modify the perception which we have of the notion of software, working platform as well as infrastructure subjected to licenses. Cloud Computing constitutes a commercial solution with a bright future. Indeed, it concerns most part of the services used in companies, going of the value for financial interesting for the acquisition of software services to the compromise between the energy consumption by the servers and the on-line acquisition of the storage spaces. Cloud Computing constitutes a system of virtual computation with the possibility of maintaining it and of managing it at a remotely. From a structural point of view, he can be characterized by the following aspects:

© ICST Institute for Computer Sciences, Social Informatics and Telecommunications Engineering 2016
Y. Zhang et al. (Eds.): CloudComp 2015, LNICST 167, pp. 269–279, 2016.
DOI: 10.1007/978-3-319-38904-2_28

- IaaS (Infrastructure as a Service).
- PaaS (Platform as a Service).
- SaaS (Software as a Service).

In this paper we make the following contributions:

- We introduce a new technique of virtualisation based on the Poincaré disk model in which a q-regular hyperbolic tree is used to model the resources through its various nodes;
- We show how the indexation of the various resources is made through a greedy routing algorithm of the requests. [6];
- We show the properties of scalability and of consistence in term of indexation;
- We perform some simulations and we show that our cloud system using based on a structured DHT is comparable and sometimes better than others structures based on existing index structures, such as Chord, MSPastry, Kademlia with possibility to run multi-attribute criteria request and multi-dimensional indexation.

The continuation of the paper is organized as follows. Section 2 provides a brief overview on the related works in the indexation in Cloud Computing. Sect. 3 presents the properties of the hyperbolic plan used in Poincaré disk model. Section 4 defines the local addressing and greedy routing algorithms of cloud computing system. Section 5 describes the mechanism of addressing and the technique of greedy routing in the hyperbolic tree. Section 6 makes an analysis of the results of the simulation of our model of Cloud Computing and we conclude in Sect. 7.

2   Related Work

We can distinguish various types of system as Distributed storage for management of big quantity of data, such as Google File System [7] (GFS), which serves Google's applications with an important volume of data. Yahoo provided PNUTS [8], a hosted, centrally controlled parallel and distributed database system for Yahoo's applications. These systems, split data and constitute some fragments, then disseminates randomly these latters into clusters to improve data access parallelism. Some central servers working as routers are responsible of the queries orientation to nodes which contain query results. Unlike these works, we propose a scalable mechanism using Poincaré disk model and which provides distributed data storage and retrieving algorithms based on the in hyperbolic space. Our indexation structure is designed to route by greedy way a big quantity of queries among a large cluster of storage nodes by hyperbolic coordinates using. Consistent hashing proposed by the previous works is designed to support key-based data retrieval but is not adapted to support range and multi-dimensional queries. It exists some solutions that support query processing over multi-dimensional data, like CAN (Content Addressable Network) [9]. It permits to build a database storage system by splitting rectangular areas.

Furthermore, a lot structured DHT algorithms (MSPastry [12], Tapestry [17], Kademlia [13], CAN, and Chord [11]) that support multi-dimensional range queries may be used to implement some cloud services such as Chord based Session Management Framework for Software as a Service Cloud (CSMC) [14], MingCloud based on Kademlia algorithm [15], Search on the Cloud is built on Pastry [16] and improves fault-tolerance, scalability and consistence.

Our work is associated to the design proposed in [18]. However, to be able to answer the multi-dimensional queries, we propose a new algorithm which uses the mechanism of greedy routing for the process data storage and data lookup. Furthermore, our structure reduces considerably the number of hops for the storage and the lookup inside of the Cloud system, so facilitating the deployment of databases for the applications.

3 Poincaré Disk Models Properties

The initial model of the hyperbolic plane that we will consider is due to the French mathematician Henri Poincaré. This model is called, Poincaré Disk Model. In this latter, the hyperbolic plane is represented by the open unit disk of radius 1 centered at the origin (coordinates associated to the origin is (0;0)). In this specific model:

- All the points are located inside of the open unit disk.
- Lines correspond to arcs of a circle intersecting the disk and meeting its boundaries at right angles.

In the Poincaré disk model, every point is identified by complex coordinates. One of the important properties of the hyperbolic plan is that we can tile by using polygons of any size, called called p-gons. Each tessellation is represented by a set {p, q} where every polygon has p faces with q of them in every vertex. The values p and q so presented obey the following relation: $(p-2)*(q-2) > 4$. In a tiling, p is associated to the number of sides of the polygons of the *primal* (indicated in black vertices and blue edges: Fig. 1) and q correspond to the number of sides of the polygons of the *dual* (indicated by the red triangles: Fig. 1). Our purpose is to split the hyperbolic plane in the aim to give an unique address to each node. We set p to infinity, thus transforming the primal into a q-regular tree. The dual is then tessellated with an infinite number of q-gons. In this way, we arrive has to create an embedded tree in the hyperbolic plan by splitting of plan into tessellation which we use to address system nodes. An example of such a hyperbolic tree with $q = 3$ is shown in Fig. 1.

The distances between any two points u and v in the Poincaré disk model are given by curves minimizing the distance between these two points. These distances are called geodesics of the hyperbolic plane. The value of a geodesic between two points u and v is represented by $d_{\mathbb{H}}$, The Poincaré metric considered as an isometric invariant is given by following relation:

$$d_{\mathbb{H}}(u,v) = argcosh(1 + 2 \times \frac{|u-v|^2}{(1-|u|^2)(1-|v|^2)}) \qquad (1)$$

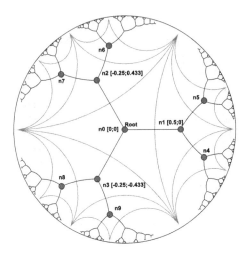

Fig. 1. 3-regular hyperbolic tree of Poincaré disk model.

This formula is used by the greedy routing algorithm shown in the next section.

4   Hyperbolic Greedy Routing

In this section we present the principle of hyperbolic addressing tree building on one hand and on the other hand, we show how various resources servers of Cloud communicate through queries. We propose in this paper a dynamic and scalable algorithm for routing's process based on greedy routing algorithm mechanism. In the initial phase, a first resource server is started and defined the number (q) of resources servers in the which it can connect (the degree of the tree). With the aim of being able to identify the various nodes of the tree associated to the resources servers, we use complex coordinates (taken in the hyperbolic plan). Each node of the hyperbolic tree has q possibilities to connect others nodes, called children of current node. The degree corresponds to addressing capacity of each resource server. The building strategy of cloud is incremental, with each new node resource joining one or more existing resources servers. This method is scalable because unlike [1], we do not have to make a two-pass algorithm over the whole cloud system to find its highest degree. In our cloud system, a node can connect to any other node at any time in the aim to obtain coordinates. The initial phase is thus to define the degree of the tree because it allows building the *dual*, namely the regular $q - gon$. We nail the root of the tree at the origin of the *primal* and we begin the tilling at the origin of the disk in function of q. The principle of splitting of the space in two separate sub-space is assured to be unique if both half-space are tangent; hence the *primal* is an infinite q-regular tree. We use the theoretical infinite q-regular tree to built the greedy embedding of our q-regular tree. So, the regular degree of the tree is the number of sides of the polygon used to build the *dual* (see Fig. 1). Furthermore, each node repeats the computation for its own half space. In half space, the space is again allocated for $q - 1$ children. Each child can distribute its addresses in its half space. Algorithm 1 shows how to calculate the coordiantes that can be given to these children. The first node takes the hyperbolic address (0;0) and is the root of the tree.

Algorithm 1. Calculating the coordinates of a nodes's children.

```
1: procedure CALCCHILDRENCOORDS(node, q)
2:     step ← argcosh(1/sin(π/q))
3:     angle ← 2π/q
4:     childCoords ← node.Coords
5:     for i ← 1, q do
6:         ChildrenCoords.rotaLeft(angle)
7:         ChildrenCoords.translat(step)
8:         ChildrenCoords.rotaRight(π)
9:         if ChildrenCoords ≠ node.ParentCoords then
10:            STORECHILDRENCOORDS(ChildrenCoords)
11:        end if
12:    end for
13: end procedure
```

Our distributed algorithm ensures that the nodes are contained in distinct spaces and have unique coordinates. All the phases of the presented algorithm are suitable for distributed and asynchronous computation. Thus, it allows the assignment of addresses as coordinates in dynamic topologies. Each node can obtain an address by asking a node already connected to system. The node supplying the address so becomes the parent of the new node. Therefore, the knowledge global of the system is not necessary. Each node wishing to connect to the system asks for an address a node of the system. If the node has not it, the query is routed in the direction of another node. Each time that node want to connects to the system, it computes its hyperbolic coordiantes of it future children. When a new node is connected to the cloud, it share these resources with others resources servers associated to the nodes of the cloud, by sending queries. The routing process from source to destination is done by step by using the greedy Algorithm 2 based on the hyperbolic distances between the nodes.

In a real context of cloud, link and node failures are expected to happen often. Indeed, if the addressing tree is broken by the failure of a node or link, we flush the addresses attributed to the nodes beyond the failed peer or link and reassign new addresses to those nodes (some nodes may have first to reconnect with other nodes in order to restore connectivity).

Algorithm 2. Routing a query in the cloud.

```
 1: function GETNEXTHOP(node, query) return Node
 2:      w = query.destNodeCoords
 3:      m = node.Coords
 4:      d_min = argcosh (1 + 2 |u-w|²/((1-|u|²)(1-|w|²)))
 5:      p_min = node
 6:      for all neighbour ∈ node.Neighbours do
 7:          n = neighbour.Coords
 8:          d = argcosh (1 + 2 |v-w|²/((1-|v|²)(1-|w|²)))
 9:          if d < d_min then
10:              d_min = d
11:              p_min = neighbour
12:          end if
13:      end for
14:      return p_min
15: end function
```

$$d_{min} = argcosh\left(1 + 2\frac{|u-w|^2}{(1-|u|^2)(1-|w|^2)}\right)$$

$$d = argcosh\left(1 + 2\frac{|v-w|^2}{(1-|v|^2)(1-|w|^2)}\right)$$

5 Strategy of Naming and Binding on Our Cloud System

We approach on this part the strategy consisting in taking the name of a server of resources then has to transform it into address with the aim of facilitating the data storage and the data lookup (this address corresponds to the virtual coordinates who allows to locate the resources server). Our solution uses a structured Distributed Hash Table (DHT) system that with the virtual addressing mechanism of resources servers associated to the greedy routing algorithms presented in Sect. 4. At the beginning, each new entity (resources server) takes a name that is associated to the service (Application, Platform, Infrastructure) that it wishes to share in the system. The name in question is kept by the entity during all its life cycle in the system. When a resources server connects to the system having obtained an address, it begins the process of storage of the various services which wishes to share on other resources servers. This storage uses a mechanism of fragmentation in sub-key of the key obtained by hashing of the entity name(as explain in the follow). When a similar sub-key is already stored in the system, an error message is generated and sent back to the resources server containing concerned service in the aim to change the service identifies. Thus, Unity of the service name is assured.

For each node is associated the pair (name, address), with the name mapping as a key is called a *binding*. Figure 2 shows the way every binding is stored in the cloud. A binder is associated to the any entity that stores these pairs. The depth corresponds among hops from given node towards the root by following the direct relationship links (including the root itself). When the cloud system is created, the system chosen a maximum depth associated to the potential binders. Thus, the depth allows to compute the maximum number of entities that can be connected to the system and potentialy share different services. Also the depth d choice must verify d that minimize the Inequality 2 with p ($p \geq 3$) corresponding to the degree:

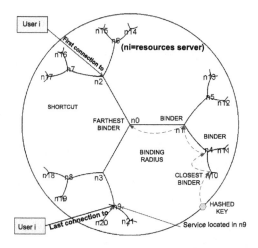

Fig. 2. Hyperbolic cloud system.

$$p \times (\frac{(1 - (p-1)^d)}{2 - p}) + 1 \geq N \tag{2}$$

This value is defined as the *binding tree depth*. When a new entity joins the system by connecting to other entities, it obtains a virtual coordinates from one of these entities. So, each service name of the resources server is transformed into a key by hashing its identifier with the SHA-1 algorithm (SHA-1 gives 160-bit key). Next, the new entity divides the 160-bit key into 5 equally sized 32-bit sub-keys (for redundant storage). One sub-key is randomly selected to be transformed into angle by use of a linear function given then. The angle is given by:

$$\alpha = 2\pi \times \frac{\texttt{32-bit sub-key}}{\texttt{0xFFFFFFFF}} \tag{3}$$

Once the obtained angle, the entity computes the virtual point v situated on the edge circle unity

$$v(x, y) \text{ with } \begin{cases} x = cos(\alpha) \\ y = sin(\alpha) \end{cases} \tag{4}$$

Next the enity identifies the locations of the closest binder to the computed virtual point above by using the given *binding tree depth*. In Fig. 2 we set the *binding tree depth* to three to avoid cluttering the figure. We have to notice that the closest entity of the circle unity can not exist. Indeed, the closest address can not have been to request by an entity. In which case, the query is redirected step by step towards the next node which contains the service either towards the root (use of the greedy algorithm of the Sect. 4). In the general way, this process continues until the query reaches to the root entity having the address (0;0) (which is the farthest binder) or the number of entities is equal to (radial strategy):

$$S \leq \lfloor \frac{1}{2} \times \frac{log(N)}{log(q)} \rfloor \tag{5}$$

with N equal to number of entities or distributed resources servers, q to degree of hyperbolic-tree.

To reduce the impact of the dynamics of the system (departures and arrived from node in the system), our system uses the redundancy mechanism which allows to guarantee a certain robustness of the cloud in the difficult contexts. This redundancy mechanism allows to store several copies of a service on a number of nodes at the radial level (according to the value of the replication radial chosen arbitrary) then at the circular level (according to the value of the circular replication chosen arbitrary).

These mechanisms entrainnent about can a not uniform growth of the system. On the other hand, they assure a bigger probability to be able to lookup or to store a service. It so maximizes the rate of success of lookup and the storages and participle in the flexibility and in the availability of the services. Our solution has the property of consistent hashing. Indeed, if one entity (or a service of the entity) fails, only its keys are lost, but the other binders are not concerned and the whole cloud system remains coherent. To avoid storing a service in a server that is going to leave later the system without the latter updates this departure. Our system requires that periodically (x this period) pair (name, address) is again stored in the system.

When a user i wants to use a service, it connects to the system and enters the name of the service. The latter is then hashed in key and splits into sub-key before to be send in the system as the lookup key. This lookup key will allow to locate the servers being able to provide this service in the cloud.

6   Experimental Results

In this section we are to focus on the results of the simulation of a model of cloud which we implemented on Peersim simulator [21] to analyze the scalability and the availability of the services. Our configuration of simulation takes into account the phenomenon of churn which shows the dynamics of the system. In our configuration, the services are uniformly distributed (i.e. each service name that is randomly generated preserves equi-probability in term of storage in the servers). For the simulation, we used the following parameters that are valid for all the DHTs that we compare:

- at beginning, number of resources servers connected and which is share services is equal to 10000;
- dynamics factors varies between 10 % and 60 % include;
- duration of simulation is equal in 2 hours;
- exponential probability law is used to qualify servers or services churn effects;
- total number of queries supposed received by our system is equal to 6 millions of queries following exponential probability law with median equal to 10 min;
- for each server we have a maximum number of services equal to 2000.

6.1   Load Balancing in Our System

Figure 3 shows the dispersal points of the cloud corresponding to the location of the various services servers in our hyperbolic addressing tree. We can easily noticed that our tree seems well-balanced. We can note that most part of nodes finds itself around the unit circle and distributed in a fair way. This implies that our builts system is balanced well and allows to realize a load balancing.

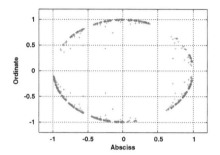

Fig. 3. Scatter plot of our system entities.

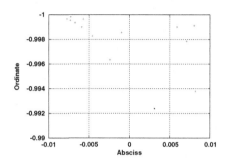

Fig. 4. Distribution of various entities in the neighborhood of the edge of the unit circle.

Figure 4 offers more precision as for the distribution of the entities around the edge of the unit circle. Indeed, more generally about is the number of entities of the system, they are all contained in the Poincaré disk and verify the relation $1 = cos^2\alpha + sin^2\alpha$.

6.2   Performances Analysis

Figure 5, shows that the rate success varies between 83 % and 88 % when the phenomenon of churn varies between 10 % and 60 %. Furthermore, in the absence

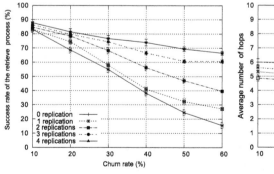

Fig. 5. Impact of the replication on the phenomenon of churn.

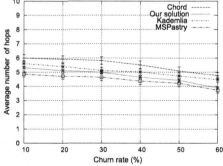

Fig. 6. Comparative analysis between different DHTs.

of replication, rate success varies between 18 % and 67 %. This result indicates that the replication has the effect of improving the rate of success of the services lookup in our cloud.

Figure 6, indicates The results obtained in term of rate of success when churn varies between 10 % and 60 % according to the various DHTs are appreciably the same. We show through this experience that our system is comparable to the existing cloud systems based on the existing DHTs such as Chord, MSPastry and Kademlia.

7 Conclusion

In this paper we propose a system of cloud which supplied scalability, flexibility and availability of the services. Very few search results proposes architecture of cloud with the which is associated a technique of muti-dimensional indexation as our. Our cloud model exploited the properties of the Poincaré disk and allows thanks to its technique of hashing it can develop strategies of replication. We showed by simulation how our system resists to the churn phenomenon. In our future works, we are going to emphasize the elaboration of a servers substitution technique in the cases of failures of these latters, in the aim to improve the rates of success of the queries. Furthermore during our future works, we consider aborderles mechanism of safeties partners in the discovery of services on our cloud

References

1. Kleinberg, R.: Geographic routing using hyperbolic space. In: IEEE Computer and Communications Societies (2007)
2. Zhang, S., Zhang, S., Chen, X., Wu, S.: Analysis and research of cloud computing system instance. In: Proceedings of the Second International Conference on Future Networks, pp. 88–92 (2010)
3. Antonin, G.: R-trees : A dynamic index structure for spatial searching. SIGMOD Rec. 14(2), 47–57 (1984)
4. Garcia-Molina, H., Ullman, J.D., Widom, J.: Database System Implementation. Prentice-Hall, Upper Saddle River (2000)
5. Wang, J., Wu, S., Gao, H., Li , J., Chin, O.B.: Indexing multi'-dimensional data in a cloud system. In: SIGMOD International Conference on Management of Data. ACM (2010)
6. Rao, A., Ratnasamy, S., Papadimitriou, C., Shenker, S., Stoica, I.: Geographic routing without location information. In: Proceedings of the 9th Annual International Conference on Mobile Computing and Networking. ACM (2003)
7. Vaquero, L.M., Luis, R.-M., Juan, C., Lindner, M.: A break in the clouds: towards a cloud definition. ACM SIGCOMM Comput. Commun. Rev. 39(1), 50–55 (2008)
8. Cooper, B.F., Ramakrishnan, R., Srivastava, U., Silberstein, A., Bohannon, P., Jacobsen, H.A., Puz, N., Weaver, D., Yerneni, R.: PNUTS: Yahoo!'s hosted data serving platform. In: VLDB Endowment (2008)
9. Ratnasamy, S., Francis, P., Handley, M., Karp, R., Shenker, S.: A Scalable Content-addressable Network. ACM, New York (2001)

10. Zhang, X., Ai, J., Wang, Z., Lu, J., Meng, X.: An Efficient multi-dimensional index for cloud data management. In: CloudDB 2009. ACM (2009)
11. Antonopoulos, N., Salter, J., Peel, R.M.A.: A multi-ring method for efficient multi-dimensional data lookup in P2P networks. In: FCS. CSREA Press (2005)
12. Castro, M., Costa, M., Rowstron, A.: Performance and dependability of structured peer-to-peer overlays. In: Proceedings of the DSN 2004 (2003)
13. Hou, X., Cao, Y., Zhang, Y.: P2P Multi-dimensional range query system based on kademlia. Comput. Eng. **20**, 14 (2008)
14. Zeeshan, P., Masood, K.A., Sungyoung, L., Lee, Y.K.: CSMC: chord based session management framework for software as a service cloud. In: ICUIMC 2011. ACM (2011)
15. Ji-yi, W., Jian-lin, Z., Tong, W., Qian-li, S.: Study on redundant strategies in peer to peer cloud storage systems. Appl. Math. Inf. Sci. **5**(2), 235S–242S (2011)
16. Savage, R., Nava, D.T., Chàvez, N.E., Savage, N.S.: Search on the cloud file system. In: PDCS: Parallel and Distributed Computing and Systems Conference (2011)
17. Zhao, B.Y., Huang, L., Stribling, J., Rhea, S.C., Joseph, A.D., Kubiatowicz, J.D.: Tapestry: a resilient global-scale overlay for service deployment. IEEE J. Sel. Areas Commun. **22**(1), 41–53 (2004)
18. Wu, S., Wu, K.L.: An indexing framework for efficient retrieval on the cloud. IEEE Data Eng. Bull. **32**(1), 75–82 (2009)
19. Lu, J., Callan, J.: Content-based retrieval in hybrid peer-to-peer networks. In: CIKM. ACM (2003)
20. Ion, S., Robert, M., David, K., Frans, K.M., Hari, B.: Chord: A scalable peer-to-peer lookup service for internet applications. ACM SIGCOMM Comput. Commun. Rev. **31**, 149–160 (2001)
21. Kazmi, I., Bukhari, S.F.Y.: PeerSim: An efficient & scalable testbed for heterogeneous cluster-based P2P network protocols. In: UkSim 2011. IEEE Computer Society (2011)

Enabling SDN Experimentation with Wired and Wireless Resources: The SmartFIRE Facility

Kostas Choumas[1]([⊠]), Thanasis Korakis[1], Hyunwoo Lee[2], Donghyun Kim[2], Junho Suh[2], Ted Taekyoung Kwon[2], Pedro Martinez-Julia[3], Antonio Skarmeta[3], Taewan You[4], Loic Baron[5], Serge Fdida[5], and JongWon Kim[6]

[1] University of Thessaly, Volos, Greece
{kohoumas,korakis}@uth.gr
[2] Seoul National University, Seoul, South Korea
{hwlee2014,dhkim,jhsuh}@mmlab.snu.ac.kr, tkkwon@snu.ac.kr
[3] University of Murcia, Murcia, Spain
{pedromj,skarmeta}@um.es
[4] Electronics and Telecommunications Research Institute, Daejeon, South Korea
twyou@etri.re.kr
[5] University Pierre and Marie Curie, Paris, France
{loic.baron,serge.fdida}@lip6.fr
[6] Gwangju Institute of Science and Technology, Gwangju, South Korea
jongwon@nm.gist.ac.kr

Abstract. Over the last few years, several experimentation platforms have been deployed around the world, providing to the computer science research community a way to remotely perform and control networking experiments. Most of the platforms, called testbeds, offer experimentation as a service. However, each testbed is specialized in a specific technology: wired, wireless or cloud. The challenge for experimenters is thus to combine different technologies in order to tackle the research questions they address. Therefore a federation framework has been developed thanks to several projects, including SmartFIRE. SmartFIRE is an intercontinental federation of SDN, wireless and cloud testbeds, aiming at providing experimentation services with resources from these various networking fields. This federation framework enables easy experimentation with the heterogeneous resources that the individual testbeds provide. In this article, we present our contributions towards the extension of the state-of-the-art control and management framework, in order to orchestrate the federated SmartFIRE facility. As a proof of concept, we demonstrate several use cases that take advantage of our contributions, providing the availability of experimentation on novel architectures.

Keywords: SDN · Wireless · Cloud · Testbed experimentation

1 Introduction

The main goal of SmartFIRE [1] is to provide a large-scale intercontinental SDN-based testbed with wireless, and wired packet switching, providing a

© ICST Institute for Computer Sciences, Social Informatics and Telecommunications Engineering 2016
Y. Zhang et al. (Eds.): CloudComp 2015, LNICST 167, pp. 280–290, 2016.
DOI: 10.1007/978-3-319-38904-2_29

federated facility that includes many smaller-scale testbeds in Europe and South Korea. The South Korean testbeds bring powerful experience in the OpenFlow connections, especially in the utilization of their outstanding capabilities for information-centric experimentation, while the European testbeds offer their knowledge in the wireless connections, enabling the perspective for enhancing OpenFlow experimentation with wireless connectivity.

SmartFIRE is the first intercontinental testbed, spanning multiple small-scale testbeds in South Korea and Europe. It exploits the building blocks of an OpenFlow-based infrastructure, wireless and cloud resources in order to construct an experimental federated testbed for researchers. The control and management of SmartFIRE is able to allow authorized and authenticated experimenters to allocate resources, run experiments and collect measurements in a given facility and across heterogeneous facilities. SmartFIRE adheres to ongoing parallel processes for improving the state-of-the-art cOntrol and Management Framework (OMF) [2], exploiting the experience and the feedback of its usage and improving its deployment in previous testbeds. Moreover, it contributes with new requirements and framework extensions as a result of its supported pilots.

2 Testbeds and Interconnections

The following subsections present the individual facilities that are federated in SmartFIRE and illustrated in Fig. 1.

2.1 South Korean Testbeds

The South Korean testbeds provide enriched experimentation in the field of SDN. The following paragraphs present their structure and their experimentation capabilities.

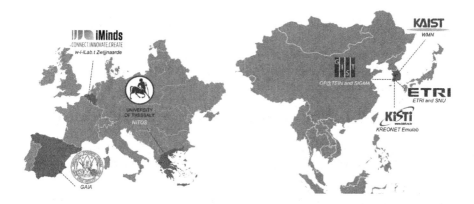

Fig. 1. The SmartFIRE federation of European and South Korean testbeds.

Gwangju Institute of Science and Technology (GIST) offers OF@TEIN, which is an aggregated OpenFlow island consisting of 7 racks, located over 7 international sites. In the OF@TEIN testbed, similar to the GENI racks, a unique rack is designed and deployed to promote the international SDN research collaboration over the intercontinental network of TEIN. OF@TEIN aims at (a) the design and verification of the racks (with domestic-vendor OpenFlow switch), (b) the site installation and verification of the OF@TEIN network, and (c) the design and development of the OF@TEIN experimentation tools. GIST has recently deployed a cloud service based on OpenStack, offering virtualized resources.

Korea Institute of Science and Technology Information (KISTI) offers an emulation based network testbed in the KREONET [3] domain. It is called KREONET-Emulab and provides the opportunity for evaluation of several network protocols. Many network protocols, which cannot perform over KREONET due to unexpected hazard, can be freely tested in KREONET-Emulab. It consists of 42 powerful servers, each of them equipped with 5 network interfaces, one for the control and four for the experimentation. Each server can work as a router with 4 paths, and each network interface can be configured up to 1 Gbps.

Electronic and Telecommunications Research Institute (ETRI) proposes the network architecture of MOFI (Mobile Oriented Future Internet) [4]. Following a completely different approach from the current IP networking, MOFI enables the development of networks with Future Internet support of mobile intrinsic environments. The evaluation of the MOFI architecture relies on the OpenFlow-based mobility testbed of ETRI. The mobility testbed is an aggregation island, consisting of four interconnected South Korean domain networks. Their interconnection is based on the KOREN [5] networking infrastructure.

Seoul National University (SNU) proposes the C-flow architecture [6], as a result of the research on the development of content delivery networks with use of SDN. In particular, C-flow is the architecture for the development of ICN-based networks using OpenFlow. It provides functionalities for caching contents at specific cache servers or caches collocated with switches, as well as for their name-based forwarding. Additionally, SNU operates the C-flow testbed which enables the experimentation on ICN.

Korea Advanced Institute of Science and Technology (KAIST) provides a wireless mesh network, named OpenWiFi+, which is a programmable testbed for experimental protocol design. It is located at the campus of the KAIST University and it consists of 56 mesh routers, 16 of them being deployed indoors and 40 outdoors, each of them equipped with three IEEE 802.11 b/g/n WiFi cards. Moreover, 50 sensor nodes are deployed at the same campus.

2.2   European Testbeds

The European testbeds share fruitful experiences in the experimentation in SDN and wireless networking. Their capabilities are presented below.

University of Thessaly (UTH) provides the NITOS facility, which is open to the research community 24/7 and it is remotely accessible. The testbed consists of 100 powerful wireless nodes, each of them equipped with 2 WiFi interfaces, some of them being 802.11n MIMO cards and the rest 802.11a/b/g cards. Several nodes are equipped with USRP/GNU-radios, cameras and temperature/humidity sensors. The nodes are interconnected through a tree topology of OpenFlow switches, enabling the creation of multiple topologies with software-defined backbones and wireless access networks [7]. The testbed features programmable WiMAX and LTE equipment, fully configurable with an SDN backbone [8].

iMinds supports the generic and heterogeneous w-iLab.t facility. It consists of two wireless sub testbeds: the w-iLab.t office and w-iLab.t Zwijnaarde. The w-iLab.t office is deployed in a real office environment while the testbed Zwijnaarde is located at a utility room. There is little external interference at the Zwijnaarde testbed as no regular human activity is present and most of its walls and ceiling are covered with metal. The majority of devices in w-iLab.t are embedded PCs equipped with WiFi interfaces and sensor nodes. Since the Zwijnaarde testbed was deployed more recently, the devices in this testbed are more powerful in terms of processing power, memory and storage.

Universidad de Murcia (UMU) offers the research and experimentation infrastructure of GAIA. GAIA comprises several network nodes interconnected with different technologies. On the one hand, they are connected to the campus network through Gigabit Ethernet switches and thus they form the point of attachment to the Internet. On the other hand, they are connected to a CWDM network, which acts as backbone/carrier network and can be adapted to different configurations, depending on the specific requirements of each experiment. GAIA has also a wide wireless and WiMAX deployment along the campus. This, together with other smaller wireless deployments, allows the experimentation with many local and wide-range wireless technologies, including mobility and vehicle (V2V) communications.

2.3   GEANT and KREONET/KOREN Interconnecting Networks

The European testbeds are interconnected through the GEANT [9] network, which is the fast and reliable pan-European communications infrastructure, enabling data transfer speeds of up to 10 Gbps. The South Korean testbeds are interconnected with the same speeds via KREONET [3] and KOREN [5].

3 Experimentation Framework and Federation Architecture

3.1 Users Management and Resources Reservation

SmartFIRE provides a web portal (http://portal.eukorea-fire.eu/) allowing experimenters to register. A distributed Public Key Infrastructure (PKI) based authentication provides users access to the different federated testbeds through a single account. The reservation of the resources is done through a GENI adopted architecture named Slice-based Facility Architecture (SFA) [10]. The goal of SFA is to provide a minimal interface, a narrow waist, that enables testbeds of different technologies and/or belonging to different administrative domains to federate without losing control of their resources. It succeeds in combining all available resources. As the name suggests, SFA is built around the central notion of a slice, which is the basic element for mapping experimenters to resources.

3.2 SFA Aggregate Manager (AM) for SmartFIRE Federation

As you see in Fig. 2, there are SFA Aggregate Manager (AM) components for each testbed. This architecture allows testbed providers to write their own driver code. A driver is responsible to translate the SFA AM calls into the specific testbed configurations. As part of the SmartFIRE project an OpenStack driver has been developed by UPMC with external partners such as KulCloud and Telecom Paris Sud. This development enabled GIST to deploy its own OpenStack instance as part of the SmartFIRE federation. The other SmartFIRE testbeds use the OMF Broker [11] developed by UTH or the Emulab framework in order to become members of the SmartFIRE federation.

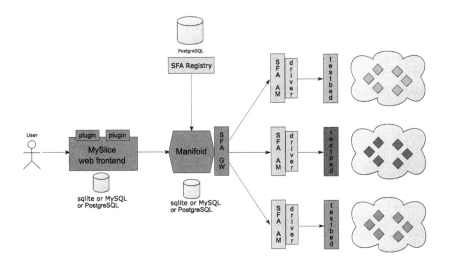

Fig. 2. SmartFIRE portal architecture.

3.3   Experiment Control: OMF

As we already mentioned, the main purpose of SmartFIRE is to extend appropriately the state-of-the-art framework of OMF [2], in order to create a unified platform that consists of multiple testbeds and is controlled from a single framework. OMF was originally created in the Orbit [12] testbed, and soon became the most widely used tool for experiment control among the majority of the testbed frameworks worldwide. OMF enables the experimenter to automate an experiment instead of setting up everything manually by logging into each node to configure/control its operation. The concept is similar to network simulators where the user describes a topology along with the applications that run during the simulation. The difference is that the topology consists of physical nodes on which OMF runs applications like a traffic generator. Also, the measurements are automatically collected with the help of the OMF Measurement Library (OML). The configuration and control of node operation occurs through specific properties, which are part of formal resource descriptions, and can be done not only at experiment setup but also during experiment runtime.

The basic components of the OMF framework are the Experiment Controller (EC) and the Resource Controllers (RCs). The role of the EC is to orchestrate the execution of the experiments, written in the OMF Experiment Description Language (OEDL). The EC interprets OEDL and sends appropriate messages to the corresponding RCs. In turn, each RC is responsible for abstracting and controlling one or more underlying physical or logical resources. It basically converts the messages received from the EC into resource-specific commands, and relays the response back to the EC. It is important to note that the message exchange between the EC and the RCs is performed using a publish-subscribe mechanism, assuming a stable and reliable communication. Thus, in case of network problems, the messages published by the EC and/or the RC are dropped.

The measurements produced by an experiment on the SmartFIRE platform are stored directly on an OML server, without any involvement of the EC. Given that several experiments can run at the same time, a separate database is maintained for each experiment. The user can inspect and retrieve the results of his experiment at any point in time. The OML software enables distributed real-time collection of data in a large-scale testbed environment, which is contextualized per experiment. While OML has been developed in the context of OMF, it has been spun out as an independent project and has already been deployed in non-OMF testbeds. It is also now being increasingly adopted for monitoring operational network and service deployments. OML is further developed to be able to collect measurements for the use cases that will be performed for the evaluation of the SmartFIRE objectives. Part of the SmartFIRE OMF and OML extensions are presented in [13,14].

4   Experimentation Capabilities Provided by SmartFIRE

4.1   ICN Experimentation

In SmartFIRE, an architecture for ICN experimentation is implemented using wireless and SDN technology. As it is depicted in Fig. 3(a), wireless devices laying on UTH (NITOS) are connected to ICN-enabled nodes on SNU, where the IP addressing scheme is replaced by a novel one based on content identifiers. The utilized resources are interconnected including Layer 2 intercontinental virtual links, based on the GEANT/KOREN services. The goal of this innovation is to use identifiers that specify only the content and not the location of this content, as the IP addresses do. Each content is cached on multiple sides on the SNU testbed, while the ICN architecture aims at forwarding the content from the most appropriate side to the wireless device that requested it. The streaming over the wireless mesh is based on a Backpressure routing scheme.

Many researchers try to replace the location-based host access with an ICN approach, where the contents are distributed and retrieved by their name, while the location of the content is not considered. Their target is the contents to be accessed not by "where", but by "what". The C-flow [6] offers the way for experimentation on ICN, using the virtual machines with the CCNx [15], the most widely known tool for ICN experimentation. More specifically, there are three entities - a publisher, a router, and a subscriber - and two types of packets - an interest-packet for the content request and a data-packet for the content encapsulation. When the subscriber broadcasts the interest-packet with the name of the wanted content, the matching data-packet is returned from the cache of an intermediate router or the repository of the publisher.

The routing over the wireless mesh is based on the Backpressure algorithm [16]. Backpressure is a throughput-optimal scheme for multihop routing and scheduling. The implementation of this scheme is not straightforward in practice, especially in the presence of 802.11 MAC, mainly because of its requirement for centralized scheduling decisions that is not aligned with the aspects of CSMA/CA. In [17] we present a novel scheme that is compatible with the decentralized operation of WiFi networks and efficiently utilizes the benefits of Backpressure, combining throughput optimality with load balancing. This scheme is implemented relying on the Click Modular Router [18] framework for routing configuration, which is another long established tool for SDN development.

SmartFIRE gathers the experience of SNU and UTH and develops the appropriate extensions of the OMF framework, supporting the experimentation in heterogeneous topologies, with information-centric data retrieval over the wired networking and load balancing schemes over the wireless access. One of the outcomes of these efforts is the ICN-OMF framework [13]: a Control and Management Framework for scalable, configurable and low-cost testbeds, that enables the experimentation with C-flow. The extended framework is able to control and manage globally dispersed ICN nodes (i.e. publishers, subscribers, or routers). The C-flow testbed architecture is depicted in Fig. 3(b), including the main OMF ICN-EC and ICN-RC components, which are extended versions of the aforementioned OMF EC and RC ones. The other outcome of SmartFIRE is the OMF support for Click Router development and experimentation [14].

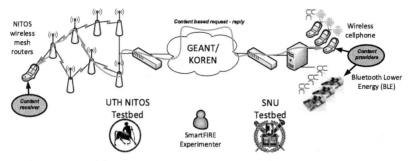

(a) The C-flow Experimentation Topology

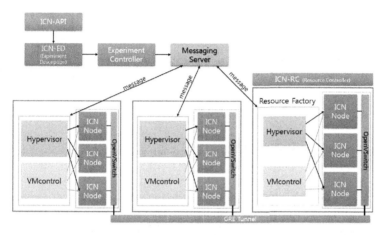

(b) The C-flow Architecture

Fig. 3. The information-centric Communication Scheme.

4.2 MOFI Experimentation

The MOFI [4] architecture is an outcome of the long-time Future Internet research in ETRI. MOFI is an identity-based network architecture that supports an environment for mobile-oriented experimentation. In MOFI, the network consists of multiple domains and multiple communication entities, having one or more global unique identifiers, named Host Identifiers (HIDs). MOFI uses an HID to identify an entity in the network, which is globally unique on the Internet. We consider the 128-bit HID format for compatibility with IPv6 application. The Locator (LOC) of each entity is used for the delivery of the data packets. In MOFI, the LOC is defined as a locally routable IP address that must only be locally unique in the concerned network. The end-to-end communication between two hosts is performed with HIDs, whereas LOCs are used for packet delivery in the access and backbone networks.

Each domain has a lot of Access Routers (ARs) enabling HID-based communication, and one or more Gateways (GWs) that interconnect the domain

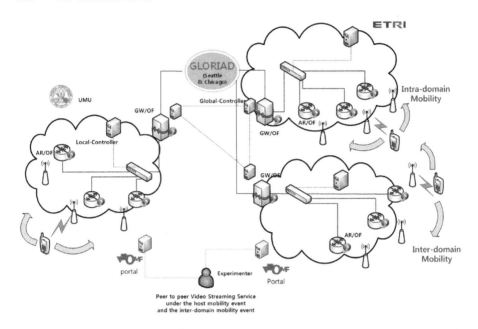

Fig. 4. The Identify-based Communication Scheme.

networks. MOFI performs better than the existing schemes for a variety of mobile network environments, in terms of signaling delays required, data transmission throughput, number of signaling messages, and handover delay. The HID-LOC mapping control is done in the distributed way, in which each AR performs the HID-LOC mapping control operations. We consider that the mapping control may be different across different network domains.

ETRI has developed an MOFI testbed over an OpenFlow-based and Linux platform, in order to evaluate the efficiency of the MOFI's architecture. This testbed is a federated facility, since it uses KOREN in order to interconnects four major South Korean domain networks. ETRI has built two MOFI-domain networks, which consist of two ARs (developed with use of virtual OpenFlow switches), a GW and an OpenFlow controller. Moreover, ETRI and UMU have developed demonstrations that showcase the capabilities of their joint experimentation, using both domain networks of ETRI and the one domain network provided by UMU, as it is depicted in Fig. 4. The experimentation on MOFI is orchestrated by the OMF framework, which is another significant contribution of SmartFIRE.

5   Conclusion

SmartFIRE can be considered as a very important complement to current available testbeds, providing considerable added value through an increased level of heterogeneity in the federated SDN-enabled infrastructure, and also through an enriched, intercontinental multi-domain, multi-layer experimental platform. The experimental facilities, which are developed in South Korea, on the one hand, and the enhancement to the experimental facilities in Europe, on the other, increase the number of involved technologies and also the level of heterogeneity. The final product is an experimental facility that provides multi-layer (layer 1 & 2), multi-domain and multi-technology testbed.

Acknowledgment. This work makes use of results produced by the SmartFIRE project, which is supported by the International Research & Development Program of the National Research Foundation of Korea (NRF) funded by the Ministry of Science, ICT and Future Planning (MSIP, Korea) (Grant number: K2013078191) and the Seventh Framework Programme (FP7) funded by the European Commission (Grant number: 611165).

References

1. SmartFIRE: Enabling SDN Experimentation in Wireless Testbeds exploiting Future Internet Infrastructures in South Korea and Europe. http://eukorea-fire.eu
2. Rakotoarivelo, T., Ott, M., Jourjon, G., Seskar, I.: OMF: a control and management framework for networking testbeds. In: Proceedings of the ACM SIGOPS (2010)
3. KREONET: Korea Research Environment Open NETwork. http://www.kreonet.re.kr/en_main/
4. Jung, H., Koh, S., Park, W.: Towards the mobile optimized future internet. In: Proceedings of the ACM CFI (2009)
5. KOREN: Korea Advanced Research Network. http://www.koren.kr/koren/eng/index.html
6. Chang, D., Kwak, M., Choi, N., Kwon, T., Choi, Y.: C-flow: an efficient content delivery framework with OpenFlow. In: Proceedings of the International Conference on Information Networking (ICOIN) (2014)
7. Choumas, K., Makris, N., Korakis, T., Tassiulas, L., Ott, M.: Exploiting openflow resources towards a content-centric LAN. In: IEEE EWSDN (2013)
8. Makris, N., Zarafetas, C., Kechagias, S., Korakis, T., Seskar, I., Tassiulas, L.: Enabling open access to LTE network components; the NITOS testbed paradigm. In: Proceedings of the IEEE Conference on Network Softwarization (NetSoft) (2015)
9. GEANT: pan-European research and education network. http://www.geant.net/Pages/default.aspx
10. Peterson, L., Ricci, R., Falk, A., Chase, J.: Slice-Based Federation Architecture. GENI, Technical report
11. Stavropoulos, D., Dadoukis, A., Rakotoarivelo, T., Ott, M., Korakis, T., Tassiulas, L.: Design, architecture and implementation of a resource discovery, reservation and provisioning framework for testbeds. In: Proceedings of the WiNMeE (2015)
12. Raychaudhuri, D., Seskar, I., Ott, M., Ganu, S., Ramachandran, K., Kremo, H., Siracusa, R., Liu, H., Singh, M.: Overview of the ORBIT radio grid testbed for evaluation of next-generation wireless network protocols. In: Proceedings of the IEEE Wireless Communications and Networking Conference (WCNC) (2005)

13. Lee, H., Kim, D., Suh, J., Kwon, T.: ICN-OMF: a control, management framework for information-centric network testbed. In: Proceedings of the International Conference on Information Networking (ICOIN) (2015)
14. Choumas, K., Makris, N., Korakis, T., Tassiulas, L., Ott, M.: Testbed innovations for experimenting with wired and wireless software defined networks. In: CNERT workshop of IEEE ICDCS (2015)
15. Mahadevan, P.: CCNx 1.0 Tutorial
16. Tassiulas, L., Ephremides, A.: Stability properties of constrained queueing systems and scheduling policies for maximum throughput in multihop radio networks. IEEE Trans. Autom. control **37**(12), 1936–1948 (1992)
17. Choumas, K., Korakis, T., Koutsopoulos, I., Tassiulas, L.: Implementation and end-to-end throughput evaluation of an IEEE 802.11 compliant version of the enhanced-backpressure algorithm. In: Korakis, T., Zink, M., Ott, M. (eds.) Testbeds and Research Infrastructure. Development of Networks and Communities. Lecture Notes of the Institute for Computer Sciences, Social Informatics and Telecommunications Engineering, vol. 44, pp. 64–80. Springer, Heidelberg (2012)
18. Kohler, E., Morris, R., Chen, B., Jannotti, J., Kaashoek, M.F.: The click modular router. ACM Trans. Comput. Syst. **18**(3), 263–297 (2000)

Cloud-Enabling Techniques and Devices

A Buffer Cache Algorithm for Hybrid Memory Architecture in Mobile Devices

Chansoo Oh[1,2], Dong Hyun Kang[1], Minho Lee[1], and Young Ik Eom[1(✉)]

[1] College of Software, Sungkyunkwan University,
Suwon 440-746, South Korea
{chansoo.oh,kkangsu,minhozx,yieom}@skku.edu
[2] Hanwha Techwin, Changwon, South Korea

Abstract. In general computing environments including mobile devices, buffer cache algorithm is generally used to mitigate the performance gap between CPU and secondary storage. However, traditional DRAM-based buffer cache architecture reveals a power consumption problem in mobile devices, because it periodically performs the refresh operations to maintain data in DRAM. In addition, traditional buffer cache algorithms never consider the states of mobile applications (e.g., foreground and background state). In this paper, we propose a novel buffer cache algorithm, which efficiently addresses the above issues based on hybrid main memory architecture that is comprised of DRAM and PCM. Our algorithm is motivated by key observation that background applications on mobile device rarely issue I/O requests as well as they can degrade the performance of foreground applications because of the interferences among the I/O requests of applications. For evaluation, we implemented our algorithm and compared its performance against two other algorithms. Our experimental results show that our algorithm reduces the elapsed time of the foreground applications by 53 % on average and the power consumption by 23 % on average without any negative performance effects on background applications.

Keywords: Hybrid memory system · Buffer cache algorithm · Mobile device · Foreground application · Background application

1 Introduction

Today's mobile devices (e.g., tablets and smartphones) require a significant amount of memory because many applications run simultaneously and they have to store their data in main memory. However, the traditional DRAM-based memory architecture suffers from the periodic refresh operations that consume the battery power of device to maintain data in DRAM (Dynamic Random Access Memory). In particular, traditional buffer cache algorithms have been designed without consideration on the dynamic state changes of mobile applications (e.g., foreground and background state). Therefore, many researchers focused on non-volatile memory, such as PCM (Phase Change Memory), to take the benefits of lower power consumption over DRAM. However, read/write latency of PCM is slower than that of DRAM and PCM has limited lifecycle (Table 1) [1]. In order to mitigate these weaknesses of PCM, some researchers proposed

© ICST Institute for Computer Sciences, Social Informatics and Telecommunications Engineering 2016
Y. Zhang et al. (Eds.): CloudComp 2015, LNICST 167, pp. 293–300, 2016.
DOI: 10.1007/978-3-319-38904-2_30

buffer cache algorithms that efficiently reduce the number of PCM writes by using hybrid main memory architecture, which consists of DRAM and PCM [2–4]. However, previous studies have only focused on desktop applications. There is no prior work which considers the state of mobile applications, such as foreground and background state.

Table 1. Characteristics of DRAM and PCM

	Read latency	Write latency	Read energy	Write energy	Static energy	Endurance
DRAM	50 ns	~20-50 ns	~0.1nJ/b	~0.1nJ/b	~W/GB	∞
PCM	50 ~ 100 ns	~1us	~0.1nJ/b	~1nJ/b	≪ 0.1 W	10^8

In this paper, we propose a novel buffer cache algorithm that saves power consumption and improves the performance of foreground applications based on hybrid main memory architecture comprised of DRAM and PCM. Our algorithm is motivated by two key observations: (1) background applications on mobile device rarely issue I/O requests and (2) they can degrade the performance of foreground applications because of interference in I/O requests between foreground and background applications. Based on these observations, we first classify I/O requests into foreground I/O and background I/O, and then place foreground I/O in DRAM and background I/O in PCM because background I/O has no direct impact on the user experience [5].

For evaluation, we implemented our algorithm and compared its performance against two representative algorithms, such as traditional LRU (Least Recently Used) and 2QLRU (2 Queue Least Recently Used) [6]. Our experimental results clearly show that our algorithm reduces the elapsed time of the foreground applications by 53 % on average and the power consumption by 23 % on average without any negative performance effects on background applications.

The remainder of the paper is organized as follows. Section 2 explains the related works, such as PCM and Android system. Then we present design of our algorithm in Sect. 3. Section 4 evaluates its performance while comparing it with previous buffer cache algorithms. We conclude our research and suggest future work in Sect. 5.

2   Background

Mobile device has a limitation in expanding hardware such as CPU, memory, and battery because it should have reasonable price, portability, and small size. Especially, high performance hardware needs much more energy to operate than old devices. Battery capacity is limited due to the fixed size of mobile device. So, various methods which try to reduce power consumption to preserve battery capacity have been studied so far [7–11]. Also, mobile device can run several applications at the same time because it provides a multitasking environment. These applications could be classified as foreground one and background one depending on its state. Only a few applications can run as foreground applications and others should run as background applications. Foreground applications produce a large number of I/O requests while interacting with the user, whereas background applications rarely issue I/O requests, which are generated by push services or audio file playbacks. Generally, foreground applications run with high priority because users can perceive performance of the foreground applications as the performance of the mobile device. On the other hand, background applications are running with lower priority than foreground ones because they do not need fast response and do not affect directly to the user.

Android is the one of the most popular software platforms for mobile devices [12]. It has been evolved to be suitable with mobile environment. Especially, Android adopts various functions from Linux kernel, such as wakelocks [13], binder [14], and lowmemorykiller [15], to customize the kernel for mobile device. In Android, many applications, which are currently not being used by user, are maintained in the background state until being killed by LMK (lowmemorykiller) or changed to foreground state. LMK kills processes to get enough memory space to run new processes. It chooses a background process which has a lowest priority at that time. Android has a standard classification about the process states called 'importance hierarchy' which consist of foreground process, visible process, service process, background process, and empty process [5]. In this classification, background process and empty process do not affect any direct effect to the foreground applications.

3   Proposed Algorithm

In this paper, we propose a novel buffer cache algorithm that exploits the characteristics of mobile devices based on the hybrid memory architecture consisting of DRAM and PCM. We are focused on managing the buffer according to the states of applications. The proposed algorithm is based on traditional LRU policy, which is most popular and easy to understand in utilizing temporal locality. Foreground applications are allowed to run in DRAM whose access latency is faster than PCM. Therefore, write operation in PCM can be minimized and preserve lifecycle of PCM because most of I/O operations on mobile device are generated by foreground applications. On the other hand, background applications run in PCM preferentially whose access latency is slower than DRAM to guarantee the performance of foreground applications. Each page in the memory has a reference count which represents the number of times it is accessed, to determine migration between DRAM and PCM. Reference count is incremented when the page hit occurs and it is decremented when the page is selected as a candidate for eviction. If the reference count of a page on the memory space is zero, the page in DRAM moves to the MRU (Most Recently Used) position of PCM and the victim page in PCM is evicted to secondary storage.

Figure 1 illustrates examples of page migration and eviction of the proposed algorithm. If the page, which is referred by foreground application, is not on the memory (page miss), it allocates a new page on the MRU position in DRAM. In case of page miss by background application, it allocates a new page on MRU position in PCM. When background application is switched to foreground state, only the page, which is being referred by the foreground application, is migrated to the MRU position in DRAM to minimize migration overhead. In contrast, when foreground application is changed to background state, the page in DRAM is not migrated to PCM and keeps in the same LRU position in DRAM. Because new foreground application generates lots of I/O requests and these pages extrude old pages to PCM, the pages of background applications are naturally migrated to PCM. Accordingly, there is no performance degradation by page migration.

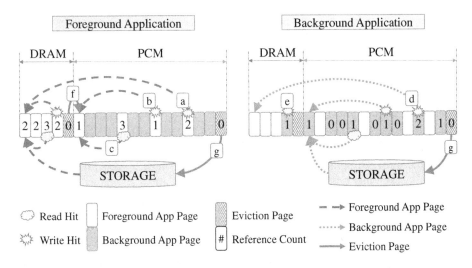

Fig. 1. Examples of page migration and eviction

In case of foreground application, new page is allocated on MRU position in DRAM and these pages are managed by LRU policy in DRAM. Cold pages that are not referred in DRAM will be migrated to PCM and they are managed by LRU policy in PCM. When page hit occurs in PCM, the page whose reference count is bigger than two is regarded as hot page and is migrated to the MRU position of DRAM (Fig. 1a). However, the pages whose reference count is lower than two are moved to the MRU position in PCM (Fig. 1b). This is for preventing performance degradation of foreground applications, which can be caused by operating hot pages in PCM which is slower than DRAM. Meanwhile, read-only pages in PCM, which are accessed by foreground application, are not migrated to DRAM but they are moved to the MRU position in PCM irrespective of its reference count (Fig. 1c). This is because read latency of PCM is not much slower than that of DRAM.

On the other hand, in case of background applications, new pages are allocated only on MRU position in PCM and these are managed by LRU policy to yield DRAM to foreground applications. When page hit occurs in PCM, every page owned by the background applications is moved to the MRU position in PCM because background applications are not sensitive about the response time. However, pages referenced more than 2 times in PCM are migrated to the MRU position in DRAM (Fig. 1d), because these hot pages are operated frequently and it can cause performance degradation of the foreground application by occupying CPU and other hardware resources.

If hot pages owned by background applications are migrated to DRAM once, these pages are not moved to MRU position in DRAM again and hold its LRU position (Fig. 1e). This is to avoid performance degradation of the foreground applications by letting background applications occupy DRAM. If there is no empty space to allocate a new page in DRAM, the proposed algorithm migrates the page on the LRU position in DRAM to the MRU position in PCM (Fig. 1f). Also, if there is no free space for a new page in PCM, the page which is on the LRU position in PCM will be evicted to secondary storage (Fig. 1g).

4 Evaluation Results

In this section, we present the performance evaluation results and analyze the proposed buffer cache algorithm, comparing it with most popular buffer cache algorithm such as LRU and 2QLRU. To extract trace data for measuring performance of the proposed algorithm, we used Google Nexus7 that are using Android kitkat version 4.2.2 based on Linux kernel version 3.4.0. Also, we modified Android kernel to get the trace data while the applications make read/write requests into the buffer cache. Kernel has oom_adj value representing process priority which can be used to classify application state as foreground or background. Mobile devices check the oom_adj value to choose processes to kill when there is not enough memory space to run other processes. Normally, foreground application has zero value and background processes have values from 1 to 15.

Above all, we measure the footprint of each workload to set up experimental environment. For first trace, we collected trace data using Chrome web browser as a foreground application and using Hangout, Gmail, and mp3 player as background applications. The I/O request ratio of foreground and background application is 15:1. Also, we obtained second trace by using multiple applications changing each applications state between foreground and background. The request ratio of the application types for second trace is 3:1. During experiments, we configured the percentage of DRAM to 5 % of total memory size to minimize power consumption at memory system and the rest percentage of memory to PCM. Our experimental results for the two types of traces are demonstrated in Figs. 2, 3, and 4. In the graphs, x-axis means memory size in each experiment and it is represented by the percentage of memory size to the total footprint. In each figure, graph (a) represents experimental results for the first trace and graph (b) represents experimental results for the second trace.

The hit ratio of our algorithm for two cases (all applications and foreground applications), our algorithm shows better performance results compared to LRU and 2QLRU policy in all range of memory sizes (Figs. 2 and 3). Also, we can see that the results for our algorithm are saturated earlier than the algorithms in the comparison group.

Especially, Figs. 2b and 3b illustrate that hit ratio of the proposed algorithm is saturated definitely earlier than other algorithms in the range of over 40 %. This means that the proposed algorithm can have better performance than other algorithms with small size of memory to run the same workload. Because every applications have been run in short interval in second workload, most of read and write requests are concentrated in small number of pages. However, experimental results for first trace indicate that hit ratio increases gradually until memory size is 70 % of the footprint (Figs. 2a and 3a). Nevertheless, the proposed algorithm has better performance than LRU and 2QLRU in whole range. In Fig. 3, hit ratio of the foreground application shows better performance than average hit ratio of all applications. Because foreground application has higher priority than background application in the proposed algorithm, many pages accessed by foreground application can be maintained in memory for a long time.

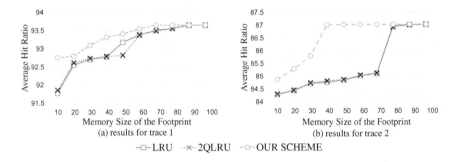

Fig. 2. Average hit ratio for all applications

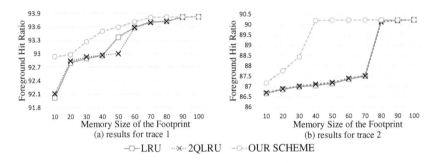

Fig. 3. Hit ratio for foreground application

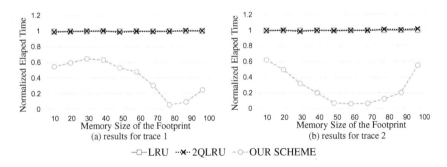

Fig. 4. Elapsed time for foreground application

In order to confirm the performance of our algorithm, we calculated the elapsed time of each algorithm based on the metrics in Table 1. Figure 4 clearly shows that our algorithm reduces the elapsed time of foreground application up to 53 % compared with other algorithms. This is because our algorithm maintains the pages, which belong to foreground applications, on DRAM as long as possible by giving higher priority to foreground applications than background application. As a result, the hit ratio of foreground applications increases. On the other hand, the hit ratio of other algorithms decreases because they give same priority to all applications for considering the temporal locality. Especially, our algorithm shows the best performance in all cases.

Since energy consumption is one of the most important issues, we finally compared it with LRU and 2QLRU algorithm. As a result, we found that our algorithm significantly reduces the power consumption by 23 % on average. This is because we can take the benefit of PCM (i.e., low power consumption) since our algorithm exploits the hybrid main memory architecture comprised of DRAM and PCM.

5   Conclusion

Generally, mobile devices employ DRAM as their main memory to mitigate performance gap between CPU and secondary storage. However, since DRAM continuously consumes the battery power of mobile device to keep data in DRAM, DRAM-based main memory architecture reveals a power consumption problem.

In this paper, we introduce a hybrid main memory architecture that is comprised of DRAM and PCM, and propose a novel buffer cache algorithm that saves battery power of device by exploiting non-volatility of PCM. In addition, our algorithm efficiently improves the performance of foreground applications because it gives higher priority to foreground applications than background applications. As a result, our algorithm shows high hit ratio by maintaining the pages, which belong to foreground application, as long as possible on DRAM. Our experimental results clearly show that our algorithm reduces the elapsed time of the foreground applications by 53 % on average and the power consumption by 23 % on average without any negative performance effects on background applications.

Acknowledgement. This research was supported by the MSIP (Ministry of Science, ICT and Future Planning), Korea, under the ITRC (Information Technology Research Center) support program (IITP-2015-(H8501-15-1015)) supervised by the IITP (Institute for Information & communications Technology Promotion). Young Ik Eom is the corresponding author of this paper.

References

1. Eilert, S., Leinwander, M., Crisenza, G.: Phase change memory: A new memory technology to enable New memory usage models. In: International Memory Workshop, pp. 1–2 (2009)
2. Qureshi, M.K., Srinivasan, V., Rivers, J.A.: Scalable high performance main memory system using phase-change memory technology. In: International Symposium on Computer Architecture, pp. 24–33 (2009)
3. Dhiman, G., Ayoub, R., Rosing, R.: PDRAM: A hybrid PRAM and DRAM main memory system. In: Design Automation Conference, pp. 664–669 (2009)

4. Lee, S., Bahn, H., Noh, S.H.: CLOCK-DWF: A write-history-aware page replacement algorithm for Hybrid PCM and DRAM memory architectures. In: IEEE Transactions on Computers, pp. 2187–2200 (2013)
5. Android Open Source Project. https://developer.android.com/guide/components/processes-and-threads.html
6. Johnson, T., Shasha, D.: 2Q: A low overhead high performance buffer management replacement algorithm. In: 20th International Conference on Very Large Data Bases, pp. 439–450 (1994)
7. Carroll, A., Heiser, G.: An analysis of power consumption in a smartphone. In: USENIX Annual Technical Conference, pp. 1–14 (2010)
8. Datta, SK., Bonnet, C., Nikaein, N.: Android power management: current and future trends. In: Enabling Technologies for Smartphone and Internet of Things, pp. 48–53 (2012)
9. Lim, G., Min, C., Kang, D.H., Eom, Y.I.: User-aware power management for mobile devices. In: Global Conference on Consumer Electronics, pp. 151–152 (2013)
10. Han, S.J., Kang, D.H., Eom, Y.I.: Low Power killer: extending the battery lifespan by reducing I/O on mobile devices. In: IEEE International Conference on Consumer Electronics, pp. 579–580 (2015)
11. Chu, S., Chen, S., Weng, S.F.: Design a low-power scheduling mechanism for a multicore android system. In: Parallel Architectures, Algorithms and Programming, pp. 25–30 (2012)
12. Gandhewar, N., Sheikh, R.: Google android: an emerging software platform for mobile devices. Int. J. Comput. Sci. Eng. **1**(1), 12–17 (2010)
13. Android Open Source Project. https://source.android.com/devices/tech/power/index.html
14. Android Open Source Project IPC. https://source.android.com/devices/#BinderIPC
15. Android Open Source Project. https://source.android.com/devices/tech/ram/low-ram.html

Protocol for a Simplified Processor-Memory Interface Using High-Speed Serial Link

HyukJe Kwon[✉] and Yongseok Choi

Electronics and Telecommunications Research Institute,
218 Gajeongdong, Yoseong-Gu, Daejeon, South Korea
{heavenwing,shine24}@etri.re.kr

Abstract. In our work, the interface protocol between a processor and memory built using an optical connection is described. We designed a serial interface protocol to simplify a parallel interface between the processor and memory, and implemented the protocol engine to be executed on the interface. There are three main roles of the protocol engines. The first is the data collection and sorting. The second is the data error detection and retransmission request. The third is packetizing the memory command and data.

Keywords: Memory · DDR · Protocol · Serial connection · Optical connection

1 Introduction

Owing to the development of the Internet and personal communication, a large amount of data and information has been recently produced and circulated. Because a large amount of data requires faster networks and a more effective processing, the requirements of more computing and more memory capacity have emerged. However, there is no memory structure satisfying the features of such applications as "small computing, big memory" [1]. In addition, the issues of more required memory bandwidth and capacity are emerging from the recently evolving "multi-core and many-core" idea [2, 3]. If the memory capacity and bandwidth per core are evenly assigned, as the number of cores increases, the capacity and bandwidth are reduced. To maintain a constant performance of the core, only increasing the capacity of the local memory is not appropriate.

A processor's memory access is made through a memory channel. More memory capacity and bandwidth are required at server-class data centers. And to ensure the stability of signals in channels, the memory should be closely attached to the server processor [2]. But the process's region to connect to memory is limited. Also, to stably transfer a normal data signal using on-board parallel channels, meticulous P&R is required.

A number of studies on improving the performance per core are still ongoing. There are several requirements to improve the performance of memory systems: the growth of the memory capacity, decreased memory latency, an expansion of the memory bandwidth, and an increased speed of the memory I/O operation, among others [4–6].

To increase the memory capacity, a stacked structure has been exploited. In recent years, other researchers have been conducting research and development for stacking the memory cells in the memory package. Such approaches include a stacked structure hybrid

© ICST Institute for Computer Sciences, Social Informatics and Telecommunications Engineering 2016
Y. Zhang et al. (Eds.): CloudComp 2015, LNICST 167, pp. 301–310, 2016.
DOI: 10.1007/978-3-319-38904-2_31

memory cube (HMC) [7, 8], high bandwidth memory (HBM), and Wide IO [2, 9]. Because memory cells with the same capacity may be stacked vertically in a limited area, they can increase the memory capacity. However, because a stacked structure is built up vertically, the die breakage is caused by an increased weight of the middle layers [10, 11].

Studies on reducing the memory latency time are carried out mainly on SDRAM, which has a relatively long latency time. Because SDRAM has a 1T1C structure, it requires a sufficient amount of time to be charged and discharged to access data stored in the capacitor. Until now, there has been no structure capable of reducing the charging or discharging time of the capacitor. Several studies on methods for improving the performance of the SDRAM cell's internal I/O by connecting to an optical fiber are ongoing [12, 13].

To increase the memory bandwidth, while the I/O operation speed has a limit of 200 Mbps, the I/O count increased by 512 and 1024, such as Wide IO(2) or HBM. These can be connected directly using external IO connections, or the connection between the memory and processor can be configured on SiP (system in package).

The focus of this paper is on memory I/O. An I/O associated with existing memory is in the form of a parallel bus interfacing with a processor. In this case, if the other memories are expanded onto the main board, the signals of those will become difficult to connect to a processor. Because there are many signals to interface with a processor. To resolve and manage these points, using high-speed serial communication and applying a packet protocol engine design, we designed protocol engines that are able to communicate a processor with memories [1, 14].

We describe the conventional structure between the CPU and memory in Sects. 2.1 and 2.2. In Sect. 3, the proposed protocol engines are described through a read and write memory operation. Section 4 then provides a description of the implementation and test of the protocol engines. Finally, in Sect. 5, some concluding remarks are provided.

2   Memory Systems and Protocol Engines

A central processing unit mainly performing the operation of each core has a separate cache for each storage device. It has from one to eight configurable cores. The memory cache for each core and the shared cache memory are interfaced. The shared cache memory, being interfaced with the memory controller and the peripheral controller, can exchange the data with those.

For the treatment of a large-capacity and high-speed main memory unit, a DDR memory is mainly used, and the interface of the data and memory controller in the processor is generally 32-bit or 64-bit. In addition to the 40-bit address and control information, more than 100 signal lines are required for a memory system to normally operate. In the case of the latest processors, the memory channel (dual) bus occupies about 50% of all package pins [16].

In [17], a bottleneck in the system performance between the processor and memory was reported. To solve this problem, the memory architecture of a 24 point-to-point method based on the memory module daisy-chain network is investigated. In [4], the SRAM memory was used in the research on memory- processor communication. In [1], it was formed in terms of a shared memory system. Specifically, rather than handling the memory I/O to improve the performance of the memory system, the memory formed by the silicon photonics to increase the operation speed in the inner memory has been studied. [3, 12].

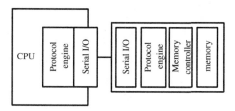

Fig. 1. Proposed memory system including the protocol engine.

In this paper, we propose a memory system to deal with communication problems between a processor and memory controller. Earlier studies dealt with a memory controller and processor, or a memory controller and memory. This paper is similar to [15] in which the memory controller is installed in the in/out side of the processor, and overrides these functional systems. We do not use the parallel communication of a conventional method between the memory controller and the memory bus, and the memory chip is built inside the memory controller. If the memory controller is located inside a memory chip, as shown in Fig. 1, the function of the memory controller can be separated. The master protocol engine of the main control processor is in charge of the memory controller and acts as a packetizer of the memory address and data generated by the processor. The memory controller has a memory part dependent control (slave) protocol engine, and the memory system can be configured together.

2.1 Proposed Memory Structure

The Double Data Rate (DDR) has a concept in which the data bandwidth is widened, that is, the memory chip latches the data on the 8 DQ (in/out) at the two edges (rising and falling) of the clock. To widen the bandwidth of the data, we have to increase the I/O clock speed, and we must also be able to afford a higher operating clock in which pre-fetched data are prepared in advance, which is a necessary task. However, the capacitor with SDRAM has a charge/discharge feature. Because of these features, the operating speed of the internal SDRAM does not increase as much as the IO operating speed, and the SDRAM internal speed is maintained without a significant change.

In this paper, we propose the reduction of the memory IO counts and the remove of the timing protocol of the DDR. The proposed scheme does not need different complex timing information to be controlled by the memory controller. The interface of the PCB or external IO can be simplified because the timings are dealt with by the inner memory because the interface is serial.

The leveling is a latching type in which the DQS signal can be able to latch the same value DQ in memory, and the use of a DQ and probe (strobe) is a way to control the DQS controlled by the memory controller. Two leveling types are used, reading and writing, and these processes are certain to be executed so that we obtain stable data in DDR3/4. Though the leveling is the skew of a method to correct a plurality (DQ count is 64) of data lines, when we are introducing a packet method, this feature may not be used.

2.2 Proposed Protocol Engines

There are three main roles of the protocol engines. The first is the data collection and sorting. The second is the data error detection and retransmission request. The third is packetizing the memory command and data. The protocol engine configuration can be divided into parts of the processor and the memory chip.

The master protocol engine is responsible for packetizing of the generated memory-related commands, data, and address by the processor. Another main role of the master protocol engine is to manage the detection and correction of the errors in the data collected, and if the re-transmission request is generated, it has to retransmit the packet that had been transmitted to the memory chip. The slave protocol engine is made up of the memory inside the chip.

The slave protocol engine re-analyzes the packet into the command, data, and address, which are transmitted by the master engine control protocol. These are then passed to the internal logic of the memory, and after the slave protocol engine generated the corresponding response packet, the packet is transmitted to the master control protocol engine. In addition, if the slave engine receives the re- transmission request, the engine has to retransmit the packet that had been transmitted to the master protocol engine.

The configuration of the master and slave control protocol engine is shown in Fig. 2. Commonly, the engine is made up of parallelizer and serializer modules. The packet generator takes on the role of reconfiguring the data obtained by the memory controller, or is configured by the processor to access the memory according to the two communication protocols. The packet sequence and CRC are used for calculating the CRC, and the CRC attached to the end of the signal packet is used for error checking. If there are more data than a fixed packet size, the data must be split into multiple packets. The packet sequence module generates the sequence number to indicate where an individual packet was generated in the entire packets. The packet checker module determines the packet processing based on the results of the packet sequence and CRC checking, i.e., whether to use or discard the received packet. At the packet checker, whether there is a

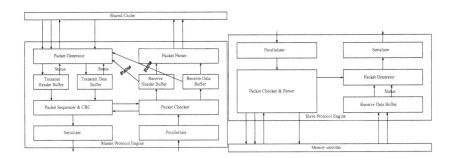

Fig. 2. Configuration of the master/slave protocol engine of connecting optical.

CRC error in a packet or the presence of duplicate packets is determined. If an error has occurred, the packet is discarded. Otherwise, the packet is stored in the receive buffer. In the stored packet, the packet parser analyzes the header and extracts the command from the memory access or collects information on the packet processing result of the other side of the protocol engine. The results collected are transmitted to the processor or memory controller.

The packet retransmission means that the transfer destination device is requested to resend the packet when an error occurs in the packet communication. For this purpose, both protocol engines should keep the transmitted packets in the buffer. If the normal memory access process is completed without the retransmission request, the data in that buffer is to be deleted or classified as not being used, and the data are then replaced with new data.

3   Operation of Protocol Engine

3.1   Write Operation

The processor holds the input data for the engine control protocols using the memory address, memory control information, burst to determine the data length, and mask information. The memory address is the entire memory address that can be accessed by the processor (Fig. 3).

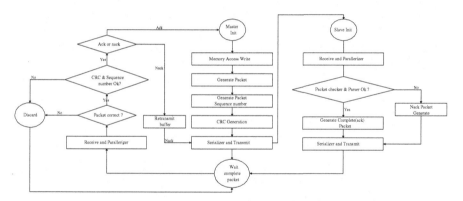

Fig. 3.   Write access flow charts.

The packet generator generates a packet and is responsible for storage and access control. The configuration factors are the transmission packet header, transmission data, and packet sequence. The generated packets are immediately transmitted depending on the circumstances of the memory access, or may be temporarily stored in a transmission header buffer and a transmission data buffer to wait for the previous packet processing to be complete. A sequence number is generated by the packet sequence, and it is argued that the master protocol engine sends this number to the slave protocol engine to confirm the order and delivery of the packet header and the data necessary for reconstruction of the factor.

The packet checker and parser in the slave control protocol are passed to the memory controller to execute a write access if a packet is received with a correct CRC. Otherwise, the packet is discarded. If that access is a completed operation, the slave protocol engine transmits the information indicating that the operation is complete to the slave control protocol. The master protocol engine proceeds to the next access after receiving a complete write access operation.

If the slave protocol engine received the packet with errors, it generates the packet based on indicating that there are problems with the write operations, and then transmits. As a result, the master protocol engine retransmits the write access packet until it receives a normal response and information for some time. Even if the received information of a normal response packet arrives later than expected, the master protocol engine judges that the write access packet sent to the main memory has not been communicated well and will retransmit that packet.

3.2 Read Operation

The slave protocol engine periodically transmits the packet to the master to be informed the state of the reception data buffer. The packet generator in the master protocol engine will consider the status of the transmission and reception header buffer and the status of reception data buffer, and also will consider the state of the reception data buffer in the slave protocol engine. Considering the above condition, a packet that includes content such as the memory address, reading field, mask information, and length of the data, is stored in the buffer (Fig. 4).

After inspecting the sequence number and CRC of the read access packet received, the packet checker and parser in the slave protocol engine transmit the memory address and the control information to the memory controller. Moreover, the slave protocol engine generates and transmits simultaneously the read access reception information to the master protocol. The packet checker and parser are redundant packet inspections and if duplicated, the packets are discarded. As the data accessed from memory by the memory controller is stored in a buffer, that data will be transmitted to the master protocol engine.

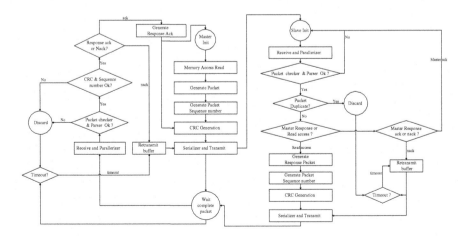

Fig. 4. Read access flow charts

The packet checker in the master protocol engine will check the sequence number and the CRC after receiving the read response packet. If there is an overlapping, it is discarded. Otherwise, it will be stored at the data buffer. Memory read data are transmitted through the processor interface, and the ACK packet is transmitted by the master protocol engine that has received a read response packet, and the read access is then completed. If the master protocol engine reads the response packet to inform it that the read access packet has not been passed to the slave protocol engine, then the packet is retransmitted and the engine waits until it receives a response packet. If the received information of a normal response packet arrives later than expected, the master protocol engine will retransmit the read access packet.

4   Test for Read and Write Access

4.1   Test Setup

To test the feasibility of the protocol engine between the memory and processor, the processor was emulated on an Altera Stratix IV FPGA. The maximum operating speed of the emulated processor is 200 MHz, the width of the system bus is 32-bit, and the processor system may be configured with a DMA, LED, LCD, inner program memory, general I/O, JTAG UART, and the master controller (protocol engine); the memory system is made up of a memory controller, LCD, memory, slave controller (protocol engine), and so on.

The configuration of the test system is as shown in Fig. 5. We constructed a single FPGA system for easier testing on a single FPGA. That is, a processor system and memory system are on a single FPGA. They are connected by an optical line in 10 Gbps, but without an internal connection.

Fig. 5. Experimental setups.

We coded a C-code that drives the process, which is used to validate the communication between the processor and memory coupled to an optical system.

The C-code executes a basic operation of the reading and writing of memory, or represents an operation between the processor and memory using three character LCD, or includes an LED control code. Two LCD shows a basic command and the data transmitted by the memory. One LCD show the reading memory data before transmitting to the processor over an optical connection.

4.2   Experimental Results

As we can see in Fig. 6, the master protocol engine generates a request packet for the read access (1). The generated packet is transmitted to the slave protocol engine. The slave protocol engine that receives the read access request (2) delivers its data to the memory controller after analyzing the packet and reconfiguring the needed data for the memory controller (3). The memory controller executes a memory access using that data over a DFI interface. The data obtained by executing a memory read access is transmitted to the master protocol engine (4). The master protocol engine receives the read-ACK in the read access response packet, and the response-ACK corresponding for the read-ACK is then transmitted to the slave protocol engine (5). The memory data are passed to the processor through the processor system bus, and displayed through the LCD (6). If the slave protocol engine receives a response-ACK generated by the master protocol engine, the protocol engine completes the read access and then waits for the next access (7).

As we can see in Fig. 7, the master protocol engine generates a request packet for the write access (1). The packet generated is transmitted to the slave protocol engine. After analyzing the packet, the slave protocol engine, which receives the write access request, delivers a write-ACK packet to the master protocol engine to confirm whether a normal packet has been received (2). The slave protocol engine delivers its data to the memory controller after analyzing the packet and reconfiguring the needed data for the memory controller (3). In addition, the memory controller executes the memory access using the data over a DFI interface (4). If the master protocol engine receives a write-ACK generated by the slave protocol engine, the protocol engine completes the write access and waits for the next access (5).

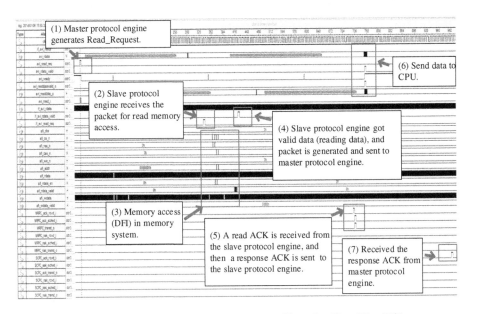

Fig. 6. Waveform of reading access captured by using SignalTap [18].

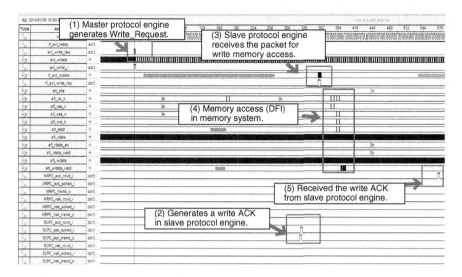

Fig. 7. Waveform of writing access captured by using SignalTap [18].

5   Conclusion

In this paper, we designed a protocol to test our proposed structure, and configured the optically connected processor and memory system. The processor system includes the master protocol engine and general processor system, and the memory system is composed of a slave protocol engine and a memory controller. We conducted an operation test of the protocol engine on each processor and memory system created within the FPGA for emulation. The operation of each system is independent of each other, and each system is supported by a 10 Gbps FPGA high-speed serial I/O connected optically.

The DIMM is configured with a memory channel in a conventional processor, which accounts for about 50 % of the number of pins in the processor. Through these proposals, if the protocol engine and memory controller can be mounted on an individual memory chip, the channel interface can be simplified. A built-in memory controller in a separate memory chip can access and control various memory, without the need to control a variety of complex timing information to the processor-memory interface, and the memory chip can control the timing internally. The change in the processor-memory interface has some advantages, i.e., a reflected signal and an inter-signal delay problem between the DIMM and a conventional memory controller may not occur.

This paper mainly described the functional aspects of the designed protocol, more experimental work is needed in the future. For this purpose, a system using a multiple memory configuration rather than a single memory configuration is necessary. In addition, we will build and test high-capacity services such as video-enabled protocols as a system for verification of the system performance.

Acknowledgement. This work was supported by the ICT R&D program of MSIP/IITP, Korea. [10038764, Silicon Nano Photonics Based Next Generation Computer Interface Platform Technology]

References

1. Li, L., et al.: Grid memory service architecture for high performance computing. In: Seventh International Conference on Grid and Cooperative Computing, pp. 24–26 (2008)
2. Okazaki, A., Katayama, Y.: Optical interconnect opportunities for future server memory systems. In: High Performance Computer Architecture, pp. 46–50 (2007)
3. Batten, C., et al.: Building many-core processor-to-DRAM networks with monolithic CMOS silicon photonics. In: HOTI 2008, pp. 21–30 (2009)
4. Yin, Y., et al.: Experimental demonstration of optical processor-memory interconnection. In: Advanced Intelligence and Awarenss Internet, pp. 23–25 (2010)
5. Hadke, A., et al.: Design and evaluation of an optical CPU-DRAM interconnect. In: ICCD, pp. 492–497 (2008)
6. Brunina, D., et al.: Building data centers with optically connected memory. J. Opt. Soc. Am. **3**(8), A40–A48 (2011)
7. H. M. C. Consortium: Hybrid Memory Cube Specification 1.0 (2013)
8. Jeddeloh, J., Keeth, B.: Hybrid memory cube new DRAM architecture increases density and performance. In: Symposium on VLSI Technology Digest of Technical Papers, pp. 87–88 (2012)
9. JEDEC: Wide I/O Single Data Rate (2011)
10. Kang, U.: 8 Gb 3D DDR3 DRAM using through-silicon-via technology. In: ISSCC 2009, pp. 130–131, 131a (2009)
11. Lee, W.S.: A Study on the effectiveness of underfill in the high bandwidth memory with TSV. In: IMAPS (2013)
12. Beamer, S., et al.: Re-architecturing DRAM memory systems with monolothically integrated silicon photonics. In: Proceedings of the 37th Annual International Symposium on Computer Architecture, ISCA 2010, pp. 129–140 (2010)
13. Udipi, A.N., et al.: Combining memory and a controller with photonics through 3D- stacking to enable scalable and energy-efficient systems. In: ISCA 2011 (2011)
14. JEDEC: DDR4 SDRAM JESD79-4, September 2012
15. Jun, H.T., et al.: Disintegrated control for energy-efficient and heterogeneous memory systems. In: HSPA2013, pp. 424–435 (2013)
16. http://www.bit-tech.net/hardware/cpus/2010/04/21/intel-sandy-bridge-details-of-the-next-gen/1
17. Brunina, D.: Building data centers with optically connected memory. IEEE/OSA J. Opt. Commun. Networking **3**(8), A40–A48 (2011)
18. http://www.altera.com/literature/hb/qts/qts_qii53009.pdf

The Trapping Device Implementation of Wireless Sensor Network

Hendrick Hendrick, Guo-Sheng Liao, Kuo-Ying Lu, Chun-Yen Lin,
and Gwo-Jia Jong[✉]

National Kaohsiung University of Applied Sciences,
No. 415, Jiangong Rd., Sanmin Dist., Kaohsiung 807, Taiwan, ROC
hendrickpnp@gmail.com, sheng800909@gmail.com,
happygoing00@yahoo.com.tw, 2103305113@gm.kuas.edu.tw,
gjjong@cc.kuas.edu.tw

Abstract. Organic agriculture is an important direction of modern agriculture development, and the biggest problem encountered in organic agriculture is the weather factor, thieves and pest problems. In this paper, we adopt wireless communication technology, micro-computing and energy saving solar technology to solve all of these problems. This system used the wireless sensor network (WSN) microcomputer judgment and wisdom of energy saving solar technology to solve all of these problems, such as the humidity, and light intensity. The purpose was to monitor the parameters of the current farm's environment.

Keywords: Organic agriculture · Wireless communication · Micro-computing · Solar technology · Wireless sensor network (WSN)

1 Introduction

Organic agriculture cannot use pesticides, the use of net house cultivation way, been able to avoid large-scale insect pest, but the use of net room cultivation, pests and diseases is still one difficult issue to face the farmer.

So we combined the internet of things (IOT) which any objects can be connected to the internet for information exchange and communication in order to achieve the objects intelligent identification, location, track, monitor and management, according to the agreed protocol, through wireless sensors such as RFID, ZigBee, Bluetooth module.

In this paper, the system is divided into the insect, anti-theft and Soil testing three functions, this function mainly through some interviews after organic farming operators set direction. We hope to reduce agricultural pests while allowing farmers about soil conditions and immediate prevention of illegal mining is not a bad guy or animals.

2 System Block Diagram and Flowchart

Figure 1 is the block diagram of the system. This system will be divided into two kinds of hanging and insert mode, we are using solar panels to light signals into electrical signals to detect whether the night and turned on the UV LED for insect phototropism were catching insects. Table 1 is the system specification.

© ICST Institute for Computer Sciences, Social Informatics and Telecommunications Engineering 2016
Y. Zhang et al. (Eds.): CloudComp 2015, LNICST 167, pp. 311–316, 2016.
DOI: 10.1007/978-3-319-38904-2_32

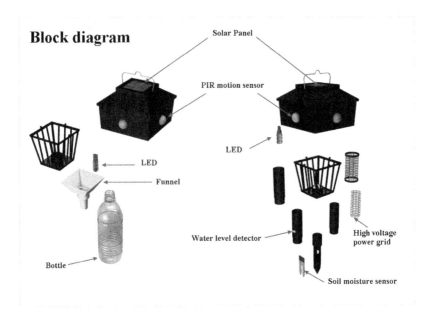

Fig. 1. The block diagram of the system

Table 1. The system specification

	Specification	Remark
Solar panel	4 V 0.14 W	Piece
Distance	200 m	ZigBee
Battery capacity	600 mAh	NiCd battery
PIR motion sensor	Wavelength 750 nm ∼ 25000 nm	Pyroelectric component
Soil moisture sensor	2.4 V to 5.5 V	SHT10
Length × Width × Height	150 mm * 150 mm * 450 mm	

Operational processes as shown in Fig. 2. Mainly, electricity provided by the solar cell to the battery, then power from the battery to the following three loops.

Anti-theft system section is the use of PIR motion sensors for a period of 10 s to determine whether there are thieves invaded, if the alarm is activated and send message to user by Zigbee; Soil detect the utilization of soil moisture is detected for a period of 30 min to determine whether the soil is too dry; Solar panel for a period of 30 min to determine whether the brightness is weak, if open LED attracting insects device utilizing optical properties tend trapping pests.

As show in Fig. 3, the system uses solar energy to provide electricity. The device is placed in the farm, one to absorb sunlight store electricity, and secondly, PIR motion sensor was used of theft. Alarm is activated and send message to user by ZigBee network, if through PIR motion sensors.

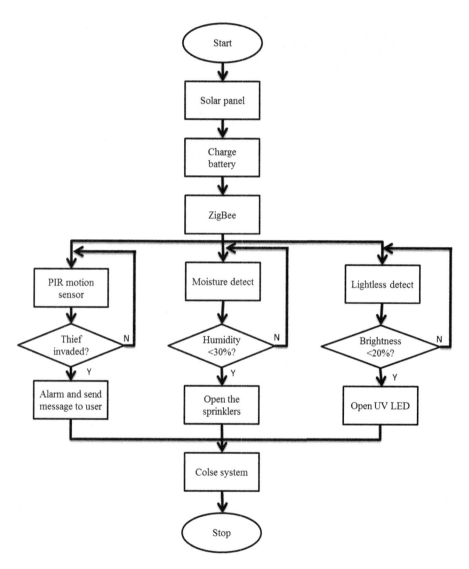

Fig. 2. The system flowchart

Fig. 3. Anti-theft system schematic

3   System Configuration

This system is mainly combined with wireless communications, PIR motion sensor, moisture sensor, and solar panel.

3.1   Solar Panel

The Amorphous silicon can be produced in a variety of shapes and sizes. Due to the universality of amorphous silicon solar cells, high efficiency, long service life and wide voltage range, etc. advantage considerations, here we choose it as a power supply, and use wisdom to determine loop solar panels do Detection action, solar panels current drops to a certain extent it is determined that night, open LED means attracting insects.

3.2   Wireless Communications

As shown in Table 2, we use low-cost ZigBee technology as a communication system of the device, according to this agreement technology is a short-range, low-power wireless communication technology to support a large number of network nodes with a variety of network topologies. Mainly applied to the field of automatic control and remote control, you can embed a variety of devices.

Table 2. Comparison between ZigBee and RFID

	ZigBee	RFID
Operating frequency	900 MHz/2.4 GHz	13.56 MHz/900 MHz
Range	Large than RFID	Less than ZigBee
Storage	More	Less
Nature	Always active	Both active and passive possible

3.3 PIR Motion Sensor

PIR main purpose as human infrared detection, because the sensor housing having a multi-layer coating can be hindered most of the infrared, only allow temperatures close to 36.5° by the wavelength of the infrared, so as suitable for human motion detection. For that reason we used it to determine whether there are thieves invaded.

3.4 Soil Moisture Sensor

We used SHT1x which is Sensations' family of surface mountable relative humidity and temperature sensors. It is a measure of temperature and humidity and very sensitive sensor module, and only through two serial to read temperature and humidity values. The sensor works with 3 or 5 V logic.

4 Conclusions

The power of this system is provided by solar energy, combined with attracting insects, security and soil moisture detection, mainly used in organic farming. We hope to use this system to improve the troubled development of organic agriculture in Taiwan, in response to energy saving but also enhance the agricultural added value. The future will be combined with private security system set up in this residential area, improve the quality of home life.

References

1. Yitong, W., Yunbo, S., Xiaoyu, Y.: Design of multi-parameter wireless sensor network monitoring system in precision agriculture. In: 2014 Fourth International Conference on Instrumentation and Measurement, Computer, Communication and Control (2014)
2. Zhang, J., Li, A., Li, J., Yang, Q., Gang, C.: Research of real-time image acquisition system based on ARM 7 for agricultural environmental monitoring. In: 2011 International Conference on Remote Sensing, Environment and Transportation Engineering (RSETE) (2011)
3. Xiao, L., Guo, L.: The realization of precision agriculture monitoring system based on wireless sensor network. In: 2010 International Conference on Computer and Communication Technologies in Agriculture Engineering (2010)
4. Gaddam, A., Mukhopadhyay, S.C., Gupta, G.S.: Trial and experimentation of a smart home monitoring system for elderly. In: 2011 IEEE Instrumentation and Measurement Technology Conference (I2MTC) (2011)
5. Meng, J., Li, Z., Wu, B., Xu, J.: Design, development and application of a satellite-based field monitoring system to support precision farming. In: Third International Conference on Agro-geoinformatics (Agro-geoinformatics 2014) (2014)
6. Wang, C., Jiang, T., Zhang, Q.: ZigBee® Network Protocols and Applications

7. John, J., Palaparthy, V.S., Sarik, S., Baghini, M.S., Kasbekar, G.S.: Design and implementation of a soil moisture wireless sensor network. In: 2015 Twenty First National Conference on Communications (NCC) (2015)
8. Datasheet SHT1x Humidity and Temperature Sensor IC. http://www.sensirion.com/fileadmin/user_upload/customers/sensirion/Dokumente/Humidity/Sensirion_Humidity_SHT1x_Datasheet_V5.pdf
9. PIR Motion Sensor - Adafruit Learning System. https://learn.adafruit.com/downloads/pdf/pir-passive-infrared-proximity-motion-sensor.pdf
10. Adriansyah, A., Dani, A.W.: Design of small smart home system based on Arduino. In: 2014 Electrical Power, Electronics, Communications, Controls, and Informatics Seminar (EECCIS) (2014)

A Formal Approach for Modeling and Verification of Distributed Systems

Gang Ren[1,2], Pan Deng[1,2(✉)], Chao Yang[1,2],
Jianwei Zhang[3], and Qingsong Hua[4]

[1] Institute of Software, Chinese Academy of Sciences, Beijing 100091, China
{rengang2013,dengpan,yangchao}@iscas.ac.cn
[2] University of Chinese Academy of Sciences, Beijing 100091, China
[3] Beihang University, Beijing 100091, China
zhangjw@nlsde.buaa.edu.cn
[4] Qingdao University, Qingdao 266071, China
8988596@qq.com

Abstract. In recent year, distributed systems have become a mainstream paradigm in industry and how to ensure correctness and reliability is a great challenge for practicing engineers. Therefore, in this paper a formal approach is proposed for modelling and verification of distributed systems, which integrates UML sequence diagram, π-calculus and NuSMV within one framework. Moreover, the practicality of the proposed approach is illuminated though a case study of scheduling road emergency service.

Keywords: UML seqence diagram · π-calculus · Model checking · Formal methods

1 Introduction

In recent year, with the rapid development of distributed systems, they have become a mainstream paradigm in industry and how to ensure correctness and reliability is a great challenge for practicing engineers [1]. They are investigating various methods and tools to address this issue.

In these methods, there are three methods widely used. One is UML sequence diagram [2], which is graphical notation for specifying dynamic interaction behaviors among system components. As it is intuitive and simple in notation and semantics, it is appealing to practicing engineer.

Another method widely used is π-calculus [3], which is a process algebra and well reputed for modelling concurrent systems and mobile systems. Due to excellent ability of expression, it has been widely applied to modelling of system dynamic behavior.

Project supported by National Nature Science Foundation of China (No. 61100066).

The third is NuSMV [4], which is a symbolic model checker which can automate verification process checking whether or not the desired temporal properties can be met.

Generally speaking, these methods improved correctness and reliability of safety-critical systems to some extent. Nevertheless, these methods and tools are always used separately. Because different methods focuses on different aspects of system, only one method can't solve this challenge very well. For example, due to intuition and simplicity, UML sequence diagram [2] is widely used in modeling of systems. However, it is a semi-formal notation and not suitable very well for distributed systems. Π-calculus [3], a process algebra, and NuSMV [4], a symbolic model checker, are another two methods used widely. However, π-calculus is only good at system specification, but not at system verification. NuSMV [4] is just the reverse.

Therefore, in this paper, a formal approach is proposed for modeling and verification of distributed systems. As shown in Fig. 1, there are 3 layers in this framework. The first is graphical layer, which utilizes sequence diagram to model system. The middle is formal specification layer which is adopted π-calculus to formalize UML sequence diagram. The third is verification layer, which adopts NuSMV as verification tool.

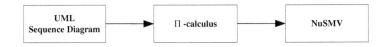

Fig. 1. A formal approach for modelling and verification of distributed systems.

2   Modelling a Scenario Using Sequence Diagram

Recently, road emergency services in Intelligent Transportation Systems have draw much attention [5,6]. In this paper, a scenario of scheduling emergency services is considered as an examination to illustrate the use of the proposed framework. As Fig. 2 shows, there are three kinds of Emergency Services (ESs): Hospital, Fire Bridge (FB) and Police Office (PO) in road network. When Road Side Unit (RSU) discoveries accident, it'll inform it to Emergency Center (EC). EC is in charge of forwarding this message into relative ESs automatically. When EC receives a request from RSU, it'll forward the message into relative ESs. Once ESs receives a reqeust from EC, it'll respond is at once. The UML sequence diagram of the scenario is described as shown in Fig. 3. Exchanging message between devices is in an asynchronous way. The combined fragment of parallel is used in sending "Request" in parallel.

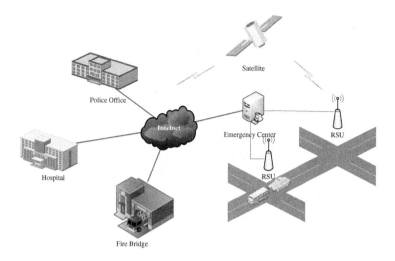

Fig. 2. A scenario of scheduling emergency services.

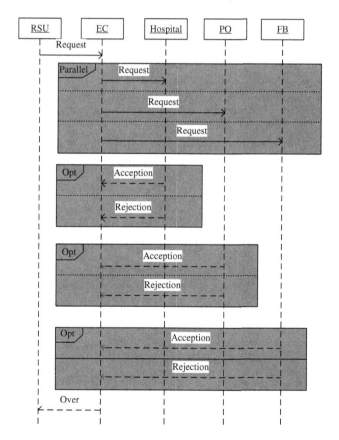

Fig. 3. Sequence diagram of emergency service.

3   From Sequence Diagram to Π-calculus

In this section, first a set of rules are defined. Then according to the above rules, π-calculus presentations of the road emergence service are specified.

Rule 1 (Sending message). *Given a device, the sending of a message is specified as an output action in π-calculus.*

Rule 2 (Receiving message). *Given a device, the receipt of a messages is specified as an input action in π-calculus.*

Rule 3 (Parallel combined fragment). *Given a device, a parallel combined fragment is specified concurrent action in π-calculus.*

Rule 4 (Optional combined fragment). *Given a device, a optional combined fragment is specified choice action in π-calculus.*

(1) **System**
$$System = RSU|EC|Hopital|FB|PO$$
(2) **RSU**
$$RSU = \overline{re}\langle Request \rangle.re(msg).[msg = Over]0$$
(3) **EC**
$$EC = EC_0|EC_1|EC_2|EC_{syn}$$
$$EC_0 = re(msg).[msg = Request]\overline{eh}\langle Request \rangle.0$$
$$EC_1 = re(msg).[msg = Request]\overline{ef}\langle Request \rangle.0$$
$$EC_2 = re(msg).[msg = Request]\overline{ep}\langle Request \rangle.0$$
$$EC_{syn} = eh(msg).([msg = Acception]ef(msg).[msg = Acception]ep(msg).$$
$$[msg = Acception]\overline{re}\langle Over \rangle.0$$
(4) **Hospital, FB and PO**
$$Hospital = ch(msg).[msg = Request](\overline{rh}\langle Acception \rangle + \overline{rh}\langle Rejection \rangle).0$$
$$FB = ef(msg).[msg = Request](\overline{rf}\langle Acception \rangle + \overline{rf}\langle Rejection \rangle).0$$
$$PO = ep(msg).[msg = Request](\overline{rp}\langle Acception \rangle + \overline{rp}\langle Rejection \rangle).0$$

4   From Π-Calculus into NuSMV

The translation rules are formally defined as follows:

Rule 1. *System process are device process are translated into main module and sub-module program and device process is translated into sub module respectively.*

Rule 2. *Given a process, its concurrent processes are translated into sub-processes executing in parallel.*

Rule 3. *In every module, there is a local enumerative scalar variable "state" which represents the transition of process states.*

Rule 4. *As for an input action, its previous state and match structure are both translated into a transition condition of "state" and its successor is translated into a next state of "state".*

Rule 5. *As for an output action, its previous state and subsequent state are respectively translated into a transition statement of "state".*

5   Model Checking for Temporal Property

In the following lists, the temporal properties to be verified are defined and translated into Computation Tree Logic (CTL) formulas which is a branching temporal logic and extends propositional logic by incorporating path quantifiers and temporal operators. For more details about syntax and semantics of CTL, please refer to [7].

Property 1 (Non-Blocking). *EC must reach the "Over" status in the future.*
$AF(re = Over)$

Property 2 (Result Reachability). *It is possible that All ECs can reach "Acception".*
$AF(eh = Acception\&ef = Acception\&ep = Acception)$

Property 3 (Forwarding Integrity). *Once EC receives a "Request" from Hospital, it must forward "Request" into ESs.*
$AF((re = Request) - > AF(eh = Request\&ef = Request\&ep = Request))$

Property 4 (Forwarding Stability). *EC can't forward message until it receives a message.*
$A[(eh! = Request\&ef! = Request\&ep! = Request)U(re = Request)]$

The execution environment comprises 8 core CPU of Intel Core i7-2600(3.40 GHz) with 4 G Memory, running Windows 7 and NuSMV 2.4.3. Firstly, the command of *"read_model"* is used in reading model file "ES.svm", which contains two parts: the one is system model generated in Sect. 4. The other one is temporal properties defined above. Secondly, the command of *"print_reachable_state"* is executed to count the number of the reachable states. As shown in Fig. 4, there are totally 318 reachable states. Finally, the command of *"check_ctlspec"* can be used in model checking temporal properties. Figure 5 shows temporal properties are all met.

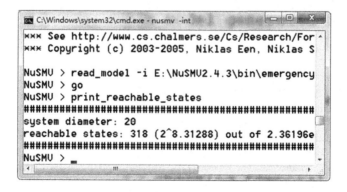

Fig. 4. Reachable states

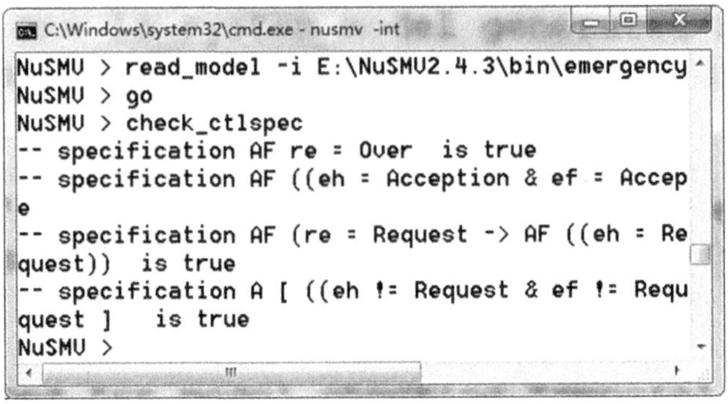

Fig. 5. Verification results

6   Conclusion

In this paper, a novel 3-layer framework is proposed for modelling and verification of safety-critical systems, which integrates three different methods and tools, and leverages their respective advantages to collaborate each other. It can improve correctness and reliability of safety-critical systems such as Industrial IoT system and applications. The major advantage of this work is that it frees the designer to know about mathematical formalisms where the learning curve might be high.

As future work, an translator from sequence diagram to π-calculus is considered to develop in order to improve automation of this framework.

References

1. Knight, J.C.: Safety critical systems: challenges and directions. In: Proceedings of the International Conference on Software Engineering, pp. 547–550, Orlando, May 2002
2. Omg unified modeling language (omg uml). Normative Reference (2013). http://www.omg.org/spec/UML/2.5
3. Milner, R., Parrow, J., Walker, D.: A calculus of mobile processes, i. Inf. Comput. **100**(1), 1–40 (1992)
4. Cimatti, A., Clarke, E., Giunchiglia, E., Giunchiglia, F., Pistore, M., Roveri, M., Sebastiani, R., Tacchella, A.: NuSMV 2: an opensource tool for symbolic model checking. In: Brinksma, E., Larsen, K.G. (eds.) CAV 2002. LNCS, vol. 2404, pp. 359–364. Springer, Heidelberg (2002)
5. Chen, C., Chen, P., Chen, W.: A novel emergency vehicle dispatching system. In: Vehicular Technology Conference, pp. 1–5, June 2013
6. Rajamaki, J.: The mobi project: designing the future emergency service vehicle. IEEE Veh. Technol. Mag. **8**(2), 92–99 (2013)
7. Clarke, E.M., Grumberg, O., Peled, D.A.: Model Checking. MIT Press, Cambridge (2000)

Design of a Security Gateway for iKaaS Platform

Seira Hidano[1]([✉]), Shinsaku Kiyomoto[1], Yosuke Murakami[2],
Panagiotis Vlacheas[3], and Klaus Moessner[4]

[1] KDDI R&D Laboratories, 2-1-15 Ohara, Fujimino-shi, Saitama 356-8502, Japan
se-hidano@kddilabs.jp
[2] KDDI Research Institute, Tokyo, Japan
[3] WINGS ICT Solutions, Athens, Greece
[4] University of Surrey, Surrey, UK

Abstract. The iKaaS (intelligent Knowledge-as-a-Service) platform integrates the data on multiple local clouds organically and provides the data to various types of applications as knowledge while taking security and privacy fully into account. However, access control on the iKaaS platform is not without complications because the application may access personal data in different countries from the one where the application exists. We thus design a security gateway that is set at the entrance of each local cloud and can control access while interpreting the differences in regulations and guidelines between countries.

Keywords: Access control · Security policy · Privacy certificate

1 Introduction

The Internet of Things (IoT) paradigm is rapidly gaining momentum in modern wireless telecommunications. IoT devices, such as smart sensors designed to monitor temperature, pressure and other environmental conditions and wearable devices to measure an individual's state of health, generate vast amounts of time sequence data. These data are accumulated on clouds and analyzed for useful information like personal preferences and to predict the environmental conditions surrounding people and the next actions that people may take. The impact will increase if the heterogeneous data stored on multiple clouds can be organically integrated. However, vast quantities of potentially correlated data have not yet been analyzed in correlated contexts for a number of reasons. As the data obtained from IoT devices are mostly sensitive information related to an individual, anxiety concerning security and privacy is an obstacle to the participation of users. A universal data model is also required for the analysis of the heterogeneous big data obtained from various types of sensors. Furthermore, there are legal considerations that complicate matters further. The compatibility of regulations related to personal data should be clearly dealt with. It is expected that with increasing trust, decentralized multi-cloud environments are about to unlock great potential for future data analysis [3,4].

© ICST Institute for Computer Sciences, Social Informatics and Telecommunications Engineering 2016
Y. Zhang et al. (Eds.): CloudComp 2015, LNICST 167, pp. 323–333, 2016.
DOI: 10.1007/978-3-319-38904-2_34

The iKaaS (intelligent Knowledge-as-a-Service) platform thus has been proposed as a way to resolve these problems [6]. On this platform, a global cloud is hierarchically built atop multiple local clouds that are set up in different countries. It integrates the data stored on the local clouds organically, and the integrated data are provided to various applications as knowledge. Security and privacy are controlled by a security gateway that is set at the entrance of each local cloud. When using the iKaaS platform, the application can access the data for different countries, conduct various-scale analyses and compare different countries. However, privacy issues have not been sufficiently resolved in the current model. When the application accesses personal data in different countries, the iKaaS platform is required to handle the data in accordance with the regulations and guidelines governing personal data in both the country where the application exists and the country where the local cloud is set up. These regulations and guidelines are complicated and there are differences between countries. For instance, a Japanese act [7] permits the transfer of personal data to the EU while an EU directive [2] does not permit the transfer of the data to Japan. Although there have been few technical studies on security and privacy for decentralized multi-cloud environments, these studies have not focused on privacy issues in relation to cross-border data [5,9]. In order to resolve these issues, there needs to be fundamental review of the architecture.

The main contribution of this paper is to design a security gateway that can interpret the differences in regulations and guidelines between countries and is capable of flexibly controlling the access permissions of the application while taking privacy into consideration. The rest of the paper is organized as follows: Sect. 2 overviews the functional capabilities of the iKaaS platform and our contributions. Section 3 proposes the security and privacy architecture for the iKaaS platform. Section 4 describes the protocol whereby the application accesses the data through the security gateway. Section 5 presents the conclusions of this paper.

2   iKaaS Platform

Intelligent Knowledge-as-a-Service (iKaaS) is a concept model where the data accumulated on multiple local clouds are organically integrated on a global cloud and the data are provided as knowledge taking security and privacy into consideration. Figure 1 shows the architecture of the iKaaS platform. The iKaaS platform encompasses a global cloud, multiple local clouds, IoT devices and third party DBs, which are hierarchically arranged. The multiple local clouds are established in different countries such as in the UK and Japan, and each local cloud has DBs for various types of data. The data are obtained not only from the newly available IoT devices but also from existing DBs designed for other purposes. The various data models are converged to a universal data model before the data are stored in the DBs on the local cloud. This resolves the issue where the models and formats of the data are different between local clouds. The global cloud is considered to be a trust component, and all data are provided to the applications through it.

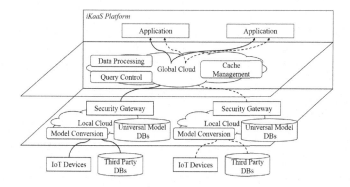

Fig. 1. Architecture of iKaaS platform.

The global cloud has three functions: query control, data processing and cache management. When the application makes a request for knowledge, the global cloud helps the application to generate queries consistent with the objective and transmits the queries to suitable local clouds. The global cloud not only deals with the raw data obtained from the local clouds but also processes the data statistically depending on the request. Massive-scale big data and heterogeneous data are combined and analyzed, and more useful knowledge is produced as a result. Self-Organizing Maps (SOMs) is an indicative technique to process the big data (in terms of disparate data formats and diversity of sources), offering user-friendly or oriented insightful knowledge visualization, for data mining with a high degree of accuracy so as to support decision making [1]. Additionally, the data are stored in a cache DB on the global cloud so that the application can access them more effectively. The global cloud manages the cache data according to the frequency with which the data are updated (because some data, like map information, for example, CityGML [10], are not useful if the data exist as an outdated version). However, the data that IoT devices extract are mostly sensitive information related to an individual, namely, personal data. Personal data should not be disclosed or provided to third parties without the consent of the data owner. There is also the case when the transfer of personal data to third parties is not permitted under the relevant regulations. The security gateway is thus arranged at the entrance of the local cloud and controls the access of the application to the data with privacy and security considerations taken into account.

Our Contributions. The contributions of our work are the following:

- We design a security gateway that can interpret the differences in the rules between the country where the application exists and the country where the local cloud is set up, to control the access permissions of the application taking the above privacy issues into account. The interpretation is realized using a privacy certificate and security and privacy policies, which are defined in Sect. 3.

326   S. Hidano et al.

- We introduce the access control with a token, which allows the process of the above interpretation to be omitted for the same application. This is because while the application may frequently request data at short intervals as the data are continuously transmitted from IoT devices, the interpretation process takes time.
- We provide a method by which the security gateway determines the validity of the application without communicating with it directly since the global platform inevitably intervenes between them. This method is achieved by combining the privacy certificate and the public and private keys of the application.
- We elucidate the concept of cache management because sensitive information could be cached. The process of determining whether the data are to be cached and the deletion of the cache data is conducted based on the cache policy defined in the local cloud. Additionally, the cache data are encrypted with the encryption algorithm recommended in each country.

3 Functions of Security Gateway

Figure 2 shows privacy-conscious architecture centered on the security gateway for the iKaaS platform. Each local cloud has a security gateway at the touch point with the global cloud. The queries from the application and the data on the local cloud are all exchanged through the security gateway. The security gateway has two functional capabilities: one is the access control of the application under the rules governing the handling of personal data both for the country of the application and the country of the local cloud, and the other is privacy control on behalf of the data owners on the local cloud. The privacy certificate issued by the privacy certificate authority (CA) and the security policy are referred to by the security gateway for access control, and the privacy policy is formulated for privacy control. The privacy certificate and the policies are defined in

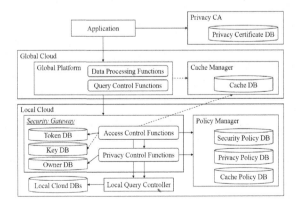

Fig. 2. Privacy-conscious model of iKaaS architecture.

Sects. 3.1, 3.2 and 3.3. The methods for both controls are explained in detail in Sect. 3.4. Furthermore, we elucidate the concept of cache management on the global cloud in Sect. 3.5. The cache manager is set up to control access to the cache data while cooperating with the security gateway. Management of the cache data is conducted taking both privacy and usability into consideration as mentioned in Sect. 2.

3.1 Privacy Certificate

The privacy certificate makes it possible for the security gateway to interpret the rules in the country where the application exists. The privacy CA is built for each country and creates the privacy certificate on the basis of the national regulations that prevail in that country and information concerning the application. It is a requirement that the application is issued a privacy certificate by the privacy CA of the same country before requesting the local cloud for data. The following parameters are listed on the privacy certificate:

- *CA Country:* The name of the country where the privacy CA is established. It also refers to the name of the country where the application exists.
- *Application IP:* The IP address of the application.
- *Application ID:* The type of service that the application provides.
- *LC Countries:* The names of the countries that the application is permitted to access.
- *LC Data IDs:* The identifiers indicate the types of data that the application is permitted to access. The values are nested in each value of *LC Countries*.
- *Expiry:* The expiry date of the privacy certificate.
- *Application PK:* The public key of the application. (The role of this key is mentioned in Sect. 3.4.)
- *Signature:* The signature is generated with the private key of the privacy CA. The public key is distributed to security gateways.

3.2 Security Policy

The security policy is created by the administrators of the local cloud based on several regulations and guidelines through the policy manager. The policy manager is provided by the privacy CA in charge of the country where the local cloud is set up, and the basic policy is formulated in accordance with the national regulations in advance. The administrator configures the security policy on the basis of the local regulations, such as a city, a town or a company, and in accordance with relevant guidelines. The security policy has two tables: the expiry periods of access permissions and the definitions related to data privacy. Tables 1 and 2 are an example of a security policy. The administrators configure the values for each type of data, namely, data ID. Each row of the tables indicates the rules related to a regulation or a guideline (including the basic policy). The expiry periods of access permissions are defined for each country as shown in Table 1. A zero value means that the data of the type indicated by the data ID

Table 1. Expiry periods.   **Table 2.** Definitions on data privacy.

No	Data 1	$\cdots$	Data N
1	UK 0/JP 2mo	$\cdots$	UK 0/JP 0
2	UK 1h/JP 2h	$\cdots$	UK 0/JP 0
$\vdots$	$\vdots$	$\ddots$	$\vdots$

No	Data 1	$\cdots$	Data N
1	Non-privacy	$\cdots$	Privacy
2	Privacy	$\cdots$	Privacy
$\vdots$	$\vdots$	$\ddots$	$\vdots$

are not permitted to be transferred to the country. This table is configured for each type of application (although Table 1 shows the configuration for a specific application). The value "Privacy" in Table 2 means that the privacy of the data of the type indicated by the data ID should be taken into account and the value "Non-privacy" means that there are no privacy-related concerns regarding the data. Even if the data are defined as "Non-privacy" in Table 2, the expiry periods are set in terms of security or with the frequency with which the local cloud DB is updated.

3.3 Privacy Policy

The status of the consent on the transfer of data to third parties for each data owner is listed on the privacy policy [8]. Personal data should be controlled by the data owner in terms of privacy as mentioned in Sect. 2. The privacy policy makes it possible for the security gateway to provide personal data to the application while preserving the privacy of the data owner. Table 3 is an example of a privacy policy. The status of the consent is defined for each data ID by each data owner. The value "Yes" means that the data owner agrees that the data can be used on the iKaaS platform and the value "No" means that the data owner does not agree. This table is configured for each type of application (although Table 3 shows the configuration for a specific application).

Table 3. Privacy policy.   **Table 4.** Cache policy.

Owner ID	Data 1	$\cdots$	Data N
1	Yes	$\cdots$	Yes
$\vdots$	$\vdots$	$\ddots$	$\vdots$
K	No	$\cdots$	Yes

No	Data 1	$\cdots$	Data N
1	2mo	$\cdots$	5days
2	2mo	$\cdots$	2wk
$\vdots$	$\vdots$	$\ddots$	$\vdots$

3.4 Access and Privacy Control

The security gateway uses a token to control the access of the application because the process involved in checking the privacy certificate and the policies takes time. When an application requests access to the local cloud DBs, the security gateway generates a token and returns it to the application. The application with the token can request the data any number of times until the token has expired. The security gateway provides two functions for access control: *Issue Token* and *Get Data*.

Issue Token. This function is called when the application obtains the token to access local cloud DBs. The application is then required to specify the data IDs that it wants to have access to and sends the privacy certificate. When issuing the token, the security gateway refers to the privacy certificate and the security policy in order to comply with the rules of both countries.

The values of parameters *LC Countries* and *LC Data IDs* listed on the privacy certificate are checked first. The security gateway uses those values to confirm whether or not the application is permitted to access the data specified by the data IDs under the rules of the country where the application exists. Meanwhile, the security gateway uses the security policy to interpret the rules of the country where the local cloud is set up. The table on the expiry periods for access permissions as shown in Table 1 is used to decide the expiry date of the token. The security gateway searches the corresponding columns of data IDs in the table using the values for the parameter *Application ID* listed on the privacy certificate and the requested data IDs. The security gateway chooses the one with the shortest expiry period for the country name corresponding to the value of the parameter *CA Country* listed on the privacy certificate and derives the expiry date by adding the current time to the chosen period. If the multiple data IDs are specified by the application, this process is carried out for each data ID, which means multiple expiry dates are set for one token. After deciding the expiry dates, the security gateway generates a token. However, if the shortest expiry period equals zero for all the data IDs, the token is not issued to the application.

Next, the security gateway refers to the table on the definitions of data privacy as shown in Table 2 to judge whether or not the privacy of the data owners is to be taken into consideration when the application with the token requests the data. The security gateway refers to the corresponding columns of data IDs in the table using the same process that was used to make the decision regarding the expiry date of the token. If the value "Non-privacy" is set for all rows, the data of the type indicated by the data ID are called non-privacy data, and the security gateway determines that there are no privacy-related concerns regarding the data. Otherwise, the data are called privacy data, and the security gateway takes the privacy of the data owner carefully into consideration when transferring the data. This process is also carried out for each data ID.

The values of the parameters *Application IP* and *Application ID* listed on the privacy certificate, the token, the data ID that the application can have access to, the expiry date of the token and the privacy type (non-privacy data or privacy data) are associated and stored in the token DB. If the application can access multiple data IDs with one token, the set of the values of the data ID, the expiry date and the privacy type are created for each of the data IDs and the multiple sets are all associated with one token. Additionally, the token is transmitted to the application after being encrypted with the value of the parameter *Application PK* listed on the privacy certificate. This is because as the security gateway does not directly communicate with the application on the iKaaS platform, conventional schemes that are used to confirm the validity of the application, such as the SSL client authentication, cannot be applied. In our architecture, the application to which the privacy certificate is issued by the privacy CA only can decrypt the token with its own private key, which prevents unauthorized use of the token by other applications.

Get Data. The application with a token calls this function via the global platform to transmit the query to the local cloud DBs. First, the security gateway verifies the authenticity of the token. This verification is conducted on the basis of a message authentication code (MAC). In other words, the token is treated as a common key. We do not assume that a specific algorithm is used to generate the MAC because the recommended algorithms are different for each country. The security gateway is thus required to inform the application of the algorithm when issuing the token. The privacy of the data owner is safeguarded when the data are transferred to the application. The security gateway checks the privacy type of the data that the application has requested to have access to. If the data is of the non-privacy type, the data is directly returned to the application. However, if there are privacy considerations, the security gateway filters the data on the basis of the privacy policy. As the relation between the ID of the data owner and the attributes is stored in the owner DB, the security gateway extracts the corresponding IDs in the owner DB with the owner attributes specified in the query. The security gateway searches the corresponding rows in the privacy policy with the extracted owner IDs and confirms the consent status on the transfer of the data for the application ID and the data IDs specified in the query. The security gateway only returns the data for which the data owner has set the value "Yes".

3.5   Cache Management

Cache functions are required when the application wants access to data more effectively. When the application obtains the data through the security gateway, the communication cost increases as compared to the case where the DBs are accessed directly. If using the cache manager, the application can access the data in fewer steps, and for that reason it is expected that the access time can be shortened.

The data on the local cloud are directly cached from the security gateway through the cache manager when the token to access the data is requested by an application. The expiry date of the cache data is decided on the basis of the cache policy. Table 4 shows an example of the cache policy. The expiry periods are configured based on various types of requirements. This is because some types of data, like map information, must be kept fully up to date, so the expiry periods should be set taking not only security and privacy into account but also the frequency with which the data need to be updated. The cache policy is formulated in the same manner as the security policy by the security gateway when the expiry date is decided.

Furthermore, it is not desirable to store sensitive information in a third party domain for an extended period of time due to security issues, and consequently there is a requirement for the cache data to be encrypted. However, because the recommended algorithms are different for each country, before transmitting the data to the cache manager, the security gateway encrypts the data using the algorithm recommended in the country of the local cloud. The encryption key is stored in the key DB and returned to the application with the token.

4   Protocol

We define the protocol for security and privacy control on the iKaaS platform. We provide the definition of a query, and then show the sequence of steps involved in issuing a token and the data request. In our architecture, the security gateway provides the functions as web APIs, and HTTPS connections only are allowed. Additionally, the global cloud instantiates a global platform for each application, and the application cannot use the global platform for any other application.

4.1   Query Formats

The security gateway has no function for interpreting the query for local cloud DBs (*LCD-query*). When the application requests the data, the headers (*SGW-headers*) are added by the global platform and the query for the security gateway (*SGW-query*) is created. The types of headers are as follows:

- *Application IP:* The IP address of the application.
- *Application ID:* The type of service that the application provides.
- *LC Data IDs:* The IDs indicate types of data that the application wants to have access to.
- *Owner Attributes:* The attributes that narrow down the data owners, for example, age and gender. This header is required when the attributes are specified as search conditions in the *LCD-query*. The security gateway uses the values to extract the corresponding owner IDs from the owner DB as mentioned in Sect. 3.4.
- *Time Stamp:* The time when the *SGW-query* is generated. It is used to prevent a replay attack.

4.2   Step Sequence

Token Issuance. The token to access data on the local cloud is issued to the application in accordance with the following procedure:

1. An application requests the privacy CA to issue the privacy certificate.
2. The application uses some functions for query control that the global platform provides in order to search the security gateway of the country where the local cloud DBs suited for the objective exist and to request the issuance of a token.
3. The global platform calls the function *Issue Token* that the security gateway provides. The global platform then specifies the data IDs that the application wants to access and sends the privacy certificate of the application.
4. The security gateway confirms the values of the parameters *Expiry* and *Signature* listed on the privacy certificate to verify the validity of the certificate. The signature is validated with the public key of the privacy CA of the country indicated by the parameter *CA Country* listed on the privacy certificate.
5. The security gateway creates a token, encrypts it with the public key of the application, which is listed on the privacy certificate, and returns the encrypted token to the application via the global platform.
6. The application decrypts the token with its own private key and stores the token on the global platform.

Data Request. The application with a token obtains the data on the local cloud as follows:

1. An application uses some query functions of the global platform and creates the *SGW-query*. The global platform generates the MAC of the *SGW-query* with the token of the application.
2. The global platform calls the function *Get Data* that the security gateway provides to transmit the *SGW-query* and the MAC to the security gateway.
3. The security gateway extracts the corresponding token from the token DB with the values of the *Application ID* and *Application IP* headers and checks the expiry date of the token.
4. The security gateway generates the MAC from the *SGW-query* and the token to verify the authenticity of the query. The value of the *Time Stamp* header is also confirmed.
5. The security gateway transmits the *LCD-query* to the local query controller.
6. When the data are returned from the local cloud DBs, the security gateway confirms the privacy type of the data while searching the token DB.
7. If the data stored as non-privacy data are returned, the security gateway returns the data to the application via the global platform without further intervention. Otherwise, the processes of Steps 8–10 are carried out.
8. The security gateway extracts the corresponding owner IDs from the owner DB using the value of the *Owner Attributes* header.
9. The security gateway searches the privacy policy using the extracted owner IDs and the values of the *Application ID* and *LC Data IDs* headers and confirms the consent status of the corresponding data owners.
10. The security gateway extracts the data on the condition that the data owner agrees to the transfer and returns the extracted data to the application via the global platform.

5 Conclusion

The iKaaS (intelligent Knowledge-as-Service) platform integrates data on multiple clouds organically and provides the data as knowledge to the cross-border application. We designed a security gateway that makes it possible to control the access of applications on the iKaaS platform. The security gateway can interpret the differences between countries in terms of their respective regulations and guidelines that govern the treatment of personal data by using the privacy certificate issued by the privacy certificate authority (CA) and the security policy on the local cloud. It also has a function that allows the availability of personal data to be controlled according to the consent status of the data owners.

Acknowledgment. The work is supported by the EUJ-1-2014 Research and Innovation action: iKaaS; EU Grant number 643262, Strategic Information and Communications ·R&D Promotion Programme (SCOPE), Ministry of Internal Affairs and Communications, Japan.

References

1. Bantouna, A., Poulios, G., Tsagkaris, K., Demestichas, P.: Network load predictions based on big data and the utilization of self-organizing maps. Springer J. Netw. Syst. Manage. **22**, 150–173 (2014)
2. EU: Directive 95/46/EC of the European Parliament and of the Council of 24 on the protection of individuals with regard to the processing of personal data and on the free movement of such data, October 1995
3. EU FP7/ICT project 257115: OPTIMIS: Optimized Infrastructure Services, June 2010–May 2013
4. EU FP7/ICT project 287708: iCore: Internet Connected Objects for Reconfigurable Eco-systems, October 2011–September 2014
5. EU FP7/ICT project 609094: RERUM: REliable, Resilient and secUre IoT for sMart city applications 2013–2016
6. EU HORIZON 2020 project 643262: iKaaS: intelligent Knowledge-as-a-Service 2014–2017
7. Japan: Act on the Protection of Personal Information, Act No. 57 of 30 May 2003
8. Kiyomoto, S., Nakamura, T., Takasaki, H., Watanabe, R., Miyake, Y.: PPM: Privacy policy manager for personalized services. In: Cuzzocrea, A., Kittl, C., Simos, D.E., Weippl, E., Xu, L. (eds.) CD-ARES Workshops 2013. LNCS, vol. 8128, pp. 377–392. Springer, Heidelberg (2013)
9. de Meer, H., Pöhls, H.C., Posegga, J., Samelin, K.: On the relation between redactable and sanitizable signature schemes. In: Jürjens, J., Piessens, F., Bielova, N. (eds.) ESSoS. LNCS, vol. 8364, pp. 113–130. Springer, Heidelberg (2014)
10. Oosterom, P.V., Zlatanova, S., Fendel, E.M.: Geo-Information for Disaster Management. Springer, Heidelberg (2005)

KVM-QEMU Virtualization with ARM64bit Server System

Jin-Suk Ma$^{(\boxtimes)}$, Hak-Young Kim, and Wan Choi

Server Platform Res Lab, ETRI,
161 Gajeong-dong, Yuseong-Gu, Daejeon, Korea
{majinsuk,h0kim,wchoi}@etri.re.kr

Abstract. In the conventional x86 or x86-64 bit system, virtualization is commonly achieved with KVM or Xen which is widely adapted in many experimental or commercial server system. At now, It is common sense that high and mid volume servers are virtualized with Xen, mid and small volume servers are virtualized with KVM. Recently, the microserver system concept was introduced, which contains low power and multicore ARM64bit sever SoCs. We present the KVM-QEMU virtualization technique and process in a real ARM64bit microserver system with ubuntu 14.04 ARM64 bit edition root file system.

Keywords: ARM64bit server SoC · KVM-QEMU · Virtualization

1 Introduction

Recently, ARM announced the ARMv8 architecture which could be used for low power and high performance server system. From ARMv7 cortex A15 architecture, ARM has supported the hardware level virtualization. ARMv8 architecture has either A57 or A53 core and both. [1] In some ARM SoC, it may have a big-little architecture with ARM57 and ARM53. ARM has licensed to APM (Applied Micro), AMD, Cavium, Broadcom and etc. One of these commercial SoC company, APM is now providing a commercial server SoC and a reference platform. The time of writing this paper, AMD is also providing the beta level test platform with NDA contract. Cavium announced the ARM64bit server SoC with 2.5 GHz clock speed, 48 ARM cores which is known to ThunderX. But it was hard to get a test level reference platform in any market.

The APM ARMv8 server SoC is called as X-Gene platform which has 4 or 8 ARMv8 cores (the code name is mustang). [2] It is widely known that APM is running the homepage webserver with X-Gene processors. As people knows that ARM architecture has been widely researched and adapted in commercial products, the microserver system which has ARMv8 server SoCs is now developing in big commercial server company such as HP, Dell and etc. We expect that the microserver will make some server product lines with not little volumes.

In view of a server software architecture, ARMv8 also supports hardware level virtualization techniques, which are basis of the conventional hardware support virtualization technique of KVM or XEN for microserver system. At current server

© ICST Institute for Computer Sciences, Social Informatics and Telecommunications Engineering 2016
Y. Zhang et al. (Eds.): CloudComp 2015, LNICST 167, pp. 334–343, 2016.
DOI: 10.1007/978-3-319-38904-2_35

technology main stream, it is essential that the server must have some virtualization capability with multiple virtual machine instances. The microserver has no exception. Unfortunately, there is not much information or paper in KVM-QEMU virtualization based on the real ARM64bit SoC platform. Alex bennee showed the buildroot based QEMU virtualization in reference [5]. He did not address the information about KVM host system. Making buildroot image is not simple even if a linux expert. There are many configuration parameters alike to linux kernel .config. And also buildroot usability is not better than ubuntu root file system in view of package management and support library. Reference [6] showed many various KVM-QEMU examples. We referenced many setup techniques about QEMU parameters on this site. We have great thanks to this site operator. It has same issue like to former work also. It seemed that ARM64 QEMU work was archived in x86 or emulation environment not real ARM64bit server system base. In this paper, we archived KVM-QEMU virtualization with APM X-Gene 883208-x1 reference platform host with ubuntu root file system, which is the real hardware not ARM simulator or x86.

2   APM X-Gene Server Reference Platform

APM X-Gene server reference board is shown in Fig. 1. Target board is provided by APM (Applied Micro Co.) and it is based on ARM licensed Cortex A57 8-core. The detail hardware shape and component locations are shown in Fig. 1 and Table 1.

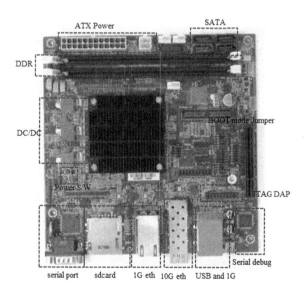

Fig. 1. APM X-Gene ARM64 server platform.

2.1   Software Development Environment

Software development environment is shown in Table 2, which is mainly supplied by APM with APM X-Gene Mustang reference platform.

Table 1. Board components and specification.

Components	Specification
Mainboard	Mustang – Applied Micro APM883208-X1-PRO-1
CPU	APM ARM64bit Cortex-A57 2.4 GHz 8Core
MEM	DRAM: ECC 16 GB @ 1600 MHz
HDD	Intel SSD 530 series 240G SATA3(for experiment)
Boot ROM	N25Q256 Serial Flash (32 MB)
Serial port	1 port
USB	2 port
Gigabit Ethernet	3 port
10G Ethernet	1 port

In this paper, we deal with the KVM-QEMU in ARM64bit server platform, so KVM version is not given in Table 1 because it is embedded in linux kernel internally. First of all, the boot disk partition is shown in Fig. 2. In Fig. 2, the system boot partition is /dev/sda1. Boot partition has kernel image (uImage) and device tree blob (apm-mustang.dtb). Kernel image is compiled from kernel source code with KVM configuration, and device tree blob is also too.

Table 2. Development software and version specifications.

Component	Version
Boot	Uboot-2013.04-mustang_sw_1.14.14
Kernel	mustang_sw-1.14.14
Root File System	AARCH64 ubuntu 14.04 LTS
Cross Compiler (GCC)	gcc-linaro-aarch64-linux-gnu-4.9 or apm-aarch64-8.0.3-le(little endian)

We will present the kernel configuration of ARM64 for KVM virtualization in Sect. 3, but the concluding result was that the complied output of uImage is about 12 MBytes and that of device tree blob(dtb) is about 26 Kbytes. So /dev/sda1 is enough disk space for housing uImage and dtb. In some case, even if you want to use ramdisk image (uInitrd), /dev/sda1 will be enough for that. /dev/sda3 is linux swap partition which is normally not included in the conventional ARM based embedded linux system. We allocated 16 Gyte of the linux swapping partition with /dev/sda3. As you know, the swap space has the double size of system RAM normally. But it is rule of thumb that the swap partition needs the almost same amount of system ram size in system with more than 8 Gbyte RAM, Actually we monitored the usage status of the swap space in working, we can not find any swapping memory use status because of the reference platform has the large system memory (16 GBytes) which is more than any other type embedded systems with the conventional ARM core. But it is common sense that the server test environment has always the various limitations in view of many user specific use case.

/dev/sda2 contains the KVM host root file system and the required space of KVM guest. so /dev/sda2 has the whole disk spaces except for boot and swap space. In Xen virtualization case, this partition may have multiple physical or logical partitions for housing a Xen guest domain. But, we didn't find any needs of sub-partitioning on /dev/sda2 in researching this work.

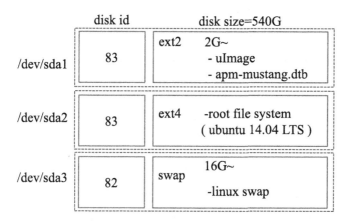

Fig. 2. Disk partition for KVM virtualization.

3   KVM-QEMU Virtualization on ARM64

3.1   KVM Kernel Configuration and Host OS

The kernel configuration for KVM virtualization in ARM64 server is essential. This is done by typing make menuconfig or manipulating .config file in linux kernel. The major kernel configuration parameters for KVM virtualization are shown in Table 3. Even thought Table 3 does not contain the whole parts of .config file due to paper space limitation, it is useful for understanding the major parts of KVM kernel configuration.

As shown in Table 3, kernel configuration parameters for KVM virtualization on ARM64 contain CPU, interrupt, IO, timer virtualization parameter setting. And also these contain the bridge network setting for host and guest OS. After we configures the linux kernel setting including Table 3 and compiles linux kernel, we could get linux kernel image (uImage) and dtb for KVM virtualization.

We select the ubuntu arm64 14.04 tar.gz style root file system for the host OS. [3, 7] Ubuntu is most widely adapted from world wide developers. Currently Canonical is quickly upgrading their public free root file system for ARMv7 (armhf) and

Table 3. Kernel parameters for KVM virtualization

Kernel parameters
CONFIG_HAVE_KVM_IRQCHIP=y
CONFIG_KVM_MMIO=y
CONFIG_VIRTUALIZATION=y
CONFIG_KVM=y
CONFIG_KVM_ARM_HOST=y
CONFIG_KVM_ARM_MAX_VCPUS=4
CONFIG_KVM_ARM_VGIC=y
CONFIG_KVM_ARM_TIMER=y
# CONFIG_AARCH32_EL0 is not set
# CONFIG_ARM64_ILP32 is not set
CONFIG_IP_ADVANCED_ROUTER=y
CONFIG_NETFILTER=y
CONFIG_NETFILTER_ADVANCED=y
CONFIG_BRIDGE_NETFILTER=y

ARMv8 (arm64). Installation and setup of ubuntu ARM64 14.04 include some complicated process if user is not a linux expert. But many references can be found in the various internet sites. So we will not deal with the installation and setup step of ubuntu ARM64 root file system. After we install ubuntu ARM64 14.04.2, we had to install the utility library such as libvirt-bin, virtinst, bridge-utils and etc. via apt-get and aptitude which are the powerful package management tool in ubuntu.

3.2 ARM64-QEMU Setup

In case of realizing the virtualization with KVM for ARM64 SoC, almost use QEMU. It supports ARM64 from QEMU ver 2.1, and at the time of writing this paper, the result of cloning of QEMU git is ver 2.3. At above Sect. 3.1, we addressed ubuntu ARM64 14.04.2 installation for host side root file system, but we could not install a qemu-system-aarch64 package via apt-get with the lack of qemu-aarch64 repository binary. So we cloned the QEMU source repository and complied a qemu-system-aarch64 binary as shown in below script.

```
#git clone git://git.qemu.org/qemu.git qemu.git
#cd qemu.git
#./configure –target-list=aarch64-softmmu --enable-debug \
 --enable-kvm
#make -j8
#make install
```

3.3 Making a qcow2 Image for Guest OS

QEMU requires a guest disk image for virtualizing an ARM64 virtual machine. Xen virtualization require some additional physical and logical partitioning for guest domain. But to get a guest disk image in QEMU, we used qemu-img command for building a guest disk image with qcow2 format with online commanding. As explained in Sect. 3.2 previously, qemu-img command had already installed with using make install command automatically. Qemu-img supports that it makes and converts a raw or qcow2 disk image file. We made a raw image file (aarch64-v1.img) with 10 GBytes size by commanding qemu-img for installing of ubuntu root file system which is used by QEMU's guest emulation. After the completion of ubuntu netboot image which will be explained in the next Section, we changed that image to aarch64-kvm.qcow2 which has qcow2 file format. By using the qcow2 with QEMU ver 2.3, we could depress the warning message by QEMU system.

3.4 Getting Netboot Image

To install an ubuntu root file system for QEMU ARM64 in guest disk image, one need netboot images. Netboot image consists of temporary kernel (vmlinuz) and ramdisk image (initrd.gz) which have the main function for supporting ubuntu network installation. One can use the reference [8, 9] to get each of them.

3.5 Guest OS Setup Using Netboot Image

One can install the root file system for guest OS with below script and the downloaded netboot images (vmlinuz, initrd.gz). More detailed command line and argument are shown in below box lines. This process will take long time to complete.

```
qemu-system-aarch64                        \
 -machine virt -cpu cortex-a57             \
 -nographic -smp 6 -m 4096                 \
 -kernel ./netboot/vmlinuz                 \
 -initrd ./netboot/initrd.gz               \
 -drive file=aarch64-v1.img,if=none,id=blk  \
 -device virtio-blk-device,drive=blk       \
 -net user,hostfwd=tcp::1014-:22           \
 -device virtio-net-device,vlan=0          \
 -append "console=ttyAMA0 --"
```

3.6   Starting Guest OS

Finally, we could start guest OS with KVM-QEMU as shown in below boxed line command script successfully. Real boot process took long time which was about more than 5 min.

```
qemu-system-aarch64                         \
 -machine virt -cpu cortex-a57              \
 -nographic -smp 4 -m 4096                  \
 -localtime                                 \
 -rtc base=utc                              \
 -kernel vmlinuz-3.13.0-49-generic          \
 -initrd initrd.img-3.13.0-49-generic       \
 -drive file=aarch64-kvm.qcow2,if=none,id=blk  \
 -device virtio-blk-device,drive=blk        \
 -net user,hostfwd=tcp::1014-:22            \
 -device virtio-net-device,vlan=0           \
 -append "root=/dev/vda2 rw console=ttyAMA0 --"  \
 -serial null
```

According to above setting procedures, we can show the whole KVM-QEMU virtualization system block diagram with ARM64 server system as shown in Fig. 3.

As known in the fact that KVM-QEMU virtualization has various benefits, we can use multiple virtual machines to increase the utilization factor of server system resources, to provide the complete independent computing environment for various

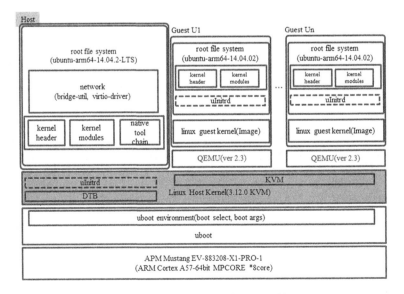

Fig. 3. KVM-QEMU virtualization with ARM64 server system

users, to migrate one physical machine to another, and etc. ARM64 server system with KVM-QEMU has the same virtualization benefits. But we have to point out the system performance degradation in our experimental system. Virtio still doesn't support the multi core in ARM64 completely. We found that the boot time of guest OS has taken long times (about more than 5 min) and some disk IOs are very slow. So we have to solve this problem for the real business deployment with ARM64 server system. This step will be the one of our next step research process.

4 Experimental Result

We installed and experimented KVM-QEMU virtualization with the ARM64bit server reference board. Our experimental system adapted the ARM64 ubuntu 14.04.2 root file system. The boot message of host OS in server board is captured and shown in Fig. 4. Host OS with KVM which has the kernel configuration described in Sect. 3.1 was good and had booted very quickly.

```
L3C: 8MB
Initializing cgroup subsys cpuset
Initializing cgroup subsys cpu
Initializing cgroup subsys cpuacct
Linux version 3.12.0-mustang_sw_1.14.14+ (root@jsma-i7) (gcc version 4.9
i Apr 10 16:51:28 KST 2015
CPU: AArch64 Processor [500f0000] revision 0
Machine: APM X-Gene Mustang board
bootconsole [earlycon0] enabled
efi: Getting parameters from FDT.
efi: Can't find System Table in device tree!
On node 0 totalpages: 4194304
   Normal zone: 57344 pages used for memmap
   Normal zone: 4194304 pages, LIFO batch:31
PERCPU: Embedded 10 pages/cpu @ffffffc3fff81000 s11776 r8192 d20992 u409
pcpu-alloc: s11776 r8192 d20992 u40960 alloc=10*4096
pcpu-alloc: [0] 0 [0] 1 [0] 2 [0] 3 [0] 4 [0] 5 [0] 6 [0] 7
Built 1 zonelists in Zone order, mobility grouping on.  Total pages: 413
Kernel command line: root=/dev/sda2 rw ip=129.254.75.125:129.254.75.123:
stang:eth0:off panic=1 console=ttyS0,115200 earlyprintk=uart8250-32bit,0
otlb=65536 pcie_ports=native
PID hash table entries: 4096 (order: 3, 32768 bytes)
Dentry cache hash table entries: 2097152 (order: 12, 16777216 bytes)
Inode-cache hash table entries: 1048576 (order: 11, 8388608 bytes)
software IO TLB [mem 0x43e8600000-0x43f0600000] (128MB) mapped at [fffff
Memory: 16379104K/16777216K available (6601K kernel code, 430K rwdata, 2
 bss, 398112K reserved)
```

Fig. 4. Host system boot messages.

After completing the boot process of host OS, verifying KVM support for host OS is done by commanding kvm-ok on system serial console. Host OS returned the support of KVM availability as shown in Fig. 5.

```
root@localhost:/# uname -a
Linux localhost.localdomain 3.12.0-mustang_sw_1.14.14+ #5 SMP Fri Apr 10 16
:51:28 KST 2015 aarch64 aarch64 aarch64 GNU/Linux
root@localhost:/# lsb_release -a
No LSB modules are available.
Distributor ID: Ubuntu
Description:    Ubuntu 14.04.2 LTS
Release:        14.04
Codename:       trusty
root@localhost:/# kvm-ok
INFO: /dev/kvm exists
KVM acceleration can be used
root@localhost:/# 
```

Fig. 5. Verification of KVM support on host OS.

As explained in Sect. 3.6, the starting messages of guest OS in host OS are shown in Fig. 6. We checked out the normal startup messages of guest OS.

```
root@localhost:~/aarch64_kvm# ./start-ubuntu-kvm.sh
[    0.000000] Initializing cgroup subsys cpuset
[    0.000000] Initializing cgroup subsys cpu
[    0.000000] Initializing cgroup subsys cpuacct
[    0.000000] Linux version 3.13.0-49-generic (buildd@twombly) (gcc versio
n 4.8.2 (Ubuntu/Linaro 4.8.2-19ubuntu1) ) #81-Ubuntu SMP Tue Mar 24 19:35:3
7 UTC 2015 (Ubuntu 3.13.0-49.81-generic 3.13.11-ckt17)
[    0.000000] CPU: AArch64 Processor [411fd070] revision 0
[    0.000000] psci: probing function IDs from device-tree
[    0.000000] PERCPU: Embedded 12 pages/cpu @ffffffc0fffa6000 s17088 r8192
d23872 u49152
[    0.000000] Built 1 zonelists in Zone order, mobility grouping on.  Tota
l pages: 1034240
[    0.000000] Kernel command line: root=/dev/vda2 rw console=ttyAMA0 --
[    0.000000] PID hash table entries: 4096 (order: 3, 32768 bytes)
[    0.000000] Dentry cache hash table entries: 524288 (order: 10, 4194304
bytes)
[    0.000000] Inode-cache hash table entries: 262144 (order: 9, 2097152 by
tes)
[    0.000000] software IO TLB [mem 0x138000000-0x13c000000] (64MB) mapped
at [ffffffc0f8000000-ffffffc0fbffffff]
[    0.000000] Memory: 4037352K/4194304K available (5718K kernel code, 590K
rwdata, 2536K rodata, 304K init, 538K bss, 156952K reserved)
```

Fig. 6. System boot messages of guest OS.

Finally we showed the normal prompt of guest OS after completing the boot process of guest OS in Fig. 7. We verified the normal operation of guest OS with KVM-QEMU virtualization in ARM64 server system successfully.

```
Ubuntu 14.04.2 LTS ubuntu ttyAMA0

ubuntu login: root
root
Password:
Last login: Tue May 12 13:52:37 KST 2015 on ttyAMA0
Welcome to Ubuntu 14.04.2 LTS (GNU/Linux 3.13.0-49-generic aarch64)

 * Documentation:  http://help.ubuntu.com/

 System information disabled due to load higher than 4.0

33 packages can be updated.
26 updates are security updates.

root@ubuntu:~# █
```

Fig. 7. Guest OS console after booting

5   Conclusions

In this paper, we explained the process of KVM-QEMU virtualization technique in ARM64bit server reference platform sequentially. KVM-QEMU virtualization in ARM64bit server system has almost the same realization processes and advantages over the conventional x86-64 system. But we identified the performance issues with related to virtio library in our experimental server system. It will be one of the next research step.

Acknowledgments. This work was supported by the ICT R&D program of MSIP/IITP. [B0101-15-0548, Low-power and High-density Micro Server System Development for Cloud Infrastructure].

References

1. ARM Technical Conference (2014). http://www.armtechcon.com/
2. APM X-Gene Mustang. https://www.apm.com/products/data-center/x-gene-family/x-gene/
3. Ubuntu on Applied Micro Circuits Corp. X-Gene 1 (Storm). http://www.ubuntu.com/certification/hardware/201407-15333/
4. https://help.ubuntu.com/community/KVM
5. http://www.bennee.com/~alex/blog/2014/05/09/running-linux-in-qemus-aarch64-system-emulation-mode/
6. https://gmplib.org/~tege/qemu.html
7. Ubuntu Core 14.04.2 LTS (Trusty Tahr). http://cdimage.ubuntu.com/ubuntu-core/releases/14.04/release/
8. http://ports.ubuntu.com/ubuntu-ports/dists/trusty-updates/main/installer-arm64/current/images/generic/netboot/vmlinuz
9. http://ports.ubuntu.com/ubuntu-ports/dists/trusty-updates/main/installer-arm64/current/images/generic/netboot/initrd.gz
10. Jinsuk, M., Hakyoung, K., Wan, C.: Software development environment for ARM64bit server system. In: Proceedings of IEIE Conference, Deajeon, Korea, pp. 56–57 (2014)

A System Interconnection Device for Small-Scale Clusters

Ye Ren[✉], Young Woo Kim, and Hag Young Kim

Electronics and Telecommunications Research Institute, 218 Gajeong-ro, Yuseong-gu,
Daejeon 34129, Republic of Korea
{yeren,bartmann,h0kim}@etri.re.kr

Abstract. The performance of a physical cluster ultimately depends on two factors. One is the capability of individual computing nodes and the other is the networking speed among them. Recent processors are being greatly developed in terms of enhancing the processing speed while lowering the monetary cost. As for the networking technologies, nowadays dominant solutions have disadvantages such as high installation price and low protocol efficiency. Such drawbacks become the bottleneck of improving the 'performance per cost' ratio of the cluster as a whole. This paper proposes an alternative system interconnection device especially for application in small-scale clusters. The non-transparent bridges in PCI Express technology are employed to allow PCI Express packets to directly transmit across networked computing nodes. The performance is measured under two kinds of data transmission schemes, with two different benchmarking tools, respectively. Currently the proposed device delivers a peak unidirectional throughput of 8.6 gigabits per second.

Keywords: Cluster · Interconnect · PCI Express · Throughput

1   Introduction

One common way of building up a small-scale cluster is to combine multiple computing nodes in the form of either boxes or blades, using networking cables and switches. Based on this method, the performance of a cluster that nests those cloud computing resources ultimately depends on the two factors. One is the performance of each individual node and the other is the networking speed among nodes of the cluster.

Recently, processors are rapidly developed to deliver more powerful processing capability while at lower cost according with the Moore's Law [1]. General-purpose CPUs clustered together can allow for an impressive performance of hundreds of giga-FLOPS (giga FLoating-point Operations Per Second) or even several teraFLOPS. In the meantime, the interconnection technologies for clusters are dominated by InfiniBand and high-performance Ethernet [2]. Those dominant networking solutions can deliver high bandwidth, but they still have disadvantages such as high price for installation and low protocol efficiency in packet transmission. Such drawbacks of system interconnects have become the bottleneck to the improvement for the cluster in terms of achieving a higher 'performance per cost' ratio as a whole.

This paper proposes an alternative system interconnection device based on the PCI Express technology and the device is especially for application in small-scale clusters.

© ICST Institute for Computer Sciences, Social Informatics and Telecommunications Engineering 2016
Y. Zhang et al. (Eds.): CloudComp 2015, LNICST 167, pp. 344–353, 2016.
DOI: 10.1007/978-3-319-38904-2_36

In the present paper an interconnection device refers to the physical interface between a local computing node and an external cable, facilitating the communication with the remote standalone node connected on the other end of the cable. The proposed device employs the non-transparent bridges to allow PCI Express packets to directly transmit across computing nodes and it is easy and flexible for ordinary consumers to install and use. Two kinds of data transmission schemes are implemented which are the memory copy and the direct memory access (DMA). The performance is measured with two different benchmarking tools, respectively, and experiments show that the proposed device outperforms the Gigabit Ethernet and is capable to deliver a peak unidirectional throughput of 8.6 gigabits per second.

The rest of paper is organized as follows. An overview of the related research work on system interconnects are depicted in Sect. 2. Section 3 presents the detailed explanation about the technology deployed in the proposed interconnection device. Next, Sect. 4 elaborates the design and implementation of the proposed generally-applicable interconnection device. Section 5 shows performance evaluation results and discussions. Finally, Sect. 6 concludes the whole paper.

2 Related Work

There are already several existing solutions for high-performance system interconnection. The 10 Gigabit Ethernet [3] and other commercial models [4, 5] provide higher performance but also induce too much power consumption and expenses for small-scale use case. Moreover, they require switches even to build up a network with just a few nodes (e.g. 2–5 nodes).

PCI Express (PCIe) [6] is a promising technology to use in system interconnection devices and this is already indicated by many previous works. Ravindran [7] examined the technology of "PCI Express External Cabling 1.0 Specification" and proposed a new technical specification named "the local mode specification" to ensure a high-bandwidth, low-latency connection between devices with independent PCI domains. Hanawa et al. proposed communication links using PCIe Gen2 (2nd generation) for embedded systems [8] and he also demonstrated an effective interconnect for direct communication between accelerators over nodes via PCIe external cables [9]. Byrne et al. [10] evaluated the benefits of using PCIe for power-efficient networking with a test-bed cluster where each node links to a central PCIe switch board and independently manages their own devices. Krishnan [11] proposed a PCIe based hardware with software for integrating IO expansion and clustering functionalities onto one PCIe interconnect, in which the solution consists of host PCIe adapters, expansion switch, and cluster switch. Such hardware would be too complicated and over-powerful in case of only two or three computing nodes are to be clustered by a consumer. In addition to the above works, a standalone system interconnection device named PCIeLINK (PCI Express Link) [12] has been proposed which can be used to integrate multiple general-purpose CPUs.

This paper elaborates the research on the proposed PCIeLINK and presents a more developed implementation with better performance compared with the prior one.

A detailed description about the adopted technology by PCIeLINK is included in this paper as well.

3   Using PCI Express for System Interconnects

3.1   Advantages and Disadvantages of PCI Express for System Interconnects

PCIe is an industrial standard system bus that delivers high-performance and low latency packet transmission between the root complex and the enumerated PCI endpoints (as shown in Fig. 1). Also, the PCIe slot is also the primary interface on a motherboard for a system to connect with various peripherals. The data rate per lane for PCIe Gen2 is 4 Gbit/s, for Gen3 is 7.877 Gbit/s, and the PCIe specification is evolving to enable higher data rates. Prevalent PCIe connectors adopt 8 or 16 lanes which contribute to a total theoretical bandwidth as good as that of many widely used system interconnection devices for supercomputers. Besides, the PCIe as an interconnect technology consumes lower power per port and also costs less money for unit price than most common commodity products [13]. Therefore, PCIe is considered as a competitive and alternative technology for system interconnections.

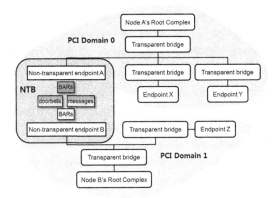

Fig. 1. PCI enumeration on two systems and the communication between the two PCI domains through the non-transparent bridge (NTB).

The PCIe standard was initially developed to allow one root complex to enumerate the PCI endpoints in one local PCI address space (or PCI domain) and provide connections between processors and IO devices within a single computing system. Therefore, there exit some restrictions in both electrical and systemic perspectives to directly apply PCIe as a system interconnect. If two PCIe domains are connected with each other using a common PCIe device directly, then the asynchronous clocking in the two different systems will hinder PCIe protocol from working properly. A more critical problem is the PCIe hierarchy enumeration problem. When two systems are powered up, BIOS of each side enumerates devices in its PCI hierarchy (PCI domain) and assign BDF (Bus, Device and Function) numbers. If two identical systems are connected with a typical

PCIe device, then the BDF number conflicts occur, which causes the two systems both fail to build up a workable PCI hierarchy.

3.2 Data Transmission Mechanism Through Non-transparent Bridges

In order to isolate the different electrical clocking and also separate the PCI bus hierarchies between individual systems, the PCIe non-transparent bridge (NTB) can be employed. As shown in Fig. 1, a typical NTB consists of two PCIe non-transparent (NT) endpoints as well as the doorbell and message registers in between to exchange status and facilitate the PCI inter-domain communication. The device discovery process of each side stops at the non-transparent endpoint during enumeration, so that the other side of NTB is not influenced at all. Doorbell registers are used to initiate interrupts on the other side of NTB and message registers can be read and written by processors on both sides of NTB. Several prior researches [10, 14, 15] about developing novel system interconnections have been conducted by employing the NTB technology.

Both sides of the NTB have their own PCI address space, i.e. PCI domain. The NTB needs to support address translation in order to direct a packet from one side to pass across the NTB and reach its destination on other side. The packet transmitting mechanism is explained based on the two-node situation as shown in Fig. 2.

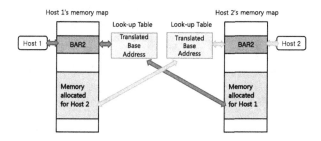

Fig. 2. Data transmission scheme between two hosts

Each NT endpoint is associated with six BARs (Base Address Register) in its configuration space. BAR0 (plus BAR1 in case of 64-bit addressing) maps this NT endpoint's configuration space into the enumerating local host's virtual memory region so that the local host can access the configuration space of this NT endpoint. BAR2 (plus BAR3 in case of 64-bit addressing) maps the endpoint-requested memory into the local host's memory region and this BAR2 (or plus BAR3) mapped region is used to serve as the aperture for local host system to access some specified memory region of the remote system on the other side of NTB. A look-up table is associated with BAR2 (or plus BAR3), and the table entries are manually programmed so that those aperture memory regions are mapped to the target memory region of the remote node. As a result, when the NT endpoint receives a memory operation (read or write) from its local host and the target address of the operation falls in the aperture, the target address of such an operation will get translated as per the associating look-up table entry, so that the memory operation goes across the NTB and is performed on the prepared memory region on the remote host. The BAR4 (plus BAR5 for 64-bit addressing) opens up an aperture for accessing remote host's memory in the same manner as the BAR2 and BAR3, except that the mapped region can also be used to access different remote hosts' configuration spaces.

4   Design and Implementation of PCIeLINK

4.1   Hardware Design and Implementation

PCIeLINK [10] was designed to have one eight-lane PCIe standard interface for connection with the local host and four four-lane external QSFP (Quad Small Form-factor Pluggable) modules for connection with remote systems. Therefore, the PCIeLINK delivers up to 16 Gbps (Gbit per second) data rate on each of its external ports and 32 Gbps on its host interface in case of using PCIe Gen2.

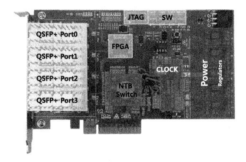

Fig. 3. The implemented PCIeLINK board [10].

The PCIeLINK board was implemented with standard full profile PCIe form factor as shown in Fig. 3. As has been designed, the board has one host connector to be inserted into the PCIe slot of the local host's motherboard and four external ports to connect with remote hosts. Every two PCIeLINKs can be connected by a QDR (quad data rate) cable without using any networking switch in between, which is easy to implement and also indicates a cheaper installation budget for a small cluster with only two to five nodes.

The board is initially configured with a firmware by which the board was divided into five different partitions, where each partition belongs to an independent PCI address domain. Also by using the firmware, the host interface is configured to operate in PCI-to-PCI (P2P) bridge plus NT endpoint plus DMA combined mode, while the external ports are all configured to operate in NT endpoint mode. The firmware also sets the value of several primary registers on the PCIeLINK to regulate the BAR's address translation method (e.g. direct address translation or lookup table translation), requirements of the claiming of memory region (e.g. prefetchable or non-prefetchable), the size of the requested memory region by the NT endpoint, and the memory addressing bits (32-bit or 64-bit addressing), etc.

4.2   Software Design and Implementation

Each node in the PCIeLINK-based cluster is identified by a unique system ID number. The device driver developed for the PCIeLINK board encompasses three layers, i.e. base layer, library layer, and virtual Ethernet interface layer as shown in Fig. 4.

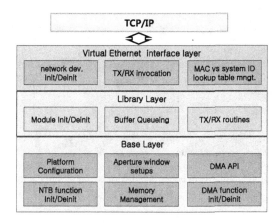

Fig. 4.   The layered structure of the implemented device driver.

The base layer abstracts away those tedious hardware registers and provides primitive functions which are called by upper-layer functions to directly manipulate the hardware. Specifically, the base layer module consists of functional blocks which enable NT endpoint initialization and de-initialization, hardware platform configuration, memory management, NT aperture window setting-ups, DMA function initialization and de-initialization, the DMA APIs that are flexible to use by upper layer, and the interrupt management. The library layer module sets up queue models and functions that operate those queues. The library module also prepares wrapped-up functions for the upper layer to manipulate the packet transmission and reception. The virtual Ethernet interface module allocates an Ethernet device structure with random MAC address and registers itself as a network device, so that the above TCP/IP layer sees the PCIeLINK device the same way as a regular Ethernet card. The virtual Ethernet interface module also has functional blocks to carry out the mapping between the network device's MAC address and the PCIeLINK's system ID number as well as the invocation of the lower-layer provided packet transmission routines. The device driver is implemented to transmit packets using either the memcpy mechanism or the DMA mechanism.

5   Evaluation and Discussion

5.1   Description of Test Environment

The initial experiment only implements the back-to-back topology in which two identical nodes are interconnected using two PCIeLINKs as illustrated in Fig. 5. The detailed description of the test environment is given in Table 1. PCIeLINK is very easy to be installed into the standard PCIe slot of a motherboard. Since a PCIeLINK board has four external ports, they are capable to interconnect a small number of hosts without using the networking switch. If a PCIe non-transparent networking switch is provided, more nodes can connect to the PCIe-networked cluster, though an upper limit exists for the total number of nodes due to the PCIe specification.

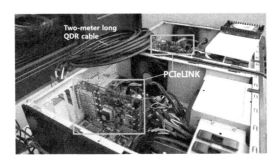

Fig. 5. The experimental platform constructed with two nodes in back-to-back topology.

Table 1. Test environment description.

Items	Description
CPU	x86 architecture, 3.4 GHz × 4 cores
Memory	DDR3 1333 MHz × 2 channels, 4 GB
NTBs on PCIeLINK board	PCIe Gen2
Motherboard slot	PCIe Gen3
OS	32-bit Open-source operating system

In this paper, the performance of PCIeLINK is compared against that of the traditional Gigabit Ethernet. The measurement approaches include using the proprietary ping-pong testing program within the device driver layer and the benchmarking tools over the TCP/IP. Experiments were made by using different testing methods, i.e. memory copy and DMA, respectively and the final results were comprehensively compared and analyzed.

5.2   Experiment Results and Performance Evaluation

Figure 6 demonstrates the unidirectional throughput results tested under the same environment with different tools and data transmission mechanisms using the same set of increasing sizes of transmitted messages. The peak value of each set of testing results is marked in the figure. A dominant pattern is reflected that PCIeLINK delivers higher saturated throughput than Gigabit Ethernet, regardless of the testing method or the data moving mechanism the driver used. The NetPIPE benchmark shows that PCIeLINK delivers a peak throughput which is, using DMA and memcpy mechanism respectively, 5.4 times and 1.6 times of the highest performance supported by Gigabit Ethernet. Likewise, the highest throughput of PCIeLINK with DMA and memcpy mechanism respectively measured by Netperf benchmark is 4.4 times and 1.8 times of that of the conventional Gigabit Ethernet. Specifically, the highest throughput is 8613 Mbps (megabit per second) at the message size of 2M bytes, which is achieved from the ping-pong testing program over PCIeLINK with DMA mechanism. This highest throughput measured of PCIeLINK with DMA is almost 9.2 times of the measured summit throughput of Gigabit Ethernet (941 Mbps by Netperf benchmarking), and for the ping-pong test of PCIeLINK with memcpy the result is 7.2 times. The highest throughput measured from PCIeLINK is 53.8 % of the designed wire speed of an external port, and this indicates that there is still much space to further improve the current driver. The reason that the ping-pong testing measures a higher performance than the NetPIPE and the Netperf benchmarking tools is that the proprietary ping-pong program runs within

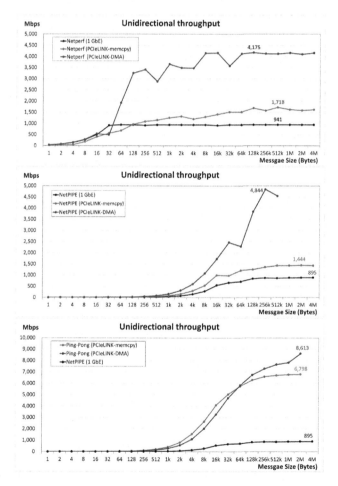

Fig. 6. The comparison of unidirectional throughput between Gigabit Ethernet (i.e. 1 GbE in the legend) and the proposed PCIeLINK. PCIeLINK-memcpy represents the results obtained with the memcpy data moving mechanism and PCIeLINK-DMA denotes the results obtained with the DMA data moving mechanism in the device driver. Peak values are noted in the figure.

the driver code, so that unlike the benchmarking tools which run over the TCP/IP protocol stack the ping-pong testing measures the raw time of data transmission between the link layer of the two nodes, saving the time consumed by copying data from and to the upper layers within the local node.

When measuring the same device's performance in the same experimental environment with two different benchmarking tools, some other patterns are discovered. For example, for the same interconnect type (and the same data moving mechanism for PCIeLINK) the throughput measured by NetPIPE gets saturated later than that measured by Netperf. Another example is that, for the same message size, in general the throughput tested by Netperf is higher than that tested by NetPIPE. Such coherent patterns shown on both PCIeLINK and Gigabit Ethernet indicate that, like the Ethernet, the performance of a PCIeLINK-based cluster is consistent and reproducible. Lastly, there is an abnormal performance noticed when testing PCIeLINK with DMA using NetPIPE that the saturated throughput degraded and cannot sustain for large message sizes, which may due to the not adapted implementation of the DMA mechanism in the device driver or the overheated NTB on the PCIeLINK. Last but not the least, it is measured that PCIeLINK with DMA mechanism does not cause additional CPU usage as compared with that of the traditional Gigabit Ethernet in the test with TCP/IP based applications.

6   Conclusions

This paper has presented an alternative system interconnection device named PCIeLINK that provides high data transmission rate and leaves out switches especially for usage in small-scale clusters. The PCIeLINK is based on the non-transparent bridging technology and is very easy and flexible to use by ordinary users. Early implementation and evaluation are conducted, which demonstrates that PCIeLINK outperforms Gigabit Ethernet in terms of delivering a much higher throughput without consuming more CPU usage. Future work includes optimizing the device driver of PCIeLINK in order to achieve the hardware-supported speed as much as possible as well as comparing the power consumption between PCIeLINK and that of traditional interconnection devices.

Acknowledgments.   This work was supported by the ICT R&D program of MSIP/IITP. [10038768, The Development of Supercomputing System for the Genome Analysis].

References

1. 50 Years of Moore's Law. http://www.intel.com/content/www/us/en/silicon-innovations/moores-law-technology.html
2. Interconnect Family System Share. http://www.top500.org/statistics/list/
3. Bencivenni, M., Bortolotti, D., Carbone, A., Cavalli, A., Chierici, A., et al.: Performance of 10 Gigabit ethernet using commodity hardware. IEEE Trans. Nucl. Sci. **57**(2), 630–641 (2010)
4. Interconnect analysis: 10 GigE and InfiniBand in high performance computing. White Paper, HPC Advisory Council (2009)

5. Koop, M.J. Huang, W., Gopalakrishnan, K., Panda, D.K.: Performance analysis and evaluation of PCIe 2.0 and quad-data rate InfiniBand. In: 16th IEEE Symposium on High Performance Interconnects, pp. 85–92, August 2008
6. PCI Express Base Specification, Revision 3.0, PCI-SIG, November 2010
7. Ravindran, M.: Extending cabled PCI express to connect devices with independent PCI domains, SysCon 2008. In: IEEE International Systems Conference, Montreal, Canada, April 2008
8. Hanawa, T., Boku, T., Miura, S., Okamoto, T., Sato, M., et al.: Low-power and high-performance communication mechanism for dependable embedded systems. In: International Workshop on Innovative Architecture for Future Generation High-Performance Processors and Systems, pp. 67–73 (2008)
9. Hanawa, T., Kodama, Y., Boku, T., Sato, T.: Interconnection network for tightly coupled accelerators architecture. In: IEEE 21st Annual Symposium on High-Performance Interconnects, San Jose, USA, pp. 79–82, August 2013
10. Byrne, J., Chang, J., Lim, K.T., Ramirez, L., Ranganathan, P.: Power-efficient networking for balanced system designs: early experiences with PCIe In: HotPower 2011 Proceedings of the 4th Workshop on Power-Aware Computing and Systems, Article No. 3 2011
11. Krishnan, V.: Evaluation of an integrated PCI express IO expansion and clustering fabric. In: 16th IEEE Symposium on High Performance Interconnects, Stanford University, USA, pp. 93–100, August 2008
12. Ren, Y., Kim, Y.W., Kim, H.Y.: Implementation of system interconnection devices using PCI express. In: IEEE International Conference on Consumer Electronics, Las Vegas, USA, pp. 300–301, January 2015
13. Percival, D.: PCI express clustering. In: PCI-SIG Developers Conference, Israel (2011)
14. Bu-Khamsin, A.: Socket direct protocol over PCI express interconnect: design, implementation and evaluation. MS thesis, Simon Fraser University (2012)
15. Cooper, S.: Using PCIe over cable for high speed CPU-to-CPU communications. PCI-SIG Developers Conference (2008)

Author Index

Al Abdulsalam, Said M.   12
Al Falasi, Asma   102
Al-Dossari, Hmood   168
Al-Ghannam, Reem   168
Alhazemi, Fawaz   22, 70
Alka, Beniwal   114
Almogren, Ahmad S.   200
Ananthalakshmi Ammal, R.   114
Aneesh Kumar, K.B.   114

Bae, Sangwook   126
Banerjee, Subhranshu   260
Baron, Loic   280
Bokhari, Fawaz S.   234
Buali, Nayef   83
Bukhari, Faisal   234

Cheikha, Jad   83
Chen, Lung-Pin   93
Cheng, Yu-Shan   93
Choi, GyuBeom   50, 176
Choi, Jisoo   50
Choi, Wan   334
Choi, Yongseok   301
Choumas, Kostas   280

Deng, Pan   317

Eom, Young Ik   30, 293

Fdida, Serge   280

Go, Gyeongmin   189

Ha, Yungi   50
Haider, Waqar   234
Hamdouch, Younes   102
Han, Younghun   189
Hendrick, Hendrick   311
Hidano, Seira   323
Hua, Qingsong   317
Hyeon, Myeongseok   60

Iqbal, Waheed   234
Ishida, Toru   244

Jaikar, Amol   126
Jang, Hyungyu   39
Jong, Gwo-Jia   311
Joo, Kyung-no   39

Kang, Dong Hyun   293
Kang, Dong-Ki   22, 39, 70, 145
Kang, Sungwon   189
Kanjo, Eiman   168
Khan, Muhammad Asif   255
Kim, Donghyun   280
Kim, Hag Young   184, 344
Kim, Hak-Young   334
Kim, Heejae   60, 176
Kim, Inhyeok   30
Kim, JongWon   3, 224, 280
Kim, Seong-Hwan   22, 39, 70, 145, 176
Kim, Seung-Hwan   136
Kim, Woojoong   136, 176
Kim, Young Woo   344
Kim, Yusik   39
Kiyomoto, Shinsaku   323
Korakis, Thanasis   280
Kwon, HyukJe   301
Kwon, Ted Taekyoung   280

Lasloum, Tariq   200
Lee, Heuijin   189
Lee, Hyunwoo   280
Lee, Minho   30, 293
Lee, Minkyeong   30
Li, Guo Wen   159
Liao, Guo-Sheng   311
Lin, Chun-Yen   311
Lu, Kuo-Ying   311

Ma, Jin-Suk   334
Martinez-Julia, Pedro   280
Mathur, Vikas   260
Moessner, Klaus   323

Murakami, Yohei   244
Murakami, Yosuke   323

Najjar, Nafez A.L.   83
Narasipur, Sreehari   260
Noh, Seo-Young   126

Oh, Chansoo   293
Opara-Martins, Justice   213

Park, Chanho   184

Ren, Gang   317
Ren, Ye   344
Renjith, B.   114
Risdianto, Aris Cahyadi   224

Sahandi, Reza   213
Serhani, Mohammed Adel   102
Shah, Syed Asif Raza   126
Shin, Junsik   3, 224
Skarmeta, Antonio   280

Song, SeongMin   176
Suh, Junho   280

Tian, Feng   213
Tiendrebeogo, Telesphore   269
Trang, Mai Xuan   244

Udoh, Vincent A.   12

Vlacheas, Panagiotis   323

Wang, Peng   159
Watfa, Mohamed K.   12, 83

Yang, Chao   317
Yang, Ling   159
Yoon, Dongsik   145
You, Taewan   280
Youn, Chan-Hyun   22, 39, 50, 60, 70, 136,
    145, 176

Zhang, Jianwei   317

Printed in the United States
By Bookmasters